READY FOR BUSINESS

Junior Certificate Business Studies

Richard Delaney

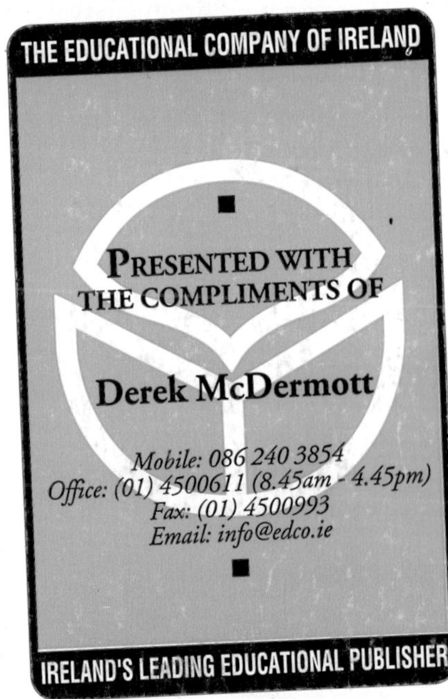

Edco

Preface

Ready For Business is a completely new and fully up-to-date textbook for Junior Certificate Business Studies. It comprehensively covers all material for both Higher and Ordinary level students and is written in student-friendly language, presented in a practical layout and an attractive, colourful design. It includes up-to-date material such as the Consumer Protection Act and the proposed Universal Social Contribution (Budget 2010).

Students using this textbook will be well prepared for all eventualities when they sit the Junior Certificate examination.

All essential definitions are highlighted throughout the book and each chapter concludes with a *Key Terms* list for easy revision.

There is a gradual introduction of accounting rules throughout the book enabling a seamless transition to the accounting section. The book also outlines methodologies that can be used in answering many of the accounting exam questions.

Each chapter, where relevant, includes worked examples of all the Junior Certificate type accounting questions and also includes exam style questions and questions which help reinforce understanding of topics.

At the request of many teachers the textbook is accompanied by a comprehensive workbook that caters for the changing layout and presentation of questions on recent Junior Certificate examination papers. It includes 'Section A' type questions, numerous budget and cash flow statement questions, numerous business document type questions, blank banking and insurance documents, business plan documents and company formation documents. It also includes up-to-date pre-printed 'fill-in' type questions and answer sheets.

Contents

The business of living

1 Budgets: Household income 1
2 Budgets: Household expenditure 8
3 Budgets: Preparing a budget 15
4 Household budgets (Higher Level) 23
5 Household accounts: The analysed cash book 31
6 Budgets revisited: Budget comparison statements 45
7 The consumer 58
8 Insurance and assurance 71
9 Money 85
10 Personal banking (commercial banks) 93
11 Bank statements 105
12 Personal saving and credit purchasing 113

The economic framework

13 Economics 1: Introduction 125
14 Economics 2: The government and the economy 135
15 Economics 3: International trade 144

Enterprise 1: Business background

16 Business ownership 155
17 Private limited companies 160
18 Business finance 165
19 The business plan & cash flow forecast 170
20 Businesses and commercial banks 178
21 Insurance for businesses 182
22 Chain of production and channels of distribution 187
23 Delivery and transport systems 194
24 Marketing 206
25 Work and employment 215
26 Employers 220
27 Industrial relations 230
28 Communication 236

Enterprise 2: Accounting

29	Record keeping and business documents	246
30	Double-entry records and the trial balance	259
31	The purchases and purchases returns books	266
32	The sales and sales returns books	280
33	Continuous balance ledger accounts	294
34	Business accounts: The analysed cash book	302
35	The petty cash book and monitoring overheads	314
36	The general journal	321
37	Debtors and creditors control accounts	330
38	Revision: Combining day books, ledgers & trial balances (HL)	341
39	End of year procedure (HL)	356
40	Final accounts 1: The trading account	365
41	Final accounts 2: Profit and loss accounts	374
42	Final accounts 3: The balance sheet	385
43	Final accounts with adjustments (HL)	394
44	Assessment and interpretation of accounts	407
45	Club accounts	418
46	Accounts for service firms	433
47	Farm accounts	442

Information technology

48	Information technology	447

Index 456

Budgets: **Household income**

The word **business** means any activity that concerns a person or a group of people.

Business concerns all aspects of our lives, i.e. our family's finances, our social (club) life, our place of work, how the government raises and spends our money, and how commercial businesses operate.

There are many items on which households *have* to spend money, e.g. food, clothes and rent or mortgage repayments. These are essentials for survival.

There are also many items on which households would *like* to spend money, e.g. holidays, presents and meals in restaurants. These are luxury goods, i.e. households can survive without them.

Therefore when a household knows its income, it must first plan to set aside money from this income to pay for the items it has to buy. Only then can it plan for the items it would like to buy. This planning is called **budgeting**.

A **budget** is a plan that matches expected spending with expected income over a period of time.

IMPORTANCE OF HOUSEHOLD BUDGETS

Household budgets help you to:

- balance expected income with expected spending, i.e. ensuring money is available when it is needed
- reduce the risk of impulse buying
- avoid unaffordable debt
- set aside money for a rainy day, i.e. to have money available for any unforeseen expenses that may arise

INCOME

Before we start planning our spending we need to know how much money we will have to finance this spending, i.e. we need to know what our **income** will be for a period of time.

Income is the money, goods or services a household receives, either regularly or irregularly.

We will look at:
1. regular income
2. irregular income
3. benefit-in-kind

1. Regular income

Regular income is income received periodically, e.g. every week, fortnight or month. We can usually predict how much we will receive.

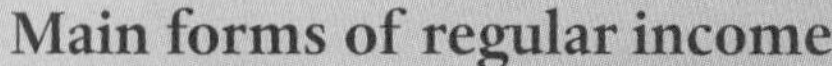

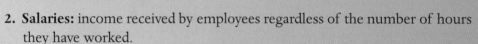

Main forms of regular income
1. **Wages:** income received by employees based on the number of hours they have worked.
2. **Salaries:** income received by employees regardless of the number of hours they have worked.
3. **Commission:** income received by salespeople. It is a payment received per unit of the goods sold.
4. **Jobseeker's benefit ('the dole'):** social welfare payments (income) received by unemployed people.
5. **Pensions:** income received by people who have retired from work.
6. **Child Benefit:** a monthly social welfare payment to parents (usually the mother), based on the number of children they have under 16 years of age (or 18 years of age if they are still in full-time education).
7. **Interest on savings:** income received from banks by people who save money with them. The income is a percentage of the amount saved.
8. **Pocket money:** income received by children from their parents or guardians.

2. Irregular or additional income

Irregular income is any extra occasional income that **may** be received; however, we cannot assume that it will be received.

Irregular income examples

1. **Overtime:** payment received for working more than the required minimum number of hours in a week. An employee may be required to work a minimum of 40 hours for a weekly wage of €800, i.e. a basic rate of €20 per hour. The employee is usually paid at a higher hourly rate for any extra hours worked.
   Examples
   Time-and-a-half means 1.5 times the basic hourly rate,
   e.g. €20 × 1.5 = €30 per hour.
   Double-time means twice the basic rate,
   e.g. €20 × 2 = €40 per hour.
2. **Bonus payments:** extra payments for employees if stated targets are reached.
3. **Dividends:** income received by owners of shares in limited companies.
4. **Lottery wins.**
5. **Money received in a will.**

3. Benefit-in-kind

Benefit-in-kind is any non-money income received for work done.

Employees sometimes receive goods or services as part of their payment. This form of payment is known as **benefit-in-kind** (**BIK**).

Benefit-in-kind examples

- **a car** provided by an employer
- **meals** received by employees of hotels and restaurants
- **club memberships** paid by employers for their employees
- **discounts** received by employees on goods provided by their employer
- **medical insurance** paid by employers for employees

In all these examples the employees are receiving something other than money for the work done by them.

Some **social welfare payments** also come in the form of benefit-in-kind. For example:

- free travel
- free TV licence
- electricity allowance
- medical card

GROSS PAY, DEDUCTIONS AND NET PAY

Gross pay

Gross pay is the total income earned by a person.

If you work 40 hours in a week and are paid €20 per hour then your gross pay is €800 per week.

Deductions from wages

Deductions from gross pay are sums of money that are taken from gross pay. There are **two groups** of deductions: statutory and voluntary.

Statutory deductions

Statutory deductions must, by law, be taken from gross wages.

The two main statutory deductions are **PAYE** and **PRSI** (**USC**). The government may, from time to time, also impose a levy on incomes. This is normally a fixed percentage of gross income.

1. PAYE

PAYE (**Pay As You Earn**) is the income tax system for employees. The money deducted by the employer for PAYE purposes is sent to the government and is part of the government's overall income.

All employees should know how to calculate the amount of PAYE payable by them.

By knowing how to calculate the amount of PAYE payable by them, employees can establish whether they are underpaying or overpaying the tax. If they are overpaying the PAYE they can arrange a **tax rebate**, i.e. get back the amount they have overpaid.

Note: PAYE calculations are covered in Chapter 26, *Employers*.

2. PRSI (USC)

PRSI (**Pay Related Social Insurance**) is a percentage of gross income taken from each employee's income and given to the government. The employer must also pay an additional percentage of the employee's income as PRSI.

Note: In the 2010 budget the Minister for Finance announced that a new **Universal Social Contribution** (**USC**) would be introduced in the 2011 budget. It is proposed that this will replace the PRSI deduction and other income levies. Therefore any future references to PRSI in this textbook will show the proposed USC in brackets.

What do you get for your PRSI (USC) contributions?

Payment of PRSI (USC) entitles employees to:

- jobseeker's benefit, if they lose their jobs
- a contributory old age pension
- maternity benefits
- sickness benefit, when temporarily out of work
- free routine dental care and other social welfare and health benefits

Voluntary deductions

Voluntary deductions are sums of money taken from the gross wage at the instruction of the employee. The employer makes these payments to a named person or organisation.

Payments into saving schemes, health insurance payments to companies such as VHI or Hibernian Aviva Health, trade union contributions, payments into pension funds and donations to charities are examples of voluntary deductions.

Net pay

Net pay is gross pay less all deductions.

Net pay is sometimes called 'take-home pay'.

WAGE SLIPS

A wage slip (or pay slip) is a written explanation of the calculation of an employee's net pay. An employee must receive one each time he or she is paid.

A simple pay slip

- Mary Murphy's standard working week is 40 hours paid @ €20 per hour.
- Any overtime is paid at time-and-a-half.
- She worked 50 hours in the week ending 22/10/2010.
- Her PAYE for the week was €125.
- Her PRSI (USC) for the week was €52.
- She paid €30 into her VHI plan and €23 into a savings plan.

Calculations

- Basic = 40 hours @ €20 per hour = €800.
- Overtime = 10 hours @ €30 per hour (€20 multiplied by 1.5) = €300

22/10/2010		WAGE SLIP – MARY MURPHY		WEEK 42
Pay	€	Deductions	€	
Basic	€800	PAYE*	€125	
Overtime	€300	PRSI (USC)*	€52	
		VHI**	€30	
		Savings plan**	€23	Net pay
Gross pay	€1,100	Total deductions	€230	€870

Explanation

- **Gross pay** of €1,100 is the total income earned by Mary (basic pay of €800 plus overtime of €300).
- **Net pay** of €870 is gross pay of €1,100 less the total deductions of €230.
- *Indicates *statutory* deductions. **Indicates *voluntary* deductions.

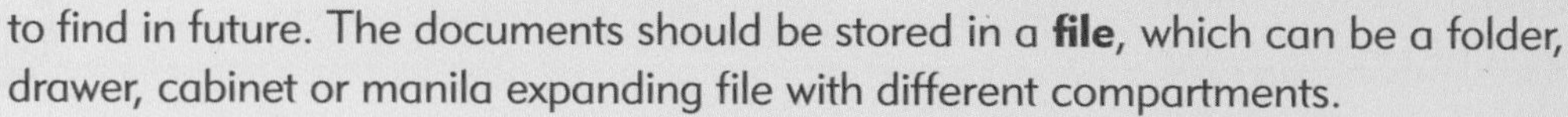

Filing

Throughout the book we talk about **filing** documents. A filing system is a method of storing documents so that they can be easy to find in future. The documents should be stored in a **file**, which can be a folder, drawer, cabinet or manila expanding file with different compartments.

The documents can be sorted in the file in different ways, e.g. alphabetically, numerically, in date order or by address.

RECORDING INCOME

Records of income received and any other documents relating to it should be filed carefully. These records will make it easy to make forecasts of income for budgeting purposes.

Example

CURRAN FAMILY REGULAR AND IRREGULAR INCOME FOR SIX MONTHS

INCOME	Jan	Feb	March	April	May	June	Total Jan–June
J. Curran – Salary	2,500	2,500	3,000	2,500	2,500	2,500	15,500
B. Curran – Salary	1,600	1,600	2,600	1,600	1,600	1,600	10,600
Child Benefit	270	270	270	270	270	270	1,620
Overtime		300			200		500
TOTAL INCOME	4,370	4,670	5,870	4,370	4,570	4,370	28,220

The figures in the *Total Jan–June* column are calculated by adding together the figures in each of the monthly columns.

In Chapter 5 we will see a more detailed method of recording income as it is received.

LEARN THE KEY TERMS

- **Income** refers to the money, goods or services a household receives either regularly or irregularly.
- **Benefit-in-kind** is any non-money income received for work done.
- **Regular income** is income received periodically, e.g. every week, fortnight or month. We can usually predict how much we will receive.
- **Irregular** or **additional income** is any extra occasional income that **may** be received. Note that we cannot assume that it will be received.
- **Overtime** is a payment received for working more than the required minimum number of hours in a week.
- **Gross pay** is the total income earned by a person.
- **Deductions** from gross pay are sums of money that are taken by the employer from gross pay.
- **Net pay** is gross pay less all deductions.

- **Statutory deductions** are deductions that must, by law, be taken from gross wages.
- **Voluntary deductions** are sums of money taken from the gross wage when the employee instructs the employer to make payments to a named person or organisation.
- **PAYE** stands for **Pay As You Earn**.
- **PRSI** stands for **Pay Related Social Insurance**.
- **USC** stands for **Universal Social Contribution**.
- A **wage slip** or **pay slip** is a written explanation of the calculation of an employee's net pay.

QUESTIONS

1. What is income?
2. What is regular income? Give two examples.
3. What is irregular income? Give two examples.
4. Joe Ryan works for a travel agency that sells holidays in Ireland and abroad. He must travel around Ireland inspecting hotels for his employer. State two examples of benefit-in-kind Joe might receive.
5. Robert Browne is unemployed. State two examples of benefit-in-kind Robert might receive from the Department of Social and Family Affairs.
6. Distinguish between statutory and voluntary deductions from wages, giving two examples of each.
7. How do employees benefit from payment of PRSI (USC)?
8. Calculate Mary White's net pay from the following information. Show your calculations. Her basic wage was €700 and she also earned €150 in overtime. She had the following deductions from her gross pay: PAYE €160; PRSI (USC) €58; VHI €40.
9. Calculate Maura Malone's net pay for the month of May from the following information: Gross pay €300.00; PAYE €50.50; PRSI (USC) €22.50; VHI €13.00; Pension €19.50. Show your calculations.
10. Niall O'Connor is paid €570 for a standard 38-hour working week. He is paid time-and-a-half for the first 8 hours' overtime he works and double-time for any hours above that. In the week ending 30 May 2010 he worked a total of 50 hours.

    (a) Calculate, showing your workings, Niall's gross basic wage per hour for a 38-hour week.
    (b) Calculate, showing your workings, Niall's gross wage for the week.

11. Joe Jordan is paid €13 per hour for a basic 38-hour week. Any overtime is paid at the rate of time-and-a-half. In the week ending 5/6/2010 he worked 48 hours. He has the following deductions: PAYE €103.35; PRSI (USC) €30.25; Trade union €20.00; CFAI (charity) €5.00.

    (a) Calculate, showing your workings, Joe's gross basic wage per hour for a 38-hour week.
    (b) Calculate, showing your workings, Joe's gross wage for the week.

See workbook for more questions.

2 Budgets: **Household expenditure**

WHAT IS EXPENDITURE?

Expenditure means spending on the goods and services we use such as televisions, food, clothes, doctors' services, school fees and transport.

When spending money:

1. Consider financial cost versus opportunity cost
2. Avoid false economies
3. Avoid impulse buying
4. Know the timing of your expenditure
5. Prioritise your expenditure
6. Check delivery notes
7. Check bills

1. Financial and opportunity cost

Most of us do not have enough money to buy all the goods and services we would like. Therefore we have to make choices about our purchases.

Assume you have €20. You would like to buy a €20 top-up for your mobile phone and a new T-shirt, which also costs €20. If you buy the T-shirt you must do without the top-up. The top-up is the **opportunity cost** of the T-shirt.

The **financial cost** of an item is the amount of money paid for that item. In this case it is €20.

Opportunity cost is the item you must do without in order to buy another item.

2. Avoid false economies

A **false economy** is spending money on something which initially appears to save you money but over a longer period of time costs you more money.

Example

You may need a new set of tyres for your car. You see one set for €240 and another set for €360. Naturally you are tempted to save yourself €120 by buying the cheaper set.

The cheaper tyres may last for only 15,000 kilometres, whereas the more expensive tyres may last for 30,000 kilometres.

It would be cheaper in the long run to buy the more expensive tyres. You would need two sets of the cheaper tyres (costing €480) to travel the same distance as you would on one set of the more expensive tyres.

3. Avoid impulse buying

Impulse buying is **unplanned spending**, i.e. buying something on the spur of the moment because it seems to be attractive at the time.

How to avoid impulse buying

1. Before you leave your house, make a list of the items you need to buy.
2. When you are going to the shop, bring only enough money to buy the items on the list.
3. When you are in the shop, buy only the items on the list. You will then have no money left for impulse purchases!

Must resist!

4. Know the timing of your expenditure

As well as knowing the items that have to be paid for, you need to know the timing of the payments.

- Some items have to be purchased every week, e.g. groceries.
- Other items have to be paid only once a month, e.g. the mortgage.
- Electricity bills are normally paid every two months.
- Some items are paid once a year, e.g. the television licence.

It is important not to spend all of your weekly income each week. If you did, there would be no money left over to pay the monthly and yearly bills.

5. Prioritise your expenditure

Most of the time there are many items we **need** to buy and many items we would **like** to buy. First we should identify all the bills that need to be paid.

If we do not pay our rent or mortgage we will have no place to live. If we do not buy food we will not survive, and if we do not pay our electricity bill we will have no light or power in our homes. Clearly these items must be paid for before we can think about things we would like to buy.

6. Check delivery notes

Some of the goods we purchase are very bulky or heavy. We request the seller to deliver them to our home. The person delivering the goods will ask us to sign a delivery note or docket. (These will be dealt with in more detail later in the book.)

You should never sign a delivery note before checking that the goods listed are the goods received and that they are the goods that were ordered.

7. Check bills

Goods and services are often purchased on credit. This means we do not pay for them at the time they are purchased and used. We receive a bill for them when payment is due.

The bill most commonly received by all households is the electricity bill. This should be checked before it is paid.

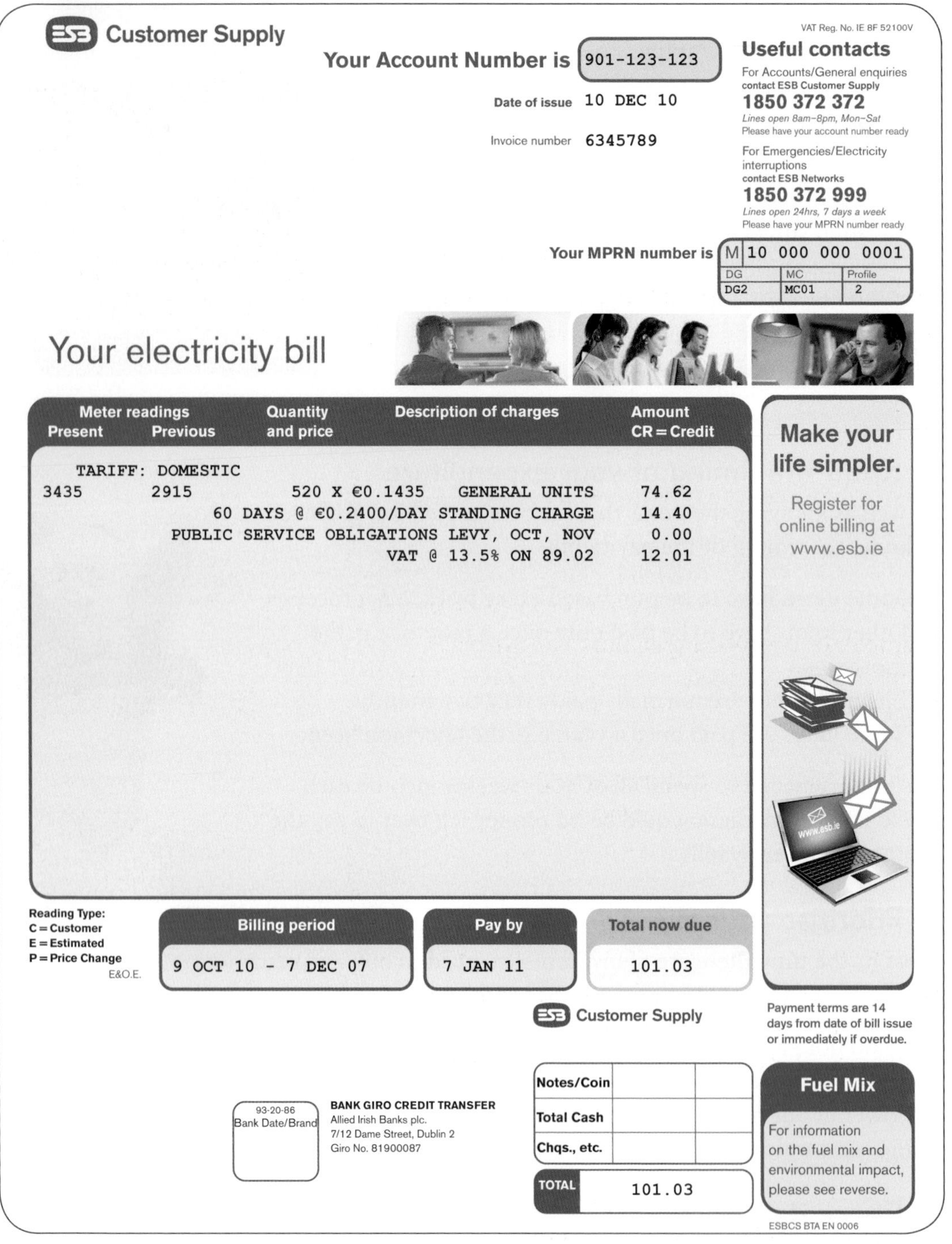
ESB Customer Supply

Your Account Number is 901-123-123

Date of issue 10 DEC 10

Invoice number 6345789

VAT Reg. No. IE 8F 52100V

Useful contacts

For Accounts/General enquiries contact ESB Customer Supply
1850 372 372
Lines open 8am–8pm, Mon–Sat
Please have your account number ready

For Emergencies/Electricity interruptions contact ESB Networks
1850 372 999
Lines open 24hrs, 7 days a week
Please have your MPRN number ready

Your MPRN number is M 10 000 000 0001

DG	MC	Profile
DG2	MC01	2

Your electricity bill

Meter readings Present	Previous	Quantity and price	Description of charges	Amount CR = Credit
TARIFF: DOMESTIC				
3435	2915	520 X €0.1435	GENERAL UNITS	74.62
		60 DAYS @ €0.2400/DAY	STANDING CHARGE	14.40
			PUBLIC SERVICE OBLIGATIONS LEVY, OCT, NOV	0.00
			VAT @ 13.5% ON 89.02	12.01

Make your life simpler.
Register for online billing at www.esb.ie

Reading Type:
C = Customer
E = Estimated
P = Price Change
E&O.E.

Billing period	Pay by	Total now due
9 OCT 10 - 7 DEC 07	7 JAN 11	101.03

ESB Customer Supply

Payment terms are 14 days from date of bill issue or immediately if overdue.

93-20-86
Bank Date/Brand

BANK GIRO CREDIT TRANSFER
Allied Irish Banks plc.
7/12 Dame Street, Dublin 2
Giro No. 81900087

Notes/Coin	
Total Cash	
Chqs., etc.	
TOTAL	101.03

Fuel Mix
For information on the fuel mix and environmental impact, please see reverse.

ESBCS BTA EN 0006

1. To check the units of electricity used, subtract the figure under *Previous meter reading* from the figure under *Present meter reading* (3435 minus 2915 = 520).
2. Multiply the number of units used by the cost per unit to get the price of the units used (520 multiplied by 0.1435 = €74.62).
3. Add *Standing charges*, which cover the cost of supplying the electricity (€14.40).
4. Add, where applicable, the Public Service Obligation (PSO) Levy. This is a charge to cover the additional costs arising from the production of electricity from native and environmentally friendly forms of fuel.
5. Finally, add the VAT (€12.01) to get the total amount due (€101.03).

EXPENDITURE TYPES

There are three types of expenditure.

1. Fixed expenditure

Fixed expenditure is spending on goods or services on a regular basis, e.g. once a week, once a month or once a year. The amount spent is fixed and does not vary with usage.

A television licence is an annual fixed expense.

Examples of fixed expenditure are TV licences, car road tax, mortgage payments, rent, loan repayments and life assurance premiums.

2. Irregular expenditure

Irregular expenditure is spending on goods and services where the amount spent and/or the timing of the spending varies with usage.

Petrol is an irregular expense.

Examples of irregular expenditure are groceries, electricity bills, telephone bills, petrol and heating costs.

3. Discretionary expenditure

Discretionary expenditure is spending on items we would like to buy but do not need for day-to-day living.

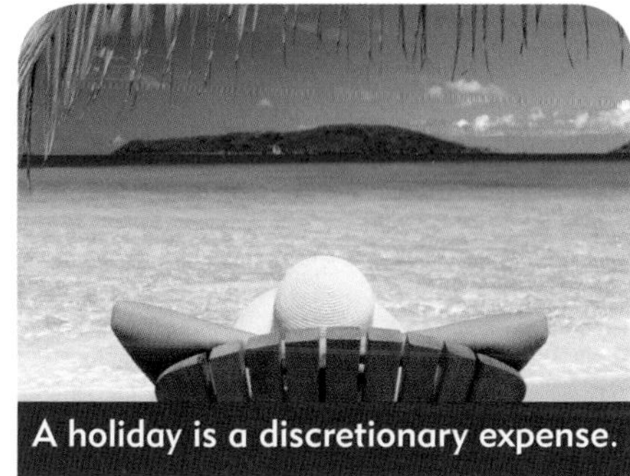

A holiday is a discretionary expense.

We could spend the remainder of our money on holidays, the cinema, eating out, iPods or presents for people. These are all examples of discretionary expenditure.

RECORD ALL EXPENDITURE

Record expenditure under the three headings used above: **fixed expenditure**, **irregular expenditure** and **discretionary expenditure**. File carefully all records of expenditure and related documents.

We can use expenditure records like the one on the next page as a guide for estimating future expenditure in budgets.

In Chapter 5 we will see a more detailed method of recording expenditure as it occurs.

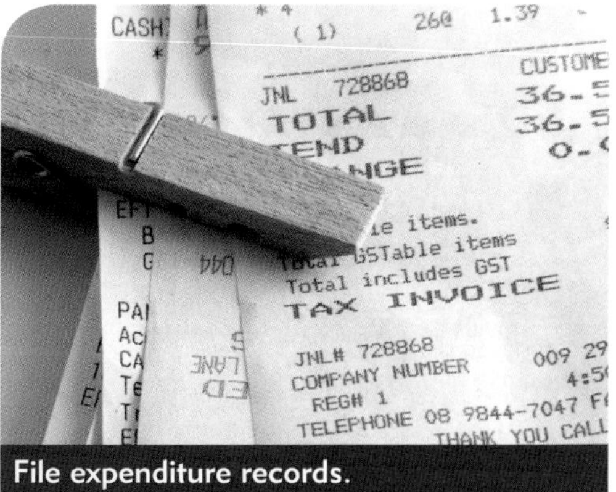

File expenditure records.

CURRAN FAMILY EXPENDITURE FOR SIX MONTHS							
EXPENDITURE	Jan	Feb	March	April	May	June	Total Jan–June
Fixed	€	€	€	€	€	€	€
Mortgage	800	800	750	750	750	750	4,600
House insurance	80	80	80	80	80	80	480
Health insurance	170	170	190	190	190	190	1,100
Subtotal (A)	**1,050**	**1,050**	**1,020**	**1,020**	**1,020**	**1,020**	**6,180**
Irregular							
Household expenses	1,300	1,300	1,300	700	1,300	1,300	7,200
Car running costs	230	230	230	230	230	230	1,380
Light and heat		1,140		290		1,200	2,630
Telephone costs	380	160	440	160	440	160	1,740
Subtotal (B)	**1,910**	**2,830**	**1,970**	**1,380**	**1,970**	**2,890**	**12,950**
Discretionary							
Holidays	500		500	1,900			2,900
Entertainment	900	900	900	1,400	900	900	5,900
Subtotal (C)	**1,400**	**900**	**1,400**	**3,300**	**900**	**900**	**8,800**
TOTAL EXPENDITURE (A +B + C)	**4,360**	**4,780**	**4,390**	**5,700**	**3,890**	**4,810**	**27,930**

Notes

1. The figures in the **total column** are calculated by adding together the figures in each of the monthly columns.
2. A **subtotal** is inserted for each form of expenditure. This allows us to see how much we spent on each of these forms of expenditure.
3. **Total expenditure** is calculated by adding the three subtotals together.
4. The figures for **fixed expenditure may vary**. Look at *Health insurance* in the record above. The amount increased in March. This may have happened because the insurance company increased its rates from 1 March.
5. The figures for **irregular expenditure do not *always* vary**. Look at the figures for *Car running costs* in our example. From January to June the Curran family may have used their car for the exact same journeys every month and had no extra costs such as servicing the car or paying for repairs.

CURRENT AND CAPITAL SPENDING

Current expenditure is ongoing spending on items that give benefit for a short period of time, usually less than one year.

If I buy groceries this week I only benefit from the expenditure this week and will have to buy more next week.

Current expenditure should be paid for out of the current year's income. Always avoid borrowing money for current expenditure.

Capital expenditure is spending on an item that will give benefit for a long period of time, usually more than one year.

If I buy a car and keep it for five years I will benefit from this expenditure for five years. Therefore I could borrow money for the car, provided I repay the loan over the five years. The loan repayments become part of future budgets.

Goods like this are known as **consumer durables**, i.e. goods that will give benefit to the buyer for a long period of time, usually more than one year.

LEARN THE KEY TERMS

- **Expenditure** is spending on the goods and services we use.
- The **financial cost** of an item is the amount of money paid for it.
- A **false economy** is spending money on something which initially appears to save money but over a longer period of time costs more money.
- **Impulse buying** is unplanned spending.
- The **opportunity cost** of a transaction is the item you must do without in order to buy another item.
- **Fixed expenditure** is spending on goods and services on a regular basis, e.g. once a week, once a month or once a year, where the amount spent is fixed and does not change with usage.
- **Irregular expenditure** is spending on goods and services where the amount spent and/or the timing of the spending varies with usage.
- **Discretionary expenditure** is spending on items we would like to buy but do not need for day-to-day living.
- **Current expenditure** is ongoing spending on items that give benefit for a short period of time, usually less than one year.
- **Capital expenditure** is spending on an item that will give benefit for a long period of time, usually more than one year.
- **Consumer durable goods** are goods that will give benefit to the buyer for a long period of time, usually more than one year.

QUESTIONS

1. What does the word **expenditure** mean?
2. Distinguish between the **financial cost** and the **opportunity cost** of an item purchased.
3. Explain the term **false economy**. Give an example of a possible false economy.
4. Mary Duggan has €15. She would like to buy a DVD which costs €15 and would also like to go to a show that costs €15. She decides to go to the show. What is the financial cost of the show and what is its opportunity cost? Explain your answer.
5. What is impulse buying?
6. Explain any steps you could take to reduce the risk of impulse buying.
7. Your electricity bill states that the present meter reading is 10,350 units and that the previous reading was 9,240 units. The charge for each unit is €0.02. There is a standing charge of €20 and VAT is charged at 10%. Calculate, showing your workings, the total electricity bill.
8. Explain the terms **fixed expenditure, irregular expenditure** and **discretionary expenditure**.
9. State any two items of expenditure that you would expect to see under each of the following headings: **fixed, irregular** and **discretionary** expenditure.
10. What is current expenditure?
11. What is capital expenditure?
12. A family spent money on the following items during the month of August:

    new car | *new suite of furniture*
    groceries | *annual car insurance*
    electricity bill | *new computer*

    List these forms of spending under the headings **capital** and **current** spending.

See workbook for more questions.

Budgets: **Preparing a budget**

We are now at the stage where we are almost ready to draw up a household budget, i.e. to draw up a plan that matches expected spending with expected income over a period of time.

Guidelines to good budgeting

1. **Be realistic about your income.** Take account only of income that you are sure you will receive. Do not rely on income you *may* receive and remember that your very old, rich and ailing grandmother may leave all her money to the home for stray cats and dogs!
2. **Be practical about your spending.** Identify all the items that you must purchase on a regular basis and the amounts you must spend on them.
3. **Identify the timing of all bills.** Some bills may be payable every two months, e.g. electricity bills; others may be payable once a year, e.g. the road tax on your car or new clothes. You may have to spend extra money at certain times of the year, e.g. Christmas. Set aside money from your regular income to pay these bills when they are due.
4. **Allow for exceptional *known* events.** For example, you may know that a family member is getting married in the near future. Set aside money to meet the extra expense that this involves.
5. **Allow for unforeseeable events.** Unexpected expenses may arise at any time. The new washing machine might break down completely, just one day after its guarantee has expired. Thus it is always important, where possible, to save money to meet these unforeseeable expenses.
6. **Avoid impulse buying.**

In Chapters 1 and 2 we saw that income and expenditure records can be used as a guide for estimating future income and expenditure in our budgets.

These records give us a pattern of past income and expenditure. Remember that a budget is a **plan** of the family's expected income and expenditure for the coming months or year. If we know there will be changes in income or expenditure we can adjust the budget accordingly.

DRAWING UP A BUDGET

Before we go into detailed budget preparation we need to understand a few basic terms. Look at the figures in a summarised budget shown here:

THE SMITH'S BUDGET JANUARY–APRIL 2010

	Jan	Feb	March	April	Total Jan–April
Total income **(A)**	€3,000	€3,000	€3,000	€3,000	€12,000
Total expenditure **(B)**	€2,600	€2,800	€3,500	€2,900	€11,800
Net cash **(A – B)**	€400	€200	(€500)	€100	€200
Opening cash	**€2,000**	€2,400	€2,600	€2,100	**€2,000**
Closing cash **(Net cash *plus* opening cash)**	€2,400	€2,600	€2,100	€2,200	€2,200

This table, firstly, shows the Smith Household's income and expenditure for the months January to April 2010. It also shows the total figures for those four months (*Total from January to April*) by adding together the figures for each of the months.

Net cash

Net cash is the difference between planned income and planned expenditure in any given period of time, e.g. in January it is €3,000 – €2,600 = €400.

- Net cash is a **surplus** (positive) when the planned income for the month is greater than the planned expenditure for that month.
- Net cash is a **deficit** (negative) when planned expenditure for the month is greater than planned income for that month.

Opening cash

Opening cash is the amount of money a household has or plans to have at the start of a month or period of time.

You will be told the *Opening cash* for the first month in any exercise. Here it is €2,000.

Closing cash

Closing cash is the amount of money a household has or plans to have at the end of a month or period of time.

It is calculated as follows:

Closing cash = Net cash + Opening cash

In January the closing cash is the net cash, €400, *plus* the opening cash, €2,000 = €2,400.

Obviously, the *closing cash* one month is the *opening cash* the next month. If you go to bed with €50 in your pocket on 31 January (closing cash) you will have €50 in your pocket on 1 February (opening cash).

We are now ready to draw up a full family budget. This will show all sources of income and will sub-divide all expenditure under the headings of fixed, irregular and discretionary.

Note: In State examinations, and in your Workbook, you will be given pre-printed forms listing all income and expenditure items. You simply fill in the figures!

BUDGET TYPE 1

Question and solution

You are to complete the budget for the Black family on the pre-printed budget document on page 19.

- Opening cash on 1 January is €500.

Black family – planned income

- Brian Black earns a net salary of €3,700 per month and expects to receive a bonus of €800 in March.
- Bernie Black earns a net salary of €3,500 per month and expects to receive a tax refund of €300 in February.
- Child Benefit is €180 per month.
- They expect to receive €300 interest on their savings in April.

Black family – planned expenditure

- The monthly mortgage of €1,800 is expected to increase by €20 in March.
- The annual car insurance premium of €500 is due for payment in January.
- The annual house insurance premium of €600 is paid in **12 equal monthly instalments**.
- Household expenses are expected to be €2,000 per month, except in April when they will be €500 **less**.
- ESB bills for light and heat are expected to be €250 in January and €200 in March. Heating oil will cost €1,000 in February.
- The Black family have a home telephone and a mobile phone. The home telephone bill is expected to be €150 in February and €180 in April. The mobile phone is expected to cost €80 per month.
- Car running costs are expected to be €120 per month for Brian and €140 per month for Bernie.
- Birthdays are expected to cost €150 in February and €200 in March.
- The Black family has booked a holiday for April costing €2,200 **in total**. They must pay a €500 booking fee in January, a €700 deposit in March, and the balance in April.
- Entertainment is expected to cost €400 per month, except in April when it will be €150 **less**.

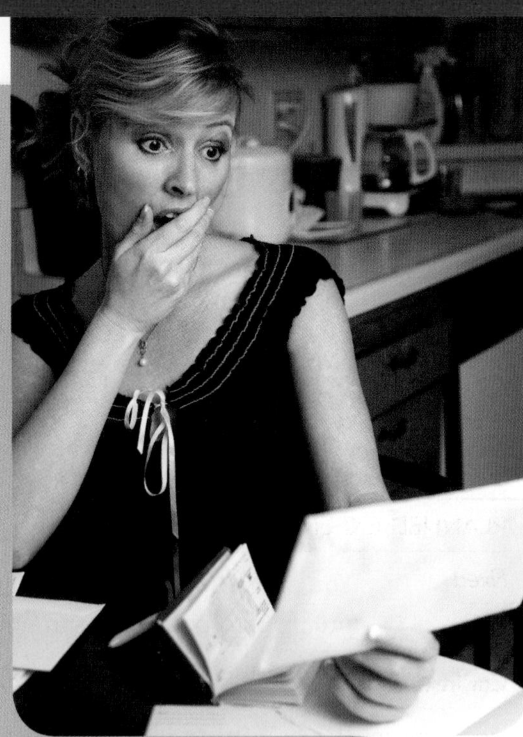

Calculations

- **Brian Black's salary in March:** €3,700 plus the bonus of €800 = €4,500.
- **Bernie Black's salary in February:** €3,500 plus the tax refund of €300 = €3,800.
- **Mortgage for March and April:** €1,800 + €20 = €1,820.
- **House insurance:** The full cost for the year is €600. It is paid in 12 equal monthly payments. Therefore each monthly payment is €600 divided by 12 = €50.
- **Telephone:** The cost of the mobile phone has to be paid each month. Therefore the full cost for telephones in **February is €230** (the mobile phone of €80 + the home phone of €150). The full cost of telephones in **April is €260** (the mobile phone of €80 + the home phone of €180).
- **Car running costs:** Add Brian and Bernie's costs together to give a monthly cost of €260.
- **Holidays:** Payment in April = (total cost of €2,200 minus the two deposits totalling €1,200) = €1,000.

Remember:

- Closing cash one month becomes the opening cash the next month.
- Opening cash in the total column is the original €500 opening cash.

BLACK FAMILY BUDGET					
	Jan	Feb	March	April	Total Jan–April
PLANNED INCOME	€	€	€	€	€
Brian Black – Salary	3,700	3,700	4,500	3,700	15,600
Bernie Black – Salary	3,500	3,800	3,500	3,500	14,300
Child Benefit	180	180	180	180	720
Interest on savings				300	300
TOTAL INCOME (A)	7,380	7,680	8,180	7,680	30,920
PLANNED EXPENDITURE					
Fixed					
Mortgage	1,800	1,800	1,820	1,820	7,240
Car insurance	500				500
House insurance	50	50	50	50	200
Subtotal	2,350	1,850	1,870	1,870	7,940
Irregular					
Household expenses	2,000	2,000	2,000	1,500	7,500
Heat and light	250	1,000	200		1,450
Telephone	80	230	80	260	650
Car running costs	260	260	260	260	1,040
Subtotal	2,590	3,490	2,540	2,020	10,640
Discretionary					
Birthdays		150	200		350
Holidays	500		700	1,000	2,200
Entertainment	400	400	400	250	1,450
Subtotal	900	550	1,300	1,250	4,000
TOTAL EXPENDITURE (B)	5,840	5,890	5,710	5,140	22,580
Net cash = A – B	1,540	1,790	2,470	2,540	8,340
Opening cash	500	2,040	3,830	6,300	500
Closing cash	2,040	3,830	6,300	8,840	8,840

In the state examinations you are normally asked two very short questions in relation to the budget you have just completed.

Typical short questions

1. Bernie Black earns a net salary of €3,500 per month. If her total deductions are €850 per month, what is her gross salary?

   Answer: Gross salary = net salary plus deductions (€3,500 + €850 = €4,350)

2. How much, per year, does the Black family expect to pay for using the mobile phone?

   Answer: €960 (€80 per month multiplied by 12)

Occasionally you are told that, each month, the family intends to save a given sum of money (as distinct from keeping it as part of their net cash). Assume it is €300.

In this case two extra rows will be inserted after *Total expenditure*: one for *Savings* and one for *Total expenditure and savings*. The monthly figures for *Net cash*, *Opening cash* and *Closing cash* are then recalculated.

Using a summary of the budget above, this would change the figures shown in blue as follows.

BLACK FAMILY BUDGET ADJUSTED FOR €300 SAVING PER MONTH

	Jan	Feb	March	April	Total Jan–April
	€	€	€	€	€
Total income (A)	7,380	7,680	8,180	7,680	30,920
Total expenditure	5,840	5,890	5,710	5,140	22,580
Savings	300	300	300	300	1,200
Total expenditure + Savings (B)	6,140	6,190	6,010	5,440	23,780
Net cash (A – B)	1,240	1,490	2,170	2,240	7,140
Opening cash	500	1,740	3,230	5,400	500
Closing cash	1,740	3,230	5,400	7,640	7,640

LEARN THE KEY TERMS

- A **budget surplus** happens when the planned income for the month is greater than the planned expenditure for that month.
- A **budget deficit** happens when the planned expenditure for the month is greater than the planned income for that month.
- **Net cash** is the difference between total planned income and total planned expenditure each month.
- **Opening cash** is the amount of money a family plans to have at the start of a month.
- **Closing cash** is the planned net cash plus the planned opening cash.

QUESTIONS

1. Copy the uncompleted budget forms into your copy book, complete them and answer any questions asked after the budgets.

BUDGET A

	Jan	Feb	March	April	Total Jan–April
Income	3,000	3,000	3,000	3,000	12,000
Expenditure + savings	1,500	2,200	2,250	2,600	8,550
Net cash	?	?	?	?	?

BUDGET B

	Jan	Feb	March	April	Total Jan–April
Income	3,000	3,000	3,000	3,000	?
Expenditure	1,500	3,200	3,000	2,600	?
Net cash	?	?	?	?	?

In Budget B above, name any one month when the net cash will be a deficit.

BUDGET C

	Jan	Feb	March	April	Total Jan–April
Income	3,000	3,000	3,000	1,500	?
Expenditure	1,800	3,200	3,250	3,600	?
Net cash	?	?	?	?	?

In Budget C above, suggest any one reason why income is expected to fall by 50% in April.

BUDGET D

	Jan	Feb	March	April	Total Jan–April
Income	3,000	3,000	3,000	3,000	?
Expenditure	2,000	2,400	2,800	3,200	?
Net cash	?	?	?	?	?

In Budget D above, do you notice any trend in this family's planned expenditure?

2. Below is Mairéad Smith's budget for January and February.

MAIRÉAD SMITH'S BUDGET FOR JANUARY AND FEBRUARY		
	January	February
Opening cash	€0	€420
Total wages	€2,000	€2,000
TOTAL AVAILABLE TO SPEND	€2,000	€2,420
PLANNED SPENDING		
Mortgage	€250	€250
Food	€300	€280
ESB	€180	€160
Telephone	€150	€120
Entertainment	€400	€300
New clothes	€300	
Annual house insurance		€750
Annual VHI		€770
TOTAL SPENDING	€1,580	€2,630
Closing cash	€420	–€210

(a) Do you think this is a good budget? Give a reason for your answer.

(b) Assuming Mairéad's income cannot be increased, what suggestions would you make to her that would eliminate the deficit at the end of February?

3. The following is Brian Greene's income and spending for January and February.

BRIAN GREENE'S INCOME AND SPENDING FOR JANUARY AND FEBRUARY		
	January	February
Opening cash	€50	€250
Total wages	€2,200	€2,200
TOTAL AVAILABLE TO SPEND	€2,250	€2,450
PLANNED SPENDING		
Rent	€350	€350
Food	€280	€280
ESB	€100	€100
Petrol	€100	€100
Telephone	€80	€80
Entertainment	€700	€500
New clothes	€390	
Car insurance		€1,240
TOTAL SPENDING	€2,000	€2,650
Closing cash	€250	–€200

Assuming Brian's income cannot be increased, what suggestions would you make to him that would eliminate the deficit at the end of February?

See workbook for more questions.

Household budgets (Higher Level)

BUDGET TYPE 2 – ESTIMATING FIGURES FOR A 9-MONTH PERIOD

Question and solution

In this second budget type question you are given a partially completed budget for the first three months of the year. You are required to complete the budget by filling in the figures for the *Estimate April–December* column and the *Total for year* column. This form of question is aimed at testing your ability to draw up a budget and testing your arithmetical skills.

Mongey family budget

- John Mongey expects to earn €200 in overtime and get a bonus of €500 in December.
- Anne Mongey expects to retire from work at the end of October and receive a lump-sum payment of €20,000 in October, in addition to her monthly salary.
- Child Benefit will increase to €200 per month from 1 October.
- Mortgage repayments are expected to increase by €50 from 1 November.
- Car insurance monthly payments will be the same as the first three months.
- Monthly household expenses are expected to increase by €20 from 1 May.
- Car running costs are expected to remain at €80 per month, with extra costs for tyres of €400 in June and a car service costing €450 in July.
- The total yearly cost for light and heat is expected to be €1,440.
- The telephone bill is paid every second month and the cost is expected to be the same as at the beginning of the year.
- Birthday presents are expected to cost €110 in June and €150 in October; and Christmas presents in December are expected to cost €700.
- Entertainment is expected to continue at the same monthly average plus **an extra** €300 in December.
- A holiday in September will cost €2,500.

Calculations for estimated figures

- **John's salary estimate:** April to December is 9 months @ €1,500, giving a salary of €13,500 + overtime of €200 + bonus €500 = €14,200.
- **Anne's salary estimate:** April to December is the 7 months' salary to October @ €1,100, i.e. €7,700 + lump-sum payment of €20,000 = €27,700.
- **Child Benefit:** 6 months @ €150, i.e. €900 + 3 months @ €200, i.e. €600 = €1,500.
- **Mortgage:** 7 months April to October @ €800 per month, i.e. €5,600 + 2 months @ €850, i.e. €1,700 = €7,300.
- **Car insurance:** 9 months @ €65 per month = €585.
- The car tax and house insurance are paid once a year, therefore there are no payments in April–December.
- **Household expenses:** 1 month @ €920 + 8 months @ €940, i.e. €7,520 = €8,440.
- **Car running costs:** 9 months @ €80 per month, i.e. €720 + tyres, €400 + service of €450 = €1,570.
- **Light and heat:** If the total for the year is expected to be €1,440 and the total for January to March is €350, then the estimate for April to December must be €1,440 less €350 = €1,090.
- **Telephone:** bills are due every second month (April, June, August, October and December). Thus five bills @ €120 each = €600.
- **Presents:** €110 + €150 + €700 = €960.
- **Entertainment:** 9 months @ €200 per month, i.e. €1,800 + €300 extra in December, giving a total of €2,100.
- **Holiday:** €2,500.

The figure for *Total for year January to December* is calculated by adding the figure for *Total for January to March* to the figure for *Estimate April to December.*

MONGEY FAMILY BUDGET	Jan	Feb	March	Total Jan–March	Estimate Apr–Dec	Total for year Jan–Dec
PLANNED INCOME	€	€	€	€	€	€
John Mongey – Salary	1,500	1,500	1,500	4,500	14,200	18,700
Anne Mongey – Salary	1,100	1,100	1,100	3,300	27,700	31,000
Child Benefit	150	150	150	450	1,500	1,950
TOTAL INCOME	2,750	2,750	2,750	8,250	43,400	51,650
PLANNED EXPENDITURE						
Fixed						
House mortgage	800	800	800	2,400	7,300	9,700
Car insurance	65	65	65	195	585	780
Annual car tax		250		250	0	250
Annual house insurance			500	500	0	500
Subtotal	865	1,115	1,365	3,345	7,885	11,230
Irregular						
Household expenses	920	920	920	2,760	8,440	11,200
Car running costs	80	80	80	240	1,570	1,810
Light and heat costs	150		200	350	1,090	1,440
Telephone		120		120	600	720
Subtotal	1,150	1,120	1,200	3,470	11,700	15,170
Discretionary						
Presents	110			110	960	1,070
Entertainment	200	200	200	600	2,100	2,700
Holidays				0	2,500	2,500
Subtotal	310	200	200	710	5,560	6,270
TOTAL EXPENDITURE	2,325	2,435	2,765	7,525	25,145	32,670
Net cash	425	315	–15	725	18,255	18,980
Opening cash	500	925	1,240	500	1,225	500
Closing cash	925	1,240	1,225	1,225	19,480	19,480

Notes on opening cash

1. The original opening cash (here €500) always appears three times:
   (a) as the opening cash in the first month
   (b) as the opening cash in the *Total Jan–March* column
   (c) as the opening cash in the column *Total for year Jan–Dec*

2. The opening cash in the *Estimate April–Dec* column (here €1,225) is always the closing cash in the *Total Jan–March* column.

BUDGET TYPE 3 – REVISED BUDGETS

Question and solution

A family's circumstances may change after it has drawn up its budget. This may happen for a variety of reasons:

- One member of the family may have been made redundant or may have obtained a better job.
- Mortgage interest rates may have increased or decreased significantly.
- Some younger adult members of the family may have moved out to their own accommodation.
- There may have been a significant change in the general cost of living.

The family would have to revise its budget for any or all of these reasons.

Galvin household budget

On the facing page there is an Original Budget and a Revised Budget form for the Galvin household from July to September 2007. After preparing the Original Budget, Mr Galvin changed jobs and his salary increased. However, Ms Galvin lost her job in the local factory after it closed down in June. The Galvin household decided to revise its budget due to the changed circumstances.

Based on Junior Certificate Higher Paper 1, 2007 with alterations

You are required to complete the Revised Budget, taking into account the following:

- Mr Galvin's annual salary will be €25,800 net, payable monthly. He also expects to receive a bonus of €1,000 net in September.
- Ms Galvin will receive €600 net monthly in unemployment benefit.
- The Galvins will sell one of their two cars and expect to receive €6,800 for it in August.
- Mortgage repayments will increase by 8% from 1 September 2007.
- The Galvin household will make one loan repayment in July and will repay the balance of the loan, €3,500, in August.
- Car insurance will reduce by €30 per month from 1 August 2007.
- Household costs will reduce by 12% per month from 1 July 2007.
- Car costs will reduce to €70 per month from 1 August 2007.
- Entertainment costs will be reduced by 50%.
- Due to their changed circumstances, the holiday planned for September will be postponed.
- All other income and expenditure will remain the same.

Approach: Go through the revised budget line-by-line. Alter figures where needed and simply copy those figures that remain unchanged.

Calculations required for changes

- Mr Galvin's monthly salary = €25,800 divided by 12 = €2,150; Sept = €2,150 + €1,000
- Ms Galvin: €600 per month as stated
- Other income = €6,800 from sale of car
- Mortgage repayment in September = €800 + 8% of €800 (€64) = €864
- Loan repayment = original (€400) in July and €3,500 in August
- Car insurance reduces to €35 (i.e. €65 less €30) in August and September

(continued overleaf)

- Household costs = 88% of €750 = €660 per month
- Car costs = these will go from €150 in July to €70 for August and September.
- Entertainment costs: 50% of €200 = €100 per month
- Holiday in September = €0
- All other figures remain unchanged

GALVIN HOUSEHOLD	ORIGINAL BUDGET				REVISED BUDGET			
	July	Aug	Sept	Total	July	Aug	Sept	Total
PLANNED INCOME	€	€	€	€	€	€	€	€
Mr Galvin – Salary	1,500	1,500	1,500	4,500	2,150	2,150	3,150	7,450
Ms Galvin – Salary	1,120	1,120	1,120	3,360	600	600	600	1,800
Child Benefit	160	160	160	480	160	160	160	480
Other					0	6,800	0	6,800
TOTAL INCOME	2,780	2,780	2,780	8,340	2,910	9,710	3,910	16,530
PLANNED EXPENDITURE								
Fixed								
Mortgage	800	800	800	2,400	800	800	864	2,464
Loan repayments	400	400	400	1,200	400	3,500	0	3,900
Car insurance	65	65	65	195	65	35	35	135
Subtotal	1,265	1,265	1,265	3,795	1,265	4,335	899	6,499
Irregular								
Household costs	750	750	750	2,250	660	660	660	1,980
Car costs	150	150	150	450	150	70	70	290
Light and heat costs	245		190	435	245	0	190	435
Telephone costs	50	50	140	240	50	50	140	240
Subtotal	1,195	950	1,230	3,375	1,105	780	1,060	2,945
Discretionary								
Entertainment costs	200	200	200	600	100	100	100	300
Presents	300		250	550	300	0	250	550
Holiday			5,000	5,000	0	0	0	0
Subtotal	500	200	5,450	6,150	400	100	350	850
TOTAL EXPENDITURE	2,960	2,415	7,945	13,320	2,770	5,215	2,309	10,294
Net cash	–180	365	–5,165	–4,980	140	4,495	1,601	6,236
Opening cash	500	320	685	500	500	640	5,135	500
Closing cash	320	685	–4,480	–4,480	640	5,135	6,736	6,736

Note: It is helpful to insert '0' in areas where no figure is applicable. When all the spaces are full you will see that you have dealt with all items of income and expenditure.

ANALYSING AND COMMENTING ON BUDGETS

In the state examinations you are normally asked questions in relation to the budget you have just completed. When answering these questions make reference to the figures in the budget wherever possible.

In relation to the Galvins' budget (page 27) you could be asked the following questions:

Questions on the Galvin budget

1. In the Original Budget, name a month in which planned income is greater than planned expenditure.

   Answer: August, because it has a positive net cash of €365.

2. In the Original Budget, by how much did the Galvin household expect to overspend in the three months?

   Answer: A household overspends when its expenditure for a period is greater than its income for that period. In this case the answer is €4,980, i.e. the value of the negative net cash in the total column.

3. Give one reason why the repayments on the mortgage might increase.

   Answer: The interest rate on the mortgage may have increased.

4. Is the Revised Budget a good one? Give two reasons for your answer.

   Answer: It is a good one because: (i) the family expects to spend €10,294, which is less than its expected income of €16,530; (ii) the family should have €6,736 in cash at the end of September compared with an opening cash of €500 on 1 July.

General guidelines for analysing budgets

1. **The family's closing cash is increasing continuously.**
   The family should plan to save money in an account that will earn interest rather than having cash at home or in a bank account that pays no interest.

2. **The family's closing cash is constantly negative.**
   The family will have to do one or more of the following:
   - **(a)** Decrease its expenditure.
   - **(b)** Get an extra source of income.
   - **(c)** Obtain a medium-term loan to clear the debt and include the repayments in a revised budget.

3. **The family's closing cash is negative for a short period.**
   The family will have to do one or more of the following:
   - **(a)** Obtain a bank overdraft for that period (see page 100).
   - **(b)** Spread large once-off annual payments over twelve equal monthly instalments, if possible.
   - **(c)** Reduce discretionary expenditure during that period of time.
   - **(d)** Use any previous savings.

Note: People who are experiencing financial difficulties, have problems paying off debts or need advice on money management can contact **MABS** (Money Advice and Budgeting Service) at www.mabs.ie. This is a national, free, confidential and independent service.

QUESTIONS

1. Mr Flanagan expects his salary to be €2,500 for the first three months of the year. He expects a salary increase of 10% in October and also expects a bonus of €1,000 in December. Calculate, showing your workings:

   (a) his expected total income from January to March
   (b) his estimated income from April to December
   (b) his total income for the year January to December

2. A family makes a monthly bank repayment of €450 per month from January to March. Due to a decrease in interest rates the monthly repayments will reduce by €10 in May. The loan will be totally paid off when the September repayment has been made. Calculate, showing your workings:

   (a) total repayments from January to March
   (b) estimated repayments from April to December
   (b) total repayments for the year January to December

3. A family pays its ESB bill every two months, starting in January with a standard bill of €150. However, due to an increase in electricity charges in July its total annual ESB bill is expected to be €1,100. Calculate, showing your workings, the estimated cost of electricity for the period April to December.

4. List the following expenditure items under the appropriate heading, i.e. *Fixed*, *Irregular* or *Discretionary* expenditure.

   Annual car insurance
   New stereo system for the family car
   Petrol for the car
   Payment of electricity bills
   Bank loan repayments
   Purchase of school books
   Birthday presents
   Equal monthly payments of house insurance
   Visits to the cinema

5. What recommendations would you make to a family whose closing cash is constantly negative and the deficit is increasing?

6. Explain three reasons why a family may revise its budget.

7. Mr Donegan, who had no opening cash, had planned a budget from January to March that showed a total income of €2,500 per month and a total expenditure of €2,200 per month.

When he was informed of a 20% monthly increase in income he revised this budget to allow for a family holiday, costing €1,500, in February. This increase was to start in January. Complete the original budget and the revised budget on the summary form below.

DONEGAN HOUSEHOLD	ORIGINAL BUDGET				REVISED BUDGET			
	Jan	Feb	March	Total	Jan	Feb	March	Total
Total planned income								
Total planned expenditure								
Net cash	0				0			
Opening cash								
Closing cash								

8. Could Mr Donegan afford the holiday mentioned in Question 7? Explain your answer.

There are four full questions on Budget Type 2 and a further four full questions on Budget Type 3 in the workbook.

Household accounts: **The analysed cash book**

5

This chapter is your first introduction to *bookkeeping* or *accounting*.

If your parents told you to be home by nine o'clock and you arrived home at ten o'clock they may ask you to *account* for your lateness. You know that this means they want an explanation for your lateness, i.e. you have to account for your whereabouts during that extra hour. So accounting means explaining something or giving a record of something.

When we have a large number of money transactions it can be very easy to forget how, where and when the money was spent. Sometimes we may even forget where all the money came from! To avoid this situation we should keep a record, or an account, of all the money we receive and all the money we spend. When we do this it is called **bookkeeping** or **accounting**. Therefore, in bookkeeping *an account* can be:

- a record of all transactions we have with a particular person or company
- a record of all our money transactions, or
- a record of all the items we have purchased or sold, and so on.

Each account is given a name. We may have an account for our cash transactions, called a **Cash account**, or an account for all our transactions with our bank, called a **Bank account**. When naming an account we usually use the abbreviation **A/C** instead of the full word *account*, e.g. *Cash A/C*.

All accounts have two sides: the left-hand side and the right-hand side. The left-hand side is known as the **debit** side and the right-hand side is known as the **credit** side. We usually use the shorthand **Dr** and **Cr** for debit and credit respectively.

- The **debit side** is used to record anything **received**, e.g. if we receive cash it will be recorded on the debit side of the Cash A/C.
- The **credit side** is used to record anything **given**, e.g. if we pay out cash it will be recorded on the credit side of the Cash A/C.

When we say 'debit an account', this means the transaction is to be entered on the debit side of that account. Likewise when we say 'credit an account', this means that the transaction is to be entered on the credit side of that account.

This leads us to our first basic rule in bookkeeping:

Debit anything received.
Credit anything given.

We could keep a record of our cash transactions in a simple Cash A/C as shown below.

Dr side (money received)			CASH A/C		Cr side (money paid out)
Date	Details	€	Date	Details	€
1/1/10	Wages	700	2/1/10	Petrol	35
6/1/10	Child Benefit	200	3/1/10	Groceries	95
8/1/10	Wages	700	4/1/10	ESB	56
			5/1/10	Groceries	25
			7/1/10	Car insurance	200
			9/1/10	Car tyres	300
			8/1/10	**Balance**	**889**
		1,600			1,600

Here you can see that all cash received was recorded on the debit side (Dr) and all cash paid out was recorded on the credit (Cr) side.

The highlighted amount, €889, is the amount of cash left over, i.e. closing cash. It was calculated by subtracting the value of the transactions on the credit side from the value of the transactions on the debit side.

This gives us a record of the cash we have received and of how we spent that money. We have accounted for our money!

We could keep a record of our bank account transactions in the very same way, as shown below.

Dr side (money received)			BANK A/C		Cr side (money paid out)
Date	Details	€	Date	Details	€
1/1/10	Lodged wages	700	2/1/10	Petrol – Chq. 1	35
6/1/10	Lodged Child Benefit	200	3/1/10	Groceries – Chq. 2	95
8/1/10	Lodged wages	700	4/1/10	ESB – Chq. 3	56
			5/1/10	Groceries – Chq. 4	25
			7/1/10	Car insurance – Chq. 5	200
			9/1/10	Car tyres – Chq. 6	300
			8/1/10	**Balance**	**889**
		1,600			1,600

However, you may recall that when we were doing our budgets we showed the total amount we expected to receive in wages and the total amount we expected to spend on items such as groceries and our car. These amounts are not *obvious* from the bank or cash account; we still have to do some arithmetic to calculate these figures.

If, however, we record all our money transactions in a **cash book** we will be able to see all these details at a glance.

Therefore, the account for all money received and all money paid out is kept in the cash book, usually called the **analysed cash book**.

The **cash book** is used to record **all money received** and **all money paid out**.

Now look at your cash book copy. Its layout is similar to that shown below.

Dr side (money received)										ANALYSED CASH BOOK									Cr side (money paid out)
Date	Details	F	Cash	Bank	1	2	3	4	5	Date	Details	F	Cash	Bank	1	2	3	4	5
2010			€	€	€	€	€	€	€	2010			€	€	€	€	€	€	€

Explanation

- In the *Date* column you should enter the date of the transaction.
- In the *Details* column you should enter a description of the transaction.
- The *Folio* (F) column is for reference numbers, which we will deal with later.
- In the *Cash* column you should enter the amount that was either received in cash (debit side) or paid out in cash (credit side).
- In the *Bank* column you should enter the amount that was received and lodged to your bank (debit side) or the amount paid out of your bank (credit side).
- The columns marked 1 to 5 are known as the analysis columns. These are used to keep a record of your regular items of income and expenditure. You may use some or all of these columns depending on the directions given to you in an exercise.

Mr Browne's cash book 1 – basic entries

On 1/2/10 Mr Browne received his salary of €2,000 in cash.

- This **money was received**, so it is entered on the **debit side**.
- The transaction took place on 1/2/10, so this date is entered in the date column.
- The transaction was for Mr Browne's salary, so the description in the details column is *Salary*.
- Because the money was received in cash (not a cheque) €2,000 is entered in the cash column.
- In order to keep a record of the total amount he received as salary income, the €2,000 is also entered in the analysis column *Salary*.

On 2/2/10 he paid rent to his landlord by cash, €250.

- This **money was given** by Mr Browne, so it is entered on the **credit side**.
- The transaction took place on 2/2/10, so this date is entered in the date column.
- The transaction was a payment of rent to the landlord, so *Rent* appears in the details column.
- Because the money was paid in cash, €250 is entered in the cash column.
- In order to keep a record of the total amount paid for rent, the €250 is also entered in the analysis column *Rent*.

Dr side (money received)										ANALYSED CASH BOOK										Cr side (money paid out)
Date	Details	F	Cash	Bank	Salary					Date	Details	F	Cash	Bank	Rent					
2010			€	€	€	€	€	€	€	2010			€	€	€	€	€	€	€	
1/2/10	Salary		2,000		2,000					2/2/10	Rent		250		250					

Every transaction is recorded in either the cash or bank column **and** in one of the analysis columns.

When we were drawing up budgets we referred to **opening cash**. This is the cash that you have at the start of the budget period. You **own** this cash.

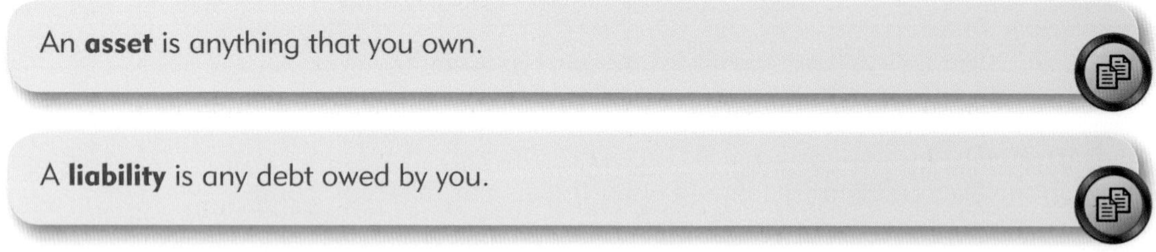

An **asset** is anything that you own.

A **liability** is any debt owed by you.

This leads us to our second basic rule in bookkeeping:

Debit assets.
Credit liabilities.

We own any cash we have at the start of a period and we own the money we have in the bank at the start of a period. Therefore they are assets. Because they are assets we enter them on the debit side of the cash book as opening balances, or simply, *Balance*.

Mr Browne's cash book 2 – more detail

We will now look at a more detailed record of another set of Mr Browne's **cash** transactions and enter them in the cash book.

Because all these transactions are cash transactions there is no need for bank columns.

The debit side has only two analysis columns. This means you will have four unused columns on the debit side of your cash book. Also there are only three analysis columns on the credit side, leaving you with three unused columns.

Mr Browne had the following transactions during the month of May 2010.

In this exercise you are to use a *Wages* analysis column and a *Child Benefit* analysis column on the debit side. On the credit side, use analysis columns for *Car*, *Light* and *Food*.

1/5/10 Cash on hand €300. (Opening cash is often described this way.) It is an asset, so it is a debit.

1/5/10 Mr Browne received his wages of €600 in cash. This is money received, so it is a debit. Because it is for his wages it is also entered in the *Wages* analysis column.

4/5/10 Paid for groceries by cash, €90. This is money paid out, so it is a credit. Because it was for groceries we also enter it in the *Food* analysis column.

6/5/10 The Brownes received Child Benefit for the month in cash of €120. This is money received, so it is a debit and it is also entered in the *Child Benefit* analysis column.

7/5/10 Paid for petrol by cash, €40. This is money paid out, so it is a credit. This cost is associated with the car so it is also entered in the *Car* analysis column.

8/5/10 Mr Browne received his wages of €600 in cash. This is money received, so it is a debit. It is also entered in the *Wages* analysis column.

12/5/10 Paid the light bill to the ESB, €150, in cash. This is money paid out, so it is a credit. It is also entered in the *Light* analysis column.

13/5/10 Paid for groceries by cash, €95. This is money paid out, so it is a credit. Because it was for groceries we also enter it in the *Food* analysis column.

14/5/10 Paid for petrol with €50 cash. This is money paid out, so it is a credit. As for the 7/5/10 amount, it is also entered in the *Car* analysis column.

15/5/10 Mr Browne received his wages of €600 in cash. This is money received, so it is a debit. It is also entered under the *Wages* analysis column.

16/5/10 Paid for car service by cash, €200. This is money paid out, so it is a credit. The cost relates to the car, so it is entered in the *Car* analysis column.

* On 16/5/10 there is a figure of €1,595 on the credit side. This is the amount of cash Mr Browne should have left at this date, i.e. the closing cash balance.

Dr side (money received) — **ANALYSED CASH BOOK** — **Cr side (money paid out)**

Date	Details	F	Cash	Wages	Child Benefit	Date	Details	F	Cash	Car	Light	Food
2010			€	€	€	2010			€	€	€	€
1/5/10	Balance		300			4/5/10	Groceries		90			90
1/5/10	Mr Browne – wages		600	600		7/5/10	Petrol		40	40		
6/5/10	Child Benefit		120		120	12/5/10	ESB		150		150	
8/5/10	Mr Browne – wages		600	600		13/5/10	Groceries		95			95
15/5/10	Mr Browne – wages		600	600		14/5/10	Petrol		50	50		
						16/5/10	Car service		200	200		
						16/5/10	**Balance c/d***		**1,595**			
			2,220	1,800	120				2,220	290	150	185
1/6/10	Balance b/d		1,595									

Explanation

The family had €300 at the start of the month, i.e. its opening cash. It received four sums of money, €600, €120, €600 and €600, during this time. Thus if the family had not spent any money it would have a total of €2,220. However, it *did* spend all the money listed on the credit side from the groceries on 4/5/10 down to the car service on 16/5/10, i.e. a total of €625. Subtract the €625 from the €2,220. This gives €1,595 which is the closing cash balance. A balance makes two sides equal to each other.

Calculating the closing balance and showing totals

These calculations should be done on a rough-work page or with your calculator.

1. After entering the last transaction, add all the figures in the cash column on the debit side. In our example this was €2,220.
2. Add up all the figures in the cash column on the credit side. In our example this was €625.
3. Subtract the two figures from each other and enter the answer, €1,595, on the next available line in the cash column, credit side, and write *Balance c/d* in the details column (c/d means 'carried down'). The balance in the cash column will always be on the credit side (you cannot spend more cash than you have received). We will see later that it can be on either side in the bank column.
4. Add up the figures in each of the analysed columns on the credit side and show the totals.
5. Add up the figures in each of the analysed columns on the debit side and show the totals **in line with the totals on the credit side**.
6. Always put a double line under totals.
7. You will recall, from your budgets, that the closing cash one month becomes the opening cash the next month. This is shown on the debit side on the first day of the next month. In the details column write *Balance b/d* and show the value in the *Cash* column (b/d means 'brought down').

By writing up the cash book in this way we are able to see immediately how much cash we should have, i.e. the closing balance. It also shows us how much income we received under the various headings and how much we spent on each area of expenditure. This information can be very useful when we are drawing up future budgets. We can also compare the information in the cash book with our budget to ensure that we are not overspending.

Contra entries

There are situations that require us to make a debit entry **and** a credit entry in the same account for the one transaction. These are called **contra entries**.

Example 1

If I go into my bank (or use an ATM) and withdraw cash from my account it will affect both my cash account and my bank account.

(**a**) I have received cash, therefore I will have to debit the *Cash* column in my cash book to show the cash received. I write *Bank* in the details column to show the source of the cash.

(**b**) Money has been paid out of my bank, so I have to credit the *Bank* column in the cash book to show this. I write *Cash* in the details column to show where the money went.

For example, I withdrew €400 from my bank on 1/1/11 (only the bank and cash columns are shown).

Dr side (money received)										ANALYSED CASH BOOK									Cr side (money paid out)		
Date	Details	F	Cash	Bank							Date	Details	F	Cash	Bank						
2010			€	€	€	€	€	€	€		2010			€	€	€	€	€	€	€	
1/1/11	Bank	¢	400								1/1/11	Cash	¢		400						

Example 2

If I take cash from home and lodge it in my bank account, the same two accounts are affected.

(a) My bank account has received money, so I will have to debit the *Bank* column in my cash book to show the money received. Write *Cash* in the details.

(b) I have paid out cash, so I will have to credit the *Cash* column in the cash book to show the money paid out. Write *Bank* in the details.

For example, I lodged €600 cash into my bank account on 3/1/11 (only the bank and cash columns are shown).

Dr side (money received)										ANALYSED CASH BOOK									Cr side (money paid out)		
Date	Details	F	Cash	Bank							Date	Details	F	Cash	Bank						
2010			€	€	€	€	€	€	€		2010			€	€	€	€	€	€	€	
3/1/11	Cash	¢		600							1/1/11	Bank	¢	600							

When recording these transactions in the cash book we place a contra sign '¢' in the folio columns on both the debit and the credit side.

Mr Browne's cash book 3 – bank account transactions

Our next example records another set of transactions for Mr Browne. This time we will also include his bank account transactions, i.e. lodgements to his bank account and payments by cheque.

Record the following transactions in Mr Browne's analysed cash book.

Instructions: On the debit side use *Cash, Bank, Child Benefit* and *Interest* columns.

On the credit side use *Cash, Bank, Groceries, Phone, Heating, Car* and *Others.*

The *Others* column (which can also be called *Sundries*) is for transactions that do not fit any of the headings you are given. Notice that we are using the *Folio* column on the credit side to record the numbers on the cheques used.

Transactions

1/5/10 Cash on hand €300 and cash at bank €1,000. These are the opening balances; they are assets, so they are a debit.

1/5/10 Mr Browne received his wages of €900 which were lodged to his bank account. This is money received and put into his bank account, so debit the *Bank* column and enter it in the *Wages* analysis column.

3/5/10 Paid for meat by cash, €100. This is money paid out so it is a credit. Because it was for food, enter it in the *Groceries* analysis column.

4/5/10 The Brownes received the Child Benefit for the month of €210 in cash. This is cash received, so it is a debit. Also enter it in the *Child Benefit* analysis column.

5/5/10 Mr Browne withdrew €500 cash from his bank account. Debit the *Cash* column and credit the *Bank* column. See explanation above.

6/5/10 Paid the house insurance of €600 with cheque no. 1. This is money paid out, so it is a credit. Because we don't have a heading for house insurance, enter it in the *Others* column.

7/5/10 Paid for petrol with cheque no. 2, €40. This is money paid out, so it is a credit. Because it was paid by cheque, enter the amount in the bank column and the *Car* analysis column.

8/5/10 Paid for heating oil, €700, with cheque no. 3. This is money paid out, so it is a credit. Because it was paid by cheque, enter the amount in the *Bank* column and the *Heating* analysis column.

9/5/10 Mr Browne received his wages of €900 which were lodged to his bank account. This is money received and put into his bank account, so debit the bank column and enter it in the *Wages* analysis column.

10/5/10 Paid the telephone bill, €150, with cheque no. 4. This is money paid out, so it is a credit. Because it was paid by cheque, enter the amount in the bank column and the *Phone* analysis column.

13/5/10 Interest earned, €100, was lodged to Mr Browne's bank account. This is money received and put into his bank account, so debit the bank column and enter it in the *Interest* analysis column.

14/5/10 Paid for petrol by cash, €50. This is cash paid out so it is a credit. Also enter it in the *Car* analysis column.

15/5/10 Mr Browne received his wages of €900 which were lodged to his bank account. This is money received and put into his bank account, so debit the bank column and enter it in the *Wages* analysis column.

18/5/10 Paid Tours Ltd €3,000 for a family holiday, with cheque no. 5. This is money paid out, so it is a credit. Because we don't have a heading for holidays, enter it in the *Others* column.

Dr side (money received)								**ANALYSED CASH BOOK**									**Cr side (money paid out)**
Date	Details	F	Cash	Bank	Wages	Child Benefit	Interest	Date	Details	F	Cash	Bank	Groceries	Phone	Heating	Car	Others
2010			€	€	€	€	€	2010			€	€	€	€	€	€	€
1/5/10	Balance		300	1,000				3/5/10	Meat		100		100				
1/5/10	Mr Browne – wages			900	900			5/5/10	Cash	¢		500					
4/5/10	Child Benefit		210			210		6/5/10	House insurance	1		600					600
5/5/10	Bank	¢	500					7/5/10	Petrol	2		40				40	
9/5/10	Mr Browne – wages			900	900			8/5/10	Heating oil	3		700			700		
13/5/10	Interest			100			100	10/5/10	Telephone	4		150		150			
15/5/10	Mr Browne – wages			900	900			14/5/10	Petrol		50					50	
18/5/10	**Balance c/d**			**1,190**				18/5/10	Tours Ltd	5		3,000					3,000
								18/5/10	**Balance c/d**		**860**						
			1,010	4,990	2,700	210	100				1,010	4,990	100	150	700	90	3,600
19/5/10	Balance b/d		860					19/5/10	Balance b/d			1,190					

Notes

1. The closing *Cash* balance is entered on the credit side because the total value, €150, of the credit transactions was less than the total value, €1,010, of the debit transactions. This is then brought down on the debit side at the start of the next period.
2. The closing *Bank* balance of €1,190 is entered on the debit side. This is because the total value of the debit transactions (€3,800) was less than the total value of the credit transactions (€4,990), a difference of €1,190. This is then brought down on the credit side at the start of the next period.
3. When the bank balance is brought down on the credit side it means that that amount of money is owed to the bank. It is called a bank overdraft. We will deal with this in more detail in Chapter 10.

If the opening bank balance is an overdraft (or if you are told that the opening bank balance is a credit balance) then it is entered in the bank column on the credit side of the cash book as it is money owed to the bank, i.e. it is a liability.

For example, 1/1/10: Cash on hand €600 and cash at bank €550 (Cr).

Dr side (money received)						ANALYSED CASH BOOK											Cr side (money paid out)		
Date	Details	F	Cash	Bank	Salary					Date	Details	F	Cash	Bank	Rent				
2010			€	€	€	€	€	€	€	2010			€	€	€	€	€	€	€
1/1/10	Balance		600							1/1/10	Balance			550					

LEARN THE KEY TERMS

- An **account** is a record of transactions.
- The **cash book** is used to record all money received and all money paid out.
- The **debit side of the cash book** is used to record money received.
- The **credit side of the cash book** is used to record money paid out.
- **Rule 1:**
  Debit anything received.
  Credit anything given.
- An **asset** is anything that you own or any debt owed to you.
- A **liability** is any debt owed by you.
- **Rule 2:**
  Debit assets.
  Credit liabilities.
- **Contra entries** are transactions that require a debit and a credit entry in the same account for any one transaction.
- **Opening cash** is the amount of cash a person or family has at the start of a period.
- **Closing cash** is the amount of cash a person or family has at the end of a period. It is calculated by finding the difference between the value of the items recorded on the debit side and the value of the items recorded on the credit side.

QUESTIONS

See workbook for Cash A/C and Bank A/C exercises.

1. What is an account?
2. Name the two sides of an account.
3. What is the cash book used to record?
4. What is meant by the term **opening cash** in the cash book?
5. What is an asset?
6. What is a liability?
7. Why is **opening cash** an asset?
8. Why is a credit opening bank balance a liability?
9. The debit side of the cash book is used to record ____________ and the credit side of the cash book is used to record ____________.
10. What is a contra entry?

Analysed cash book exercises – Questions 11 and 12 deal with cash transactions only

11. The Maguire household use an analysed cash book to record all income and expenditure. All transactions are by means of cash. From the following information you are required to write up and balance their analysed cash book. Use the following headings:

Dr side *Cash, Wages* **Cr side** *Cash, Heating, Car, Groceries*

1/3/10	Received wages	€800
4/3/10	Paid for petrol	€40
6/3/10	Paid for groceries	€120
5/3/10	Paid for heating oil	€600
8/3/10	Received wages	€800
9/3/10	Paid for groceries	€100
12/3/10	Paid for petrol	€35
13/3/10	Purchased bottled gas for gas heater	€70

12. The Duffy household use an analysed cash book to record all income and expenditure. All transactions are by means of cash. From the following information you are required to write up and balance their analysed cash book. Use the following headings:

Dr side *Cash, Wages, Child Benefit* **Cr side** *Cash, Light, Car, Groceries*

1/6/10	Cash on hand	€400
2/6/10	Paid for petrol	€50
4/6/10	Received wages	€500
5/6/10	Paid for groceries	€100
10/6/10	Received Child Benefit	€210
11/6/10	Received wages	€500
12/6/10	Paid for groceries	€110
15/6/10	Paid ESB bill for light	€85
18/6/10	Received wages	€500
20/6/10	Paid for new tyres for the car	€360

Bank transactions only

13. The Murphy household use an analysed cash book to record all income and expenditure. All income is lodged to the bank and all payments are by cheque. From the following information you are required to write up and balance their analysed cash book. Use the following headings:

Dr side *Bank, Wages*
Cr side *Bank, Groceries, Car, Telephone*

1/7/10	Opening bank balance	€2,000	
2/7/10	Paid telephone bill	€200	Chq. no. 1
4/7/10	Received wages	€850	
5/7/10	Paid for groceries	€85	Chq. no. 2
10/7/10	Paid for petrol	€55	Chq. no. 3
11/7/10	Received wages	€850	
12/7/10	Paid for groceries	€110	Chq. no. 4
15/7/10	Paid for car service	€350	Chq. no. 5
18/7/10	Received wages	€850	
19/7/10	Paid for 'top-up' for mobile phone	€60	Chq. no. 6

Questions 14 to 18 deal with cash and bank transactions

14. The Keane household use an analysed cash book to record all income and expenditure. From the following information you are required to write up and balance their analysed cash book. Use the following headings:

Dr side *Cash, Bank, Wages, Child Benefit*
Cr side *Cash, Bank, Car, Groceries, Light, Others*

1/8/11	Cash on hand	€400	
1/8/10	Cash at bank	€2,000	
2/8/10	Paid for petrol	€60	Chq. no. 1
4/8/10	Received wages, which were lodged	€700	
5/8/10	Paid for groceries by cash	€100	
10/8/10	Received Child Benefit in cash	€210	
11/8/10	Received wages, which were lodged	€700	
12/8/10	Paid for groceries by cash	€95	
13/8/10	Family outing to the cinema cost, cash	€60	
15/8/10	Paid ESB bill for light	€85	Chq. no. 2
18/8/10	Received wages, which were lodged	€700	
19/8/10	Paid for groceries by cash	€105	
20/8/10	Paid for new tyres for the car	€380	Chq. no. 3
23/8/10	Paid rent	€800	Chq. no. 4
25/8/10	Paid cash for new light bulbs	€40	

15. The Byrne household use an analysed cash book to record all receipts and payments. From the following information you are required to write up and balance their analysed cash book. Use the following headings:

Dr side *Cash, Bank, Wages, Child Benefit, Others*
Cr side *Cash, Bank, Groceries, Telephone, Heating, Entertainment*

1/9/10	Cash on hand	€800	
1/9/10	Cash at bank	€3,500	
2/9/10	Paid landline telephone bill	€120	Chq. no. 8
4/9/10	Received wages, which were lodged	€500	
5/9/10	Paid for groceries by cash	€120	
10/9/10	Received Child Benefit in cash	€115	
12/9/10	Won cash in local club raffle	€500	
14/9/10	Rented videos by cash	€40	(entertainment)
15/9/10	Purchased heating oil	€750	Chq. no. 9
16/9/10	Withdrew cash from the bank	€500	(contra entry)
18/9/10	Received wages, which were lodged	€500	
20/9/10	Paid for groceries by cash	€105	
22/9/10	Purchased 'top-up' for mobile phones	€80	Chq. no. 10
23/9/10	Family outing to a restaurant cost	€250	Chq. no. 11
25/9/10	Paid cash for groceries	€85	

16. The Tchaikovsky household use an analysed cash book to record all receipts and payments. From the following information you are required to write up and balance their analysed cash book. Use the following headings:

Dr side *Cash, Bank, Wages, Child Benefit*
Cr side *Cash, Bank, Groceries, Telephone, Car, Clothes, Others*

1/10/10	Cash on hand	€1,000	
1/10/10	Cash at bank	€200	
3/10/10	Paid for groceries by cash	€180	
5/10/10	Received wages, which were lodged	€600	
7/10/10	Paid for clothes	€420	Chq. no. 19
10/10/10	Received Child Benefit in cash	€220	
11/10/10	Paid for petrol	€55	Chq. no. 20
12/10/10	Received wages, which were lodged	€600	
13/10/10	Paid deposit for holiday	€600	Chq. no. 21
14/10/10	Purchased new mobile phone	€180	Chq. no. 22
16/10/10	Withdrew cash from bank	€400	
19/10'10	Received wages, which were lodged	€600	
20/10/10	Paid for groceries by cash	€105	
21/10/10	Purchased new stereo system for car	€500	Chq. no. 23
22/10/10	Paid for new suit	€350	Chq. no. 24
25/10/10	Paid telephone bill	€185	Chq. no. 25

17. The Smith household use an analysed cash book to record all receipts and payments. From the following information you are required to write up and balance their analysed cash book. Use the following headings:

Dr side *Cash, Bank, Wages, Child Benefit*
Cr side *Cash, Bank, Groceries, Light & Heat, Car, Entertainment, Others*

1/11/10	Cash on hand	€200	
1/11/10	Bank balance	€500	credit, i.e. overdraft
2/11/10	Paid for groceries by cash	€180	
4/11/10	Received wages, which were lodged	€500	
6/11/10	Paid ESB bill	€185	Chq. no. 26
9/11/10	Received Child Benefit in cash	€140	
10/11/10	Paid for petrol	€60	Chq. no. 27
11/11/10	Received wages, which were lodged	€500	
13/11/10	Paid for heating oil	€600	Chq. no. 28
15/11/10	Purchased tickets for the theatre	€120	Chq. no. 29
16/11/10	Withdrew cash from bank	€600	
17/11/10	Paid for car service by cash	€420	
18/11/10	Received wages, which were lodged	€500	
19/11/10	Paid for groceries by cash	€105	
20/11/10	Purchased new sitting room carpet	€1,500	Chq. no. 30

18. The Turner household use an analysed cash book to record all income and expenditure. From the following information you are required to write up and balance their analysed cash book. Use the following headings:

Dr side *Cash, Bank, Wages, Child Benefit*
Cr side *Cash, Bank, Groceries, Telephone, Car, Others*

1/12/10	Cash on hand	€1,500	
1/12/10	Bank balance	€200	credit
3/12/10	Paid for groceries by cash	€220	
5/12/10	Received wages, which were lodged	€900	
6/12/10	Paid telephone bill	€205	Chq. no. 32
9/12/10	Received Child Benefit, which was lodged	€240	
10/12/10	Paid for petrol	€50	Chq. no. 33
12/12/10	Received wages, which were lodged	€900	
13/12/10	Paid for repairs to roof	€350	Chq. no. 34
13/12/10	Paid for petrol by cash	€45	
15/12/10	Purchased tickets for football match	€75	cash
16/12/10	Withdrew cash from bank	€200	
17/12/10	Paid car insurance	€420	Chq. no. 35
19/12/10	Received wages, which were lodged	€900	
19/12/10	Paid for groceries by cash	€85	
20/12/10	Purchased new TV	€1,100	Chq. no. 36
21/12/10	Received Christmas bonus wages, which were lodged	€800	
22/12/10	Lodged cash in bank	€100	
23/12/10	Paid for Christmas presents	€800	Chq. no. 37

See workbook for more questions.

Budgets revisited: **Budget comparison statements**

6

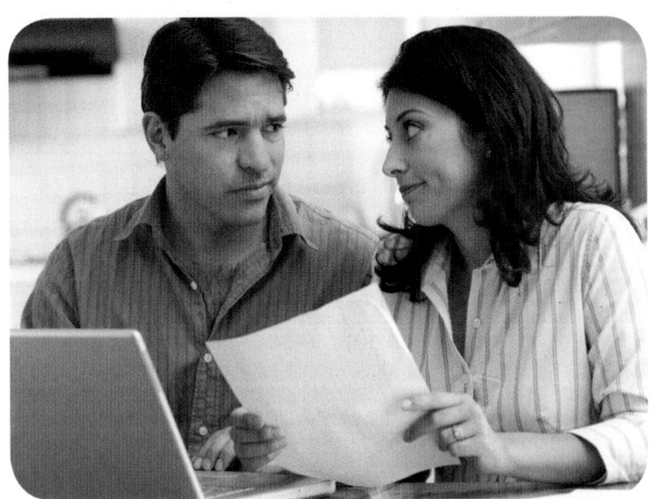

Our household budget outlined how we planned to spend our expected income. In the last chapter we saw how to record the actual amount of income we received and how we spent that income.

It is very easy to have a planned budget at the start of a period and then forget about it. We should compare our plan with what actually happened on a regular basis. This will help us to keep within budget or, if necessary, revise our budget or change our spending pattern.

We compare our budgeted figures with our actual figures by drawing up a **budget comparison statement**.

A budget comparison statement shows:

- the **budgeted** figures
- the **actual** figures taken from the analysed cash book
- the **difference** between them

Thus we can conclude that a budget comparison statement is used to compare and highlight the difference between *budgeted* income and expenditure and *actual* income and expenditure.

We will first look at a budget comparison statement and then at two different ways you could be asked to draw up one of these statements.

BUDGET COMPARISON STATEMENT			
	Budget	Actual	Difference
INCOME	€	€	€
Wages	10,280	10,347	**+ 67**
Child Benefit	70	60	**– 10**
Lotto win	______	10,000	**+ 10,000**
TOTAL INCOME	10,350	20,407	**+ 10,057**
EXPENDITURE			
Fixed			
Mortgage	3,000	2,750	**– 250**
House insurance	500	560	**+ 60**
Subtotal	3,500	3,310	**– 190**
Irregular			
Groceries	270	143	**–127**
House	390	245	**–145**
Shoes and clothes	120	145	**+ 25**
Car	100	84	**– 16**
Subtotal	880	617	**– 263**
Discretionary			
Presents	600	800	**+ 200**
Holidays	2,500	2,100	**– 400**
Subtotal	3,100	2,900	**– 200**
TOTAL EXPENDITURE	7,480	6,827	**– 653**
Net cash	2,870	13,580	**+ 10,710**
Opening cash	200	200	
Closing cash	3,070	13,780	

- The figures in the *Budget* column are taken from the household budget.
- The figures in the *Actual* column are taken from the analysed cash book.
- The figures in the *Difference* column are calculated by subtracting the *Budget* figures from the *Actual* figures, i.e. **Actual** minus **Budget** = **Difference**.
- It is essential to show the + and – signs to indicate when the *Actual* figures are greater than (+) or less than (–) the *Budget* figures.

Examples

Wages		Groceries	
Actual	€10,347	Actual	€143
Less Budget	€10,280	Less Budget	€270
Difference	+ €67	Difference	– €127

By inserting the + and – signs we can see clearly that the actual wages received were greater than planned and that the actual expenditure on groceries was less than planned.

The sum of the individual figures in the *Difference* columns should equal the difference between *Total Actual* and *Total Budgeted* figures. Look at the income figures in the example above.

The figures in the *Difference* column are: + €67 – €10 + €10,000 = + €10,057

Total actual income of €20,407 minus *Total budgeted income* of €10,350 = + €10,057

Remember:

Total expenditure = the three subtotals added together.

Net cash = *Total income* less *Total expenditure*.

Opening cash is always stated in any question you may have to do.

Closing cash = *Net cash* + *Opening cash*.

In real life drawing up a budget comparison statement is very simple. We just compare the figures in the budget with the figures in the analysed cash book and calculate the difference between them.

However, in questions or exams the information you require may be presented to you in a number of different ways The two most common ways are outlined below.

1. You are given the budget figures and sufficient information to calculate the actual income and expenditure figures. These calculations are very similar to the calculations you used when you were drawing up revised budgets.

2. You are given budget figures, but this time you are also given actual figures to be used to write up the analysed cash book. You then use the information from this to get the actual figures to be used in the budget comparison statement.

QUESTION TYPE 1

When the Jones household checked their analysed cash book at the end of December 2010, they discovered that their actual income and expenditure for the 12 months differed from the budgeted figures in the partially completed budget comparison statement, for the following reasons:

- The salaries of the Jones household increased by 6%.
- There are two children in the household. The monthly Child Benefit increased by €10 per child from 1 October 2010.
- Mortgage payments decreased by €10 per month from 1 July 2010.
- Mr Jones incurred penalty points on his driving licence resulting in a 20% increase in his motor insurance.
- The house insurance was €250 for the year.
- Household costs were 7.5% greater than budgeted.
- Car costs were €120 less than budgeted.
- Light and heat costs were 10% less than budgeted.
- Entertainment costs averaged €150 per month except for the two months of June and December, which averaged €200.
- Presents cost 20% more than budgeted.
- Holidays cost €2,750.

Complete the budget comparison statement by entering the appropriate figures into the *Actual* and *Difference* columns.

Note: Use plus sign if *Actual* is **greater** than the *Budget* figure. Use minus sign if *Actual* is **less** than the *Budget* figure.

Calculations

The *Actual* figures shown in blue in the budget comparison statement opposite are calculated as follows:

- **Salaries:** 106% of €25,000 = **€26,500**
- **Child Benefit:** increased by €20 per month for three months (€60), giving budgeted €600 + €60 = **€660**
- **Mortgage:** decreased by €60, giving budgeted €3,600 less €60 = **€3,540**
- **Car insurance:** 120% of €700 = **€840**
- **House insurance: €250** (stated in the question)
- **Household costs:** 107.5% of €9,000 = **€9,675**
- **Car costs:** Budgeted figure of €1,200 less €120 = **€1,080**
- **Light and heat costs:** €2,000 less €200 (i.e. 10% of €2,000) = **€1,800**
- **Entertainment:** 10 months @ €150 per month (€1,500) + 2 months @ €200 (€400) = **€1,900**
- **Presents:** €600 plus €120 (i.e. 20% of €600) = **€720**
- **Holidays: €2,750** (stated in the question)

Note: The change in the net cash should equal the difference between the *Actual* and the *Budgeted* closing cash, i.e. €6,005 minus €5,900 = + €105.

The supplementary questions below the budget comparison statement opposite are typical of those asked in the Junior Certificate examination. They require simple, brief answers based on your budget comparison statement.

BUDGET COMPARISON STATEMENT FOR 2010			
	Budget	Actual	Difference
INCOME	€	€	€
Salaries	25,000	26,500	+ 1,500
Child Benefit	600	660	+ 60
TOTAL INCOME	25,600	27,160	+ 1,560
EXPENDITURE			
Fixed			
Mortgage	3,600	3,540	– 60
Car insurance	700	840	+ 140
House insurance	300	250	– 50
Subtotal	4,600	4,630	+ 30
Irregular			
Household costs	9,000	9,675	+ 675
Car costs	1,200	1,080	– 120
Light and heat costs	2,000	1,800	– 200
Subtotal	12,200	12,555	+ 355
Discretionary			
Entertainment	1,700	1,900	+ 200
Presents	600	720	+ 120
Holidays	2,000	2,750	+ 750
Subtotal	4,300	5,370	+ 1,070
TOTAL EXPENDITURE	21,100	22,555	+ 1,455
Net cash	4,500	4,605	+ 105
Opening cash	1,400	1,400	
Closing cash	5,900	6,005	

1. What was the budgeted closing cash at the end of 2010?
   Answer: €5,900, i.e. the closing cash in the *Budget* column.

2. How much had the Jones household budgeted to save during 2010?
   Answer: €4,500, i.e. the net cash in the *Budget* column, or the difference between the budgeted opening cash and budgeted closing cash.

3. What was the actual closing cash at the end of 2010?
   Answer: €6,005, i.e. the closing cash in the *Actual* column.

4. State by how much the Jones household exceeded their budgeted total expenditure.
   Answer: €1,455, i.e. the figure in the *Difference* column in *Total expenditure*.

QUESTION TYPE 2

The McCauley family keeps a record of all financial transactions in an analysed cash book. On 1 March 2010 they had €200 in the bank.

During March the family had the following transactions:

Date	Transaction	€
1 March	Purchased paint for house by cheque no. 1	80
5 March	Lodged wages cheque	2,500
9 March	Paid for groceries with cheque no. 2	150
11 March	Paid for new clothes with cheque no. 3	350
12 March	Lodged wages cheque	2,700
15 March	Lodged Child Benefit	210
18 March	Paid house insurance with cheque no. 4	550
19 March	Lodged wages cheque	2,700
22 March	Paid for petrol with cheque no. 5	50
23 March	Paid for groceries with cheque no. 6	180
25 March	Paid TV licence with cheque no. 7	200
26 March	Lodged wages cheque	2,500
28 March	Paid for holidays with cheque no. 8	2,100

A. Enter the above transactions in the analysed cash book using the following headings:
Debit side: *Bank, Wages, Child Benefit*
Credit side: *Bank, Groceries, House, Clothes, Car, Other*

B. Using the partially completed budget comparison statement on page 51, enter the appropriate figures (from the analysed cash book you have prepared), in the *Actual* and *Difference* columns.

Note: In the *Difference* column use a plus sign if *Actual* is **greater** than the *Budget* figure. Use a minus sign if *Actual* is **less** than the *Budget* figure.

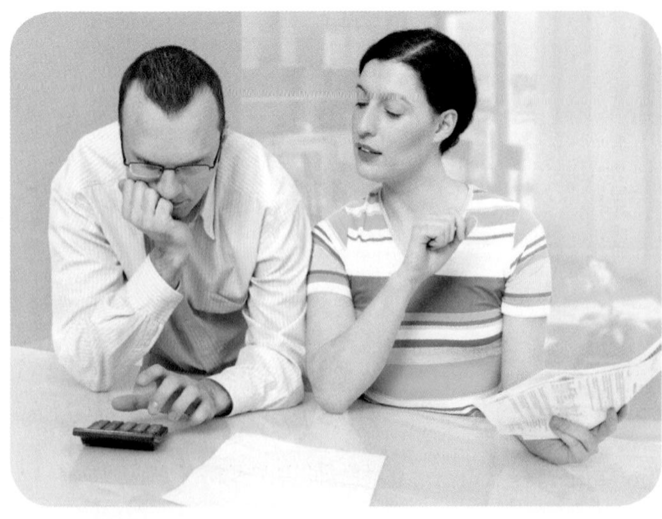

A. Complete the analysed cash book in the normal way, remembering to debit money received and credit money given.

Don't forget to enter the opening cash at the start. This is shown in **bold type** in the solution below.

Dr side (money received)					ANALYSED CASH BOOK								Cr side (money paid out)
Date	Details	Bank	Wages	Child Benefit	Date	Details	Bank	Groceries	House	Clothes	Car	Others	
2010		€	€	€	2010		€	€	€	€	€	€	
01/03/10	**Balance**	**200**			01/03/10	House paint Chq. no. 1	80		80				
05/03/10	Wages	2,500	2,500		09/03/10	Groceries Chq. no. 2	150	150					
12/03/10	Wages	2,700	2,700		11/03/10	Clothes Chq. no. 3	350			350			
15/03/10	Child Benefit	210		210	18/03/10	House insurance Chq. no. 4	550		550				
19/03/10	Wages	2,700	2,700		22/03/10	Petrol Chq. no. 5	50				50		
26/03/10	Wages	2,500	2,500		23/03/10	Groceries Chq. no. 6	180	180					
					25/03/10	TV licence Chq. no. 7	200					200	
					28/03/10	Holidays Chq. no. 8	2,100					2,100	
					30/03/10	Balance c/d	7,150						
		10,810	**10,400**	**210**			10,810	**330**	**630**	**350**	**50**	**2,300**	
01/04/10	Balance b/d	7,150											

B. The **totals** of each of the analysed columns, shown in blue, are now entered as the *Actual* figures in the budget comparison statement.

PARTIALLY COMPLETED BUDGET COMPARISON STATEMENT

	Budget	Actual	Difference
INCOME	€	€	€
Wages	10,000	10,400	+ 400
Child Benefit	190	210	+ 20
TOTAL INCOME	10,190	10,610	+ 420
EXPENDITURE			
Groceries	400	330	– 70
House	600	630	+ 30
Clothes	300	350	+ 50
Car	40	50	+ 10
Other	2,500	2,300	– 200
TOTAL EXPENDITURE	3,840	3,660	– 180
Net cash	6,350	6,950	+ 600
Opening cash	200	200	
Closing cash	6,550	7,150	

Do not fill in the shaded area.

Notes on completing the budget comparison statement

1. You may have noticed that *Net cash*, *Opening cash* and *Closing cash* in the *Budget* column were not shown in the partially completed budget comparison statement. **You must insert these figures when completing the budget comparison statement.**
   - (a) *Net cash* is the total budgeted income of €10,190 less total budgeted expenditure of €3,840, which gives €6,350.
   - (b) The *Opening cash* is the original opening cash given at the start of the question, i.e. €200.
   - (c) The *Closing cash* is calculated in the normal way, *Net cash* of €6,350 plus *Opening cash* of €200, which gives €6,550.
2. The figures in the *Actual* column are, as already stated, the relevant total figures from the analysed columns in the analysed cash book. These are shown in blue in the completed budget comparison statement.
3. When you calculate the *Closing cash* in the *Actual* column it should automatically equal the *Closing cash* in the analysed cash book.
4. Remember that the figures in the *Difference* column are calculated by subtracting the figures in the *Budget* column from the figures in the *Actual* column. Use a plus sign if the *Actual* figure is **greater** than the *Budget* figure and use a minus sign if the *Actual* figure is **less** than the *Budget* figure. All these figures are shown in red in the completed budget comparison statement.
5. Finally, check that the figure in *Net cash* in the *Difference* column is equal to the difference between the *Budget Closing cash* and the *Actual Closing cash*.

LEARN THE KEY TERMS

- A **budget comparison statement** is used to compare and highlight the difference between budgeted income and expenditure and actual income and expenditure.

QUESTIONS

1. What is a budget comparison statement?
2. Why should a family draw up a budget comparison statement?
3. Complete the following family budget comparison statement and insert the appropriate plus and minus signs.

FAMILY BUDGET COMPARISON STATEMENT AUGUST 2010

	Budget	Actual	Difference
INCOME	€	€	€
Wages	2,500	2,400	
Child Benefit	300	300	
TOTAL INCOME	2,800	2,700	
EXPENDITURE			
Mortgage	670	600	
Groceries	600	580	
Petrol	90	110	
House insurance	450	500	
Light and heat	120	110	
TOTAL EXPENDITURE			
Net cash			
Opening cash	100		
Closing cash			

Do not fill in the shaded area.

4. The O'Reilly family obtained the following information concerning their bank account from their analysed cash book on 31 October 2010.

Opening cash on 1 October 2010: €150

Total income: Salary €2,500, Child Benefit €350 and Interest €180

Total payments: Mortgage €700, Motoring expenses €250, Light and heat €120, Groceries €600 and Holiday €1,800

Using this information, complete the O'Reillys' budget comparison statement below and insert the appropriate plus and minus signs in the *Difference* column.

O'REILLYS' BUDGET COMPARISON STATEMENT OCTOBER 2010

	Budget	Actual	Difference
INCOME	€	€	€
Salary	2,700		
Child Benefit	350		
Interest	190		
TOTAL INCOME			
EXPENDITURE			
Mortgage	650		
Motoring expenses	300		
Light and heat	110		
Groceries	500		
Holiday	1,500		
TOTAL EXPENDITURE			
Net cash			
Opening cash			
Closing cash			

Do not fill in the shaded area.

(a) Comment on the original budget.

(b) Is there anything in the *Budget* figures which might indicate that the O'Reilly family have money somewhere else other than in this particular bank account?

(c) Both the interest that the family expected to earn and their mortgage repayments decreased. Suggest a possible reason for this.

(d) Show how to check the accuracy of the closing cash you calculated in the *Actual* column.

5. The Quinn family keeps a record of all financial transactions in an analysed cash book. On 1 June 2010 they had €600 in the bank. During June they had the following transactions:

Date	Transaction	€
June 1	Paid telephone bill with cheque no. 21	120
June 5	Lodged wages cheque	1,670
June 9	Paid for groceries with cheque no. 22	140
June 11	Paid for car service with cheque no. 23	450
June 12	Lodged wages cheque	1,670
June 15	Lodged Child Benefit	230
June 18	Paid for new clothes with cheque no. 24	550
June 19	Lodged wages cheque	1,970
June 22	Paid for petrol with cheque no. 25	70
June 23	Paid for groceries with cheque no. 26	180
June 25	Purchased top-ups for mobile phones with cheque no. 27	80
June 26	Lodged wages cheque	1,670
June 28	Paid for holidays with cheque no. 28	1,800
June 29	Paid rent to landlord with cheque no. 29	600

A. Enter the above transactions in the analysed cash book using the following headings:
Debit side: *Bank, Wages, Child Benefit*
Credit side: *Bank, Groceries, Telephone, Clothes, Car, Rent, Other*

B. Using the partially completed budget comparison statement on the next page, enter the appropriate figures (from the analysed cash book you have prepared) in the *Actual* and *Difference* columns. Insert plus and minus signs in the *Difference* column as appropriate.

(a) What is the value of the *Actual* closing cash?
(b) Suggest any one reason why the wages on the 19th were greater than in other weeks.
(c) How much money had the Quinn family intended to save during June?
(d) How much money did the Quinn family actually save during June?
(e) Name two items of discretionary expenditure undertaken by the Quinn family during June.
(f) Do the Quinn family own their home? Give a reason for your answer.

PARTIALLY COMPLETED COMPARISON STATEMENT

	Budget	Actual	Difference
INCOME	€	€	€
Wages	6,610		
Child Benefit	230		
TOTAL INCOME	6,840		
EXPENDITURE			
Groceries	300		
Telephone	250		
Clothes	400		
Car	490		
Rent	600		
Other	1,700		
TOTAL EXPENDITURE	3,740		
Net cash			
Opening cash			
Closing cash			

Do not fill in the shaded area.

6. When the Whelan family checked their analysed cash book at the end of December 2010, they discovered that their actual income and expenditure for the 12 months differed from the budgeted figures, shown below in the partially completed budget comparison statement, due to the following reasons.

- The salaries of the Whelan family increased by 10%.
- Child Benefit was €500 less than the budget figure as one of the older children took up full-time employment.
- Interest was €50 more than budgeted.
- The Whelan family won €3,000 in a Prize Bond draw.
- Mortgage payments increased by €25 per month from 1 June.
- The Whelan family benefited from an increase in their No Claims Bonus, resulting in their car insurance premium being €80 less than the budget figure.
- The house insurance remained as budgeted.
- Groceries costs were 7½% less than budgeted.
- Car costs were €550 greater than budgeted.
- Light and heat costs were 5% greater than budgeted.
- Due to the child taking full-time employment, school and college expenses were €1,200 less than budgeted.
- Entertainment costs averaged €300 per month.
- Due to their prize bond win they gave more expensive presents to all the family at Christmas, which increased the cost of presents by €1,500 more than budgeted.
- The family holiday cost €300 less than budgeted.

Complete the budget comparison statement by entering the appropriate figures into the *Actual* column. Show the differences between the *Actual* and *Budget* figures by completing the column marked *Difference*. Use a plus or minus sign in front of each figure in that column.

PARTIALLY COMPLETED COMPARISON STATEMENT

	Budget	Actual	Difference
INCOME	€	€	€
Salaries	50,000		
Child Benefit	1,500		
Interest	500		
TOTAL INCOME	52,000		
EXPENDITURE			
Fixed			
Mortgage	6,000		
Car insurance	700		
House insurance	540		
Subtotal	7,240		
Irregular			
Groceries	6,240		
Car costs	3,600		
Light and heat	3,000		
School and College expenses	5,500		
Subtotal	18,340		
Discretionary			
Entertainment	3,000		
Presents	800		
Family holiday	1,800		
Subtotal	5,600		
TOTAL EXPENDITURE	31,180		
Net cash	20,820		
Opening cash	300		
Closing cash	21,120		

Do not fill in the shaded area.

See workbook for more questions.

7 The consumer

People buy goods for different reasons.

- **Consumers** buy goods for their personal use: e.g. you may buy a TV to watch it at home.
- **Traders** buy goods to resell them: e.g. the owner of a shop may buy TVs in the hope of reselling them at a profit.

Different laws apply to the rights and obligations of consumers and traders. This chapter deals with consumers only.

According to law, **consumers** are people who buy goods or services for their personal use from someone whose business it is to sell goods and services.

The chapter is divided into five learning sections:

1. The wise consumer
2. The consumer and the law
3. Consumer rights
4. Making complaints
5. Consumer organisations

SECTION 1: THE WISE CONSUMER

Guidelines for the wise consumer

Before buying goods or services, you should ask yourself the following questions.

1. **Do you need it?** You may already have a similar product that is in perfectly good order. Do you really need to replace your computer with the latest model? It may be a luxury item that you will hardly ever use.

2. **Can you afford it?** What effect will the purchase have on your budget? Will it cause you financial hardship? Buying it may force you to do without some other essential item. Remember the concept of opportunity cost!

3. **Is it value for money?** If you purchased it in a larger or smaller quantity would you get better value? Do not assume that the largest packet of a product gives the best value.

   Example: A 10-kilo bag of potatoes may be selling for €10, while a 2-kilo bag may be selling for €1.50. The smaller bag is better value as it works out at 75 cent per kilo, whereas the larger bag works out at €1 per kilo. Also, even if the larger bag did give better value, would you use all the potatoes in that bag? Remember the concept of false economies.

4. **Have you checked prices elsewhere?** Even if you need something and can afford it, it always pays to shop around for the best price.

Finally, when you buy a product:

5. **Get proof of purchase (a receipt) and keep it safely (file it).** This could be essential if you have to return the item. A receipt may be as simple as an automatic one from a supermarket till, or it may be a formal one as shown below. A formal receipt should show: the date of the payment, the amount paid, the name of the person who paid the money, the signature of the person to whom the money was paid and the receipt number.

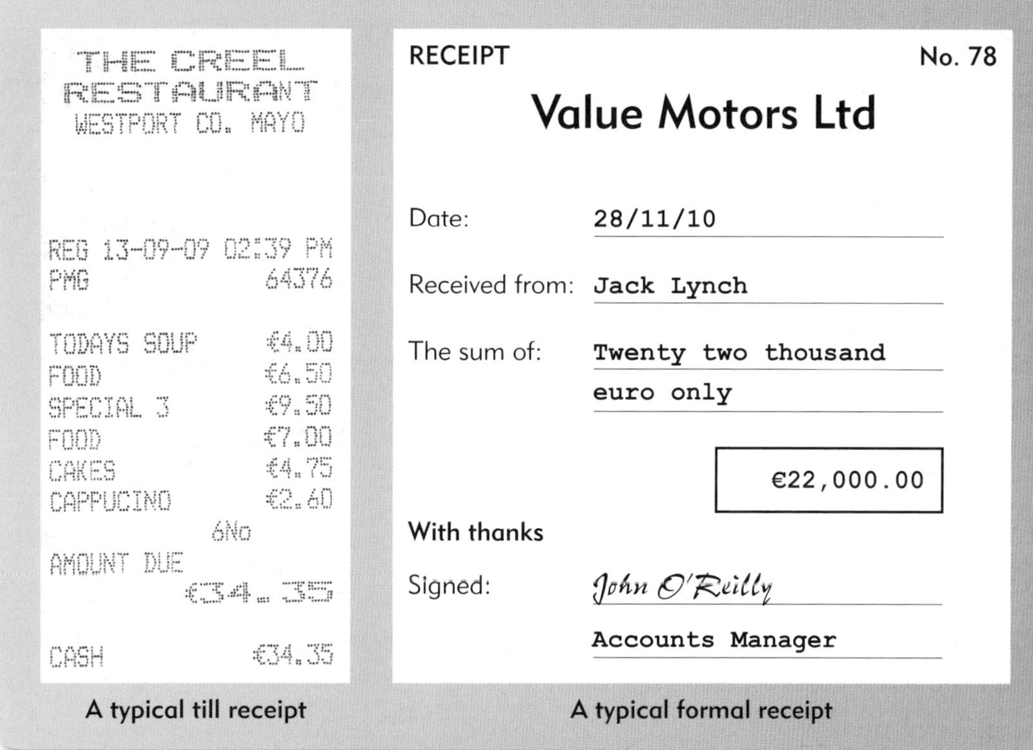

THE CREEL
RESTAURANT
WESTPORT CO. MAYO

REG 13-09-09 02:39 PM
PMG 64376

TODAYS SOUP	€4.00
FOOD	€6.50
SPECIAL 3	€9.50
FOOD	€7.00
CAKES	€4.75
CAPPUCINO	€2.60

6No

AMOUNT DUE
€34.35

CASH €34.35

A typical till receipt

RECEIPT No. 78

Value Motors Ltd

Date: 28/11/10

Received from: Jack Lynch

The sum of: Twenty two thousand euro only

€22,000.00

With thanks

Signed: John O'Reilly

Accounts Manager

A typical formal receipt

More consumer information

1. Brand names

A brand name is a unique name given to a product to distinguish it from similar products made by other companies.

Many brands have reputations for good value or for being exclusive. A knowledge of brands could save you money in the long run.

2. Symbols

Likewise you should understand the **tags** and **symbols** attached to certain products. Here are some of the better-known ones.

3. Labelling

All pre-packed food products must be clearly labelled. These labels should include:

- The **name** under which the product is sold.
- A list of all the **ingredients** in descending order of weight or volume.
- The **net quantity** of the product in the packet, i.e. the weight or volume excluding the weight of the packet.
- The **best before date** for long-lasting products or the **use by date** for more perishable products.
- Any special **storage conditions** required to keep the product in good condition or any conditions concerning the use of the product, e.g. 'Use within 3 days of opening'

4. Bar codes

A bar code is a series of lines and numbers on a product. The bar code is read by a computer to identify the country of origin of the product, the product itself, the name of the manufacturer and the price of the product. These help to speed up check-out at the supermarket and are also used for stock control by the seller.

5. Loss leaders

Many shops offer some products at very low prices in order to attract customers into their shops in the hope that they will also buy other products that are highly profitable to sell. The low-priced products are known loss leaders.

SECTION 2: **THE CONSUMER AND THE LAW**

The law of contract

When you buy a good you enter into a contract.

A **contract** is a legally binding agreement, i.e. it can be enforced by law.

The people involved in a contract are called the **parties** to the contract.

For example, if you buy goods in a shop the parties to the contract are you and the owner of the shop. Everybody else is called a 'third party'.

Contracts are valid only when the following three elements exist:

1. An **offer** is made by one person, e.g. you make an offer to buy goods for €5 from a shop-owner.
2. There is **acceptance** of that offer by another person, e.g. the shop-owner accepts your offer of €5 for those goods.
3. There is **consideration**, i.e. something of value passes between the parties to the contract, e.g. you get the goods and the shop-owner gets €5.

Price tags

When you go into a shop and pick up a product with a price tag on it, this price tag is simply a guideline to you to make an offer of that price to the shop-owner. In the vast majority of cases the owner of the shop is **not offering** the product for sale at the price stated on the tag. A price tag can be defined as 'an invitation to offer'.

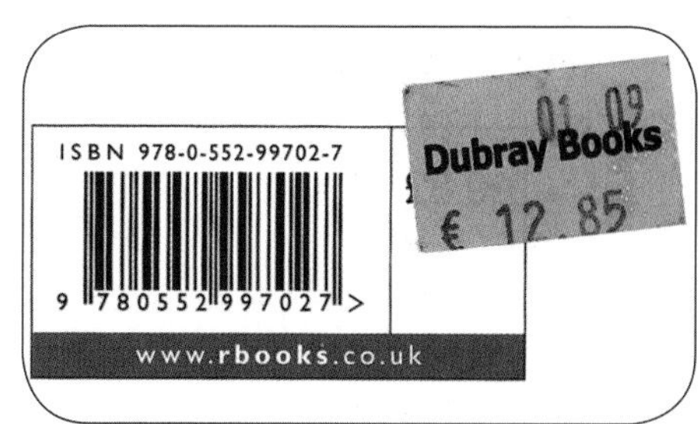

Consumer legislation (laws) protecting consumers' rights

Consumers in Ireland are protected by laws passed by the Dáil and by EU Directives. It is important to realise that consumer legislation **does not apply** if:

1. You have received the goods as a gift.
2. You buy goods for private use that are normally used for business purposes.
3. You buy goods from an individual who is not in business, e.g. you buy a secondhand car from a neighbour who wants to sell it to get money to put towards the purchase of a new car.

The Sale of Goods and Supply of Services Act 1980

Under this Act the **buyer** of goods and services has the **right** to assume:

1. **That the seller has title to the goods**, i.e. that the seller has the legal right to sell the goods.
2. **That the goods are of merchantable quality**, i.e. the goods must be able to perform the basic function for which they were designed. If I buy a watch I can assume that the watch supplied will actually keep time!
3. **That the goods are fit for the purpose** described by the seller to the buyer when the buyer informs the seller that he or she is relying on the seller's expert knowledge.
4. **That the goods supplied are as described** in a catalogue or that they match a sample displayed.
5. That **services** are carried out by **suitably qualified people**.
6. That **parts** supplied during a service are of **merchantable quality**.

These are known as **implied conditions** in the contract for the sale of goods or the supply of services. An implied condition is one that is legally enforceable even though it is not written into the contract.

The Consumer Protection Act 2007

From our point of view there are **four** main elements in this Act.

- **Element 1** deals with misleading claims regarding goods, services and prices.
- **Element 2** deals with EU Directives on unfair, misleading or aggressive commercial practices.
- **Element 3** deals with EU directives concerning pyramid schemes.
- **Element 4** deals with the National Consumer Agency.

Element 1
Under the act it is an offence for any manufacturer, retailer, service provider or advertiser to make a false or misleading claim about **(i) goods**, **(ii) services** and **(iii) prices**. It is also an offence **to sell** goods that bear a false or misleading description.

Misleading advertising means advertising that deceives (i.e. misinforms or deliberately does not tell the full truth about something) or is likely to deceive anyone that sees it. Notices in shops or claims made by a sales assistant could come under the definition of misleading advertising.

(a) **Goods**
Claims about the **weight**, **ingredients** and **performance** of goods must be stated truthfully.

Examples of misleading claims about products:

1. It is an offence to state that a packet of a given product contains 5 kg of the product when it only contains 4.5 kg.
2. It is an offence to state that there are no artificial ingredients in a product when it contains an artificial sweetener.
3. It is an offence to state that using the product will cure baldness when there is no proof that it will do so.

(b) **Services**
Claims about the **time**, **place** or **manner** in which a service is provided and claims about the **effect** of a service and the service providers must also be true.

Examples of misleading claims about services:

1. It is an offence to state that the service is available nationwide when it is not.
2. It is an offence to claim that there are no side effects arising from a medical procedure if there is any possibility that there may be side effects.
3. It is an offence for the provider of a service to make false claims about his or her qualifications and experience.

(c) **Prices**
Actual prices, **previous prices** and **recommended prices** of goods and services must be stated truthfully. Where a price is stated, it should be clear which item it relates to.

Examples of offences related to pricing:

1. It is an offence to state a price for a product if the stated price is not the total price, i.e. there should be no *hidden* extras. However, it is legal to state that the price of a car is €28,000 plus delivery and related charges, i.e. these extra costs are not hidden.

2. It is an offence to claim that a product was previously offered for sale at a different price, or at a particular price, if it was not, previously, openly offered for sale **at that price** and **at the same place** for a reasonable period of time.
3. It is an offence for a business to claim that it is selling a product below the recommended price if there is no recommended price for this product. A stated 'recommended price' implies that this is the price publicly recommended by the manufacturer or distributor of the product.
4. It is an offence to give a false impression of a price. A retailer may state in an advertisement that the price range of its products starts at €1,000. The advertisement might show a photograph of the most expensive model in the range that costs €2,500. This is misleading the consumer into believing that the price of €1,000 applies to that model.

Element 2

The Consumer Protection Act brings into Irish law **EU Directives** on (a) **unfair**, (b) **misleading** or (c) **aggressive commercial practices**.

These refer to any practices used by sellers that would result in people buying products that they would not buy under normal circumstances.

Examples:

1. Applying a quality mark (e.g. pure new wool) or symbol (e.g. flame-resistant) to a product without having permission to do so.
2. False claims that the product is recommended by leading doctors.
3. Pressurising people into buying a product today by making them believe that the price will increase tomorrow.

Element 3

The Directives ban the establishment, operation, promotion and participation in **pyramid schemes**. Penalties for offences relating to pyramid schemes involve a fine of up to €150,000 and a prison term of up to five years.

These schemes are unsustainable as they depend on an infinite number of people being available to participate.

Pyramid schemes take many different forms. A common form is a chain letter. For example:

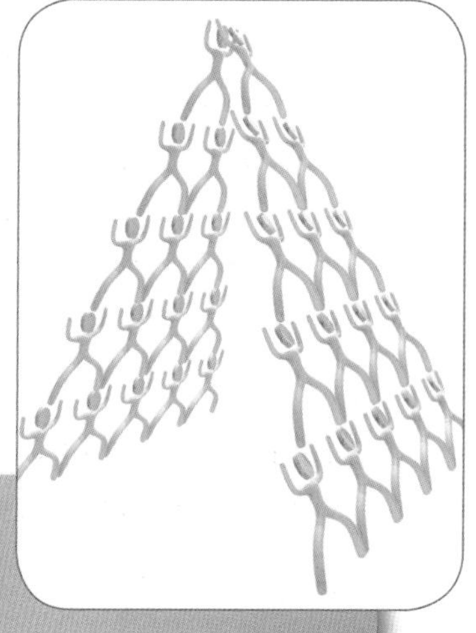

You receive a letter requesting you to send €100 to a named person and you are promised that you will receive €1,000 if you pass that letter on to ten more people. Sounds simple!
Now take a look at how quickly the scheme will collapse due to the need to recruit sufficient people:

- **Step 1:** Send €100 to person 'A' and pass the letter on to **10** more people who will each send you €100. Therefore you receive €1,000, making a profit of €900.

- **Step 2:** Each of the 10 people to whom you send the letter must then send the letter on to 10 more people in order to make their €900 profit. Already there are **100** people involved.
- **Step 3:** Each of these must send the letter to another 10 people. Now there are **1,000** people involved.
- **Step 4:** Each of these must send the letter to another 10 people. Now there are **10,000** people involved.
- **Step 5:** Each of these must send the letter to another 10 people. Now there are **100,000** people involved.
- **Step 6:** Each of these must send the letter to another 10 people. Now there are **1,000,000** people involved.
- **Step 7:** Each of these must send the letter to another 10 people. Now there are **10,000,000** people involved. This is roughly 2½ times the population of the Republic of Ireland!

Thus you can see that the scheme is unsustainable.

Element 4
The National Consumer Agency (NCA)

The main functions of the National Consumer Agency are to:

- promote and protect the interests and welfare of consumers
- enforce consumer laws
- encourage retailers and other sellers to comply with consumer laws
- investigate suspected offences under consumer laws
- refer cases to the Director of Public Prosecutions where appropriate

SECTION 3: **CONSUMER RIGHTS**

When a consumer purchases a product in a shop, or any other type of retail outlet, the contract is between **the consumer and the seller**. The seller cannot pass on his or her responsibilities under the contract to anybody else, e.g. to the manufacturer. Thus the shop-owner **cannot** tell you to take the complaint to the manufacturer of the item.

Resolution of a consumer's genuine complaint

It is important to return faulty goods as quickly as possible. Your claim becomes weaker the longer you delay returning goods.

When a consumer has a genuine legal complaint it may be resolved by:

1. a full **refund**, or
2. a **replacement** product, or
3. a **repair**

These are known as **the 3Rs of consumers' rights**.

Illegal signs

It is illegal for shops to display signs that give the impression that the consumers' rights are being disregarded.

NO REFUNDS GIVEN	CREDIT NOTES ONLY, IN CASE OF RETURNS	NO RETURN OF GOODS PURCHASED DURING SALE

Credit notes

Sometimes a seller will offer the customer a **credit note**, instead of cash, when goods are returned. This is a written document giving the customer permission to select goods in that shop (or chain of shops) up to the value stated on it.

The seller cannot force you to accept a credit note in exchange for **faulty goods**. Of course you may accept one if it suits you!

However, the shop *may* offer a credit note to a customer who purchased a product and later discovered that he or she did not need or want that particular product. This may be done as a gesture of goodwill to retain this person's custom.

You do not have a valid claim if:

1. You were told about the fault before you bought the item. Sometimes goods are sold as 'seconds' or 'shop-soiled'. In this situation you know there is a defect in the goods.
2. You examined the item before you bought it and the fault is so obvious that you should have seen the defect.
3. You bought the item knowing that it wasn't fit for the purpose required by you.
4. You broke or damaged the product.
5. You made a mistake when buying the item, e.g. you thought the handbag would match the shoes you had at home but found, when you went home, that they did not match.
6. You change your mind and you no longer want that item.

Retailers are *not obliged* to give refunds or credit notes under the above circumstances, even if you show proof of purchase.

A guarantee or warranty

Consumers should know that the conditions stated in a guarantee or warranty that comes with a product cannot override their rights as consumers.

A **guarantee** or **warranty** is a written undertaking that the manufacturer, or somebody appointed by the manufacturer, will repair or replace an item within a stated period of time after the purchase date.

SECTION 4: **MAKING COMPLAINTS**

General guidelines for consumers making complaints

1. Return to the shop where you purchased the good and make your complaint and your desired resolution known to somebody who has the authority to deal with it, e.g. the shop manager. Make sure you have your receipt or any other proof of purchase. Do not part with this.
2. If you are not satisfied then write a letter of complaint to the shop-owner or manager outlining your problem. Keep a copy of the letter. (See sample letter on page 67.)
3. If your complaint has not been resolved you should now write to the shop's trade association* outlining your complaint and the steps you have taken to date to have it resolved. Enclose copies of your receipt and any correspondence you have had with the shop.
4. If your complaint is still not resolved you should write to the National Consumer Agency. Give the Agency a full record of your attempts to have the problem resolved, including all receipts and correspondence with the shop and the Trade Association. The NCA will then attempt to resolve the problem on your behalf.
5. Finally, if your complaint is still not resolved, apply to the Small Claims Court to resolve your dispute (see *Small Claims Court*, page 68).

*Trade Associations

A trade association is an organisation representing all or most of the producers or sellers in a particular industry. It exists for the benefit of its members, but also insists that its members adhere to good standards in their dealings with consumers.

The following are some of Ireland's better-known trade associations.

- CIF Construction Industry Federation
- IASC Irish Association of Seafood Companies
- IHF Irish Hotels Federation
- IIF Irish Insurance Federation
- ISIA Irish Security Industry Association
- ITAA Irish Travel Agents' Association
- RECI Register of Electrical Contractors of Ireland
- SIMI Society of the Irish Motor Industry

Writing a letter of complaint

1. Give details of the product or service concerned, including price and date of purchase.
2. Enclose copies of receipts and other relevant documents (keep the originals).
3. State the nature of the complaint, i.e. what is wrong with the product.
4. Remind the shop of its legal obligations under the Sale of Goods and Supply of Services Act 1980.
5. State the resolution you are seeking.

There are nine elements in a letter of complaint.

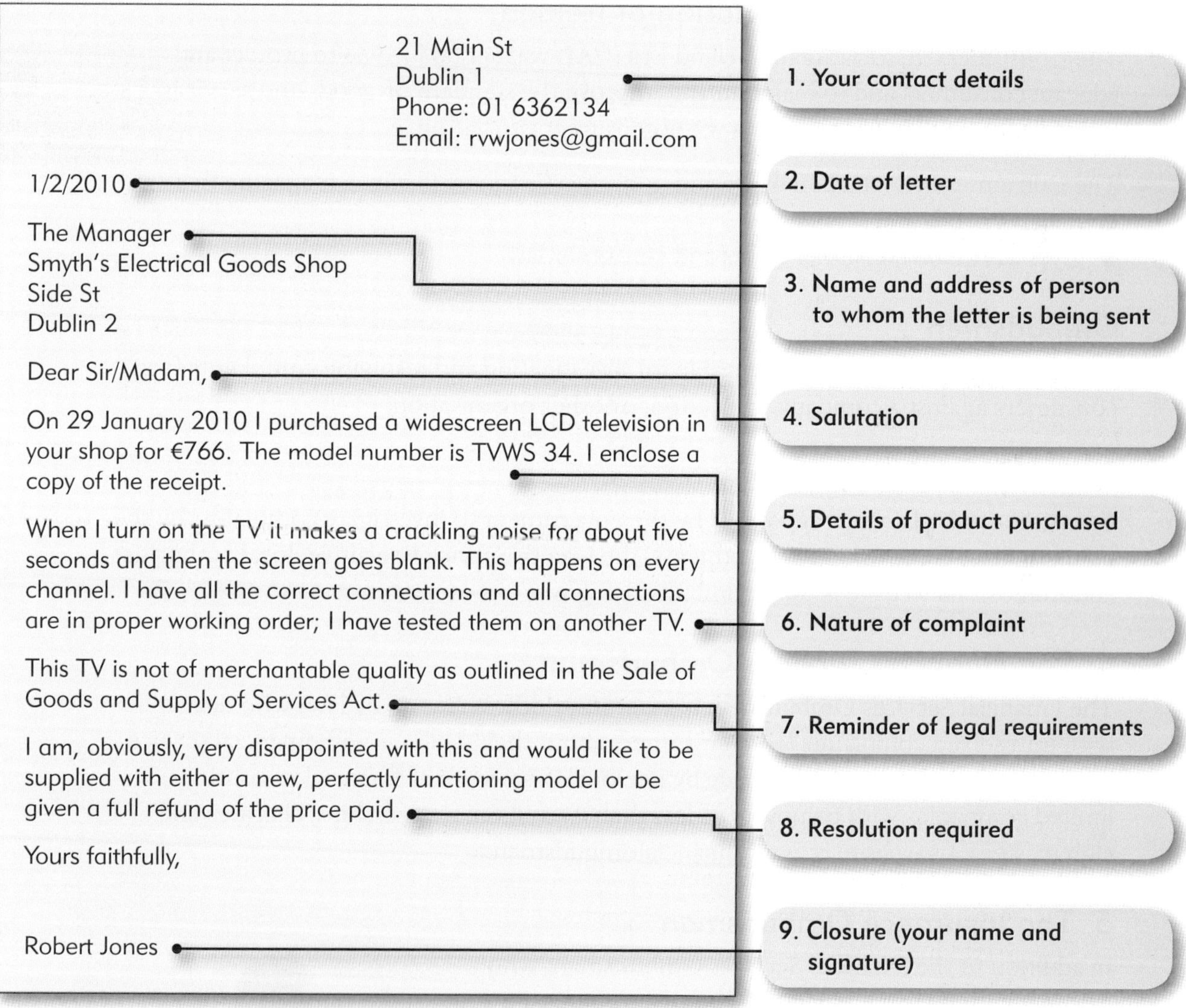

21 Main St
Dublin 1
Phone: 01 6362134
Email: rvwjones@gmail.com

1/2/2010

The Manager
Smyth's Electrical Goods Shop
Side St
Dublin 2

Dear Sir/Madam,

On 29 January 2010 I purchased a widescreen LCD television in your shop for €766. The model number is TVWS 34. I enclose a copy of the receipt.

When I turn on the TV it makes a crackling noise for about five seconds and then the screen goes blank. This happens on every channel. I have all the correct connections and all connections are in proper working order; I have tested them on another TV.

This TV is not of merchantable quality as outlined in the Sale of Goods and Supply of Services Act.

I am, obviously, very disappointed with this and would like to be supplied with either a new, perfectly functioning model or be given a full refund of the price paid.

Yours faithfully,

Robert Jones

SECTION 5: **CONSUMER ORGANISATIONS**

A number of organisations can assist consumers to resolve disputes.

1. The Small Claims Court

The Small Claims Court provides a cheap, fast and easy way for consumers to resolve their disputes with providers of goods and services without the need to employ a solicitor. Claims can be made for faulty goods or bad workmanship. Claims can also be made for minor damage to property.

At present the Small Claims Court deals only with claims up to €2,000. The current fee for making a claim in the Small Claims Court is €15.

2. The Consumers' Association of Ireland

The Consumers' Association of Ireland Ltd (CAI) was set up in 1966 to protect and educate consumers and to maintain and improve the standard of goods and services offered to the public. Its website is www.consumerassociation.ie

The Consumers' Association of Ireland publishes *Consumer Choice*, a magazine that:

- reviews goods and services
- gives advice on consumer rights and consumer law

Ombudsmen

An ombudsman is a person responsible for investigating and resolving complaints from consumers against a company, institution, or other organisation.

3. The State Ombudsman

The State Ombudsman is appointed by the government to investigate complaints by the public against Government Departments, the Health Service Executive, local authorities and An Post. Its website is: www.ombudsman.gov.ie

4. The Financial Services Ombudsman

The Financial Services Ombudsman is a statutory officer (set up by law) who deals with unresolved complaints from customers about their dealings with financial service providers. Complaints may be made by personal customers of financial institutions, limited companies with turnovers of less than €3 million, partnerships, charities and club trustees. Its website is: www.financialombudsman.ie

5. The Insurance Ombudsman

In addition to the Financial Services Ombudsman, who can deal with financial aspects of complaints against insurance companies, there is also a private sector Insurance Ombudsman.

The Insurance Ombudsman attempts to resolve disputes between personal insurance policyholders and their insurance company. If complaints made by policyholders have not been settled satisfactorily through the normal complaints procedures then they can be referred to the insurance ombudsman.

LEARN THE KEY TERMS

- A **consumer** is a person who buys goods and services for personal use from someone whose business it is to sell goods and services.
- A **trader** buys goods to sell them.
- A **brand name** is a unique name given to a product to distinguish it from similar products made by other companies.
- A **contract** is a legally binding agreement.
- **Consideration** is something of value that passes between the parties to a contract.
- **Implied conditions** are conditions that are not written into a contract but are legally deemed to be part of the contract.
- The **3Rs** of consumers' rights are: refund, replacement and repair.
- A **guarantee** or **warranty** is a written undertaking that the manufacturer, or somebody appointed by the manufacturer, will repair or replace an item within a stated period of time after the purchase date.
- A **trade association** is an organisation representing all or most of the producers or sellers in a particular industry.
- An **ombudsman** is a person responsible for investigating and resolving complaints from consumers or other members of the public against a company, institution, or other organisation.

QUESTIONS

1. Explain the difference between a consumer and a trader.
2. State and explain four basic points a consumer should consider before purchasing a product.
3. What is meant by the term **brand name**?
4. Name five items that should appear on the labels of pre-packed food products.
5. State the three essential elements for a valid contract.
6. A customer picked up a product from a supermarket shelf. Attached to the product was a price tag of €20. However, when the customer offered €20 at the checkout it is refused by the shop-owner who stated that the price on the tag should be €200. The customer stated that the product should be sold for €20 as that was the price stated on the tag. The shop-owner still refused the €20, repeating that the price on the tag was a mistake. Who is legally correct? Explain your answer.
7. What is an **implied condition** in a contract?
8. State the six implied conditions in any contract for the sale of goods or the supply of services.
9. Name the **3Rs** of consumers' rights.

10. Outline the steps a customer should take when he or she has a genuine complaint about a product.

11. What is a **credit note**?

12. A customer purchased a blue raincoat as a birthday present for her cousin. However, two days later, her cousin returned the coat to the shop, looking for a replacement coat and stating that blue did not suit her. State two valid reasons why the shop-owner might refuse to give a replacement.

13. Another customer also purchased a raincoat for himself during a sale. The first time he wore it the rain seeped through the seams of the raincoat onto his inside jacket. He returned it to shop the next day, demanding either a refund of his money or a replacement raincoat. The shop-owner refused his request. The shop-owner told the customer to return the coat to the manufacturer. State two valid reasons why the customer was within his rights to look for a redress of his problem from the shop-owner.

14. What is meant by **misleading advertising**?

15. On 1/3/2010 Joan O'Sullivan, of 23 High St, Newbridge, Co. Kildare, saw a computer, model XZ21, on display in Electrical Traders Ltd, 12 Low St, Naas, Co. Kildare, for €500. She ordered that model of computer. The computer was given to her in a box. When Joan brought it home and took it out of the box it was not the same model as the one displayed in the shop. She returned the computer to the shop but was told by the sales assistant that he could not give Joan a refund or a replacement but would offer her a credit note to purchase any other product in the shop. Joan refused this and on 5/3/2010 wrote a letter of complaint to the manager of the shop demanding either a refund or a replacement. Assume you are Joan and write the letter of complaint.

16. Outline the major offences under the Consumer Protection Act with regard to goods, prices and services.

17. State the full names of the following associations: ITAA, SIMI and CIF.

18. What are the functions of the National Consumer Agency?

19. What are the aims of the Consumer Association of Ireland?

20. Distinguish between the role of the (State) Ombudsman and the Financial Services Ombudsman.

See workbook for more questions.

Insurance and assurance

An **insurance** policy is a contract between an insured person and an insurance company that gives the insured person protection against the occurrence of a risk that **might** happen. For example, the driver of a car might have a crash, but on the other hand he or she might never crash.

An **assurance** policy gives protection against the occurrence of something that **will** happen, e.g. a life assurance policy. Everybody will die!

THE CONCEPT OF INSURANCE

Many people share common risks, e.g. the contents of their houses could be destroyed by fire. So it makes sense for all households to pay a relatively small fee into a fund each year so that there is sufficient money available for those who lose their contents to replace their losses.

Insurance companies organise such funds. When people pay into such a fund they are buying an **insurance policy**. The amount of money that each person pays into this fund is known as the **premium**.

The **price paid** for insurance cover is called the **premium**.

Some insurance companies pass on some or all of the risk to an **underwriter**, i.e. an individual or company who will take on the risk of having to pay insurance claims when they arise.

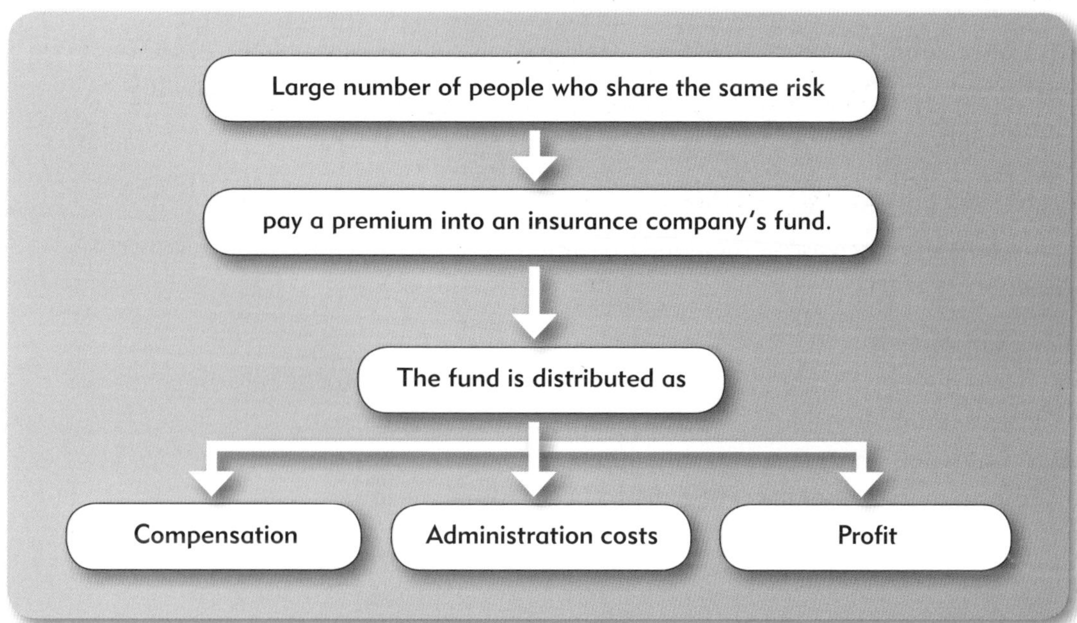

Insurance premiums

The value or size of an insurance premium is based on:

1. the degree of risk involved
2. the potential sum of money involved
3. the administration costs of the insurance company

1. The degree of risk involved

This refers to the probability, or likelihood, of the risk occurring.

For example, motor insurance companies have compiled statistics that show that young, inexperienced drivers are more likely to be involved in a motor accident than mature, experienced drivers. The premium therefore for young drivers tends to be greater than that for older drivers. Thus as the degree of risk increases, the size of the premium also increases, and vice versa.

2. The potential sum of money involved

This refers to the amount of money that the insurance company may have to pay out in the event of a claim being made against the policy. The premium goes up in line with the amount of money.

3. The administration costs of the insurance company

Insurance companies must employ people to manage their insurance policies. The cost of this is spread over all the policies. Therefore each policy has a small administration cost added to it.

Insurance companies calculate standard premiums for standard policies based on past experience. These premiums can be increased or decreased if an individual's circumstances are not standard.

Increases in standard premiums

A **loading** is an increase in the standard premium due to an extra risk in a particular situation.

For example:

- A taxi driver pays a higher premium than an ordinary motorist because he or she drives more often and is therefore more likely to have a crash.
- A house left unoccupied for more than 30 consecutive days in a year carries a higher premium than one that is occupied all year round.

Reductions in standard premiums

A **no-claims bonus** is a reduction in the standard premium if the insured person has not made a claim against the policy for a given period of time.

This is common in motor insurance policies. Insurance companies also offer premium reductions for other types of policies.

For example:

- a premium reduction for house contents insurance if the house is fitted with a burglar alarm
- a premium reduction for house fire insurance if the house is fitted with a sprinkler system

See page 81 for exam-type sample methods of calculating premiums.

PRINCIPLES OF AN INSURANCE OR ASSURANCE CONTRACT

All contracts of insurance are subject to five principles. These must be followed to protect insurance companies against fraudulent claims and to make insurance companies fully aware of the degree of risk they are undertaking and so apply the correct premium in each case.

1. the principle of utmost good faith
2. the principle of insurable interest
3. the principle of indemnity
4. the principle of contribution
5. the principle of subrogation

1. The principle of utmost good faith

This means that the person applying for insurance must reveal all relevant information to the insurance company.

Relevant information means any information that affects the degree of risk and so affects the calculation of the premium.

When applying for insurance you usually fill out a standard application form containing a list of standard questions. Utmost good faith dictates that as well as answering these questions honestly, you must also provide any other information, not covered by the questions, that affects the degree of risk, e.g. your house is located near a munitions factory.

2. The principle of insurable interest

According to this principle a person is only entitled to insure something if that person benefits from its existence or stands to suffer a real loss (usually monetary) if the item is damaged, lost or destroyed.

You have an insurable interest in something if you own or are responsible for it.

For example:

- I have an insurable interest in my own TV set. I do not have an insurable interest in my cousin's TV set. However, if I borrowed her TV set I would have an insurable interest in it because I would have to buy a new one for her if it was stolen from my house.
- Likewise I do not have an insurable interest in my neighbour's house. Just think of the possible consequences if we could all insure property we did not own!

3. The principle of indemnity

This principle means that the insurance company is obliged to indemnify the insured person only when the insured risk occurs.

To **indemnify** means to pay compensation equal to the value of the loss or damage suffered by the insured person.

The insured person cannot make a profit from the insurance.

The next two principles are really sub-sections of the principle of indemnity.

4. The principle of contribution

This principle states that the insurance companies involved will share the indemnity between them if somebody **fully** insures an item with more than one insurance company.

It is a waste of money to pay three premiums to three separate insurance companies hoping to claim from the three of them if the risk occurs.

All insurance claims are registered on a central registry. It is easy for insurance companies to see if someone is making more than one claim for a single risk occurring.

5. The principle of subrogation

This principle covers two different possible situations.

Subrogation – situation A

Once an insurance company fully indemnifies the insured person then all legal claims the insured may have against a third party pass to the insurance company.

For example, you are hospitalised arising from a car crash caused by another driver. You have a private health care insurance policy. If you claim your medical expenses under the health insurance policy you cannot also claim these expenses from the other driver's car insurance policy. This right passes to your health insurance company. Thus you cannot profit from insurance.

Subrogation – situation B
Once an insurance company fully indemnifies the insured person then all salvage rights pass to the insurance company.

Salvage, in this situation, means any money that can be raised from the sale of damaged items.

For example, your car is deemed to be a write-off as a result of a crash. Your insurance company fully indemnifies you. The insurance company now has the right to any money that can be raised from the sale of any parts of the car.

APPLYING FOR INSURANCE OR ASSURANCE

Step 1. The person applying for insurance fills out a **proposal form**.

A typical proposal form (from JC Ordinary Level Paper, 1998)

Proposal form for House and Contents Insurance

Gander Insurance Co. Ltd, Race St, Castlebar

Name______________________ Occupation______________

Address______________________________________

____

Insurance required from________________ to________________

Tick (✓) Yes or No in answer to each of the following:

	Yes	No
1. Is your house:		
(i) built of stone or concrete?	☐	☐
(ii) subject to flooding?	☐	☐
(iii) detached?	☐	☐
2. Has your house been previously damaged?	☐	☐
3. Have you or your family:		
(i) been convicted of any crime?	☐	☐
(ii) ever been refused insurance?	☐	☐

4. State how much cover you require: €____________

5. Apart from furniture and clothing, name any articles valued over €1,000.

____

____

Signature______________________ Date______________

Step 2. If the application is accepted an **actuary**[1] will assess the degree of risk and decide the size of the premium.

Step 3. The insurance company will usually issue a **cover note**[2] on receipt of the first premium.

Step 4. Finally, the insurance company will issue the **insurance policy**[3].

Notes

1. An **actuary** is a statistician who calculates insurance premiums based on the degree of risk involved.
2. A **cover note** is a document stating that the insurance cover exists.
3. The **insurance policy** is the actual contract of insurance setting out all its details.

MAKING A CLAIM

Step 1. The insured person fills out a claim form stating how, where and when the loss occurred, and the estimated value being claimed. In some cases (where a crime is suspected), the Gardaí may also have to be informed of the loss.

HOUSEHOLD INSURANCE

CLAIM NOTIFICATION FORM

QUINN direct

DETAILS OF POLICYHOLDER

Policy Number | Full Name

Address | Daytime Telephone Number

Evening Telephone Number

Postcode

Are you registered for VAT? Yes/No | If so, please detail your VAT number ....

DETAILS OF CLAIM

Date and Time of Loss/Damage | Place where it occurred (if different from address above)

Describe fully how it happened *(can continue on adddditional pages if needed)*

NOTE—Enter details of loss, damaged or stolen property overleaf.
Have you had any other losses within the last 3 years (insured or otherwise)? Yes/No
If YES, please give brief details (e.g. year, amount, cause, insurers).

If theft from the home, were the locks in operation? Yes/No

DETAILS OF PREMISES

Are you the owner of the premises? (i.e. the address as above) Yes/No

If the buildings are rented are you responsible for repairs? Yes/No

Is any part of the buildings lent, let, sub-let or shared? Yes/No

Were the buildings occupied at the time of the loss? Yes/No

If NO, when were they last occupied prior to the loss?

DECLARATION

I declare that the particulars given are true and claim the amount of:

€ | Stg.£

Signature | **Date**

Policy Excesses: Please refer to your policy booklet for full details of your policy excesses.
Have you completed the details overleaf and attached all available receipts/estimates?

CERTIFICATION FOR COMPLETION BY GARDA / POLICE

Name, Address and Telephone Number of Investigating Station: ______________________

Name of Investigating Officer: ______________________

Is the loss reported the result of theft, attempted theft or malicious damage? ____________

TO: QUINN DIRECT INSURANCE

This is to certify that (name) ______________________

of (address) ______________________

reported to this station on the undernoted date the loss of property, as outlined in this claim form.

Date and Time reported: ______________

The interest of Quinn Direct Insurance has been noted.

Signed ______________ Date ______________

Garda/ Police Verification Stamp

Date ______________

Step 2. The insurance company will then send out an assessor or a loss adjuster to calculate the value of the loss.

Assessors are employed by insurance companies to make sure that claims made are covered by the terms of the policy and to investigate the cause of the loss or damage.

Loss adjusters are independent investigators who become involved when there may be disagreement between the insured and the insurance company. This only happens in complicated claims and the loss adjuster acts as a negotiator between insurers and the insured.

Step 3. Finally, if the insured person's policy covers the claim and the person has fully insured the risk, the insurance company will fully indemnify (compensate) the insured person.

THE AVERAGE CLAUSE

The **average clause** is a condition included in insurance policies that limits the value of a claim if you are under-insured.

Claims are limited in proportion to the risk covered by the insurance company.

Assume you own a house worth €400,000. You decide (in order to save money on your premium) that you will only insure it for €300,000 in the belief that the house will never be completely destroyed and that the €300,000 should cover any damage. You are now only insuring ¾ of the value of the house.

Legally you are deemed to be undertaking ¼ of the risk yourself.

If a fire occurs in your house causing €20,000 worth of damage, you will receive compensation for only ¾ of the damage, i.e. €15,000.

This situation arises from the principle of utmost good faith. The insurance company must be made fully aware of the risk it is undertaking.

Calculating the average clause

Use the formula below to calculate the average clause.

$$\textbf{Average clause} = \frac{\text{Sum insured}}{\text{True value}} \times \text{Loss}$$

In the example above this is: $\frac{€300{,}000}{€400{,}000} \times €20{,}000 = €15{,}000$

INSURANCE REQUIREMENTS OR 'ADEQUATE INSURANCE'

The amount and nature of insurance required by individuals and households obviously will depend on their circumstances. If you don't own a house or a car then you don't need these forms of insurance.

On the other hand, if you own valuable pieces of jewellery you would need to have them individually insured. Each individual or household should identify their insurance needs and then obtain the cover required.

OBTAINING INSURANCE

An insurance policy can be obtained by:

- Applying directly to an insurance company
- Applying to an insurance **agent** who is employed by one insurance company and sells policies on behalf of that company. The agent receives commission on each policy sold.
- Applying to an insurance **broker** who is a self-employed individual (or company) and sells policies on behalf of many different insurance companies. The broker should be able to advise customers about the best policies for their needs.

HOUSEHOLD INSURANCE

Household insurance policies are usually classified under four headings:

1. Personal insurance
2. Property insurance
3. Life assurance
4. Motor insurance

1. Personal insurance

There are six basic types of personal insurance.

1. Personal accident insurance

This gives a lump sum payment to the insured in the event of an accident causing death or permanent disability, e.g. loss of sight, speech, hearing, or a limb.

2. Private medical health insurance
This covers hospital fees, medical consultants' fees and other medical expenses.

3. Income protection insurance
This provides a regular income if the insured is no longer able to work due to a long-term illness or disability. The premium paid is normally a percentage of the income being earned. The regular income paid under the insurance is also a percentage of the income earned.

4. Travel insurance
This covers expenses resulting from: loss of, damage to or delay of your luggage; cancelled or delayed flights; loss or theft of money or passport; and illness or injury while travelling.

5. PRSI/USC (Pay Related Social Insurance/ Universal Social Contribution)
See page 4.

6. Loan repayment protection insurance
This covers loan repayments if you are unable to pay due to accident, illness, death or redundancy. This kind of insurance is important for anybody with large borrowings such as a mortgage.

2. Property insurance

There are three basic types of property insurance.

1. Buildings insurance
This covers damage to the structure of a house and to permanent or unmovable fixtures such as fitted kitchens and bathroom equipment.

2. Contents insurance
This covers damage to or the theft of moveable items in a home such as furniture, TVs, computers, paintings and clothes.

3. All risks insurance
This covers the loss of, theft of, or accidental damage to items **outside your home as well as inside it**. This can be 'unspecified all risks' that covers all unnamed objects up to a combined stated maximum value or 'specified all risks' that covers individually named items up to a certain value.

Note: We have listed three forms of property insurance, but most insurance companies combine all three into one policy. This is generally cheaper than separate policies.

Exclusion and excess clauses

Many property insurance policies contain **exclusion** and **excess clauses**.

Exclusion clauses point out the occasions when the insurance company will not pay out on the policy, e.g. Acts of God.

Excess clauses state the value of the risk being incurred by the insured, e.g. the first €400 on any claim.

3. Life assurance

There are three basic types of life assurance.

1. A term policy

A term policy pays out a lump sum of money if the insured person dies before an agreed date. The money is paid to the next-of-kin or to somebody nominated by the insured person.

2. A whole-life policy

Under this policy the insured pays an agreed premium each year, month or week. When the insured person dies an agreed sum of money is paid to the insured's next-of-kin or somebody nominated by the insured.

A whole-life policy carries a bigger premium than a term policy because the assurance company **will** have to pay out on it at some stage.

3. An endowment policy

An endowment policy is taken out for an agreed period of time. It either gives the insured person a lump sum at the end of that period (known as the maturity date) **or** pays an agreed amount if the person dies before the maturity date.

The premium is greater than for term or whole-life policies because the assurance company knows that it **will** have to pay out a minimum sum by a definite date.

Endowment policies can be surrendered or 'cashed in' before the maturity date. However, the insured person will not get the full value of the policy at that date. The amount received is known as the **surrender value**.

4. Motor insurance

There are three basic types of motor insurance.

1. Third party policies

This policy compensates for the death of or injury to a third party or for damage to any property of a third party caused by the insured. (Remember that there are two parties to a policy, i.e. the insurance company and the insured person. Anybody else is called a third party.) **Third party insurance is compulsory for all motorists.**

2. Third party fire and theft policies

In addition to the risks covered by a third party policy, this policy also covers the owner for damage arising from a fire in the car, and also compensates the owner if the car is stolen.

3. Fully comprehensive policies

These give the same cover as third party fire and theft, but also cover damage to your own car, even if it is your own fault.

Most insurance premiums must be paid by a stated date (expiry date) if they are to be renewed for the following year. However, many insurance companies allow **days of grace** to renew the policy. This is the number of days allowed to renew the premium after the expiry date. If the premium is not paid within the stated number of days the policy lapses.

NON-INSURABLE RISKS

Not all risks are insurable. An insurance company will refuse insurance if a risk has any or all of the following characteristics:

1. An actuary, due to lack of statistics, cannot calculate the probability of the risk occurring.
2. There are not enough people seeking similar insurance to share the risk.
3. The loss is **imminently inevitable** (bound to happen in the near future). For example, a terminally ill person could not take out life assurance.
4. The **damage is gradual** (loss in value of an asset due to normal wear and tear).
5. The occurrence of the risk would be catastrophic for the insurance company, i.e. the potential cost of the pay-out by the insurance company would be ruinous for it. Insurance companies will not insure against the flood damage in areas that are flooded regularly.

SAMPLE INSURANCE PREMIUM CALCULATIONS

1. Property

Daniel O'Connell, who lives at 22 Clune Road, Ashtown, Co. Dublin, wants to insure his house and contents. His house is valued at €600,000 and the contents at €20,000. He has a burglar alarm installed and is a member of a Community Alert Scheme.

On 5 June 2010, he received the following insurance quote from Property Insurances Ltd:

INSURANCE	QUOTE
Buildings	€30 per €10,000
Contents	€8.50 per €1,000
Alarm installed	10% discount
Member of Community Alert Scheme	5% discount

Using the information in the above insurance quote, calculate the total net cost of insuring Daniel O'Connell's house and contents.

Solution

(a) **Buildings**

Divide value of the house, €600,000 by €10,000 to find the number of '€10,000s' in €600,000.

600,000 ÷ 10,000 = 60

Multiply €30 by 60 to get the cost of insuring the buildings = **€1,800.00**

(b) **Contents**

Divide value of the contents, €20,000, by €1,000 to find the number of '€1,000s' in €20,000.

This gives an answer of 20.

Multiply €8.50 by 20 to get the cost of insuring the contents = **€170.00**

Cost of buildings plus contents = €1,800 + €170	=	€1,970.00
Deduct the combined discounts of 15%	–	€295.50
Total net cost of insurance	=	**€1,674.50**

2. Motor insurance

Helen Grogan wants to insure her car. She received the following quotation from Best Motors Insurance Ltd:

INSURANCE	QUOTE
Basic premium	€2,200
Loading for 8 penalty points	40%
No claims bonus	70%

Using the information in the above insurance quote, calculate the total net cost of insuring Helen Grogan's car.

Solution

Note: Add loadings before applying any discounts.

Basic premium	€2,200
Plus loading (40% of €2,200)	+ €880
	€3,080
Less no claims bonus (70% of €3,080)	– €2,156
Total net cost of insurance	**€924**

3. Life assurance

Mr O'Reilly is a 40-year-old steeplejack. His hobby is aero gliding (piloting a motorless aircraft). He applied to Life Assurance Ltd for a life assurance policy on himself for €200,000 and received the following quotation:

ASSURANCE	QUOTE
Basic premium per annum	€2 per €1,000
Loading for over 35 years of age	10%
Loading for dangerous occupation	5%
Loading for dangerous hobbies	2%

Using the information in the above quote calculate the annual premium Mr O'Reilly would have to pay for the life assurance.

Solution

Divide €200,000 by €1,000 to find the number of '€1,000s' in €200,000 = 200.

Multiply 200 by €2 to calculate the basic premium	€400
Add the combined loadings (17% of €400)	+ €68
Total annual cost of premium	**€468**

LEARN THE KEY TERMS

- An **insurance broker** sells insurance policies on behalf of different insurance companies and can advise customers about the policy best suited to their needs.
- An **insurance agent** sells insurance policies on behalf of one insurance company only.
- A **proposal form** is an application form filled out by the person applying for insurance.
- A **cover note** is a document proving that an insurance policy exists.
- An **insurance policy** is the contract between the insurance company (the insurer) and the insured person. This normally outlines the exclusion clauses and the excess clauses.
- **Exclusion clauses** point out the occasions when the insurance company will not pay out on the policy, e.g. Acts of God.
- **Excess clauses** state the value of the risk being incurred by the insured, e.g. the first €400 on any claim.
- An **actuary** is a person who calculates the degree of risk involved and so sets the premium.
- An **underwriter** is an individual or company who will take on the risk of having to pay insurance claims when they arise.
- A **loading** is an increase in the standard premium due to an extra risk involved.
- A **claim form** is a form filled out by the insured when making a claim for compensation.
- The **average clause** is a condition included in insurance policies that limits the value of a claim if you are under-insured.

  Example: A person who has a house valued at €500,000 insures it for €375,000, which is only ¾ of its value. A fire occurs in the house and causes €20,000 worth of damage. The insurance company will pay out only €15,000, i.e. ¾ of the value of the damage.
- **Days of grace:** the number of days allowed to renew the premium after the expiry date.

QUESTIONS

1. Explain the difference between an **insurance** and an **assurance** policy.
2. Explain the difference between a **cover note** and a **policy**.
3. What is meant by the **premium** in insurance?
4. Explain three factors that influence the size of a premium.
5. What is a **loading** in insurance?
6. Explain the principle of utmost good faith.
7. Explain how a person could have an insurable interest in an object.
8. Explain the principle of indemnity.
9. Explain fully why it is a waste of money for an individual to fully insure his or her house with more than one insurance company.
10. Explain the principle of subrogation.
11. What is the difference between an **exclusion clause** and an **excess clause**?
12. Under what circumstances might an insurance company deem a risk to be non-insurable?
13. What is covered by an **all risks policy** in property insurance?
14. With regard to life assurance explain the difference between a **whole life policy** and a **term policy**.
15. Explain why it is more important for the owner of a very expensive car to have a fully comprehensive motor insurance policy than it is for the owner of a car of very little value.
16. Eileen Jones has a €400,000 mortgage on her house, has five young children, owns a car and travels abroad at least five times a year. Give a very brief explanation of the types of insurance or assurance policies you would expect Eileen Jones to have.
17. Explain the difference between an **insurance agent** and an **insurance broker**.
18. Explain the role of an **assessor**.
19. What is the role of an actuary in insurance?
20. What is the difference between a **proposal form** and a **claim form**?

See workbook for more questions.

Money

MONEY

Money is anything that is generally accepted by the majority of people in exchange for goods and services.

Before our modern money system developed people used the barter system to obtain the goods they could not make themselves.

BARTER

Barter is the exchanging (swapping) of one good for another without the use of money.

The barter system has many disadvantages.

Disadvantages of barter

1. The biggest problem with barter is the **double coincidence of needs and wants**. This means that a person who wishes to exchange goods must not only find somebody who has the good that he or she needs, but who must also want the good that he or she has to exchange.

   Thus if Mr Murphy wants a shirt and has socks to exchange, he must find somebody who has a shirt to exchange and who also just happens to need socks.

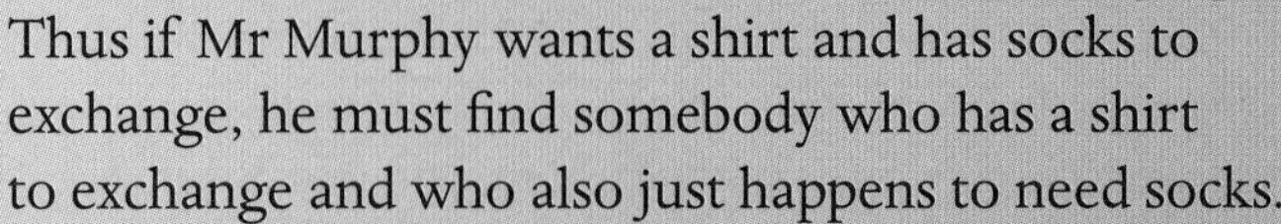

2. Under the barter system it is very difficult to decide the exchange value of any one product. How many pairs of socks must be given for a shirt?

3. Saving is a big problem under the barter system. What do I do with the goods I have produced but do not need for exchange at the moment? I may have to build a warehouse in which to store them. Even worse, the goods might be perishable and so become worthless.

4. What happens if I don't have enough goods to exchange for a good that I need? It is extremely difficult to get goods on credit. What builder would agree to build a house for somebody in exchange for a supply of socks every month for the following twenty years!

To overcome these disadvantages people began to exchange objects that were useful and valuable in their own right, as well as acting as a means of exchange. Early examples include cattle, pigs, seashells, iron nails, salt and pepper.

Eventually precious metals such as gold and silver became widely used. People often deposited their gold and silver with goldsmiths for safe-keeping. The goldsmith gave them a written receipt. These receipts were then passed from one person to another as a form of payment for goods and services.

Such receipts were perfectly acceptable as people knew they could convert them to gold at any time. The receipts became the basis for our use of notes and coins as a means of exchange.

FUNCTIONS OF MONEY

We use money for a number of things.

1. A means of exchange

By taking money in exchange for a good, we are not limited by the double coincidence of needs and wants. We simply give money to somebody who has what we need.

2. A measure of value (unit of account)

The amount of money that must be given for a product reflects its relative value. For example, if a shirt costs €30 and a suit costs €240, then the suit is eight times more valuable than the shirt. This eliminates a lot of the haggling associated with barter.

3. A store of wealth (a means of saving)

If I produce more goods than I need for exchange purposes I can simply exchange them for money. Then I can keep the money until I need to spend it. This also has the advantage that I may earn interest on the money saved, if I put the money into a bank.

4. A means of deferred payments (an efficient credit system)

When most people buy a house they do not have enough money to pay for it from their own savings. However, they can borrow money from a bank or building society, and repay that money over a long period of time. This would not be possible under the barter system.

Look back at the disadvantages of barter and notice how the use of money has overcome these.

Over time we have developed different forms of money. But experience has shown that the form of money we use must have certain characteristics.

CHARACTERISTICS OF MONEY

1. **It must be instantly recognisable as money.** If people have doubts about the item being used as money it will not be acceptable as a means of exchange, therefore it would not be money! All our notes and coins are identical.
2. It must be **easy to carry around** in relatively large values, unnoticed. It is very easy to carry a few hundred euro in your pocket without anybody being aware that you are doing so.
3. It must be **divisible** into units of small value. This enables people to buy goods of small value and shopkeepers to give back change. Our basic unit is the euro. It is also issued in subdivisions of 50c, 20c, 10c, 5c, 2c and 1c coins.
4. In order to have value it must be **scarce in supply**. Our Central Bank controls the amount of money in circulation.
5. It must be reasonably **durable**, i.e. it must be something that will not wear out too quickly when it is being continuously passed from person to person. We use the small units of our money (coins) more often than other forms. Hence coins are made of metal, which can stand up to constant use.

MODERN FORMS OF MONEY

1. Cash or currency (notes and coins)

You are all familiar with cash. The euro (€) notes and coins in circulation are issued by our Central Bank on behalf of the European Central Bank (ECB).

2. Cheques

Traditionally people have used cheques to transfer money from their bank accounts to somebody else without having to physically withdraw cash from their accounts.

A **cheque** is a written instruction to a bank to pay a stated sum of money to a named person or to the bearer (the person who has it) of the cheque.

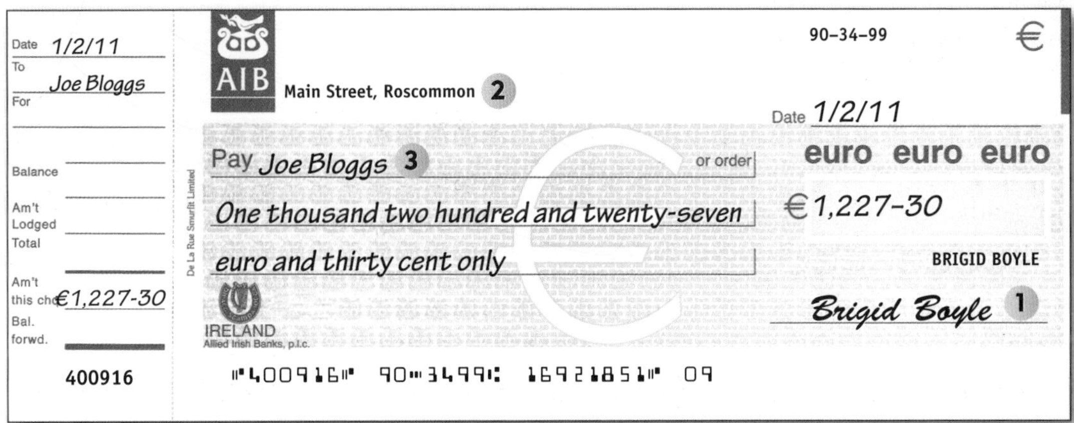

Date 1/2/11
To Joe Bloggs
For
Balance
Am't Lodged
Total
Am't this cheque €1,227-30
Bal. forwd.
400916

AIB Main Street, Roscommon 2
90-34-99 €
Date 1/2/11
Pay Joe Bloggs 3 or order
euro euro euro
One thousand two hundred and twenty-seven €1,227-30
euro and thirty cent only
BRIGID BOYLE
Brigid Boyle 1
IRELAND
Allied Irish Banks, p.l.c.
De La Rue Smurfit Limited
⑈400916⑈ 90⑉34991⑆ 16921851⑈ 09

This is an instruction written on 1/2/11 by Brigid Boyle to her bank, AIB, to pay Joe Bloggs €1,227 and 30 cent.

- The person writing the cheque (1 Brigid Boyle) is the **drawer** of the cheque.
- The drawer's bank (2 AIB) is the **drawee** of the cheque.
- The person to whom the cheque is made payable (3 Joe Bloggs) is the **payee**.

We will return to cheques in more detail in the next chapter.

Bank drafts

A bank draft is a cheque where the bank is both the drawer and the drawee. People can 'buy' a bank draft for a fee by lodging money with the bank and having the draft made payable to a specific payee. These are normally used to pay large sums of money where personal cheques are not acceptable.

Traveller's cheques

These are pre-printed and numbered cheques made out for specific amounts of a foreign currency, e.g. $100 or $50. They are purchased from banks and other financial institutions. They must be signed by the buyer in the presence of the seller (the bank or other financial institution). The buyer should keep a record of the number on each of the cheques.

The signed traveller's cheques can then be exchanged for cash in a bank or Bureau de Change in the appropriate country. They must be signed again when they are being cashed and the bank cashing them will usually ask for a passport as proof of identity.

Traveller's cheques can be cancelled by the buyer if they are lost or stolen; hence the importance of keeping a record of the number on each of the cheques.

3. Plastic money cards

The development of computers and electronic payment systems have allowed the use of 'plastic money'. Plastic money transactions are often referred to as **electronic funds transfer at point of sale (EFTPOS)**.

An EFTPOS terminal

(a) Debit cards (Laser cards)

Debit cards are issued by banks to people who have bank accounts. They enable the cardholder to pay for goods without using either cash or cheques.

- When purchasing goods the cardholder presents the card to the seller.
- The Laser card is swiped through a terminal at the cash desk and the amount being paid is keyed in.
- The cardholder checks that the amount keyed in is correct and then enters his or her **personal identity number (PIN number)**. This authorises the bank to transfer the amount from the customer's current account to the shop's bank account, provided of course there is enough money in the customer's account.

This system is known as **chip and PIN**. The terminal at the cash desk reads the computer chip embedded in the card and the customer enters the PIN number.

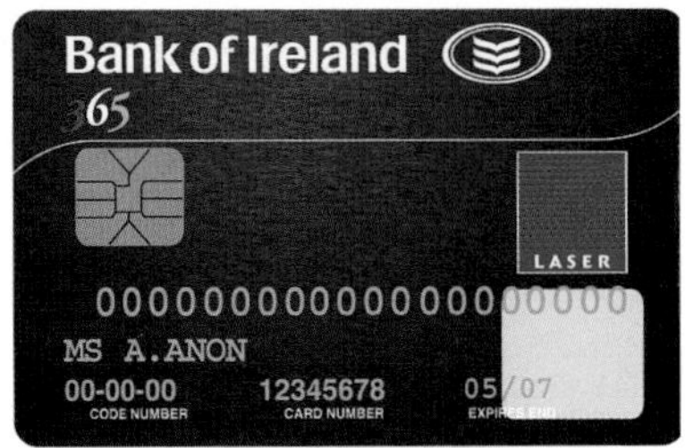

Cardholders can also use debit or Laser cards to withdraw cash from their accounts at **automated teller machines (ATMs)**, see page 100.

Most Laser cards have a **Cirrus** facility that allows the cardholder to withdraw cash from ATMs in over 120 countries. **Maestro** is the most commonly used debit card.

(b) Credit cards

Credit cards are used in the same way as Laser cards when purchasing goods, i.e. the chip and PIN system. But they differ from Laser cards in that the money is not instantly transferred from the cardholder's bank account to the shop's bank account. The shop is paid by the credit card company within a few days. Shops are charged a fee by the credit card company.

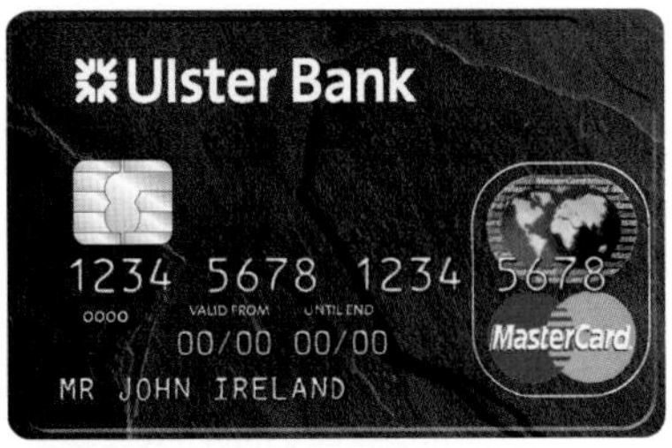

The use of the credit card allows the cardholders to purchase goods on credit up to a certain credit limit.

The cardholder receives a statement of his or her transactions each month and has 28 days from receipt of the statement to pay the outstanding balance.

No interest is charged if the full amount due is paid within the 28 days. If the full amount is *not paid* then a very high rate of interest is charged on the amount owed. When using a credit card make sure you do not overspend to the point where you cannot pay the full amount outstanding by the due date.

Credit cards can also be used to withdraw cash from ATMs, but interest is charged on this cash from the moment it is withdrawn. This is a very expensive way of obtaining cash.

(c) Charge cards

From a purchasing point of view, charge cards operate in the same way as credit cards. However, the amount owed on the card must be paid in full when the statement is received.

Charge cards have the advantage of being acceptable all over the developed world. American Express and Diners Club are the two most widely used ones.

(d) Smart cards

Smart cards can be used by both bank and non-bank customers. They operate in a similar way to prepaid phone accounts. The cardholder preloads his or her card with an amount of money (credit) and can pay for goods in the same way as a Laser cardholder until the amount is used up.

The disadvantage of a smart card is the fact that you are paying for goods even before you buy them, and somebody else has the use of your money in the meantime. However, unlike a credit card, it does have the advantage of preventing you from over-spending. Thus smart cards are good from a budgeting point of view.

OTHER METHODS OF PAYING FOR GOODS AND SERVICES

Standing order (SO)

A standing order is an instruction from a bank account holder to the bank to pay from his or her account, on a regular basis, a fixed sum of money to a stated person.

Standing orders are often used to pay bills that recur on a regular basis for a regular amount, e.g. life assurance premiums and mortgage repayments.

A direct debit (DD)

To understand direct debits you need to know about creditors and debtors.

- A **creditor** is a person to whom money is owed.
- A **debtor** is a person who owes money.

A direct debit gives a creditor permission to apply to his or her debtor's bank account for a variable sum of money (up to a stated maximum amount) on a regular basis.

Direct debits are often used to pay monthly bills of a variable amount, such as electricity and telephone bills. The debtor fills out a direct debit **mandate** or **instruction** to allow the creditor to apply for the money due.

A typical direct debit mandate is shown below.

ESB Direct Debit Instruction											
Your Electricity Account Number:	7	5	3	-	8	8	9	-	4	6	2
I wish to pay my electricity bill every two months.											
To	The Manager										
Bank	**AIB Bank**										
Bank Address	**The Mall,**										
	Westport										
	Co. Mayo										
I give permission to ESB to charge variable amounts to my bank account.											
Name of Bank Account to be debited	**John Murphy**										
Account type	**Current**										
Bank Account Number	1	7	9	4	0	8	3	2			
Branch Sorting Code	9	3	-	2	6	-	0	5			
Contact Telephone Number	**087 – 4536281**										
Signature	*John Murphy*										
Date	**5 June 2008**										

Source: Junior Certificate Marking Scheme 2008

Credit transfer (CT)

A credit transfer allows you to transfer money from your own bank account to another person's bank account.

To do this you must fill out a pre-printed form supplied by the payee and give the required amount of money to a teller in the bank. This contains all information on the payee's bank account. The bank then transfers the money to the payee's bank account.

Alternatively you can set up a credit transfer system via your Internet banking facility.

Paypath

Paypath is an electronic means of transferring an employee's wages from the employer's bank account to an employee's bank account.

PayPal

PayPal is a safe way to pay for goods online without disclosing your credit card, debit card or bank account details to a great number of different sellers. You register your account details with PayPal only. It transfers money from your account to the seller without the seller getting your account details.

Legal tender

Legal tender is the form of money that a creditor is legally obliged to accept in payment of a debt. **Notes and coins are legal tender**. Cheques and plastic money are not legal tender.

LEARN THE KEY TERMS

- **Money** is anything that is generally accepted by the majority of people in exchange for goods and services.
- An **ATM** is an automated teller machine.
- **Barter** is the exchanging (swapping) of one good for another.
- A **cheque** is a written instruction to a bank to pay a stated sum of money to a named person or to the bearer (the person who has it) of the cheque.
- **PIN** stands for personal identity number.
- **EFTPOS** stands for electronic funds transfer at point of sale.
- A **bank draft** is a cheque where the bank is both the drawer and the drawee.
- A **standing order** (SO) is an instruction from a bank account holder to the bank to pay from his or her account, on a regular basis, a fixed sum of money to a stated person.
- A **direct debit** gives a creditor permission to apply to his or her debtor's bank account for a variable sum of money (up to a stated maximum amount), on a regular basis.
- A **credit transfer** (CT) is a system whereby a person can transfer money from his or her own bank account to another person's bank account.
- **Paypath** is an electronic means of transferring an employee's wages from the employer's bank account to an employee's bank account.
- **Legal tender** is the form of money that a creditor is legally obliged to accept in payment of a debt.

QUESTIONS

1. What is money?
2. What is barter?
3. What does 'the double coincidence of needs and wants' mean in relation to the barter system?
4. What are the other major disadvantages of the barter system?
5. What are the functions of money?
6. Name the characteristics of a good money form.
7. What is a cheque?
8. Explain how traveller's cheques are used.
9. Explain how goods can be purchased using credit cards or Laser cards, i.e. explain 'chip and PIN'.
10. What is the major difference between purchasing goods by credit card and purchasing goods by Laser card?
11. What is the major difference between a credit card and a charge card?
12. Explain what each of the following stands for:

    (a) ATM
    (b) PIN
    (c) EFTPOS.
13. What is a standing order?
14. What is a credit transfer?
15. What is a direct debit?
16. Explain smart cards.
17. What advantage does a smart card have over a credit card for somebody operating on a very strict budget?
18. Who uses Paypath, and when?
19. What is legal tender?
20. Explain any reason why cheques are not legal tender.

See workbook for more questions.

Personal banking (commercial banks)

10

There are many different types of financial institutions operating in Ireland. These include commercial banks, merchant banks, industrial banks, building societies, post offices and credit unions.

In this chapter we will look at commercial banks. They are sometimes referred to as the *Associated banks* or *high street banks*. As well as accepting deposits, these banks give loans to personal and commercial borrowers. These are the banks that are familiar to most people – AIB, Bank of Ireland, Irish Life and Permanent (Permanent TSB), Ulster Bank and National Irish Bank.

Bank of Ireland

Ulster Bank

National Irish Bank

EBS

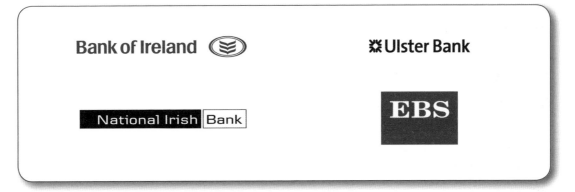

FUNCTIONS OF A COMMERCIAL BANK

1. Current accounts, including overdrafts
2. Deposit accounts (see Chapter 12)
3. Payment services for customers (see Chapter 9)
4. ATM machines
5. Loans (see Chapter 12)
6. Night safes
7. 24-hour banking services
8. Foreign currency exchange

Note: Functions 3, 4, 6 and 7 are normally additional services provided by the bank to current account holders.

CURRENT ACCOUNTS

These are accounts to which people lodge money that is then available to them to pay for their day-to-day expenses. (Hence the word *current*, i.e. on-going.)

Money lodged into current accounts does not *normally* earn interest. There is *usually* a charge for each transaction.

Some banks, under certain circumstances, may offer interest on money in these accounts and may not have any transaction charges. You are all familiar with the expression 'terms and conditions apply'.

Opening a current account

Banks require you to fill out a very detailed application form when opening a current account. As well as your name and address, the form requires your **employment details** (architect, plumber, chef, etc.), **employer's name and address, length of time working at that employment**, your **gross wages** and details of **any other bank accounts** you hold. All this information is required in order to establish your credit worthiness and to prevent money laundering.

Money laundering is the practice of hiding the source of money because it may have been earned illegally or because the tax due on it was not paid.

The bank will also require a specimen of the applicant's signature that will then be used to compare with the signature on cheques written on that person's account.

THE SHAMROCK BANK **Personal current account application form**

*Please use BLOCK CAPITALS and ✓ where appropriate. Sections marked * are mandatory and must be completed in full.*

Personal details: *Title: Mr ☐ Mrs ☐ Miss ☐ Ms ☐

*First name: ____________ *Surname: ____________

*Home address: ____________

*County: ____________ *Country: ____________

*Date of birth: ______ *Country of birth: ______ *(as per identity documents)* County/City of birth: ______

***PPS no.** ____________ Other bank accounts: ____________

***Employment details:** Employee ☐ Self-employed ☐ Retired ☐ Not currently employed ☐

Job description: ____________ Employer's name: ____________

*Basic gross annual income: € ____________ Number of years in this employment: ______

Contact details: Home tel. ______ Mobile tel. ______ Email: ______

I certify the accuracy of the information given and I agree the bank may make such enquiries about me as it considers necessary in relation to this application.

Signed: ____________ Date: ____________

When the application is accepted, money must be lodged to the account and the applicant will be given an account number, a cheque book and an ATM card or Laser card that also acts as a banker's card (also known as a cheque guarantee card).

Banker's card (cheque guarantee card)

A banker's card (cheque guarantee card) is a card presented by the drawer of a cheque to the payee when paying by cheque. The presentation and proper use of the card ensures that the bank will honour the cheque up to a sum of €130 even if the drawer has no money in his or her account. When accepting a cheque the payee should:

1. Ensure that the cheque is signed in his or her presence.
2. Ensure that the signature on the cheque matches the signature on the card.
3. Ensure that the card is still in-date (there is an expiry date embossed on the front of the card).
4. Write the card number on the back of the cheque.

Note: Irish banks are phasing out cheque guarantee cards to encourage greater use of electronic payment methods such as debit cards. The banks are expected to follow moves in Britain where **new** customers cannot obtain the cheque guarantee facility.

Lodging money to a current account

A lodgement docket should be filled out. This should show the following:

1. Name and address of the account holder
2. Account number
3. Amount being lodged, sub-divided into notes, coins and cheques
4. Signature of the person lodging the money
5. Date of the lodgement

Express / Lodgment / Credit Transfer

Account Name: ______

Branch Code Number: 90-__-__

Account Number: ______

Amount: € 856 00

Date: ___/___/___

Subject to verification, please see over.

Bank of Ireland. A member of the Bank of Ireland Group. Bank of Ireland is regulated by the Financial Regulator.

Please tear along this line

Express / Lodgment / Credit Transfer — Bank of Ireland

To: Bank of Ireland Date: ______

Account Holding Branch: ______

Account Name: ______

Address: ______

Brand/Initials

Paid in by: ______

Phone No.: ______ (in case we need to contact you)

Branch Code Number: 90

Account Number: ______

Please itemise cash and cheques overleaf

Notes	750	00
Coin	6	00
Total Cash		
Chq. Total	100	00
Other		
Total €	856	00

Bank of Ireland. A member of the Bank of Ireland Group. Bank of Ireland is regulated by the Financial Regulator.

4-717RU.5 (10/09) Please do not write or mark below this line or fold this docket

023285 ⑈023285⑈ 81

Money lodged to a current account can be withdrawn at any time without having to give the bank advance notice of withdrawal, i.e. the money is 'on demand'.

Withdrawing money from a current account

A current account holder can withdraw the money in the account by:

- using a cheque
- withdrawing cash from an ATM (see page 100)
- using a Laser card
- using direct debits and standing orders
- going into the bank and getting the money 'over-the-counter', i.e. filling out a withdrawal slip and obtaining cash from a teller

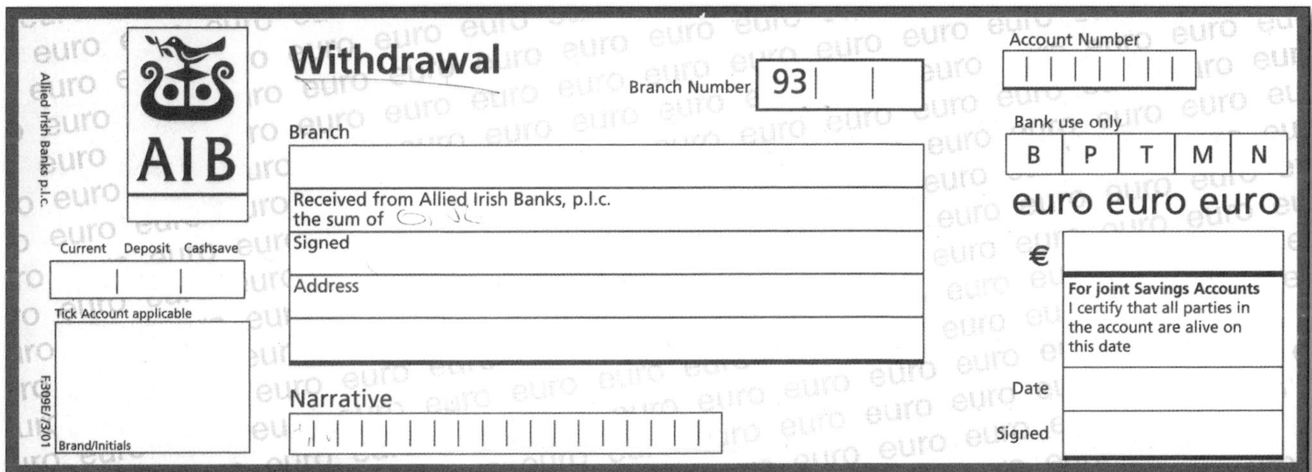

Allied Irish Banks p.l.c.

AIB

Withdrawal

Branch Number 93

Account Number

Bank use only

B	P	T	M	N

euro euro euro

Branch

Received from Allied Irish Banks, p.l.c. the sum of

Signed

Address

€

For joint Savings Accounts I certify that all parties in the account are alive on this date

Date

Signed

Current Deposit Cashsave

Tick Account applicable

Narrative

Brand/Initials

F309E/3/01

CHEQUES

In the previous chapter we defined a cheque as a written instruction to a bank to pay a stated sum of money to a named person or to the bearer of the cheque.

Below is an example of a cheque.

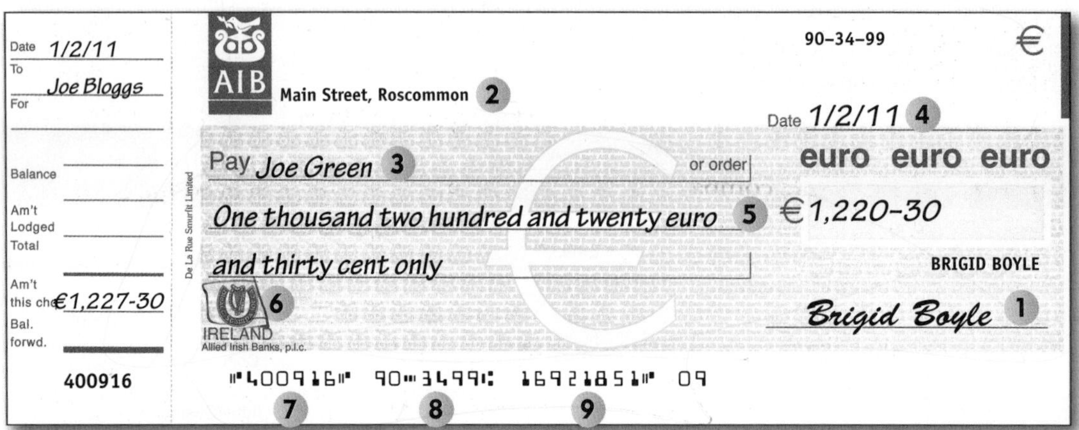

The parties to a cheque

1. The **drawer** is the person who makes out and signs the cheque. In the above example it is Brigid Boyle.
2. The **drawee** is the drawer's bank. In this case it is AIB.
3. The **payee** is the person to whom the cheque is payable – Joe Green in this case.

Most banks provide their customers with pre-printed cheques and strongly encourage their use. A cheque is valid, so long as the written instruction contains the following **six essential items**:

1. **Signature** of the drawer
2. Name of the **drawee**
3. Name of the **payee**
4. The **date** the cheque was written
5. The **amount** in both words and figures
6. A **revenue stamp** (which is really a tax on the use of a cheque)

Three other items normally appear on pre-printed cheques.

7. The **cheque number** (400916). All cheques are numbered in sequence to make it easier to keep a record of them.
8. The bank's **sort code** (90-3499). All banks have an individual identity number. This is always a six-digit number subdivided into three two-digit numbers.
9. The customer's **bank account number** (16921851).

The drawer should always fill out the cheque's counterfoil. The **counterfoil** is a record of the cheque payment and the details on it are used by the drawer to write up his or her cash book. Brigid Boyle would record the above cheque in her cash book as follows (only the *Bank* columns of the cash book are shown).

BANK A/C							
Date	Details	No.	€	Date	Details	No.	€
				1/2/11	Joe Green	16	1,220.30

The cash book should be compared with the bank statement that is sent to the current account holder by the bank. These bank statements will be dealt with in Chapter 11.

Obtaining the money due on a cheque

The payee can get the money due on a cheque by:

1. **Lodging** it to his or her own bank account. The payee's bank will then collect the money from the drawee and credit it to the payee's account.
2. **Cashing** it, i.e. going to the drawee and getting the money from the bank (the payee must have some identification).
3. **Selling** it, i.e. **endorsing** it (signing the back of the cheque) and giving it to somebody else for cash. Many retailers will accept such cheques from customers who are well known to them. When the payee endorses a cheque he or she is giving all rights to the cheque to the bearer of the cheque.

A **stale cheque** is one that has not been cashed or lodged within six months of the date written on it, i.e. a cheque is only valid for six months. A bank cannot accept a stale cheque.

A **post-dated cheque** is one with a future date on it and cannot be cashed until that date.

A person might post-date a cheque when buying goods that are to be delivered at some future date. If the goods are not delivered on or before that date the drawer will cancel (stop) the cheque.

An **ante-dated cheque** is one that bears a date prior to the date the cheque was written.

Ante-dated cheques

A drawer writing a cheque on 1/1/2011 may date it for 1/10/2010. This shortens the life of the cheque because it must be cashed within six months of the date written on it. This is sometimes done by the drawer to encourage the payee to lodge or cash the cheque quickly.

Making a cheque safe (crossing a cheque)

A **crossing** on a cheque makes it more difficult for a person who has found or stolen a cheque to cash it.

A **crossing** on a cheque is an instruction to the bank to pay the money due on the cheque only into a bank account.

A crossing is written between two parallel lines across the face of the cheque.

1. A general crossing

A general crossing is an instruction to the bank to pay the money into any bank account.

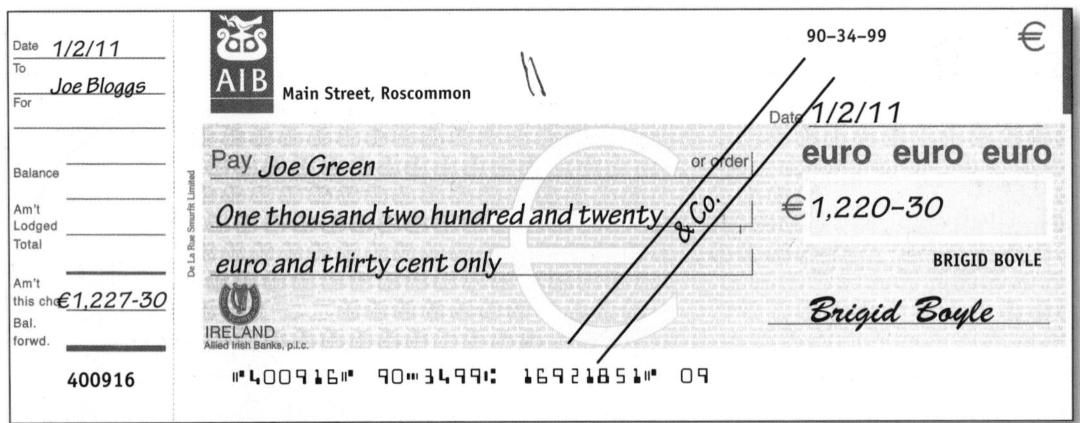

Date 1/2/11
To Joe Bloggs
For
Balance
Am't Lodged
Total
Am't this che €1,227-30
Bal. forwd.
400916

AIB Main Street, Roscommon
90-34-99 €
Date 1/2/11
Pay Joe Green or order
euro euro euro
One thousand two hundred and twenty
€1,220-30
euro and thirty cent only
& Co.
BRIGID BOYLE
Brigid Boyle
IRELAND Allied Irish Banks, p.l.c.
De La Rue Smurfit Limited
⑈400916⑈ 90⑉34991⑆ 16921851⑈ 09

2. A special crossing

A special crossing is an instruction to the bank to pay the money into a named bank account only.

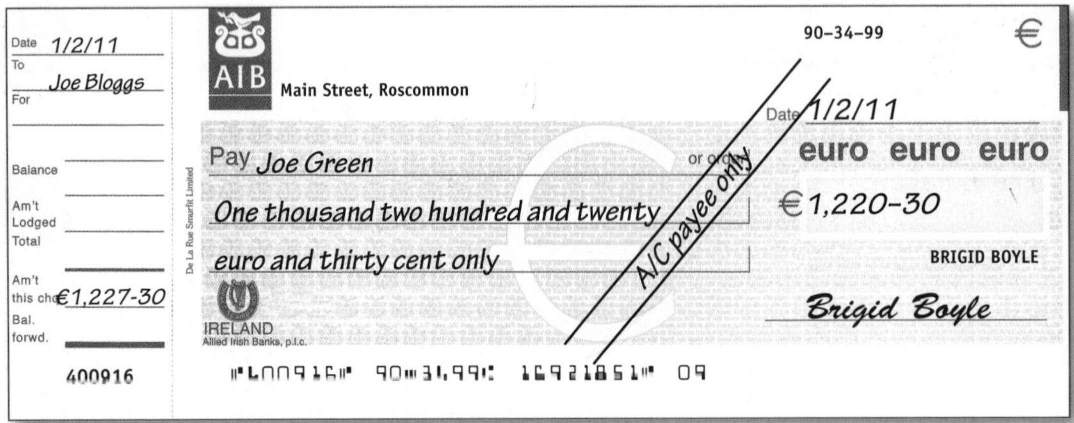

Date 1/2/11
To Joe Bloggs
For
Balance
Am't Lodged
Total
Am't this che €1,227-30
Bal. forwd.
400916

AIB Main Street, Roscommon
90-34-99 €
Date 1/2/11
Pay Joe Green or order
euro euro euro
One thousand two hundred and twenty
€1,220-30
euro and thirty cent only
A/C payee only
BRIGID BOYLE
Brigid Boyle
IRELAND Allied Irish Banks, p.l.c.
De La Rue Smurfit Limited
⑈400916⑈ 90⑉34991⑆ 16921851⑈ 09

If you put a special crossing on a cheque you must be sure that the payee has a bank account.

3. A restrictive crossing

A restrictive crossing is an instruction to the bank to pay the money into a named bank account in a named bank.

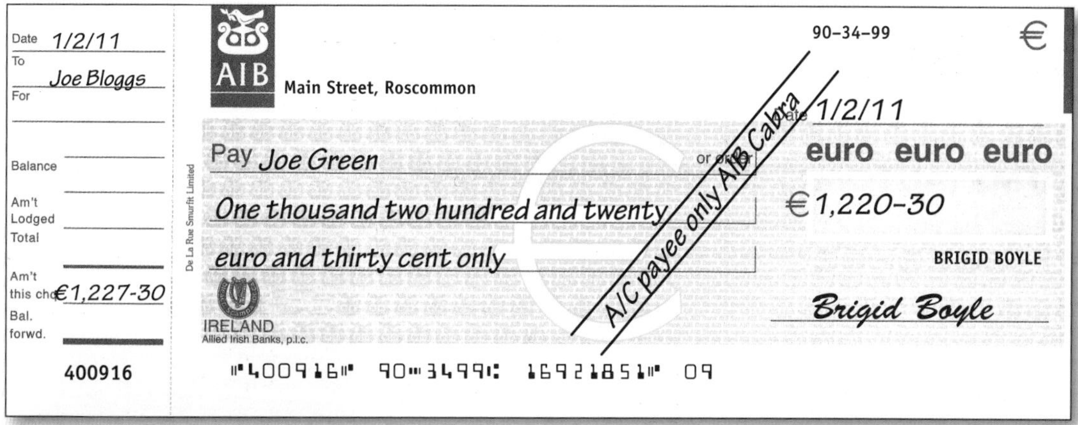

It is obvious that the drawer must know where the payee's bank account is held when putting a restrictive crossing on a cheque.

If a payee receives a cheque **without a crossing** on it he or she can cross it.

Dishonouring a cheque

A bank may refuse to honour a cheque (refuse to pay the money due on it) for any of the following reasons:

1. One of the six essentials is missing from the cheque.
2. The cheque is post-dated, i.e. the date on the cheque is for some time in the future.
3. The cheque is a stale cheque, i.e. more than six months have elapsed since it was dated.
4. The bank is suspicious of the signature on the cheque.
5. The drawer does not have enough money in his or her bank account.
6. The drawer instructs the bank to do so.
7. There is a Garnishee order on the account, i.e. a court order freezing all transactions on the account.

When a bank dishonours a cheque it marks it R/D and returns it to the payee.

R/D stands for *Refer to drawer.* The payee must return the cheque to the drawer and seek either a new cheque or cash instead of the cheque.

Bank overdraft

A bank overdraft allows a current account holder to withdraw more money from the account than is in it. Interest is charged on the amount overdrawn.

An overdraft is the equivalent of obtaining a short-term loan from the bank. It is shown as a credit balance in a cash book because the money is **owed** to the bank. Remember: 'Credit liabilities!'

ATMS (AUTOMATED TELLER MACHINES)

Before banks had ATMs we had to go into our banks to lodge or withdraw cash. The bank employee accepting or giving out the cash was known as a bank-teller.

Nowadays we can access our accounts without having to go into the bank by using automated teller machines. In this context the word 'automated' means robotic or computerised. Thus the bank-teller has been replaced by a computer!

ATMs are preloaded with cash and are linked to the banks' computers. We insert the ATM card supplied by the bank into the ATM. It reads the computer chip embedded in the card and we enter our PIN number.

Providing our account contains enough money, an ATM allows us to:

- withdraw cash
- pay bills
- check account balance
- order a statement or cheque book
- transfer money to another account
- purchase 'top-ups' for mobile phones
- top-up smart cards

Laser cards (described in the previous chapter) can also be used at ATMs.

Some ATM cards and Laser cards have a **Cirrus** facility that allows the cardholder to withdraw cash in foreign currencies from ATMs in over 120 countries. **Maestro** cards automatically provide a Cirrus facility.

NIGHT SAFES

Night safes are vaults provided by the banks for their customers' use. These safes allow customers to deposit cash and cheques after hours. They are accessed from outside the bank. The door to the vault is located on an outside wall of the bank and leads down to the safe through a long chute.

The customer is provided with a key to open this door and is also provided with lockable or sealable wallets by the bank. The customer places cash or cheques in these wallets along with a lodgement slip. The wallet is deposited in the night safe and is opened the next morning by a bank clerk who then credits the customer's account.

24-HOUR BANKING SERVICES

The major commercial banks now provide an Internet banking service that can be accessed 24 hours a day. This allows the customer to:

- make balance enquiries
- get online bank statements
- order printed statements
- transfer funds to other bank accounts
- pay utility bills, Visa card bills and so on
- search for cheques paid and other transactions on the account
- order cheque books
- request text alerts when there is any unusual transaction on the account

Banks also offer a telephone service for many of the above, but some services may not be available 24 hours a day.

FOREIGN CURRENCY EXCHANGE

Banks will exchange euro for foreign currency and exchange foreign currency for euro.

The **exchange rate** is the number of units of a foreign currency given in exchange for one euro.

Banks always show two exchange rates when dealing in foreign currencies. For instance, in the case of pounds sterling:

We buy	We sell
0.79	0.77

A bank regards the foreign exchange that it holds as part of the stock it has *for sale.*

Thus if you want to get pounds sterling from the bank, it is *selling* sterling to you, so you would use the *We sell* rate.

If you want to exchange pounds sterling for euro, the bank is *buying* sterling from you, so you would use the *We buy* rate.

Example 1

You are going to London and want to exchange €300 for pounds sterling. Multiply 300 by the *sell* rate. This gives $300 \times 0.77 = £231$

Example 2

Assume you want to exchange £100 sterling for euro when you return from London. Divide 100 by 0.79. This gives $100 \div 0.79 = €126.58$

Exchange Rates
We Sell
AUSTRALIA
BRAZIL
CANADA
CHINA
Costa Rica
Euro
HONG KONG
JAPAN
MEXICO
NEW ZEALAND
S Korea
SINGAPORE

Currency exchange – general rule

(a) When exchanging **euro for foreign currency**, multiply the *We sell* rate by the number of euro you are exchanging.

This gives the number of units of the foreign currency you will receive.

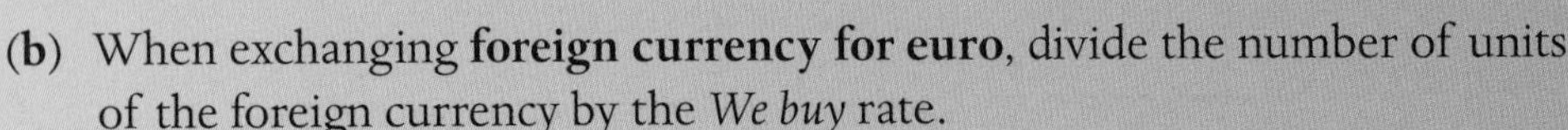

(b) When exchanging **foreign currency for euro**, divide the number of units of the foreign currency by the *We buy* rate.

This gives the number of euro you will receive.

LEARN THE KEY TERMS

- **Current accounts** are accounts to which people lodge money, which is then available to them, on demand, to pay for their day-to-day expenses.
- A **banker's card (cheque guarantee card)** is a card presented by the drawer of a cheque that ensures that the bank will honour the cheque up to a sum of €130.
- **Money laundering** is the practice of hiding the source of money because it may have been earned illegally or because the tax due on it was not paid.
- The **drawer** is the person who makes out and signs the cheque.
- The **drawee** is the drawer's bank.
- The **payee** is the person to whom the cheque is payable.
- The **counterfoil** is a record of the cheque payment.
- A **stale cheque** is one that has not been cashed or lodged within six months of the date written on it.
- A **post-dated cheque** is one dated some time in the future. It cannot be cashed until that date.
- An **ante-dated cheque** is one that bears a date prior to the date the cheque was written.
- A **crossing** on a cheque is an instruction to the bank to pay the money due on the cheque only into a bank account.
- A **bank overdraft** is a facility whereby permission is given to a current account holder to withdraw more money from the account than is in the account.
- **ATMs** are automated teller machines.
- The **exchange rate** is the number of units of a foreign currency given in exchange for one euro.

QUESTIONS

1. What are the functions of a commercial bank?
2. Name any three commercial banks in Ireland.
3. What are the main characteristics of a current account?
4. What is a cheque?
5. Name the six essential items that must appear on a cheque.
6. Name and explain the three means by which a payee can receive the money due on a cheque.
7. What is a banker's card (cheque guarantee card)?
8. Outline the correct procedure to be followed when using a cheque guarantee card.
9. Name the drawer, the drawee and the payee on this cheque.

10. (a) Name the type of crossing shown on this cheque.
    (b) What is the effect of this crossing?

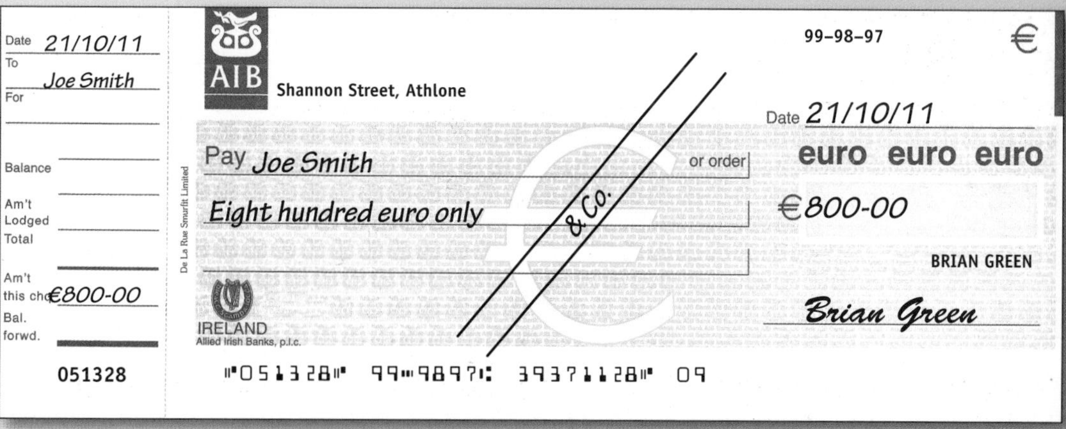

11. If Joe Smith's local grocer accepted this cheque from him what must Joe Smith write on the cheque and where must he write it?

12. Show how Brian Green would enter this cheque in his cash book showing the *Bank* columns only.

BANK A/C							
Date	Details	No.	€	Date	Details	No.	€

13. What is a stale cheque? When would each of the cheques in questions 9 and 10 become stale cheques?

14. List five items that are inserted in a lodgement docket by a person lodging money to a current account.

15. State and explain any four circumstances when a bank might dishonour a cheque.

16. What services, other than the withdrawal of cash, are normally provided by banks through the ATMs?

17. How can banks provide a '24-hour banking service' when they are closed almost sixteen hours every day?

18. What is meant by the term 'euro exchange rate'?

19. A bank displays the following exchange rates for the euro against the £ sterling.

John Smith is going on a school tour and needs to exchange €200 for pounds sterling. How much sterling will he receive? Show your workings.

20. John Smith has £30 sterling left over when he returns from his school tour. He goes back to the same bank to exchange this for euro. How many euro will he receive? Show your workings.

See workbook for more questions.

Bank statements

11

A BANK STATEMENT

A bank statement is a copy of the bank's record of a customer's transactions with the bank. It is sent to the customer periodically by the bank.

It allows the customer to compare his or her transactions record with the bank's record and so find any errors in either record.

A bank statement can show only the transactions that have gone through the bank by the last date of the statement.

Bank statement vs. cash book

Shown below are Joe Green's cash book (bank columns only) for January 2011 and a copy of his bank statement for that month.

CASH BOOK

Date	Details	F	Bank €	Date	Details	F	Bank €
1/1/11	Opening balance		1,000	2/1/11	ESB, Chq. no. 1		120
3/1/11	Salary		800	5/1/11	G. Green, Chq. no. 2		250
10/1/11	Salary		800	8/1/11	S. Smith, Chq. no. 3		600
17/1/11	Salary		800	10/1/11	ATM		150
18/1/11	Child Benefit		200	18/1/11	Groceries, Chq. no. 4		150
24/1/11	Salary		800	22/1/11	Car service, Chq. no. 5		400
31/1/11	Salary		800	28/1/11	Telephone, Chq. no. 6		180
				31/1/11	Balance		3,350
			5,200				5,200
1/2/11	Balance b/d		3,350				

BANK STATEMENT
Galway Bank Ltd, Main Street, Athenry, Co. Galway
90-06-11

Joe Green
Main Street
Athenry

A/C No. 00184541 09

Date: 31/01/11

Date	Details	payments Debit €	receipts Credit €	Balance €
01/01/11	Opening balance			1,000
03/01/11	Lodgement		800	1,800
05/01/11	Cheque no. 1	120		1,680
05/01/11	Direct Debit Irish Life	95		1,585
10/01/11	ATM Athenry	150		1,435
10/01/11	Lodgement		800	2,235
11/01/11	Cheque no. 3	600		1,635
17/01/11	Lodgement		800	2,435
18/01/11	Lodgement		200	2,635
20/01/11	Bank charges	15		2,620
21/01/11	Cheque no. 4	150		2,470
22/01/11	Credit transfer		300	2,770
24/01/11	Lodgement		800	3,570
25/01/11	Cheque no. 5	400		3,170

Layout of cash book and bank statement
The cash book is presented as a **T-ledger** account whereas the bank statement is presented as a **continuous balance ledger**. These ledger types will be dealt with in detail in Chapter 33.

Notice that items that are debits in the cash book appear as credits in the bank statement and items that are credits in the cash book appear as debits in the bank statement.

For example, Cheque no. 1 payable to the ESB is entered on the credit side of the cash book but is shown in the debit column in the bank statement.

When the bank is recording transactions on your account it regards any withdrawals as money being **received by you**.

It also regards any lodgements made by you as money **given by you** to them. This brings us to the next bookkeeping rule:

Debit the receiver of goods or money.
Credit the giver of goods or money.

Cheque transactions on a bank statement show that it is a **current account statement**. Cheques may not be used with any other type of account.

When you receive a bank statement, the balance shown on the statement will rarely match the balance shown in your own cash book. This is because:

1. The bank made or received payments on your behalf that you had not recorded in your cash book, e.g. direct debits, standing orders, credit transfers, and bank charges such as transaction charges and interest.
2. Some of the cheques paid out by you and recorded in your cash book may not yet have been presented to your bank for payment.
3. Lodgements made by you and recorded in your cash book may have been made too late to be included in the bank statement.

To establish the correct cash balance you need to update your cash book from any extra information contained in the bank statement.

When you receive a bank statement you should compare it with your cash book.

Make out two lists:

(a) A list of items that appear in the bank statement but do not appear in your cash book.
(b) A list of items that appear in your cash book but do not appear in the bank statement.

Simply tick, in both the cash book and the bank statement, the items that appear in both.

Now let us revisit our cash book and bank statement and do this.

EXAMPLE

Using the cash book and bank statement provided, update Joe Green's cash book and draw up a bank reconciliation statement at 31/1/11.

DR		CASH BOOK					CR
Date	Details	F	Bank €	Date	Details	F	Bank €
1/1/11	Opening balance	✓	1,000	2/1/11	ESB, Chq. no. 1	✓	120
3/1/11	Salary	✓	800	5/1/11	G. Green, Chq. no. 2		250
10/1/11	Salary	✓	800	8/1/11	S. Smith, Chq. no. 3	✓	600
17/1/11	Salary	✓	800	10/1/11	ATM	✓	150
18/1/11	Child Benefit	✓	200	18/1/11	Groceries, Chq. no. 4	✓	150
24/1/11	Salary	✓	800	22/1/11	Car Service, Chq. no. 5	✓	400
31/1/11	Salary	✓	800	28/1/11	Telephone, Chq. no. 6	✓	180
				31/1/11	Balance	✓	3,350
			5,200				5,200
1/2/11	Balance b/d		3,350				

BANK STATEMENT
Galway Bank Ltd, Main Street, Athenry, Co. Galway
90-06-11

Joe Green
Main Street
Athenry

A/C No. 00184541 09

Date: 31/01/11

Date	Details	Debit €	Credit €	Balance €
01/01/11	Opening balance ✓			1,000
03/01/11	Lodgement ✓		800	1,800
05/01/11	Cheque no. 1 ✓	120		1,680
05/01/11	Direct debit Irish Life	95		1,585
10/01/11	ATM Athenry ✓	150		1,435
10/01/11	Lodgement ✓		800	2,235
11/01/11	Cheque no. 3 ✓	600		1,635
17/01/11	Lodgement ✓		800	2,435
18/01/11	Lodgement ✓		200	2,635
20/01/11	Bank charges	15		2,620
21/01/11	Cheque no. 4 ✓	150		2,470
22/01/11	Credit transfer		300	2,770
24/01/11	Lodgement ✓		800	3,570
25/01/11	Cheque no. 5 ✓	400		3,170

You can see that the two closing balances are not the same.

Updating cash book and bank reconciliation statement

Updating the cash book

Use the first list to bring your cash book up to date, i.e. enter the information contained in the bank statement that you had not recorded in your cash book.

This is often referred to as a **cash correction account**. It will give you your real (correct) cash balance.

Use List 1, i.e. the unticked items in the bank statement.

List 1

1. Direct debit Irish Life €95
2. Bank charges €15
3. Credit transfer €300

CASH CORRECTION ACCOUNT AT 31/1/11

Balance as per cash book	€3,350		Direct debit Irish Life		€95
Credit transfer	€300		Bank charges		€15
			Correct cash balance		**€3,540**
	€3,650				€3,650

Notes

(a) Start by entering the **closing balance** from the cash book, i.e. €3,350.
(b) Debit the cash correction account with any credits that were in the bank statement that did not appear in the cash book. These increase your correct cash balance. Here it is €300.
(c) Credit the cash correction account with any debits that did not appear in the cash book. These decrease your correct cash balance. Here they are the direct debit (DD) Irish Life, €95 and bank charges, €15.
(d) Calculate the new balance, i.e. debits of €3,650 minus credits of €110.
(e) This gives the **correct cash balance**, i.e. the true amount of money you have, i.e. €3,540.

Bank reconciliation statement

A bank reconciliation statement is a procedure carried out to ensure that the difference between the correct cash balance and the balance shown in the bank statement is due to the items that have not yet been recorded in the bank statement but have been recorded in the cash book.

Use List 2, i.e. the unticked items in the cash book.

List 2

1. Salary lodgement €800 — *The bank has not yet received this money.*
2. Cheque no. 2, €250
3. Cheque no. 6, €180 — *The money due on these cheques is still in your account.*

BANK RECONCILIATION STATEMENT AT 31/1/11		
Correct cash balance		€3,540
Less lodgement not yet credited		
Salary		€800
		€2,740
Plus cheques not yet cashed		
Cheque no. 2	€250	
Cheque no. 6	€180	€430
Balance as per bank statement		**€3,170**

Notes

1. Start with the **correct cash balance**.
2. Subtract any lodgements that have not yet been credited by the bank. As far as the bank is concerned this money is not yet in your account.
3. Add any cheques, entered in the cash book, that do not appear in the bank statement. As far as the bank is concerned the money due on these cheques is still in your account.
4. The answer at Step 2 should equal the balance of the bank statement.

This shows that we are able to explain the difference between the balance as per bank statement and the correct cash balance. If we cannot reconcile the two balances then there must be a mistake in either the cash book or the bank statement that must be found and corrected.

Bank reconciliation statement – alternative method

An alternative method of drawing up the bank reconciliation statement is to start with the *Balance as per bank statement* and then add lodgements not yet credited and subtract cheques not yet cashed. This should give you the *Correct cash balance.*

BANK RECONCILIATION STATEMENT AT 31/1/11		
Balance as per bank statement		€3,170
Plus lodgements not yet credited		
Salary		€800
		€3,970
Less cheques not yet cashed (or presented)		
Cheque no. 2	€250	
Cheque no. 6	€180	€430
Correct cash balance		**€3,540**

Overdrawn accounts

If the bank account is **overdrawn** (indicated by a **Dr** after the balance), the *Balance as per bank statement* should be treated as a negative (minus) number.

If the difference between the two balances cannot be resolved then there is a mistake (or mistakes) in either the cash book or the bank statement. This will lead to a further investigation of the cash book and of the bank statement to correct any mistakes.

This is a very important procedure because any mistakes, particularly made by the bank, could affect your credit worthiness with the bank. This could make it difficult to borrow money from the bank at some future date.

It is also important because it highlights any inaccuracies in your own cash book.

Note

In some questions you are given the bank statement but you have to write up the **cash book** (bank columns only) from given information, and then do the **cash correction account** and the **bank reconciliation statement**.

LEARN THE KEY TERMS

- A **bank statement** is a copy of the bank's record of a customer's transactions with the bank.
- Rule: **Debit the receiver** of goods or money. **Credit the giver** of goods or money.

- A **cash correction account** (updating the cash book) is used to establish the true amount of money a person really has.
- A **bank reconciliation statement** is used to give a verifiable reason for the difference between the correct cash balance and the balance shown in the bank statement.

QUESTIONS

1. What is a bank statement?
2. State any three reasons why the balance in a cash book would differ from the balance in the corresponding bank statement.
3. What is the purpose of a cash correction account? *or*
   Why is it necessary to update a cash book when a bank statement is received?
4. What is a bank reconciliation statement?
5. Martina Malone received the following statement from her bank:

BANK STATEMENT
The Shamrock Bank Ltd, Main Street, Lusk
90-06-13

Martina Malone
High Street, Swords

A/C No. 12348765

Date: 31/01/11

Date	Details	Debit €	Credit €	Balance €
01/01/11	Opening Balance			5,000
03/01/11	Lodgement		600	5,600
05/01/11	Cheque no. 31	500		5,100
05/01/11	DD EBS	1,200		6,300
9/01/11	ATM O'Connell St	300		6,000
10/01/11	Lodgement		3,000	9,000
11/01/11	Cheque no. 33	600		9,400
17/01/11	Lodgement		1,500	10,900
18/1/11	Cheque no. 34		11,000	100 DR
20/01/11	Bank charges	30		130 DR
21/01/11	SO Irish Life	200		330 DR
22/01/11	Credit transfer		12,000	11,670
24/01/11	Lodgement		800	3,570
25/01/11	Cheque no. 35	400		3,170
30/01/11	Interest	3		3,167

(a) What is the name and address of Martina Malone's bank?
(b) What evidence is there in the statement that this is a current account?
(c) What, according to the bank, is the balance on the account at the end of the month?
(d) Explain the entry on 9/01/11.

(e) Explain the balance on 20/01/11.
(f) Explain the interest charge on 30/01/11.
(g) Martina Malone wrote all cheques in numerical sequence and did not stop any cheque. Explain why cheque no. 32 does not appear on the statement.

6. Rita Dunne opened a current account on 1 September 2011 with *permanent tsb* by lodging €2,200.

You are provided with a record of her own cash book (bank columns only) and a copy of the bank statement she received from the bank.

You are required to bring her **cash book** up to date (i.e. a cash correction account) and prepare a **bank reconciliation statement** at 14/09/2011.

DR				CASH BOOK			CR
Date	Details		Bank €	Date	Details	Chq	Bank €
01/09/11	Lodgement		2,200	01/09/11	Groceries	1	200
13/09/11	Lodgement		500	01/09/11	Clothes	2	150
14/09/11	Lodgement		1,000	05/09/11	ATM		250
				06/09/11	ATM		100
				10/09/11	Car insurance	3	350
				12/09/11	Groceries	4	215
				14/09/11	Balance		2,435
			3,700				3,700

BANK STATEMENT
permanent tsb, Main St, Blanchardstown, Dublin 15
90-06-17

Rita Dunne **A/C No. 00184541 07** **Date: 14/0/11**
Main Street, Dublin 1

Date	Details	Debit €	Credit €	Balance €
01/09/11	Lodgement		2,200	2,200
02/09/11	Cheque no. 1	200		2,000
03/09/11	Direct Debit ESB	95		1,905
04/09/11	Cheque no. 2	150		1,755
05/09/11	ATM Castleknock	250		1,505
06/09/11	ATM Cabra	100		1,405
07/09/11	Paypath		1,000	2,405
09/09/11	Credit transfer		500	2,905
12/09/11	Bank charges	15		2,890
13/09/11	Lodgement		500	3,390

See workbook for more questions.

Personal saving and credit purchasing

12

At any given time some people can afford to save some of their income, while others need to borrow money to buy an expensive product.

The financial institutions (banks) cater for both sets of people by accepting deposits from savers and using these savings as the basis for loans to borrowers.

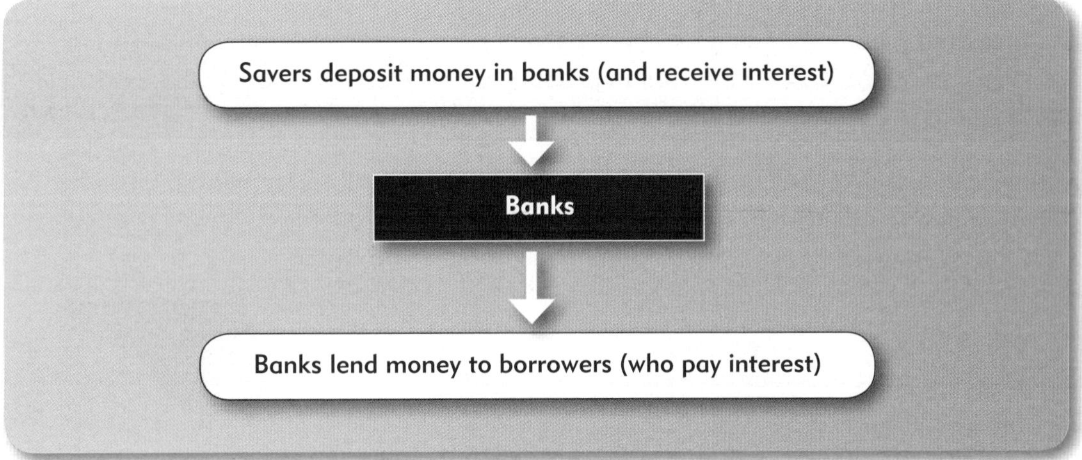

This chapter covers both saving and borrowing.

When we say *financial institutions* we are usually referring to commercial banks, building societies and An Post. We looked at commercial banks in Chapter 10.

BUILDING SOCIETIES

Building societies are financial institutions owned by their members. They were originally established to provide mortgages* but now also offer loans for purposes other than the purchase of houses.

*A **mortgage** is a contract where a property (usually a house) is signed over to a lender of money for the duration of the loan. The lender can only force the sale of the property if the borrower fails to meet the repayments due on the loan.

CREDIT UNIONS

A credit union is a co-operative (see Chapter 16) owned by a group of savers and borrowers who have something in common, such as living in the same area or working in the same industry.

Credit unions lend to their members at an affordable rate of interest. Each credit union is run by volunteers from its membership. Every member has an equal say in the running of the credit union.

AN POST

An Post is a limited company (see Chapter 16) owned by the Minister for Finance and the Minister for Communications, Marine and Natural Resources. As well as offering postal services, it also provides various saving schemes. (Details of these schemes are outlined on page 116).

SAVING AND INVESTING

Saving means not spending some of your income.

Investing means **spending** on capital goods such as factories, machines and land, i.e. goods that will be used to produce other goods and services.

However, in reality, little distinction is made between saving and investing. Financial institutions frequently run advertising campaigns inviting people to 'invest your money with us'. These banks are really asking people to save with them.

Why do people save and invest?

1. **To purchase some expensive item in the future:** Many people save to pay for holidays or cars. Many others save to get a deposit for a house.
2. **For thrift purposes:** Some people deliberately save part of their income so that they do not waste it on unnecessary luxury goods or to prevent impulse buying.
3. **To earn interest.**
4. **For precautionary purposes:** To have money available for unforeseen events such as unexpected medical expenses or car repairs.
5. **To provide for children's education.**
6. **To provide for retirement.**
7. **To earn a credit rating for possible future borrowings:** Many financial institutions will grant loans only to people who can prove they have the ability to repay them. When people save on a **regular** basis they are proving they have this ability.

SAVING SCHEMES

Banks and building societies

Banks and building societies operate deposit accounts.

Deposit accounts

1. A deposit account is a form of savings account. The account holders receive interest on the money in the account.
2. Money can be withdrawn only through an ATM or 'over-the-counter'.
3. Chequebooks are not used.

Deposit account types

There are two basic types of deposit account:

1. **Demand deposit accounts.** Money can be withdrawn at any time.
2. **Term or time deposit accounts.** Money can be withdrawn only by giving a minimum amount of notice, e.g. 7 days, a month or after an agreed period of time. Money in time deposit accounts cannot be withdrawn at ATMs.

DIRT and its effect on interest received

Interest earned on money in deposit accounts is subject to a **Deposit Interest Retention Tax**, commonly known as **DIRT**. Thus DIRT is a tax on interest earned from a financial institution and it decreases the real rate of interest received on the savings.

Example of the effect of DIRT	
Deposit	€1,000
Interest **earned** at 10% (i.e.10% of €1,000)	€100
Less 25% DIRT (i.e. 25% of €100)	- €25
Interest received	€75
True rate of interest **received** (75 ÷ 1000 × 100)	7.50%

Credit union deposit accounts

Most credit unions operate two types of deposit account:

1. A **regular share account**, which receives a share of the profits earned by the credit union. You do not pay DIRT on these accounts.
2. A **normal deposit account**, which operates in the same manner as bank deposit accounts. Interest on these deposit accounts is subject to DIRT.

An Post saving schemes

An Post operates a number of different saving schemes.

1. **Savings Certificates** are for people who want to save a lump sum of money. These currently offer a 21% rate of interest over a period of five years and six months that is tax-free. The money is state guaranteed.
2. **Savings Bonds**, again, are for people who want to save a lump sum for a shorter period of time. These currently offer a 10% rate of interest over a period of three years that is tax-free. The money is state guaranteed.
3. **Instalment Savings Agreements:** These cater for people who want to save any regular amount between €25 and €1,000 per month for a minimum of twelve months. The money is then left on deposit for a further five years and earns 20% interest tax-free. If the money is withdrawn before the end of the five-year period a lower rate of interest is applied.

Note: Interest rates quoted here were correct at the time of writing. Interest rates can change from time to time. As an ongoing exercise you should check these rates.

Proof of your name, address and your PPS number (tax number) is required when opening an account with An Post. You must also state your date of birth and An Post may request proof of this.

INVESTMENT SCHEMES

Life assurance schemes

Endowment life assurance policies are a form of investment (see page 80). The life assurance companies invest the premiums received and the insured person receives a share of the profits from these investments when the policy matures. Endownment policies normally have good returns over a long period of time. But remember that the value of these investments may decrease if share market prices go down.

Shares

When you purchase shares you are buying a part ownership in a business. The major attraction is the *possibility* that you could sell these shares in the near future at a greater price than you paid for them. This profit is called a **capital gain**. Of course if the value of the shares goes down you will lose money!

Some people purchase shares to get a dividend from them. A **dividend** is a payment to the shareholder based on the amount of profit earned by the business. If the business makes big profits on an ongoing basis then the dividend may be greater than the annual interest rate earned on a similar sum of money in a deposit account.

From this you can see that investing in shares is a risky business.

INTEREST ON SAVINGS

Interest can be calculated as **simple interest** or as **compound interest**.

Simple interest

Here interest is paid each year only on the amount saved in that year.

Compound interest

Here interest is paid each year on the total sum of money in the account, i.e. the amount saved *plus* the amount previously earned in interest. This means you earn interest on interest you have already earned! It is often called the **Compound Annual Rate** or **CAR**.

The difference between simple and compound interest

Assume you lodge €10,000 to a deposit account on 1 January 2011 and leave the money in the account for three years at an interest rate of 10%.

Interest earned at simple interest rate			Interest earned at compound interest rate		
	Amount	Interest		Amount	Interest
Year 1	€10,000	€1,000	Year 1	€10,000	€1,000
Year 2	€10,000	€1,000	Year 2	€11,000	€1,100
Year 3	€10,000	€1,000	Year 3	€12,100	€1,210
Total interest		**€3,000**	**Total interest**		**€3,310**

You earn €310 more interest under the compound rate of interest, i.e. the total interest earned over the three-year period is more than 10% greater than that earned under the simple interest rate.

Many financial institutions are now using the terms **Equivalent Annual Rate** (**EAR**) or **Annual Equivalent Rate** (**AER**) instead of CAR, i.e. the full rate of interest earned if the full sum of money is left in the account for a full year.

CHOOSING A SAVING OR INVESTMENT SCHEME

Consider the following factors before deciding on a saving or investment scheme.

1. **Safety:** Are your savings guaranteed to be repaid to you? Some schemes give a guarantee that you will not lose any of your own capital, while others have State guarantees. If you buy shares you may lose all your money.

2. **Interest rates:** Always shop around for the best interest rate for the saving scheme best suited to your needs. Is the interest rate at least equal to the rate of inflation, i.e. could the purchasing power of your money go down? (See Chapter 13.)

3. **Liquidity:** An asset is liquid if it can be exchanged for cash very quickly. Your savings are an asset. Do not put money into a time deposit account if there is any possibility that you may need that money during the notice period. Nor should you invest in funds that attach a high penalty if cashed before the maturity date.

4. **Convenience:** Do you have to travel long distances to a particular bank to get access to your savings? Is it possible to access the savings via an ATM? Do the opening hours of the bank suit you? Can the savings be accessed online?

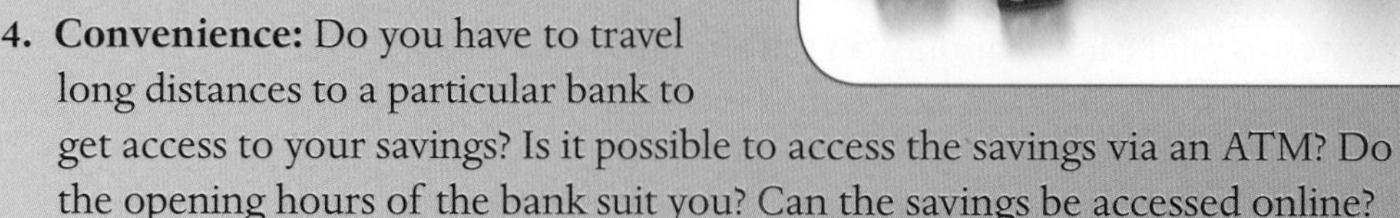

5. **Secondary benefits:** If it concerns you, will the record of your saving help to obtain a mortgage for you? Are there any bonus benefits if you leave your money on deposit for a stated period of time?

6. **Tax:** Is the interest tax free? Does the rate of DIRT substantially reduce the true rate of interest you are earning? Are there any income tax concessions on the regular payments into the investment fund?

BUYING ON CREDIT (BORROWING)

Paying by cash is generally the cheapest way to buy goods. However, if we borrow to buy goods we must pay interest on the borrowings. The full annual rate of interest charged on the loan is known as the Annual Percentage Rate (APR). The APR is calculated each year only on that part of the loan still outstanding.

Some financial institutions calculate the repayments on a loan on the basis of a flat rate of interest. Under this system the borrower is charged a fixed rate of interest each year on the original sum of money borrowed. This works out at a much higher interest charge than that calculated by the APR.

Flat rate of interest versus APR

Sum of money borrowed is €3,000 to be repaid over three years at 10% per annum. We will assume that one payment, including interest, is made at the end of each year.

	FLAT RATE OF INTEREST			APR		
	Balance	Repayment	Interest	Balance	Repayment	Interest
Year 1	€3,000	€1,300	€300	€3,000	€1,300	€300
Year 2	€2,000	€1,300	€300	€2,000	€1,200	€200
Year 3	€1,000	€1,300	€300	€1,000	€1,100	€100
Total interest			**€900**			**€600**

Before borrowing to pay for a product consider:

1. Do you really need this product now?
2. How long would it take you to save for the product, allowing that you will earn interest on your saving?
3. Do you know the difference between the cash price and the full price you will have to pay for the product, allowing for interest payments?
4. Do you know the monthly repayments on the loan?
5. Can you afford these repayments?
6. Do you know the consequences for failure to meet the repayments? You might lose your house!

BORROWING AND DEFERRED PAYMENT

1. Bank overdraft

This was explained in Chapter 10. The rate of interest charged on overdrafts tends to be cheaper than that charged on credit cards, if the money is being borrowed for a few months. This makes overdrafts a relatively cheap form of short-term borrowing, provided the money is repaid quickly and within the stated period.

Overdrafts should be used only when a person has a temporary shortage of cash, e.g. at Christmas or for payment of college fees.

2. A term loan

This is where a customer borrows a sum of money for a fixed period of time (term), and repays it on a regular basis in agreed instalments. This is suitable for the financing of expensive, durable goods such as cars and furniture, but the term of the loan should never exceed the life of the good being purchased. Sometimes banks will look for collateral for a loan.

Collateral is something of value used as security against a loan that a bank can sell if the loan is not repaid. The ownership of the collateral is assigned to (i.e. transferred to) the bank for the period of the loan.

A **loan application form** must be completed when applying for a loan (see next page). This gives the bank a full record of the financial situation of the person applying for the loan. The bank uses the information to determine the ability of the applicant to repay the loan.

When the loan is approved, the borrower then signs a loan agreement that outlines the terms and conditions attached to the loan.

Credit unions also offer term loans to their members. The major advantages of borrowing from a credit union are:

- The repayment agreement includes an element of saving so that the borrower has some savings at the end of the loan period.
- The credit union provides free insurance on the loan so that no debt remains due to the credit union if the borrower dies before the loan is fully repaid.

PERSONAL LOAN APPLICATION

The Shamrock Bank

PERSONAL DETAILS

Title: Tick (✓) appropriate box: Mr ☐ Mrs ☐ Ms ☐

Forename:

Surname:

Address:

Home phone no. Mobile phone no.

Number of years living at this address:

Do you own or rent the house?

Mortgage amount (if any):

EMPLOYMENT DETAILS

Occupation:

Employer's name:

Number of years in your present employment:

INCOME DETAILS

Gross annual income in this employment:

Other income:

LOAN DETAILS

Amount of loan required:

Loan repayment period (in months):

Purpose of loan:

Signature: Date:

3. A mortgage

Traditionally mortgages were offered only by building societies. Today the majority of commercial banks also offer mortgages.

A mortgage is a relatively cheap method of financing long-term expenditure, particularly the purchase of a house or an apartment.

The borrower agrees to repay a fixed or variable amount of money each month. The interest rate charged can be either a fixed rate or a variable rate.

However, the borrower must assign the property to the bank or building society so that in the event of the borrower defaulting on the repayments the property can be sold to regain the amount outstanding to the lender.

4. Hire purchase

This literally means what it states, i.e. you are hiring (renting) a product until you have fully paid for it (purchased it). It is often used by people who cannot or do not want to get a bank loan to purchase an expensive, consumer durable product.

There are three parties to a hire purchase agreement:
1. the buyer of the goods
2. the seller of the goods
3. a finance company or bank

The seller sells the goods to the customer (hirer) and is paid in full by the finance company, which then collects the purchase price plus interest from the hirer. The hirer does not own the goods until the final payment is made to the finance company. The rate of interest on hire purchase agreements tends to be high, but the finance company usually does not look for collateral.

Hire purchase agreements

All hire purchase agreements (contracts) must show:
1. Name and address of the buyer
2. Name and address of the seller
3. Cash price of the goods
4. Full hire purchase price of the goods
5. APR being charged
6. Deposit, if any, that must be paid
7. Number of payments to be made
8. Amount of each payment to be made

Remember that, subject to certain conditions, the hire purchase company can repossess the goods if the repayments are not made on time.

5. Leasing

Leasing means renting a good on a contractual basis. This is suitable for acquiring a good that you may not need to keep for a long time and do not want ownership of.

Leasing saves you from paying out the full purchase price of the good or borrowing the purchase price from a bank. However, no matter how long you pay the lease you never own the good. Some people lease a house when they only need it for a short time and do not want to have to take out a mortgage.

6. Credit and store cards

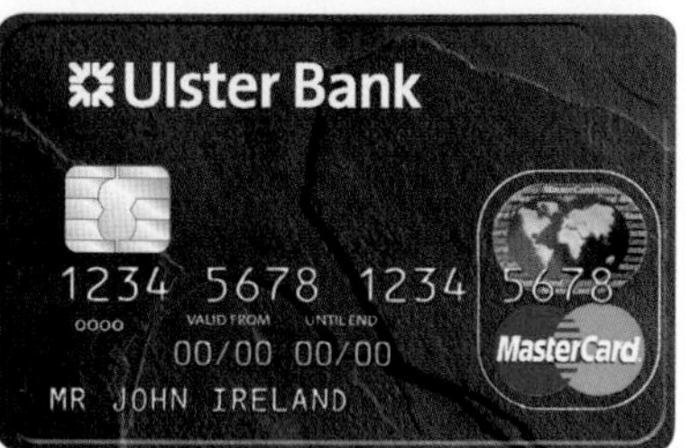

Credit cards were explained on page 89. They should be used only for obtaining very short-term credit because the interest rates are extremely high. Remember that if a balance (including interest) on a statement is not paid in full by the due date, you will pay interest on the interest outstanding over the following months.

Store cards operate in the same manner as credit cards except that purchases are confined to the particular chain of stores, e.g. Debenhams, Topshop or IKEA. These store cards offer extra benefits to the cardholder such as 10% privilege weeks, sale preview evenings and cardholder-only shopping events. But, as the APR on these varies between 17% and 20%, they should be used only for short-term credit.

7. Money lenders

Money lenders should be used only when a person, for any reason, cannot borrow from a bank, a building society, or a credit union, or obtain a hire purchase agreement.

A **money lender** is defined by the Financial Regulator as 'a person who carries on the business of money lending or who advertises or announces himself or holds himself out in any way as carrying on that business' and is the holder of a licence granted for that purpose by the Financial Regulator.

Also, the total cost of credit to the consumer under official money-lending agreements is **in excess of an APR of 23 per cent**. In most cases the APR is even higher than this.

Here we are only examining the role of licensed money lenders. There are, of course, many unlicensed and unscrupulous money lenders in operation.

Money lenders usually give loans for relatively short periods of time only, e.g. six months.

When obtaining a loan from a money lender the borrower should ensure there is a written agreement and that the written agreement should show, in a prominent position, the words *Money lending agreement*.

The money lender should provide a repayment book or loan statement sheet to keep track of what has been paid and what is still owed. This should be kept safely as it is the only record of the repayments.

LEARN THE KEY TERMS

- **Saving** means not spending some of your income.
- **Investing** means spending on capital goods.
- **Demand deposit account:** money can be withdrawn at any time.
- **Time deposit account:** money can only be withdrawn by giving a minimum amount of notice.
- **Deposit Interest Retention Tax (DIRT)** is a tax on interest earned from a financial institution.
- A **credit union** is a co-operative owned by a group of savers and borrowers who have common characteristics.
- **Simple interest** means that interest is only paid each year on the amount saved.
- **Compound Interest Rate** (or **Compound Annual Rate** or **CAR**) means that interest on savings is paid each year on the total sum of money in the account.
- **AER** is the Annual Estimated Rate of interest on savings.
- **EAR** is the Estimated Annual Rate of interest on savings.
- **APR** (Annual Percentage Rate) is the full annual rate of interest charged on a loan. The interest each year is only charged on the balance that remains unpaid.
- **Flat rate of interest** means a fixed rate of interest **each year** on the original sum of money borrowed.

QUESTIONS

1. Name and explain any five reasons why people might save.
2. Distinguish between saving and investing.
3. What are the major characteristics of deposit accounts?
4. Distinguish between (i) a demand deposit account and (ii) a time deposit account.
5. What do the initials DIRT stand for?
6. Joe Murphy saves €1,000 in a deposit account. He receives simple interest at the rate of 5% per annum (per year). How much interest will he earn at the end of two years? Show your calculations.
7. Mary O'Brien saves €1,000 in a deposit account. She receives a compound annual rate of interest of 5% per annum. How much interest will she earn at the end of two years? Show your calculations.
8. Calculate the **total value** of Mary O'Brien's savings at the end of the second year if DIRT of 20% was charged **each year**.
9. James Jones has €10,000 that he will not need for the next three years. His local Building Society is offering an annual interest rate of 4% EAR for three years subject to DIRT of 20% on the total interest earned. An Post is offering Savings Bonds at 10% gross interest at the end of three years, tax-free. Which option would you recommend to James? Show all your calculations.

10. Distinguish between interest on loans charged as an APR and interest charged as a flat rate.

11. Robert Jones has a choice of borrowing €6,000 over a three-year period at a flat rate of interest of 5% per annum or at an APR of 8% per annum. Robert will repay €2,000 capital each year. Which of these loan offers would you recommend to Robert? Show all your calculations.

12. Celine O'Hanlon wishes to purchase house furniture costing €3,000. She has two options:

Option 1: Hire purchase: €200 deposit and 36 instalments of €110 each

Option 2: Loan at 8% APR over three years with the loan amount reduced by €1,000 each year.

(a) Calculate the total cost of each option.
(b) Which option would you recommend? Give one reason for your answer.

See workbook for more questions.

Economics 1: **Introduction**

13

We often hear statements similar to the following:

- 'I can't afford a new car this year because I have to replace all the old windows in our house.'
- 'This year, as Minister for Finance, I can spend more money on educational facilities or I can spend more money on health-care facilities – I can't do both.'
- 'Our business has only enough capital to produce one of the two products we would like to produce.'

These statements show that all sections of our society – families, governments and businesses – must, from time to time, make choices. This happens because we don't have enough income to do everything we would like to do.

We earn our incomes by using the resources available to us to produce goods and to provide services.

But our country only has a limited amount of resources with which we can produce these goods and provide these services.

Therefore we have to decide on our priorities, i.e. what actions are most important to us at any given time.

Economics is the study of how we make the best possible use of scarce resources in order to satisfy the requirements of as many people as possible.

The *requirements* mentioned in this definition refer to our **needs** and **wants**.

Needs are the essential items we require to survive.

We have three needs:

- basic food
- basic clothing
- basic shelter

At a more advanced level our needs can also depend on circumstances, e.g. students need to spend money on books, farmers need to spend money on fertilisers and a household needs to spend money on electricity.

Wants are items we would like to have in addition to our needs.

Examples
- Meals in a restaurant
- Designer clothes
- A holiday home
- A wide-screen plasma TV set
- A hi-fi system

The list is endless.

The *resources* mentioned in the definition of economics refer to the items that are available to us to produce goods and services. There are not enough resources available to us to produce everything we would like to produce. These resources are called the factors of production.

THE FACTORS OF PRODUCTION

The **factors of production** are those resources that help to produce a product or provide a service.

The products we produce and the services we supply are called **wealth**.

We need an enormous amount of different resources to make any given product. For example:

Resources needed to make a wooden chair:
- Land on which to grow trees
- People to plant the seeds for the trees
- Saws of all shapes and sizes to cut down the trees
- People to use these saws
- Forms of transport to get the trees from the forest to the carpenter's workshop
- Roads on which this transport can travel
- Bricks and mortar to build the carpenter's factory
- People to build the factory
- Machinery needed in the factory
- People to operate these machines
- Other materials such as nails and glue that are used in the making of the chair
- More forms of transport to get the chair from the factory to a shop
- The shop itself
- The energy needed at all the above stages
- People who can organise or coordinate all of this activity

This is not a complete list of all the resources required. See if you can add to it. Nevertheless it gives a good indication of the amount of resources needed to produce any product.

For convenience purposes we classify the **factors of production** under four headings:

1. Land
2. Labour
3. Capital
4. Enterprise

Land

Land is anything provided by nature that helps to produce goods and services.

Examples
- The sea
- Soil
- Gas
- Metals such as lead, zinc, gold and copper
- Even climate can be considered as land because it is provided by nature. Many countries are able to exploit their climate to create a tourism industry.

The payment made to people who supply land is called **rent**.

Labour

Labour is any human effort that helps to produce goods and services.

Examples
- Factory workers
- Accountants
- Carpenters
- Doctors
- Janitors

In fact any human activity for which people are willing to pay a price is regarded as labour.

The payment made to people who supply labour is called **wages**.

Capital

Capital is anything that is made by humans that is then used to help to produce other goods and services.

Examples
- Machines
- Trucks
- Computers
- Factories
- Roads

Many people regard the money that is invested in a business as its capital. However, from Chapter 9 you will recall that money is simply a means of exchange.

The money invested in a business is used to purchase such items as machines, computers, and buildings. It is these items that are used to make other goods and services. The people who loan the money, e.g. banks, receive interest on that money. Thus the payment for capital is **interest**.

Enterprise

Enterprise is that special form of human activity that **organises** the other factors of production and **bears the risk** involved in production.

Features
1. The people who supply enterprise are called **entrepreneurs.** These are the people who arrange the **financing** of businesses and who **run** businesses.
2. Land, on its own, is not very productive. Labour can produce very little without the use of capital goods. Capital goods cannot do anything on their own. People are needed to operate these capital goods. Thus entrepreneurs are needed to **coordinate the other three factors of production** into a productive and, hopefully, profitable business unit.
3. The payment to enterprise is **profit**, if the business is successful. If it is not then the entrepreneur suffers a loss. This is why we state that **enterprise bears the risk** involved in production.

ECONOMIC SYSTEMS

As countries developed they devised different economic systems, i.e. ways of organising and running their economic activities. Any economic system must decide:

(**a**) What goods and services are to be produced?
(**b**) How are these goods and services to be produced?
(**c**) Who is to benefit from the production of these goods and services?

Over time three basic systems evolved.

Free-enterprise system (sometimes referred to as capitalism)

Under the free-enterprise system, all resources (the factors of production) are owned by private individuals or by companies and used for their benefit only. The government plays no role in this type of economy.

Centrally planned systems (sometimes referred to as communism)

In a centrally planned system all resources are publicly owned, i.e. owned by the government on behalf of all its citizens. The government controls all economic activity.

Mixed economies

Mixed economies allow most of the major economic decisions to be made by the private sector, but the government intervenes to ensure the supply of essential goods to everybody.

From time to time the government also involves itself in planning the organisation and future development of the economy. Ireland's economy is a mixed economy.

COSTS

We are all familiar with the **financial cost** of buying a good or service, i.e. the amount of money we must pay for it. However, because resources are scarce and because we must make choices, there is always an **opportunity cost** involved in all transactions.

Opportunity cost is the item we do without (forego) when we have to make a choice between two or more actions.

Example 1
I own a piece of land. I would like to build a shop on it and I would also like to build a factory on it. But it is only big enough for one of these. If I build the shop then the factory is the opportunity cost of the shop.

Example 2
The government has €2m that can be spent building a new school **or** it can be spent on new medical equipment in a hospital. If the government builds the new school the opportunity cost of the school is the medical equipment.

From this you can see that it is impossible to satisfy everybody's needs and wants at any given time.

INFLATION

One of the biggest problems facing any economy is inflation.

Inflation is the increase in the general level of the price of goods and services over a period of time.

The **rate of inflation** is the percentage by which the general level of prices increases. It is usually shown as an annual rate of inflation.

Formula for measuring the rate of inflation:

$$\frac{\text{The **increase** in prices in Year 2}}{\text{The level of prices in Year 1}} \times 100$$

Example

- Price of goods for a typical household in Year 1 = €3,000
- Price of goods for a typical household in Year 2 = €3,150

Thus prices increased by €150. Therefore the rate of inflation is:

$$\frac{€150}{€3,000} \times 100 = 5\%$$

The official measurement of inflation is known as the **consumer price index (CPI)**.

Causes of inflation

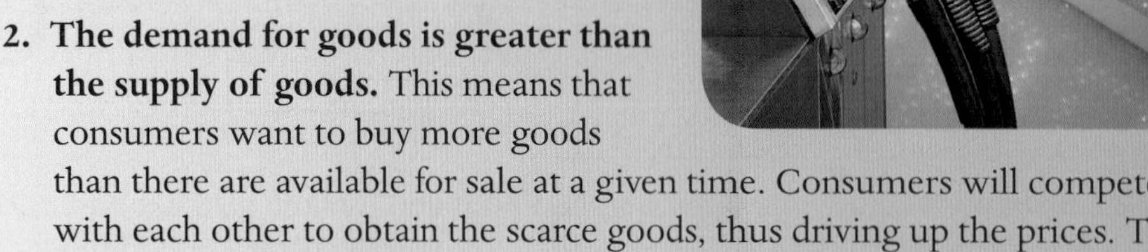

1. **An increase in the cost of producing goods** is passed on to the consumer so that the manufacturer can maintain profits.
2. **The demand for goods is greater than the supply of goods.** This means that consumers want to buy more goods than there are available for sale at a given time. Consumers will compete with each other to obtain the scarce goods, thus driving up the prices. Think of an auction situation.
3. **The cost of importing goods increases.** This is 'imported inflation'. We either pay the extra prices or do without the goods.
4. **Increases in indirect taxes.** Any time the government increases the VAT on products the price of these products automatically increases.

Effects of inflation

Inflation is harmful because:

1. It increases the cost of living, i.e. households have to pay higher prices for goods and services.
2. It causes demands for wage increases to compensate for the inflation. Wage increases can then cause further inflation as producers increase their prices to recoup the extra cost of the increased wages.
3. It discourages saving because people decide to spend their money before its value decreases any further.
4. It causes the price of our exports to increase, which makes it more difficult to sell them.
5. It may cause Irish people to buy cheaper imports instead of goods made in Ireland.

Note: Deflation is a decrease in the general level of the price of goods and services over a period of time.

GROSS DOMESTIC PRODUCT

Gross domestic product (GDP) is the total amount of goods and services produced in an economy in one period.

GDP is usually measured on an annual basis and in money terms.

Example

Number of goods produced in a year = 1,000,000.
Average price per unit = €10

GDP = €10,000,000.

Gross national product (GNP) is the gross domestic product *less* profits sent out of the country by foreign-owned companies located in the country, *plus* profits returned to the country by local firms based abroad.

The distinction between GDP and GNP is very important in Ireland because there is a net outflow of profit from Ireland of over €25,000 million (€25 billion) annually.

GNP is our national income because it is the amount of money left in the country for spending or saving purposes.

ECONOMIC GROWTH

Economic growth occurs when more goods are produced in a country one year than were produced the previous year.

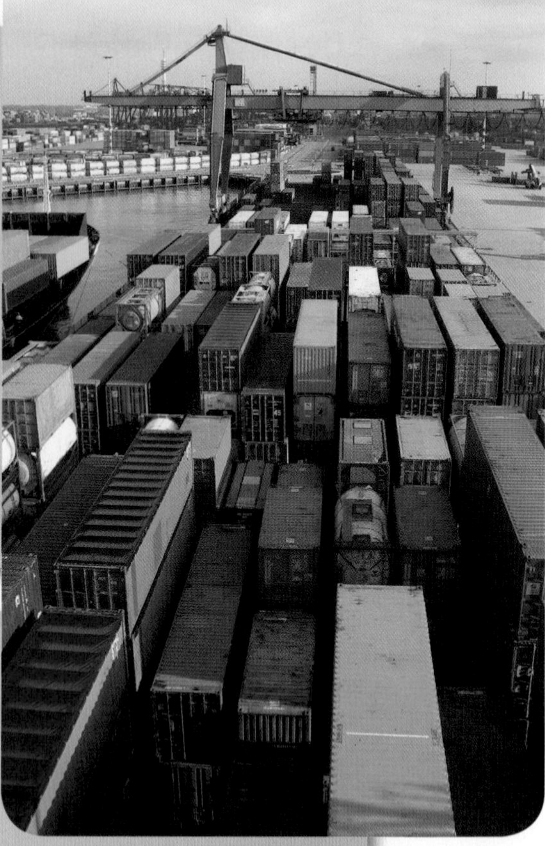

Example 1

Year 1
Number of goods produced = 1,000,000.
Average price = €10 each.

GDP = €10m.

Year 2
Number of goods produced = 1,100,000.
Average price = €10 each.

GDP = €10.1m.

Here economic growth **has** occurred because the quantity of goods produced in year 2 has increased.

Example 2

Year 1
Number of goods produced = 100,000.
Average price = €10 each.

GDP = €1m.

Year 2
Number of goods produced = 100,000.
Average price = €11 each.

GDP = €1.1m.

Here economic growth **has not** taken place, because the quantity of goods produced has not increased in year 2. The increase in the GDP figure was caused by inflation.

Negative economic growth occurs when the amount of goods and services produced one year is less than the amount produced the previous year.

Benefits of economic growth

1. **Improves the standard of living.** A large percentage of the population will now have access to a greater quantity and better quality of goods and services.
2. **Creates employment.** There is a greater number of, and variety of, employment opportunities and it is easier for people to get employment to match their talents.
3. **Improves the government's finances.** Government revenue increases when employment and the sale of goods increase. This allows the government to provide more services in areas such as education and health.
4. **Alleviates poverty.** As the economy develops the government can afford to implement a social welfare system. Although poverty can never be eliminated, it can be alleviated.

RECESSIONS

The Central Statistics Office measures the amount of goods and services produced on a quarterly basis (i.e. every three months). If less goods and services are produced in two consecutive quarters then the national economy is officially in a **recession**.

LEARN THE KEY TERMS

- **Economics** is the study of how we make the best possible use of the world's scarce resources in order to satisfy the requirements of as many people as possible.
- **Needs** are the essential items required for survival in life.
- **Wants** are any items we would like to have in addition to our needs.
- **Factors of production** are those resources that help to produce a product or provide a service.
- **Land** is anything provided by nature that helps to produce goods and services.
- **Labour** is any human effort that helps to produce goods and services.
- **Capital** is anything that is made by humans that is then used to help to produce other goods and services.
- **Enterprise** is that special form of human activity that organises the other factors of production and bears the risk involved in production.
- **Inflation** is the increase in the general level of the price of goods and services over a period of time.
- **Deflation** is the decrease in the general level of the price of goods and services over a period of time.
- The **consumer price index (CPI)** is the official measurement of the rate of inflation.
- **Gross domestic product (GDP)** is the total amount of goods and services produced in an economy in one period.
- **Gross national product (GNP)** is the Gross Domestic Product **less** profits sent out of the country by foreign-owned companies located in the country, **plus** profits returned to the country by local firms based abroad.
- **Economic growth** occurs when more goods are produced in a country one year than were produced in the previous year.
- **Negative economic growth** occurs when the amount of goods and services produced one year is less than the amount produced the previous year.

QUESTIONS

1. What is economics?
2. Define **needs** and give two examples.
3. Define **wants** and give two examples.
4. What is land? Give two examples of land.
5. What is labour? Give two examples.
6. What is enterprise? Give one example of an entrepreneur in your locality.
7. What is capital? Give two examples of capital goods.
8. 'Joe O'Brien and Helen Green have combined their savings to set up and run a shoemaking business. They buy land from a farmer and hire bricklayers, carpenters and electricians to build a workshop for them on the land. They also buy machines to use in the workshop and computers to use in their office.'

   Identify one example of each of the factors of production in the above situation.
9. Kerry County Council is faced with the choice of spending money on a new public park or spending it on a new library. It chooses to build the new library. What is the opportunity cost of the library? Explain your answer.
10. What are the three basic problems facing the organisers of any economic system?
11. Define **inflation**.
12. Define **the rate of inflation**.
13. What index measures the official rate of inflation?
14. Explain any two disadvantages of inflation.
15. Name and explain any three causes of inflation.
16. Define **deflation**.
17. Define **gross domestic product**.
18. Explain the difference between gross domestic product and gross national product.
19. Define **economic growth**.
20. What is a **recession**?

See workbook for more questions.

Economics 2: The government and the economy

14

We saw in Chapter 13 that the Irish economy is a **mixed economy**. This means that although most goods and services are provided by privately owned businesses, there is also some government involvement in the economy.

The word *government* refers to both central government (the Dáil) and local government (County Councils and Urban District Councils).

Reasons for government involvement in the economy

- **To provide merit goods.** These are goods that society considers should be available to everybody at some minimum quantity, regardless of income. Examples are shelter, education and medical services.
- **To provide sociably desirable goods or services** that are not supplied by privately owned businesses because it is unprofitable to do so. Examples are the provision of public transport to sparsely populated areas, public libraries and public parks.

- **To provide an income** for people who cannot provide one for themselves. This involves taxing one set of people and passing the money to another set of people in the form of social welfare benefits.
- **To provide services that are too important to be controlled by the private sector.** An Garda Síochána and the Army provide such services, for example.

- **To provide finance for industries** when the private sector is unable to provide it. Historically this was important. In the 1920s the government was the only body that could raise enough money to set up the ESB to provide an expensive electricity generation system in Ireland. Much of this form of investment is now provided by the private sector, e.g. some of our electricity is now generated by privately owned wind farms.
- **To make regulations concerning the running of the economy**, e.g. health and safety regulations and minimum wage rates.

Many of the goods and services provided by central and local government are called **public utilities** or **public services** as they are of benefit to, or are used by, the general public.

Public utilities are part of the **infrastructure** of the country. The infrastructure of a country is made up of capital goods (see Chapter 13) that do not directly produce goods and services but are necessary for efficient production to take place.

Infrastructure examples

1. A transport system (including roads, railways, airports and harbours)
2. A waste disposal system
3. A postal and telecommunications system
4. A water supply system
5. An electricity supply system

CENTRAL AND LOCAL GOVERNMENT

Central government is responsible for overall national economic issues and the provision of goods and services such as national roads, railways, electricity supply and health care.

Local government is responsible for the provision and maintenance of local roads, water services, waste disposal services, public housing and libraries.

THE NATIONAL BUDGET

The national budget is the government's estimate of its income and expenditure for the coming year.

Organisation of the national budget

Towards the end of a year each government department makes out an estimate of its expenditure for the coming year. These are submitted to the Minister for Finance.

The Minister then calculates how much money the government will have to collect from existing taxes, from new taxes and maybe even from borrowings to finance the total expenditure by all the government departments.

These figures are *normally* published as the Budget and presented to the Dáil by the Minister on the first Wednesday in December each year.

The government makes a clear distinction between **current expenditure** and **capital expenditure.**

Government current (day-to-day) expenditure is spending by the government on the provision of goods and services that will be totally consumed (used up) in that year.

Current expenditure

- Social welfare payments
- Salaries of all government employees
- Payments for the running of schools
- Interest payments on the national debt
- Day-to-day running costs of the health services
- Grants to sporting bodies to run their organisations

Government capital expenditure is spending by the government on assets that will benefit the country for some years into the future.

Capital expenditure

- Building new schools
- Building new roads
- Building new hospitals
- Providing computers for schools
- Giving grants to CIÉ to purchase new trains
- Providing new sporting facilities

Therefore the government subdivides its budget into two separate sections.

1. The government's current budget

The current budget is the government's estimate of its current income and current expenditure for the coming year.

Sources of current income

1. **Income tax (PAYE)**
2. **VAT**
3. **Stamp duty:** Taxes on cheques, credit and Laser cards and on the transfer of property, e.g. the stamp duty payable when buying a house
4. **Customs duty:** Taxes placed on goods imported from non-EU countries
5. **Excise duties:** Taxes placed on specific goods produced or distributed in the country such as petrol, alcoholic drinks and tobacco products
6. **DIRT:** Deposit Interest Retention Tax
7. **Corporation tax:** Taxes on profits made by companies
8. **Capital gains tax:** Taxes on profits made from the sale of assets such as shares
9. **Capital acquisition tax:** Taxes on inheritances or gifts
10. **EU receipts**
11. **Charges for services:** Fees charged by government departments and semi-state bodies: e.g. hospital charges
12. **National Lottery**
13. **Profit from the Central Bank**

Currently, in addition to the Department of the Taoiseach, there are fourteen government departments.

MAIN SPENDING GOVERNMENT DEPARTMENTS AND THEIR SERVICES	
Department	**Services**
Department of Health and Children	Hospital and other medical services
Department of Social and Family Affairs	Jobseeker's Benefit and other social welfare benefits
Department of Education and Science	Teaching and other educational services, from primary to third-level education
Department of Justice, Equality and Law Reform	Garda and policing services and crime and law enforcement services
Department of Enterprise, Trade and Employment	Industrial relations services, consumer rights services and services to the self-employed and EU services
Department of the Environment, Heritage and Local Government	Works with local governments to protect the environment (clean water and waste services), to develop our roads, to protect our heritage and to provide social housing
Department of Defence	Provides the Army, Naval and Air Corps services

2. The government's capital budget

This is the government's estimate of its capital expenditure for the coming year and the sources of money needed to finance it.

Sources of income for capital expenditure:

1. Surplus, if any, on the current budget
2. Income from the sale of semi-state bodies, e.g. Aer Lingus
3. EU grants
4. Borrowings

See page 137 for examples of capital expenditure.

Types of current budgets

1. A **balanced** current budget happens when the planned current income equals the planned current expenditure.
2. A **surplus** current budget happens when the planned current income is greater than the planned current expenditure.
3. A **deficit** current budget happens when the planned current expenditure is greater than the planned current income. (In this case the government must borrow money.)

The **exchequer balance** is the difference between total government revenue and total government expenditure (current and capital) in any one year.

If the government has to borrow money to pay for its spending then the amount borrowed is added to our national debt.

The **national debt** is the total amount of money owed by the central government at any given time.

The **general government debt (GG debt)** is the national debt plus all local government debt at any given time.

Debt servicing is the term used to describe the payment of interest on the national debt.

Budget options

1. When, at the planning stage, the Minister for Finance is faced with a **deficit** current budget he may decide to increase taxes, decrease expenditure or borrow for the deficit.
2. When, at the planning stage, the Minister for Finance is faced with a **surplus** current budget he may decide to reduce taxes, increase current expenditure or use the surplus to either pay for some of the capital expenditure or pay off some of the national debt.

Typical examination question on drafting a budget

The following figures have been prepared by the Minister for Finance prior to drawing up the current budget for 2011. You are to use these figures to draw up the budget for the Minister.

Items of revenue and expenditure	Estimated amounts in millions of €
Health services	2,500
Social welfare services	2,400
Income tax (PAYE)	4,000
Education and Science services	2,000
VAT	2,300
DIRT	300
Debt servicing	80
Customs and excise duties	1,200
Corporation tax	1,500
Agriculture services	800
Defence services	400

Solution

Step 1: Identify items of revenue, make a list of them and show a sub total as *Total revenue*.

Step 2: Identify items of expenditure, make a list of them and show a sub total as *Total expenditure*.

Step 3: Subtract the *Total expenditure* from the *Total revenue* to get the balance and identify it as a *surplus* or a *deficit*.

NATIONAL BUDGET FOR 2011 (€M)		
Revenue		
Income tax (PAYE)	4,000	
VAT	2,300	
DIRT	300	
Customs and excise duties	1,200	
Corporation tax	1,500	
Total revenue		**9,300**
Expenditure		
Health services	2,500	
Social welfare services	2,400	
Education and Science services	2,000	
Debt servicing	80	
Agriculture services	800	
Defence services	400	
Total expenditure		**8,180**
Budget surplus		**1,120**

The following questions are typical of those asked about national budgets.

Questions

1. Identify the government department responsible for preparing Ireland's national budget.
2. Distinguish between capital expenditure and current expenditure for the government. Use one example of each type of expenditure to explain your answer.
3. Explain the term 'excise duties'.
4. State **two** effects of an increase in employment on the national budget.

Answers

1. The Department of Finance.
2. Capital expenditure is spending on assets that will benefit the country for a number of years into the future, while current expenditure is spending on items that will be fully consumed in the year of the spending.
   Example: Government spending on the building of a hospital is capital expenditure; spending on the wages of nurses and doctors working in the hospital is current expenditure.
3. Excise duties are taxes placed on specific goods produced in, or distributed in the country such as petrol, alcohol drinks and tobacco products.
4. **(a)** It will increase government revenue because more people will pay PAYE and **(b)** it will decrease government expenditure because less money will be paid out on Jobseeker's Benefit.

LEARN THE KEY TERMS

- **Public utilities** or **public services** are goods or services provided by central and local government that are of benefit to, or are used by, the general public.
- The **infrastructure** of a country is made up of capital goods that do not directly produce goods and services but are necessary for production to take place.
- The **national budget** is the government's estimate of its income and expenditure for the coming year.
- Government **current expenditure** is spending by the government on the provision of goods and services that will be totally consumed in that year.
- Government **capital expenditure** is spending by the government on assets that will benefit the country for some years into the future.
- The government **current budget** is the government's estimate of its current income and current expenditure for the coming year.
- The government's **capital budget** is the government's estimate of its capital expenditure for the coming year and the sources of money needed to finance it.
- A **balanced current budget** happens when the planned current income equals the planned current expenditure.
- A **surplus current budget** happens when the planned current income is greater than the planned current expenditure.
- A **deficit current budget** happens when the planned current expenditure is greater than the planned current income.
- The **exchequer balance** is the difference between total government revenue and total government expenditure (current and capital) in any one year.
- The **national debt** is the total amount of money owed by the central government at any given time.
- The **general government debt** (GG debt) is the national debt plus all local government debt at any given time.

QUESTIONS

1. Why does the government become involved in the economy?
2. What are merit goods?
3. What are public utilities? Name any three public utilities.
4. What is the national budget?
5. Distinguish between **government current expenditure** and **government capital expenditure**. Give examples to highlight the differences between them.

6. Explain each of the following forms of government revenue:

   (a) Customs duties
   (b) Excise duties
   (c) Capital gains tax

7. Name three of the biggest-spending government departments and state a service supplied by each of them.

8. Who is the current Minister for Finance?

9. Name any two sources of income for government capital expenditure.

10. Name any three items of government capital expenditure.

11. What is the exchequer balance?

12. What is the national debt?

13. What is the general government debt?

14. How would a decrease in the level of employment affect the government's current budget?

15. Name two forms of taxation that would be affected by a decision of the majority of people to reduce their expenditure and increase their savings.

16. What is debt servicing?

17. What is a current budget surplus?

18. When is a current budget described as being a balanced budget?

19. Prepare the government's current budget from the following information:

Revenue	
VAT	€500m
PAYE	€600m
Corporation tax	€300m
Customs and excise duty	€150m
Expenditure	
Social welfare services	€300
Education and Science services	€250m
Health services	€280m
Debt servicing	€20m
Defence services	€100m

   (a) Is this budget a deficit or a surplus budget? Give a reason for your answer.
   (b) What percentage of total expenditure was spent on education? Show your workings.

(continued overleaf)

20. Prepare the government's current budget from the following information:

Revenue

Customs duties	€500m
VAT	€800m
PAYE	€900m
DIRT	€50m
Capital gains tax	€100m
Corporation tax	€750m

Expenditure

Social welfare services	€1,000m
Health services	€900m
Education and Science services	€800m
Agriculture services	€500m
Debt servicing	€30m
Defence services	€250m

(a) Is this budget a deficit or a surplus budget? Give a reason for your answer.
(b) What percentage of total income was received as VAT? Show your workings.

21. Prepare the government's current budget from the following information:

Items of revenue and expenditure	Estimated amounts in millions of €
Social welfare services	5,000
Income tax (PAYE)	7,000
Health services	4,500
Customs and excise duty	2,000
Education and Science services	4,000
DIRT	600
Debt servicing	90
VAT	6,500
Agriculture services	2,500
Corporation tax	4,500
Equality and Law Reform services	2,000
Capital gains tax	550
Local government services	2,400

(a) Is this budget a deficit or a surplus budget? Give a reason for your answer.
(b) Name any two payments made under the heading of *Social welfare services*.
(c) What is a capital gains tax?
(d) What percentage of total expenditure was spent on health services? Show your workings.

See workbook for more questions.

15 Economics 3: International trade

FOREIGN TRADE

Foreign trade (or international trade) means selling goods and services to, and buying goods and services from, other counties.

Most countries have a natural advantage over other countries in the production of one or more goods or services. This may be due to the existence of natural resources or skills and traditions in each country.

Therefore most countries tend to concentrate on the production of the goods and services in which they have an advantage and import the other goods they need.

An **export** is a good or service provided by the residents of a country that causes money to come into the country when sold.

Remember: exports cause money to *come into* a country

An **import** is a good or service purchased by the residents of a country that causes money to go out of the country.

Remember: imports cause money to *go out of* a country

International trade is subdivided into visible and invisible trade.

Visible trade

Visible trade deals with physical products that can be seen going out of, or coming into the country.

Visible exports are physical products produced by the residents of a country that cause money to come into the country when sold.

Examples of Ireland's visible exports:

- food products
- computer chips
- pharmaceutical products
- beverages

Visible imports are physical goods purchased by the residents of a country that cause money to go out of the country.

Examples of Ireland's visible imports:

- cars
- household electrical products
- timber
- fruit

Invisible trade

Invisible trade deals with services. No physical product can be seen going out of, or coming into the country. Money comes into or goes out of the country as a result of the sale or purchase of services.

Invisible exports are services provided by the residents of a country that cause money to come into the country.

Examples of Ireland's invisible exports:

- incoming tourists: they use the services provided by hotels, restaurants, theatres and other leisure facilities
- residents of a foreign country using the services of an Irish transport firm
- earnings from abroad, by Irish musicians, that are returned to Ireland

Invisible imports are services purchased by the residents of a country that cause money to go out of the country.

Examples of Ireland's invisible imports:

- residents of Ireland going abroad for holidays
- a resident of Ireland using the services of a foreign-based insurance company
- foreign musicians performing in Ireland and taking their earnings out of the country

THE BALANCE OF PAYMENTS

The **balance of payments** is a record of a country's economic transactions with the rest of the world.

There are three sections in the balance of payments:

1. the balance of trade
2. the balance on the current account
3. the capital account

1. The balance of trade

The **balance of trade** is the difference between the value of visible exports and the value of visible imports.

Example

BALANCE OF TRADE	
Total value of visible exports	€20,000m
Less total value of visible imports	€15,000m
Balance of trade	€5,000m

If the value of the visible exports is greater than the value of the visible imports we say there is a surplus on the balance of trade or that there is a **favourable balance of trade**. The balance would be a **positive** figure. See above.

If the value of the visible imports is greater than the value of the visible exports we say there is a deficit on the balance of trade or that there is an **unfavourable balance of trade**. In this case the balance would be a **negative** figure. See below.

BALANCE OF TRADE	
Total value of visible exports	€20,000m
Less total value of visible imports	€28,000m
Balance of trade	(€8,000m)

If the value of the visible exports is equal to the value of the visible imports then there is a **balanced balance of trade**.

2. Balance on the current account

The **balance on the current account** is the balance of trade *plus or minus* the difference between the value of the invisible exports and the value of the invisible imports.

Example

BALANCE OF TRADE		
Balance of trade		€5,000m
Total value of invisible exports	€18,000m	
Less total value of invisible imports	€20,000m	(€2,000m)
Balance on the current account		€3,000m

The same terminology regarding a surplus or a deficit applies to the balance on the current account as applied to the balance of trade.

Correcting a deficit on the current account

If a country's balance on the current account is a deficit then this can be corrected by either increasing exports or decreasing imports.

- **Increasing exports:** There are many State-owned companies or bodies (see Chapter 16) that can help Irish firms to find new export markets and to develop existing ones. These include Enterprise Ireland, Bord Bia and Fáilte Ireland.
- **Decreasing imports:** Many countries try to decrease imports by implementing an import substitution policy.

Import substitution is the replacing of imported goods with domestically produced goods on the home market.

In this situation the government encourages domestic firms to manufacture goods that are being imported and also encourages domestic consumers to buy these goods.

3. The capital account

The **capital account** shows the flow of all money into and out of the country.

Money can come into or go out of the country because of international trade, payments to and from the EU, and net direct foreign investment.

Net direct foreign investment is the difference between money invested in Ireland from abroad and money invested abroad by Irish residents.

REASONS FOR INTERNATIONAL TRADE

Why import?

1. Countries import to obtain raw materials not available in their own country that are needed by their domestic industries.
2. Countries import to obtain capital goods (e.g. machinery) not available in their own country that are needed by their domestic industries.
3. Countries import to obtain consumer goods that cannot be made, or cannot be made at a reasonable price, in their own countries.

Why export?

1. Countries export to earn money from abroad to pay for their imports. Countries try to earn enough income from their exports to pay for their imports, i.e. international trade should be self-financing.
2. Countries export in order to create employment in their own countries that would not otherwise be created.
3. Countries export in order to sell off their surplus production. Countries often produce greater quantities of goods than are needed in their own countries. Selling the surplus goods abroad earns extra income for these countries.

IRELAND'S MAIN TRADED GOODS	
Exports	**Imports**
Beverages	Cars
Bloodstock	Chemicals and pharmaceuticals
Chemicals and pharmaceuticals	Clothing
Clothing (expensive end of the market)	Electrical household goods
Computer software and hardware	Food and beverages
Crystal	Fruit and vegetables
Dairy and food products	Industrial machinery
Livestock	Oil
	Tobacco

IRELAND'S MAIN TRADING PARTNERS (2008)	
Exports	**Imports**
USA	UK
UK	USA
Belgium	France
Germany	Germany
France	China

IRELAND AND THE EU

The EU is an economic and political partnership between 27 democratic European countries.

Its motto is *United in diversity*. This implies that all member counties are working together to achieve peace and prosperity, while still recognising the different cultures, languages and traditions of each member country.

Ireland is one of the 27 members of the European Union (EU) (see following table). These countries make up the Single European Market. Fifteen of these countries now make up the **euro zone**, i.e. the euro is the common currency in each of these countries.

Countries in the EU

COUNTRIES IN THE EU		
Country	**Official EU language(s)**	**Currency**
Austria	German	Euro
Belgium	French, German and Dutch	Euro
Bulgaria	Bulgarian	Lev
Cyprus	Greek and English	Euro
Czech Republic	Czech	Czech Koruna
Denmark	Danish	Danish Krone
Estonia	Estonian	Estonian Kroon
Finland	Finnish and Swedish	Euro
France	French	Euro
Germany	German	Euro
Greece	Greek	Euro
Hungary	Hungarian	Forint
Ireland	English and Irish	Euro
Italy	Italian	Euro
Latvia	Latvian	Lats
Lithuania	Lithuanian	Litas
Luxembourg	French and German	Euro
Malta	Maltese and English	Euro
Netherlands	Dutch	Euro
Poland	Polish	Zloty
Portugal	Portuguese	Euro
Romania	Romanian	Romanian Leu
Slovakia	Slovak	Slovak Koruna
Slovenia	Slovenian	Euro
Spain	Spanish	Euro
Sweden	Swedish	Krona
United Kingdom	English	Pound Sterling
Candidate countries		
Croatia		Kuna
Republic of Macedonia*		Denar
Turkey		Turkish Lira

*This is a disputed name for this country. Many still refer to it as the Former Yugoslav Republic of Macedonia.

The aim of the Single European Market is to have free movement of people, goods, services and capital (money) between the member countries.

This means that there is **free trade** between the member countries, i.e. there are no restrictions placed on the importing or exporting of goods between the member countries.

Benefits to Ireland from EU membership

1. Irish exporters now have free access to a market of over 493 million people. This has helped to substantially increase Irish exports. Over 60% of Ireland's exports are to EU member countries.
2. Many non-EU companies have located in Ireland to get free access to the EU market. This has resulted in very big investment and job creation in Ireland.
3. Ireland has received over €37,000 million in grants and subsidies since joining the EU. As well as increasing our standard of living, this has helped to make us a more competitive country on the international market.
4. Irish consumers now have access to a greater range of goods and services and at a lower price than before our membership
5. Membership of the euro zone simplifies trade with the other member countries.

Ireland's other trading partners

OTHER TRADING PARTNERS

Country	Official language(s)	Currency
Australia	English	Australian Dollar
Canada	English and French	Canadian Dollar
China	Chinese	Yuan
Japan	Japanese	Yen
New Zealand	English	New Zealand Dollar
Norway	Norwegian	Krone
Russia	Russian	Rouble
South Africa	Afrikaans and English	Rand
Switzerland	French and German	Swiss Franc
USA	English	US Dollar

Problems facing Irish firms in international trade

Language: Communication between exporters and importers can be difficult when they don't have a common language. Translators may have to be employed, which adds to the overall cost of transactions.

Transport: Ireland is an island with no direct connections to mainland Europe. This means that all exports must bear the additional cost of sea or air transport, as well as the normal road or rail transport.

Insurance: Insurance costs are high due to the additional handling of goods arising from extra transport methods required. There is an extra risk the goods could be damaged or stolen when being transferred to ships and aeroplanes.

Standards and specifications: Different countries set different minimum standards of production and different specifications for products. Irish exporters may have to change their standard production methods to meet these requirements.

Currencies: Irish importers dealing with countries outside the euro zone will have to buy foreign currencies to pay for the imported goods. This involves extra banking charges and could also involve extra expenses due to changes in the exchange rates between currencies.

Currency differences

At this stage you should revise the section on foreign currency exchange on page 101.

Remember:

1. Multiply the *We sell* rate by the number of euro being exchanged to calculate the amount of foreign currency you will receive.
   or
   Divide the number of units of a foreign currency sought by the *We sell* rate to calculate the number of euro that must be paid for that number of units of the foreign currency.
2. Divide the amount of foreign currency being exchanged by the *We buy* rate to calculate the amount of euro you will receive.

Example 1

An Irish importer receives a bill for $1,500 from an American supplier. The bank quotes the importer two exchange rates. *US Dollars: We buy 1.40. We sell 1.45.* How many euro must the importer pay the bank to get $1,500?

Solution
In this situation the bank is selling dollars to the importer, so divide 1,500 by the *We sell* rate.

Answer: 1,500 ÷ 1.45 = €1,034.483

Example 2

An Irish exporter was paid $1,500 by an American buyer. Using the same rates of exchange, calculate how many euro the exporter will receive when the dollars are converted to euro.

Solution
In this situation the bank is buying dollars from the exporter, so divide the 1,500 by the *We buy* rate.

Answer: 1,500 ÷ 1.40 = €1,071.429

LEARN THE KEY TERMS

- An **export** is a good or service provided by the residents of a country that causes money to come into the country when sold.
- An **import** is a good or service purchased by the residents of a country that causes money to go out of the country.
- **Visible exports** are physical products produced by the residents of a country that cause money to come into the country when sold.
- **Visible imports** are physical goods purchased by the residents of a country that cause money to go out of the country.
- **Invisible exports** are services provided by the residents of a country that cause money to come into the country.
- **Invisible imports** are services purchased by the residents of a country that cause money to go out the country.
- The **balance of payments** is a record of a country's economic transactions with the rest of the world.
- The **balance of trade** is the difference between the value of visible exports and the value of visible imports.
- **Import substitution** is the replacing of imported goods with domestically produced goods on the home market.
- The **balance on the current account** is the balance of trade *plus* or *minus* the difference between the value of the invisible exports and the value of the invisible imports.
- The **capital account** shows the flow of all money into and out of the country.
- **Free trade** means there are no restrictions placed on the import or export of goods between countries.

QUESTIONS

1. Define **exports**.
2. Define **imports**.
3. What is a visible export? Give one example of an Irish visible export.
4. What is an **invisible export**? Give one example of an Irish invisible export.
5. What is a **visible import**? Give one example a visible import into Ireland.
6. What is an **invisible import**? Give one example an invisible import from Ireland's point of view.
7. What is the **balance of trade**?
8. Describe a **surplus** on the balance of trade.
9. Describe a **deficit** on the balance of trade.
10. Show how to calculate the **balance on the current account**.
11. What is shown in the **capital account**?
12. From the following figures calculate the **balance of trade** and state whether the balance is a deficit or a surplus. Show your workings.

Visible exports	€500m
Visible imports	€750m

13. From the following figures calculate the **balance of trade** and state whether the balance is a deficit or a surplus. Show your workings.

Visible exports	€800m
Visible imports	€650m

14. From the following figures calculate the **balance of the current account** and state whether the balance is a deficit or a surplus. Show your workings.

Visible exports	€500m
Invisible exports	€400m
Visible imports	€450m
Invisible imports	€500m

15. From the following figures calculate the **balance of the current account** and state whether the balance is a deficit or a surplus. Show your workings.

Invisible imports	€670m
Visible exports	€800m
Visible imports	€650m
Invisible exports	€550m

16. What is meant by the term **import substitution**?
17. Name any four counties, other than Ireland, in the euro zone.

18. Fill in the blanks in the box below.

Country	Currency
USA	
	Yen
South Africa	
	Lev

19. An Irish exporter received US $2,200 from an American customer. When the exporter went into the bank the following rates were quoted.

How many euro did the exporter receive for the €2,200? Show your workings.

20. A student returned home from the UK after a school tour with £150. She wanted to convert the pounds back to dollars. When she went into the bank she saw the following rates being quoted.

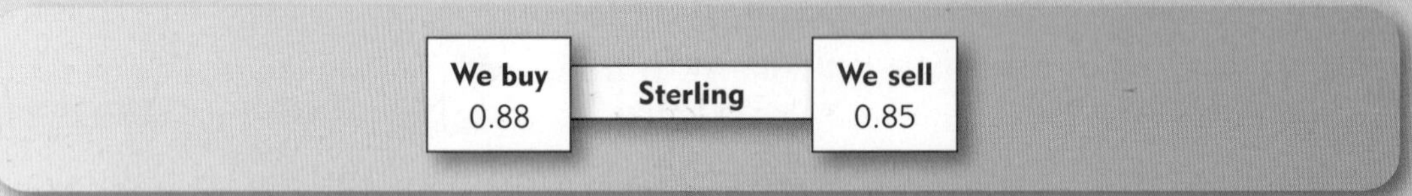

How many euro did she receive for her £150? Show your workings

21. An Irish importer received a bill from a South African exporter for 10,000 South African Rand. The bank quoted the following rates of exchange.

What was the cost of the imports to the Irish importer in euro? Show your workings.

See workbook for more questions.

Business ownership 16

Business ownership takes many forms. The most common forms are:

1. Sole traders
2. Private limited companies
3. Co-operatives
4. State-owned companies

SOLE TRADERS

A **sole trader** is a person who owns, manages and provides the money (capital) for a business.

Advantages of a sole trader

1. The owner has full control over the business. This means the sole trader can make business decisions very quickly.
2. The sole trader keeps all the profit. The profits don't have to be shared with anybody else because there is only one owner.

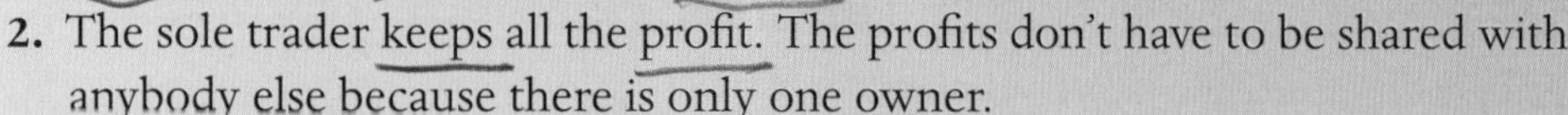

3. It is easy and cheap to set up a sole trader business. A licence may be needed for some forms of business activities, e.g. a bookmaker and a publican. If the sole trader wishes to use a trading name (e.g. *Jumping Jeans*) other than his or her own name, the trading name must be registered with the Companies Registration Office.
4. Sole traders may find it easy to adapt their business hours to suit the needs of their customers, e.g. if an accountant sets up as a sole trader he or she can arrange to meet clients after normal working hours so that clients can carry on their businesses during their own normal working hours.

Disadvantages of a sole trader

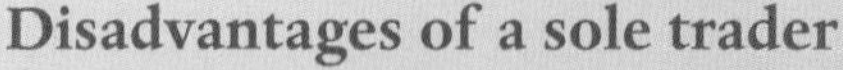

1. The business has unlimited liability, i.e. the owner of this type of business can lose his or her private property to pay for the debts of the business.
2. If the business suffers a loss the sole trader must bear this loss alone.
3. The business may find it difficult to expand due to lack of capital because there is only one person contributing capital to the business.
4. The owner has to make all business decisions alone and may not have sufficient knowledge of all aspects of the business, e.g. no one individual can be an expert in all areas of sales, production and finance.
5. The business ceases to exist when the owner dies.

PRIVATE LIMITED COMPANIES

- Private limited companies are owned by **shareholders**.
- The money invested in the business by the shareholders is called its **capital**.
- This capital is **owed to** the shareholders.
- If the company makes a profit the shareholders receive a **dividend**.
- The dividend received by a shareholder depends on the number of shares that that shareholder has in the company because the dividend is a payment per share.
- The shareholders have **limited liability**. This means the shareholders cannot lose their private property to pay for the debts of the business. Their loss is limited to the money they invested in the company.

Characteristics of private limited companies

1. They have a minimum of 1 and a maximum of 50 shareholders.
2. Shares cannot be sold to the general public. Hence they are not quoted on the Stock Exchange.
3. A shareholder must obtain permission to sell his or her shares to a new shareholder.
4. These companies must have the word *Limited* (Ltd) or *Teoranta* (Teo) after their name.
5. They do not have to publish their annual accounts.

Advantages of a private limited company

1. A limited company can expand more easily than a sole trader because it has more people providing capital.
2. All the shareholders have limited liability.
3. When a shareholder dies the business continues because the shares are passed on to the shareholder's next of kin or a person named in the shareholder's will.
4. As the company expands it can afford to employ more experts in each department.

Disadvantages of a private limited company

1. Profits have to be shared between all the shareholders.
2. It is more expensive to set up a limited company than a sole trader business.
3. There are many legal requirements that a limited company must honour.
4. The original founders or owners may lose control of the company if they end up with less than half of the issued share capital. (See *Recording the issued share capital* page 163.)

CO-OPERATIVES

A **co-operative** (often called a **co-op**) is a business organisation set up by and run for the benefit of a group of people who share a common interest.

A group of farmers may set up a co-op in order to get a market for their products. A group of employees may form a co-operative to purchase their place of employment. Residents of a particular area may set up a credit union for their own financial security.

Features of a co-operative

1. Each member must purchase at least one share in the co-operative.
2. Members receive interest on these shares.
3. Each member has only one vote, regardless of the number of shares held by each member.
4. Profits are divided in accordance with the value of transactions that the member has with the co-operative.
5. If the co-operative registers with the Registrar of Friendly Societies the members can have limited liability.

Forms of co-operatives

1. Producers' co-operatives are owned by the people who supply the raw materials to the co-operative (these include agricultural co-operatives).
2. Workers' co-operatives are owned by employees.
3. Retail co-operatives are owned by customers.
4. Service co-operatives, e.g. credit unions.

Advantages of co-operatives

1. When people join together in a co-operative they can usually achieve more collectively than they could by acting individually.
2. Because profits are shared, based on the value of transactions the members have with the co-operative, members are encouraged to do as much business as possible with the co-operative.
3. All members have an equal say in the running of the business.
4. Co-operatives create employment in their local region which may not otherwise be created.
5. The members can have limited liability.

Disadvantages of co-operatives

1. Co-operatives are usually too small to compete with larger public limited companies that have more capital.
2. Appointments to management positions are sometimes based on a person's popularity rather than on that person's ability. This can lead to poor organisation of the business.

STATE-OWNED COMPANIES

State-owned companies are formed by an Act of the Dáil and owned by the State. The State finances the companies and appoints boards of directors to manage them, but does not get involved in their day-to-day running.

Reasons why there are State companies

- Some essential services cannot be provided by private enterprise at a reasonable price, e.g. public transport and electricity in remote rural areas.
- Private enterprise may not have sufficient capital to set up the business. (This was one of the main reasons why so many State companies were established in Ireland.)
- The profitable ones are a source of income for the State.
- The State can keep control over some natural resources, e.g. natural gas and peat.

In the recent past the Irish government has sold some State-owned companies to private investors. The most recent example was Aer Lingus. When the government sells a State-owned business it is called **privatisation**.

If the government buys or takes over a privately owned company we say the company has been **nationalised**.

Public private partnerships (PPPs) are business **partnerships** between the government bodies (**public** sector) and the **private** sector. Many of the new motorways in Ireland were built using public private partnerships.

EXAMPLES OF STATE COMPANIES

Economic sector	Name	Activities
Transport	CIÉ	Bus Éireann Dublin Bus Iarnród Éireann
Production	ESB Bord na Móna	Production of electricity Production of turf and related products
Communications	An Post RTÉ	Postal service National radio and TV service
Training	FÁS FETAC	Both provide training and education in industrial skills
Marketing	Bord Iascaigh Mhara Bord Bia Enterprise Ireland	Development and marketing body for the Irish fishing industry Develops markets for Irish food products throughout the world Helps to develop new export markets and expand existing ones
Finance	Industrial Development Agency (IDA)	Attracts and develops foreign investment in Ireland
Insurance	VHI	Provides private health insurance
Services	Dublin City Enterprise Board	Helps new firms with enterprise information, advice, and training

LEARN THE KEY TERMS

- A **sole trader** is a person who owns, manages and provides the money (capital) for a business.
- A **private limited company** is a business owned by shareholders (1 to 50) who provide the capital of the business. The shareholders have limited liability and receive a dividend if the company makes a profit.
- **Limited liability** means the shareholders cannot lose their private property to pay for the debts of the business.
- A **co-operative** is a business organisation set up by and run for the benefit of a group of people who share a common interest.
- **State-owned companies** are formed by an Act of the Dáil and owned by the State. The State finances the companies and appoints boards of directors to manage them.
- **Privatisation** means the government sells a State-owned company to the private sector.
- **Nationalisation** means the government buys or takes over a privately owned company.
- **Public private partnerships** are business partnerships between government bodies and the private sector.

QUESTIONS

1. What is a sole trader?
2. Mention two actions that Brian Byrne would need to take if he, as a sole trader, wished to set up as a publican trading as *The Local*.
3. Explain three advantages and three disadvantages of a sole trader as a form of business ownership.
4. What is a private limited company?
5. What does the term **limited liability** mean?
6. Explain three advantages and three disadvantages of a private limited company as a form of business ownership.
7. What is a co-operative?
8. Explain three advantages and three disadvantages of a co-operative as a form of business ownership.
9. Co-operatives and private limited companies have different methods of sharing profits. Explain the different methods.
10. What is a State-owned company? Give three reasons for the setting up of State-owned companies.
11. Name five State-owned companies and explain their function. See www.gov.ie/en/sites/
12. Explain the difference between privatisation and nationalisation.
13. Name a State-owned company that was privatised in recent years.
14. What are public private partnerships?

See workbook for more questions.

17 Private limited companies

FORMATION OF A PRIVATE LIMITED COMPANY

The people who are setting up a company are known as the **promoters** of the company.

(A) In conjunction with a solicitor they draw up five documents:

1. the Memorandum of Association
2. the Articles of Association
3. a statement of the names of the directors of the company and their consent to become directors (see page 162)
4. a declaration of compliance with the Companies Act (see page 162)
5. a statement of the nominal share capital

(B) These documents are then sent to the **Registrar of Companies** at the Companies Registration Office (CRO).

(C) If all the documents are in order the registrar then issues a Certificate of Incorporation (see page 162). This Certificate of Incorporation makes the company a legal person that can sue or be sued like any private individual. It is now a separate entity from the promoters. This is really the birth certificate of the company.

At this stage the private limited company also receives a Trading Certificate and can now do business in the name of the company.

THE MEMORANDUM OF ASSOCIATION

This sets out the **relationship** between the company and the general public. It states:

1. the name of the company with the letters *Ltd* after it
2. the objectives of the company (what the company was set up to do), e.g. to publish magazines
3. the capital of the company, i.e. the authorised share capital
4. that the company has limited liability

The Memorandum of Association is signed by the directors. See next page.

THE ARTICLES OF ASSOCIATION

This sets out the **internal rules** of the company. These include:

1. the name of the company
2. the share capital of the company
3. the voting rights of shareholders
4. how the directors are to be appointed
5. powers of directors
6. how meetings are to be called
7. the procedure for winding-up the company

Companies may adopt all or any of the regulations found in a standard set of Articles of Association contained in the Companies Act, known as Table A, or they may draw up their own Articles of Association.

COMPANIES ACT 1963 TO 2001
COMPANY LIMITED BY SHARES
MEMORANDUM OF ASSOCIATION
OF
EDUCATIONAL ENTERPRISES LTD

1. The name of the company is: Educational Enterprises Ltd.
2. The objects for which the company is established are:
   (a) To establish an educational facility for second and third level pupils
   (b) To supply educational and learning materials
   (c) To publish and distribute teaching CDs, videos and other related materials.
3. The liability of the members is limited.
4. The share capital of the company is:
   EURO 100,000, divided into 100,000 ordinary shares of EURO 1.00 each with the power to increase the share capital
5. We, the several persons whose names and addresses are subscribed, wish to be formed into a company in pursuance of the Memorandum of Association, and we agree to take the number of shares in the capital of the company set opposite our respective names.

NAMES, ADDRESSES AND DESCRIPTION OF SUBSCRIBERS		Number of shares taken by each subscriber
JOSEPH GREENE 20 HIGH STREET CLONSILLA DUBLIN 15 COMPANY DIRECTOR	*Joseph Greene*	TWENTY THOUSAND
MARY GREENE 20 HIGH STREET CLONSILLA DUBLIN 15 COMPANY DIRECTOR	*Mary Greene*	TWENTY THOUSAND
TOTAL SHARES TAKEN		FORTY THOUSAND

DATED THE 8TH DAY OF DECEMBER 2008
WITNESS TO THE ABOVE SIGNATURES:

Rosemary Smith

ROSEMARY SMITH
20 MAIN STREET
DUBLIN 2

DECLARATION OF COMPLIANCE WITH THE COMPANIES ACT 1963 TO 2001

We, the directors of **Educational Enterprises Ltd**, agree to comply with the requirements of The Companies Act.

Signed: *Joseph Greene* and *Mary Greene* Date: 18/12/08

DECLARATION OF CONSENT TO BE DIRECTORS

We, the undersigned, consent to become directors of **Educational Enterprises Ltd**.

Signed: *Joseph Greene* and *Mary Greene* Date: 18/12/08

No. 456789

Certificate of Incorporation

I hereby certify that

EDUCATIONAL ENTERPRISES LTD

is this day incorporated under the Companies Acts 1963 to 2001 and that the company is limited and I have entered such name on the Register accordingly.

Given under my hand at Dublin, this Tuesday 26th day of December 2008

Michael Browne

For Registrar of Companies

Certificate handed to/posted to* John O'Hagan and Co.
Solicitors
Dublin 15

Signed: *Michael Browne* Date: 26/12/08

* Delete as appropriate

ANNUAL GENERAL MEETING

A company is obliged by law to hold a meeting of all the shareholders once a year. This is known as the Annual General Meeting (AGM) of the company. At the AGM:

1. The directors of the company give a report on the performance of the company during the previous year.
2. The annual accounts are presented to the meeting.
3. If required, new directors will be elected at the meeting.
4. Formal resolutions concerning the company may be passed at the meeting.
5. The directors usually declare the dividend being paid to the shareholders for the year.

RECORDING THE ISSUED SHARE CAPITAL

All companies must keep a full record of all money received by it and paid out by it. It must also keep a record of its assets and liabilities.

You will recall from Chapter 5 that assets are items owned by or due to somebody and liabilities are debts owed.

When the shareholders give money to the company, this money is technically owed to the shareholders and has to be repaid if and when the company ceases to exist. Thus the **issued share capital** is a **liability**.

The company has received this money. It is now an **asset** of the company.

You will recall a basic rule of bookkeeping.

Debit assets
Credit liabilities

The company has received this money (an asset) from the shareholders and now owes it (a liability) to the shareholders.

Therefore we must **debit** the company's *bank account* to record the receipt of the money and **credit** its *issued share capital account* to record the liability.

Debit (Dr) side			BANK A/C		Credit (Cr) side
Date	Details	€	Date	Details	€
8/12/08	Issued share capital	40,000			

Dr			SHARE CAPITAL A/C		Cr
Date	Details	€	Date	Details	€
			8/12/08	Bank	40,000

You will have noticed that the one transaction, i.e. the receipt of money from the shareholders, had to be recorded in two different accounts. This is known as double-entry accounting.

Double-entry accounting is the recording of the debit and the credit aspect of any one transaction.

Therefore for every debit entry in our records there must be a corresponding credit entry.

This makes it easy to check the accuracy of our accounting because the value of all our debit balances must equal the value of all our credit balances. This is done by drawing up a **trial balance** at a given date showing these debit and credit balances. The trial balance for **Educational Enterprises Ltd** at the 31/12/08, assuming there were no other transactions, would be that as shown here.

TRIAL BALANCE AT 31/12/08		
	Dr	Cr
Bank A/C	40,000	
Share capital A/C		40,000
	40,000	40,000

LEARN THE KEY TERMS

- The **promoters** of a company are the people who wish to set up a company.
- The **Memorandum of Association** sets out the relationship between the company and the general public.
- The **Articles of Association** set out the internal rules of the company.
- A **Certificate of Incorporation** is a document that makes the company a legal person that can sue or be sued like any private individual.
- An **annual general meeting** is a meeting of all the shareholders that must be held once a year.

QUESTIONS

1. Who are known as the **promoters** of a company?
2. Name the five documents that must be drawn up when setting up a private limited company.
3. What is the Memorandum of Association?
4. Name any four items that appear in the Memorandum of Association
5. What are the Articles of Association?
6. Name any four items that normally appear in the Articles of Association.
7. 'A Certificate of Incorporation is the birth certificate of a company.' Explain this statement.

See workbook for more questions.

Business finance 18

Businesses always need money to finance their expenditure. When a business is being established it needs money for premises, machinery and equipment. It also needs money to pay the day-to-day expenses of running the business and of course it needs money for expansion, hopefully!

A firm divides its expenditure into:
(**a**) current (or revenue) expenditure
(**b**) capital expenditure

Current expenditure is spending on the on-going or repetitive costs of running a business.

This form of spending occurs at least once a year, but usually much more often, e.g. spending on wages, stock, electricity, insurance and delivery costs.

Capital expenditure is spending on fixed assets.

A **fixed asset** is anything owned by the business whose value is not directly changed by the normal daily transactions of the business.

The normal daily transactions of a business refer to the current expenditure of the business.

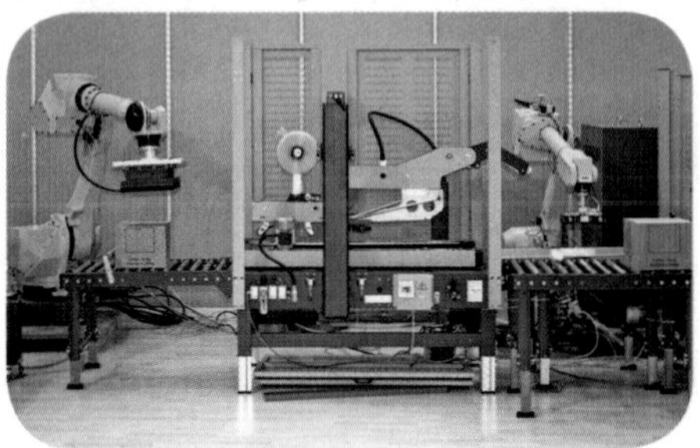

Items such as computers, buildings, machinery and land owned by the business do not change in value on a day-to-day basis.

Capital expenditure is subdivided into **medium-term** and **long-term expenditure**.

Medium-term expenditure is spending on assets that will have to be replaced within the foreseeable future, normally within a 3- to 5-year period. Examples are delivery vans, furniture, computers and machinery.

Long-term expenditure is spending on assets that the business does not intend to replace in the foreseeable future. Examples are land and buildings.

EXAMPLES OF EXPENDITURE		
Short-term expenditure	**Medium-term expenditure**	**Long-term expenditure**
Wages	Computers	Land
Insurance	Delivery vans	Buildings
Stock	Furniture	Fixtures
Electricity	Photocopiers	Plant

Businesses must always match the source of finance to the nature of the spending. There is no point in obtaining a long-term loan to pay weekly wages or an overdraft to buy premises that will benefit the business for many years.

INTERNAL AND EXTERNAL FINANCE

Sources of finance can be classified as either internal or external. The source of finance is internal when the business is using its own money. It is external when the money is obtained from outside the business.

Sources of short-term finance

1. The firm's own cash (internal)
Many businesses have enough cash to pay the running costs of the business. However, they must always take into account the opportunity cost of using this cash, e.g. the interest the money could earn on deposit in a bank.

2. The use of creditors (external)
A creditor is a firm that has supplied goods on credit, i.e. a firm that has allowed another firm to purchase stock now and pay for it in a month's time. The buyer does this in the hope that the stock will be sold before the payment has to be made. This means a business has, temporarily, the use of some other firm's money. However, the business should be aware of any extra discounts obtainable for cash payments.

3. Bank overdraft (external)
Many businesses sell goods on credit and may have to wait 30 days for payment. In the meantime they can obtain permission from the banks to overdraw their account to pay their current expenses. This can be done in the knowledge that the firm can clear the overdraft at the end of the 30 days.

4. Factoring of debtors (external)
A debtor is a person or company to whom goods have been sold on credit. Factoring means a business passes on (sells), at a discount, the debts owed to it, in exchange for cash. The business gets cash quickly, and does not have to collect the debt. However, the business loses some of the value of the debts. The factoring company gets the debt and has to collect it. It makes a profit by paying less cash than the full value of the debts.

5. Accruals/expenses due (external)
Many firms delay payment of bills due in order to keep money in their bank accounts and earn interest on the balance. Some firms also delay payment of a bill in order to avoid overdraft charges. From time-to-time businesses delay the

payment of the VAT, PAYE and PRSI (USC) that they have collected in order to use that money to pay wages or to buy stock. Likewise they delay payment of electricity and telephone bills. Just like creditors, as in point 2, this means the businesses are using somebody else's money to finance their activities.

However, businesses must be careful when using this form of finance because essential services, such as electricity, may be cut off. They also run the risk of facing heavy penalties for late payment of PAYE and VAT.

Sources of medium-term finance

1. A bank term loan (external)
The firm borrows money from a bank to be used to purchase an asset. It agrees to repay the loan by fixed repayments, per month, over an agreed term. The term should never be longer than the life of the asset being purchased. The firm owns the asset as soon as it is purchased.

2. Hire purchase (external)
This is similar to a bank loan, except the firm does not own the asset until the final payment has been made. The rate of interest on hire purchase agreements tends to be much higher than on term loans.

3. Leasing (external)
A lease is a contract to rent an asset for an agreed period of time. The profit made by using the asset should be more than enough to meet the cost of the lease. The major disadvantage of leasing is that the lessee never gets ownership of the asset.

Sources of long-term finance

1. Issue of shares (internal)
The firm sells shares to the general public. This is 'free' money in the sense that no interest is paid and no repayment has to be made until the firm closes down.

However, any profit the firm makes will have to be shared by more people.

2. Long-term loans (external)
This involves taking out a mortgage on property for a period of 20 years or so. The idea is that the firm will have the property for this period of time and so can spread the repayments on the mortgage over the time period and keep any cash it has for current expenditure.

3. Retained profits (internal)
This means reinvesting some of the profit made by the company back into the business, rather than giving it all to the shareholders in dividends. Again it is 'free' money, but if the shareholders do not get a worthwhile return on their investment they may decide to sell their shares and thereby lower the value of the business.

4. Issue of debentures (external)
A debenture is a certificate acknowledging the existence of a loan or a debt. It is normally issued in the case of a long-term loan secured against the assets or an asset of the business. No annual repayments have to be made on the loan but interest must be paid each year. The sum of money borrowed is repaid in one lump sum at the end of the period of the loan. The firm must ensure that the annual interest is paid; otherwise the debenture holder (the lender) can force the sale of the asset or assets.

5. Sale and leaseback (external)
A firm may find itself in a position where it has little or no cash, but at the same time owns valuable fixed assets such as land or buildings. In this case the firm may sell the fixed asset to a finance company and then lease the asset back over a long-term agreement. The firm receives a large injection of cash and still has use of the asset. The disadvantages of this are that the firm also has the additional cost of the lease each year and loses out on any increasing value of the fixed asset.

6. Government/semi-state/EU grants (external)
Grants are non-repayable sums of money given to a firm by the government (or a government agency) and by the EU in order to set up or expand a business.

Examples:
- The IDA gives grants for setting up new factories or will supply 'advance' (prebuilt) factories.
- Enterprise Ireland provides grants to businesses in the exporting sector of the economy.
- Fáilte Ireland gives grants to businesses in the tourism sector.
- Bord Iascaigh Mhara provides grants to the fishing industry.
- FÁS provides grants towards the training of employees.
- EU grants are available through the European Investment Bank and the European Regional Development Fund.

SOURCES OF FINANCE		
Short-term finance	**Medium-term finance**	**Long-term finance**
Own cash	Term loan	Issue of shares
Creditors	Hire purchase	Long-term loans
Bank overdraft	Leasing	Retained profits
Factoring		Issue of debentures
Accruals/expenses due		Sale and leaseback
		Government and EU grants

LEARN THE KEY TERMS

- **Current** or **short-term expenditure** is spending on the on-going or repetitive costs of running a business.
- **Capital expenditure** is spending on fixed assets.
- **Medium-term expenditure** is spending on assets that will have to be replaced within the foreseeable future, normally within a 3- to 5-year period.
- **Long-term expenditure** is spending on assets that the firm does not intend to replace in the foreseeable future.
- **Factoring** means a business passes on (sells), at a discount, the debts owed to it, in exchange for immediate cash.
- A **debenture** is a certificate acknowledging the existence of a debt. It is normally issued in the case of a long-term loan secured against the assets or an asset of the business.
- **Sale and leaseback** occurs when a firm sells a fixed asset to a finance company and then leases the asset from it over a long-term agreement.

QUESTIONS

1. Distinguish between short-term, medium-term and long-term expenditure.
2. Name two items of expenditure that would appear under each of the following headings:
   Short-term expenditure   *Medium-term expenditure*   *Long-term expenditure*
3. Distinguish between internal and external sources of finance.
4. A firm needs raw materials to manufacture its product. Name and explain one internal source of finance and two external sources of finance that it could use for this purpose.
5. A firm needs to obtain new machinery for its factory. The firm expects that the machinery will have to be replaced in three years. Explain, fully, three sources of finance that could be used for this purpose.
6. Explain, fully, two internal and two external sources of finance available to a firm that needs to purchase land and build a new factory in order to expand its business.
7. Distinguish between the use of creditors and the use of accruals as sources of short-term finance.
8. Explain why it would not be advisable for a firm to take a three-year term loan for payment of one month's wages owed to its employees.
9. Distinguish between a loan and a grant.
10. Name any two public bodies that make grants available to Irish industries.

See workbook for more questions.

19 The business plan & cash flow forecast

THE BUSINESS PLAN

Sports coaches often use a quote from Benjamin Franklin: 'By failing to prepare, you are preparing to fail.'

The same idea applies to a business. A firm must be able to identify clearly its present situation, set goals or targets for the future (either short-term or long-term) and have a stated plan of action that will help it attain those goals.

A **business plan** is a formal document that describes the present status of a business, identifies clear goals for its future development and lays down methods by which the goals are to be achieved.

Main elements of a business plan

1. **Company details, including:**
   (a) Name and address of the company
   (b) Names of the key people in the organisation such as owners, directors and managers
   (c) Qualifications and experience of the key people
2. **The company's product(s) or service(s):**
   A brief description of the products sold by the business
3. **Market research information, including:**
   (a) Potential size of the market, along with sales targets over a period of time
   (b) Level of competition in the industry
   (c) Price that can be charged for the product
4. **Sales promotions policy, including:**
   (a) Advertising methods
   (b) Bulk purchase discounts (if any)
   (c) Sponsorship policy
5. **Financial details, including:**
   (a) Present cash situation
   (b) Present value of the business's assets
   (c) Possible grants available to the business
   (d) Amount of cash needed for future development
6. **Directors' signatures**

Many businesses include a **cash flow forecast** in the business plan (see page 174).

A business plan is essential because:

1. It states definite measurable targets to be achieved by the business, e.g. increasing sales by 2% per month.
2. It puts in place work practices to be used to achieve the targets, e.g. methods of advertising and sales promotions.
3. It identifies the finances required by the firm at all times, e.g. cash flow statements (see page 174).
4. It provides essential information required by banks and future shareholders when seeking money for expansion purposes.

Example business plan

Murdel Ltd is located at 10 High Street, Dublin 4. The shareholders and directors are Michael Murphy and Richard Delahunty. Richard Delahunty is also the managing director. The company has its bank account with the **AIB, O'Connell Street, Dublin 1.**

It produces sets of team football jerseys and also distributes individual replica jerseys on the Irish market.

Market research has indicated that there is a potential to sell 30,000 individual replica jerseys and 2,000 sets of team jerseys each year. The individual replica jerseys sell at €50 each and each set of team jerseys sells for €400. There are four other similar firms in the industry nationwide.

Murdel Ltd promotes its products by distributing catalogues to individual clubs around the country and by advertising on local radio stations. It also sponsors inter-club competitions in all the leading national sporting organisations.

On 1/1/2012 Murdel Ltd's premises and equipment is valued at €1,500,000. It wishes to expand its business at a total cost of €1,000,000. It has €500,000 of its own cash reserves and will receive a grant of €100,000 from the government.

It hopes to raise the remaining finance by issuing shares in the company. (See the note below the business plan.)

Prepare the business plan for Murdel Ltd on 1/1/2012 for the above situation.

BUSINESS PLAN FOR MURDEL LTD

COMPANY DETAILS

Name of Company	Murdel Ltd
Address of Company	10 High Street, Dublin 4.
Shareholders / Directors	Michael Murphy Richard Delahunty
Managing Director	Richard Delahunty
Company Bank	AIB, O'Connell Street, Dublin 1

PRODUCTS

(i) Sets of team football jerseys
(ii) Individual replica jerseys

MARKET RESEARCH

Annual size of market	
Sets of team football jerseys	2,000 sets
Individual replica jerseys	30,000 units
Prices	
Sets of team football jerseys	€400 per set
Individual replica jerseys	€50 each
Competition	There are four other similar firms in the industry nationwide.

SALES PROMOTIONS

Sets of jerseys	(i) Distributing catalogues to individual clubs (ii) Sponsoring inter-club competitions in all leading national sporting organisations.
Individual replica jerseys	Advertising on local radio stations

FINANCIAL DETAILS

Present value of premises and equipment	€1,500,000
Cost of expansion	**€1,000,000**
Less amounts available	
Reserves	€500,000
Grants	€100,000
Share investment required	**€400,000**

SIGNED

(i) *Michael Murphy*
(ii) *Richard Delahunty*

DATE 1/1/2012

Note: Amount of finance required for expansion is calculated as follows:

Total cost of expansion
Less firm's own reserves
Less grants available
***Equals* finance required**

Example, applied to Murdel Ltd

Cost of financing expansion	
Buy new machinery	€500,000
Extend its premises	€400,000
Update its computer network	€60,000
Acquire more cash to run the business on a day-to-day basis (called working capital)	€40,000
Total cost of expansion	**€1,000,000**
Less own cash reserves	€500,000
Less grant available	€100,000
Finance required (issue of new shares)	**€400,000**

Fixed and variable costs

A business's total cost of production is made up of its **fixed costs** and its **variable costs**.

Fixed costs are costs that **do not change** as the volume of goods produced or sold changes.

Examples of fixed costs:

- the lease or rent on a factory
- the cost of a delivery van
- the cost of a computer
- repayments on a term loan

Variable costs are costs that **change** as the volume of goods produced or sold changes.

Examples of variable costs:

- the cost of raw materials
- the cost of electricity
- petrol used by a delivery van
- interest payment on an overdraft

CASH FLOW FORECASTS (STATEMENTS)

A cash flow forecast is to a business what a household budget is to a family. *Cash* in this context means any form of money.

A **cash flow forecast** is a business's estimate of the future timing and source of its income and the future timing and nature of its expenditure.

Once a business's opening cash is established the cash flow forecast can be used to calculate estimated future net cash, opening cash and closing cash figures. These are shown in the simplified version below.

A business has an opening cash of €2,500 on 1/1/2012. The following is its cash flow forecast.

Note: The word *receipts* is often used as an alternative for *income* in cash flow forecasts.

CASH FLOW FORECAST: JANUARY TO MARCH 2012

	Jan	Feb	March	Total Jan–March
RECEIPTS	€	€	€	€
Cash sales	30,000	35,000	40,000	105,000
New share issue			100,000	100,000
(A) TOTAL RECEIPTS	**30,000**	**35,000**	**140,000**	**205,000**
PAYMENTS				
Purchases	15,000	15,000	20,000	50,000
Wages	5,000	5,000	8,000	18,000
Electricity	1,000	1,200	1,400	3,600
Purchase of machinery			75,000	75,000
(B) TOTAL PAYMENTS	**21,000**	**21,200**	**104,400**	**146,600**
(C) Net cash (A – B)	**9,000**	**13,800**	**35,600**	**58,400**
(D) Opening cash	**2,500**	**11,500**	**25,300**	**2,500**
Closing cash (C + D)	**11,500**	**25,300**	**60,900**	**60,900**

You should recall from your household budget that:
(**a**) Net cash is total receipts/income minus total payments
(**b**) The closing cash one month becomes the opening cash the next month
(**c**) The opening cash in the total Jan–March column is the original opening cash.

Importance of cash flow forecasts

Cash flow forecasting enables a firm to:

1. Predict the months that they expect to have a cash surplus.
2. Predict the months that they are likely to suffer a shortage of cash.
3. Plan borrowing.
4. Support an application for a bank loan. Banks require cash flow forecasts to assess a business's ability to repay a loan.

Example of a cash flow forecast question

Adapted from Junior Certificate Higher Level 2007 Paper II Question 3

Part A

Provided below is a partially completed cash flow forecast for HARP Ltd.

CASH FLOW FORECAST FOR HARP LTD FOR FEBRUARY TO JULY 2008							
	Feb	March	April	May	June	July	Total Feb–July
RECEIPTS	€	€	€	€	€	€	€
Cash sales	85,000	85,000					
Loan							
(A) TOTAL RECEIPTS	**85,000**	**85,000**					
PAYMENTS							
Cash purchases	40,000	40,000					
Light and heat		8,000					
Wages	30,000	30,000					
Motor vehicles							
Dividend							
Rent	4,000	4,000					
(B) TOTAL PAYMENTS	**74,000**	**82,000**					
Net cash (A – B)	11,000	3,000					
Opening cash	1,000	12,000	15,000				
Closing cash	12,000	15,000					

You are required to complete the forecast for the months of April, May, June and July 2008 together with the total column.

The following information should be taken into account:

- Monthly cash sales are expected to increase by 25% beginning in July.
- HARP Ltd expects to receive a loan of €150,000 in May.
- Monthly cash purchases are expected to increase by 15% beginning in July.
- Light and heat is expected to increase by 25% in the months of May and July.
- Wages are expected to remain the same, except in May, when an additional bonus of €8,000 will be paid.
- New motor vehicles will be purchased in May for €155,000.
- Shareholders will be paid a dividend of €15,000 in July.
- Rent is expected to remain the same every month.

Part B

Name **two** items, other than cash sales and loans, that could be entered in the *Receipts* section of a cash flow forecast.

Solution

Part A

Calculations required:

- Cash sales in July = €85,000 + (25% of €85,000) €21,250 = €106,250
- Cash purchases in July = €40,000 + (15% of €40,000) €6,000 = €46,000
- Wages in May = €30,000 + bonus of €8,000 = €38,000

CASH FLOW FORECAST FOR HARP LTD FOR FEBRUARY TO JULY 2008							
	Feb	March	April	May	June	July	Total Feb–July
RECEIPTS	€	€	€	€	€	€	€
Cash sales	85,000	85,000	85,000	85,000	85,000	106,250	531,250
Loan				150,000			150,000
(A) TOTAL RECEIPTS	**85,000**	**85,000**	85,000	235,000	85,000	106,250	681,250
PAYMENTS							
Cash purchases	40,000	40,000	40,000	40,000	40,000	46,000	246,000
Light and heat		8,000		10,000		10,000	28,000
Wages	30,000	30,000	30,000	38,000	30,000	30,000	188,000
Motor vehicles				155,000			155,000
Dividend						15,000	15,000
Rent	4,000	4,000	4,000	4,000	4,000	4,000	24,000
(B) TOTAL PAYMENTS	**74,000**	**82,000**	74,000	247,000	74,000	105,000	656,000
Net cash (A – B)	11,000	3,000	11,000	(12,000)	11,000	1,250	25,250
Opening cash	1,000	12,000	15,000	26,000	14,000	25,000	1,000
Closing cash	12,000	15,000	26,000	14,000	25,000	26,250	26,250

Part B

Newly issued share capital and government/EU grants could also be entered as receipts.

LEARN THE KEY TERMS

- A **business plan** is a formal document that describes the present status of a business, identifies clear goals for its future development and lays down methods by which the goals are to be achieved.
- **Fixed costs** are costs that do not change as the volume of goods produced or sold changes.
- **Variable costs** are costs that change as the volume of goods produced or sold changes.
- A **cash flow forecast** (statement) is a business's estimate of the future timing and source of its income and the future timing and nature of its expenditure.

QUESTIONS

1. What is a business plan?
2. Excluding the signatures and date, name the five main headings in a business plan.
3. Explain any three reasons a business would prepare a business plan.
4. Distinguish between fixed costs and variable costs.
5. Give two examples each of fixed and variable costs for a typical factory.
6. What is a cash flow forecast (statement)?
7. Why is it important for a firm to prepare a cash flow forecast?
8. Fill in the missing figures (?) in the following cash flow forecast.

CASH FLOW FORECAST FOR 'X' LTD FOR JANUARY TO MARCH 2012

	Jan	Feb	March	Total Jan–March
RECEIPTS	€	€	€	€
Cash sales	35,000	35,000	45,000	?
New share issue			50,000	?
(A) TOTAL RECEIPTS	?	?	?	?
PAYMENTS				
Purchases	20,000	19,000	20,000	?
Wages	3,000	3,000	3,500	?
Delivery costs	500	500	580	?
New computer			15,000	?
(B) TOTAL PAYMENTS	?	?	?	?
(C) Net cash (A – B)	?	?	?	?
(D) Opening cash	4,000	?	?	?
Closing cash (C + D)	?	?	?	?

See workbook for more questions.

20 Businesses and commercial banks

Chapter 10 outlined the services available from commercial banks to the householder. All of these services are also available to the business sector. In addition, the banks offer other services to businesses.

SERVICES PROVIDED BY COMMERCIAL BANKS TO BUSINESSES

1. **Current accounts**, including cheque payments, direct debits and standing orders as well as an on-line banking facility that allows access to the bank accounts via the internet.
2. **Loans and overdrafts**
3. **Foreign exchange facilities** including making payments for imports
4. **Business credit cards** and all the services required by businesses to accept credit card and debit card payments
5. **Night safes** for overnight cash deposits
6. **Leasing** facilities for items such as equipment and vehicles
7. **Advice** on such items as business formation, drawing up business plans, taxation and **franchising**. A franchise is a licence to produce and/or sell another well-known company's products and to use that company's name. The product sold or produced must conform strictly to guidelines laid down by the company granting the licence. A fee is paid to obtain the licence and the company receiving the franchise (franchisee) must pay a percentage of its sales to the franchiser. The franchiser undertakes most of the advertising and marketing. Examples are McDonald's, prontaprint and Abrakebabra.
8. **Paypath** facilities. This is an electronic means of paying wages directly from the employer's bank account to the employee's bank account.

Opening a business bank account

When opening a bank account a business must fill out an application form like that shown on page 94. If the business is a limited company it must also provide:

(a) The company's Certificate of Incorporation
(b) The company's Articles of Association
(c) The company's Memorandum of Association
(d) A signed copy of a resolution passed by the directors of the company to open a business bank account
(e) The signatures of the people authorised to sign the cheques. Most companies require the signatures of two people on a cheque.
(f) A Non-Personal Customer Identification Form or money laundering certificate. This is proof that the money being deposited into the account is not laundered.

Good banking practices

1. All lodgements to and payments from the bank account should be recorded in the company's cash book.
2. Only authorised people should sign cheques and there should be two people's signatures on every cheque. The counterfoil of the cheque or a cheque requisition form should always be completed.
3. The cheques in the company's chequebook should be used in numerical sequence (in number order).
4. A bank reconciliation statement should be prepared each time a bank statement is received from the bank (see Chapter 11).

Applying for a bank loan

A bank will require the following information when a company applies for a loan:

(a) The name of the company and the address of the company's registered office (the company's address that is recorded in the Companies Registration Office and to which all official correspondence is sent)

(b) A brief history of the business

(c) The qualifications and experience of the owners and/or managers of the company

(d) The amount of the loan required

(e) The purpose of the loan, e.g. to purchase new equipment

(f) The time period for which the loan is required

(g) Bank accounts held by the business

(h) The company's business plan

(i) A cash flow forecast to show that the company will have the ability to repay the loan

(j) Audited accounts of the business (these are independently verified accounts that give an accurate statement of the business's financial position)

(k) The security or collateral* being offered by the business and/or the name and signature of a **guarantor** (an individual who guarantees to repay the loan if the company fails to do so)

***Collateral** is an item of value that is assigned to the bank (i.e. the bank receives temporary ownership of it), which the bank can sell if the loan is not repaid. It is usually an asset of the business such as land or buildings. Obviously the value of the collateral should be at least equal to the value of the loan and should not be something that is likely to decrease in value.

Cando Bank Ltd

LOAN APPLICATION FORM

APPLICANT

Name of company	Murdel Ltd
Company's registered office	10 High Street, Dublin 4

BUSINESS HISTORY

Murdel Ltd has been trading, profitably, in sportswear for the past seven years

PERSONNEL: Qualifications and Experience

Michael Murphy, director	Qualified accountant with 10 years' general experience
Richard Delahunty, director	Materials engineer with experience in UK and USA

DETAILS OF LOAN REQUIRED

Amount	€200,000
Purpose of loan	To purchase new equipment
Period of loan	36 months

COMPANY'S BANKER	AIB, O'Connell Street, Dublin 1
ATTACHMENTS	Business plan, cash flow statement and audited accounts
COLLATERAL	Freehold premises located at 10 High Street, Dublin 4
SIGNED	*Michael Murphy* *Richard Delahunty* Date 1/8/2012

Note: A **freehold property** is one that is owned by a business and is not being used as security for a loan, i.e. the company is free to sell it.

Recording the receipt of a loan in the company's accounts

When a bank gives a loan to a company, it puts the money into the company's bank account. The company not only **receives** money from the bank, but it now also **owes** money to the bank.

In Chapter 5 (*The Analysed Cash Book*) we saw that any money received and lodged to the bank is entered on the **debit side** of the bank account.

We also saw that any money owed to the bank is a **liability**. Liabilities are recorded on the **credit side** of the liability account, which in this case is the **bank loan account**.

Therefore when a bank loan is received:

Debit the bank account and
Credit the bank loan account with the value of the loan

This would be shown in Murdel Ltd's account as follows:

Debit (Dr) side		BANK A/C			Credit (Cr) side
Date	Details	€	Date	Details	€
1/8/12	Cando Bank	200,000			

Dr		CANDO BANK LOAN A/C			Cr
Date	Details	€	Date	Details	€
			1/8/12	Bank	200,000

LEARN THE KEY TERMS

- A **franchise** is a licence to produce and/or sell another well-known company's products and use that company's name.
- **Paypath** is an electronic means of paying wages directly from an employer's bank account to an employee's bank account.
- A **guarantor** is a person who guarantees to repay a loan if a company fails to do so.
- **Collateral** is an item of value that is assigned to a bank, which the bank can sell if a loan is not repaid.
- **Audited accounts** of a business are independently verified accounts that give a true and accurate statement of the business's financial position.
- A **freehold property** is one that is owned by a business and is not being used as security for a loan, i.e. the company is free to sell it.

QUESTIONS

1. Name any five services provided by commercial banks to businesses.
2. What is a **franchise**?
3. Name any six items or pieces of information that a company must provide to a bank when opening a bank account.
4. Give a brief outline of the information a bank will require when a company applies for a loan.
5. Who or what is a **guarantor**?
6. What is **collateral**?
7. Why would a bank seek a freehold property collateral for a loan?
8. What is meant by the term **audited accounts**?
9. Outline four procedures a business should put in place to ensure accurate checks on its banking transactions.

See workbook for more questions.

21 Insurance for businesses

Businesses have many valuable assets – their factories, offices, stock, delivery vans and computers. They could not function properly if any of these assets were lost, damaged, stolen or destroyed.

Many businesses run similar risks, so they seek insurance policies to protect them in the event of any of the risks occurring.

If you have forgotten the concepts of insurance and assurance you should revise the **five principles of insurance** and the **average clause** in Chapter 8.

NON-INSURABLE RISKS

You will recall from Chapter 8 that insurance companies will not insure against the occurrence of a risk when they cannot calculate the likelihood of the risk occurring.

Non-insurable risks are risks faced by a business for which insurance is not available.

These include:

1. Loss of profit due to sudden increases in the cost of production
2. Loss of profit due to strikes
3. Loss of profit due to changes in consumers' tastes and fashions
4. Loss of profit due to the entry of new rival firms into the industry
5. Loss of profit due to the adverse effects of new legislation, e.g. new health and safety regulations
6. Loss of profit due to adverse effects of international trade agreements, e.g. cheap imports may now be allowed into the country that were not allowed before the trade agreement
7. Loss of profit due to bad management

The amount and type of insurance a firm needs will depend on the business the firm is involved in. The following list shows some common policies.

TYPES OF BUSINESS INSURANCE POLICIES

TYPE OF POLICY	PROTECTION AGAINST
Bad debts insurance	Failure of individual debtors to pay amount owed
Building insurance	Damage to buildings arising from construction defects
Burglary/theft insurance	Losses arising from either theft or burglary
Cash in transit insurance	Loss of money while being transferred to or from the business's premises
Consequential loss insurance	Loss of profit arising from the occurrence of an insurable risk
Employer's liability insurance	Claims for injuries suffered by the employees arising from their employment
Fidelity bond insurance	Dishonesty by individual employees in a position of trust, e.g. the cashier stealing cash
Fire insurance	Damage to any property arising from a fire on the premises
Goods in transit insurance	Loss of goods while being transferred to or from the business's premises
Motor insurance	Third party injuries or damage. Comprehensive policies should also be considered
Plate glass insurance	Loss arising from breakage of or damage to large, expensive shop windows
Product liability insurance	Claims from consumers for injuries/illnesses arising from the proper use of the firm's product
PRSI (USC)	Employers must contribute to employees' PRSI (USC)
Professional indemnity insurance	Claims against people in professional practices (e.g. doctors, solicitors and auditors) for negligence arising out of their professional work
Public liability insurance	Claims by the general public for injuries incurred while on or about the firm's premises
Sprinkler leakage insurance	Damage caused by accidental water discharge from an automatic sprinkler system

Both motor insurance and PRSI (USC) are compulsory insurance policies.

A **compulsory insurance policy** is a policy that must, by law, be taken out by a person or business.

CALCULATING THE COST OF INSURANCE

There are many companies in Ireland offering insurance policies. Firms seeking insurance should obtain quotations from a number of different companies to get the best possible prices for their insurance requirements. Remember, it always pays to shop around!

Examination type question

On 15/12/2011 Murdel Ltd requested a quotation from Best Insurances Ltd for the following assets:

- Buildings €400,000
- Machinery €60,000
- 4 delivery vans €30,000 each
- Stock €50,000
- Cash in the office €3,000, which is transferred to a bank 10 kilometres from the office once a week

Best Insurances sent the following quotation for an annual policy for the assets:

- Buildings €7 per €1,000
- Machinery €5 per €1,000
- Delivery vans €950 each
- Stock €14 per €1,000
- Cash in transit €20 per €500

They also offered a 10% no-claims bonus on the delivery vans.

Best Insurances Ltd also offered an introductory offer of 10% discount on the gross total premium.

Murdel Ltd accepted the quotation and paid the premium by cheque on 1 January 2012.

You are required to:

(a) Calculate the premium payable on 1/1/2012 showing all your calculations.

(b) Complete the cheque, signed by Michael Murphy, paid by Murdel Ltd on that date.

(c) Complete the entry in Murdel Ltd's analysed cash book and insurance account for the transaction.

Solution

(a) Calculation of premium

ASSET	VALUE	CALCULATION	COST
Buildings	€400,000	€400,000 ÷ €1,000 = 400 400 × €7	€2,800
Machinery	€60,000	€60,000 ÷ €1,000 = 60 60 × €5	€300
Delivery vans	€30,000 each	€950 × 4 = €3,800 *Less* 10% = €380	€3,420
Stock	€50,000	€50,000 ÷ €1,000 = 50 50 × €14	€700
Cash in transit	€3,000	€3,000 ÷ €500 = 6 6 × €20	€120
Gross total premium due			**€7,340**
Less 10% introductory offer			€734
Total premium due			**€6,606**

(b) Complete the cheque

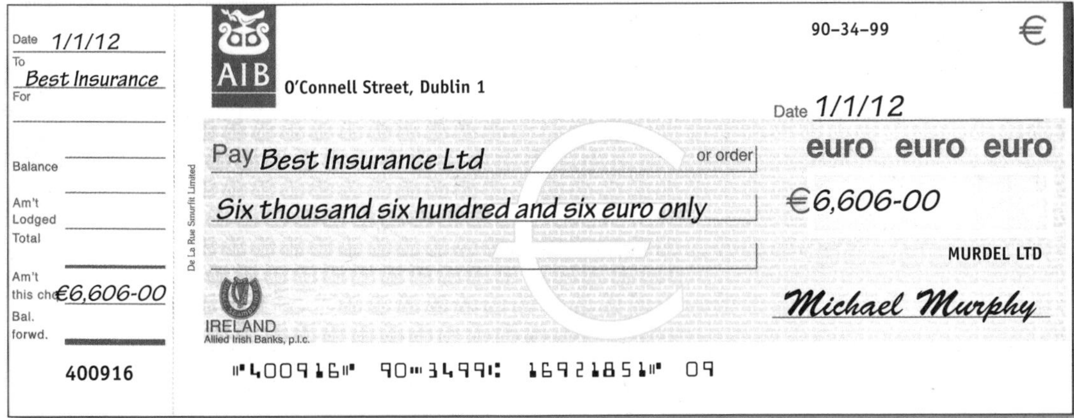
Date 1/1/12
To Best Insurance
For
Balance
Am't Lodged
Total
Am't this che €6,606-00
Bal. forwd.
400916

AIB O'Connell Street, Dublin 1
90-34-99 €
Date 1/1/12
Pay Best Insurance Ltd or order
Six thousand six hundred and six euro only
euro euro euro
€6,606-00
MURDEL LTD
Michael Murphy
De La Rue Smurfit Limited
IRELAND
Allied Irish Banks, p.l.c.
⑈400916⑈ 90⑉34991⑆ 16921851⑈ 09

(c) Complete the cash book

ANALYSED CASH BOOK (CREDIT SIDE)				
Date	Details	Chq no.	Bank	Insurance
1/1/12	Best Insurance Ltd	400916	€6,606.00	€6,606.00

Dr		INSURANCE A/C			Cr
Date	Details	€	Date	Details	€
1/12/12	Bank	6,606.00			

LEARN THE KEY TERMS

- **Non-insurable risks** are risks faced by a business for which insurance is not available.
- A **compulsory insurance policy** is any policy that must, by law, be taken out by a person or business.

QUESTIONS

1. Why should businesses insure their assets?
2. What is a non-insurable risk?
3. Name any four uninsurable risks.
4. What is a consequential loss policy?
5. What is covered by an employer's liability insurance policy?
6. What is covered by a product liability insurance policy?
7. What is covered by a professional indemnity insurance policy?
8. What is a compulsory insurance policy?
9. Name two compulsory insurance policies.

10. Green Enterprises have the following assets:

Premises	€200,000
Equipment	€50,000
3 motor vans	€20,000 each
Stock	€10,000
Cash	€5,000

On 15/1/12 it received the following quotation from Best Insurance Ltd:

Premises	€6 per €1,000
Equipment	€4 per €1,000
Motor vans	€700 each
Stock	€5 per €1,000
Cash	€8 per €500

Best Insurance Ltd also offer a 10% discount on the total premium due if Green Enterprises accepts the quotation by 1/2/12.

Calculate the total premium due if Green Enterprises accepts the quotation by the stated date. Show all your calculations.

See workbook for more questions.

Chain of production and channels of distribution

22

THE CHAIN OF PRODUCTION

The **chain of production** refers to the various production or processing stages that a good or service goes through before it is sold to the consumer.

'Consumers want cakes'

Think about the process of providing consumers with cakes.

1. Farmers grow wheat.
2. Wheat is sent to millers who make flour.
3. Flour is sent to bakers who make cakes.
4. Cakes may be sold to wholesalers, who sell them to retailers.
5. Retailers sell cakes to consumers.

The farmers, millers, bakeries and shops need banking and insurance services for their businesses. They also need transport services to distribute their end products.

From this we can identify three distinct sectors involved in the manufacturing and distribution of products.

The primary sector (extractive industries)

These industries take (extract) materials from the land or the sea. Farming, fishing, mining, and oil and gas production are primary industries.

The secondary sector (secondary production)

This is the manufacturing and construction sector of the economy. The firms in this sector use the goods produced by the primary sector and change them into finished products.

Examples are the clothing, food processing and building industries.

The tertiary sector (service providers)

The tertiary sector is made up of firms that provide services to all other sectors of the economy. Producers and manufacturers could not operate efficiently without these services.

Examples are the insurance, banking, transport, communications and advertising industries.

Wholesalers and **retailers** also provide services to both the producers and the consumers of goods. Tailors, hairdressers, mechanics, entertainers and solicitors provide services to consumers.

CHANNELS OF DISTRIBUTION

Channels of distribution are the methods used to transfer finished goods from manufacturers to consumers.

Different channels of distribution

1. Manufacturer ⟶ Wholesaler ⟶ Retailer ⟶ Consumer

This channel is used to distribute popular household consumer goods that are sold in small quantities to many small retailers, e.g. tea, coffee, milk, bread, washing-up liquids and greeting cards.

2. Manufacturer → Retailer → Consumer

This channel is used to distribute popular household consumer goods that are sold in large quantities to large retail outlets, such as large supermarkets.

3. Manufacturer → Consumer

This channel is usually used when goods are made to order, e.g. aeroplanes or tailor-made clothes.

You are aware from Chapter 15 on international trade that many products sold in Ireland are not manufactured here but are imported from abroad.

This can add an extra unit to the channel of distribution – the **importing agent**. Thus we could have a channel of distribution as follows:

4. Foreign manufacturer → Importing agent → Wholesaler → Retailer → Consumer

Wholesaling

A **wholesaler** is a company or person that buys large quantities of goods from many manufacturers and sells them in smaller quantities to retailers.

The traditional wholesaler benefits the **manufacturer**.

ROLE PLAYED BY WHOLESALER	BENEFIT TO MANUFACTURER
Buys very large quantities	Manufacturers only have a small number of customers, which reduces their administration and distribution costs
Stores the goods	Manufacturers are saved the cost of warehousing the goods
Promotes the goods to retailers and consumers	Reduces advertising costs as the manufacturers need only promote their goods to the wholesalers
Pays promptly for the goods	Gives the manufacturers the working capital they need for current expenditure
Provides the manufacturer with information received from retailers about market trends	Prevents the manufacturers from making goods that may be going out of fashion

The traditional wholesaler also benefits the **retailer**.

ROLE PLAYED BY WHOLESALER	BENEFIT TO RETAILER
Provides a wide range of goods	Retailers need deal with only a small number of wholesalers rather than many manufacturers
Sells goods in small quantities	Retailers are saved the cost of storing large quantities of goods
Delivers goods	Reduces transport costs for retailers and allows them more time at their own business
Provides credit facilities	Retailers may be able to sell all their stock before payment is due
Provides information about new products coming on to the market	Prevents the retailers over-stocking goods that may be going out of fashion

Cash and carry wholesalers

Today 'cash and carry' wholesalers are located in most large towns. These differ from traditional wholesalers in the following ways.

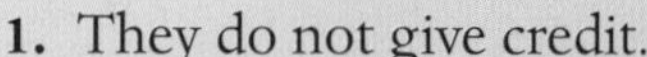

1. They do not give credit.
2. They do not deliver goods.
3. They operate on a self-service basis.
4. They provide ample parking space for retailers.
5. Their prices tend to be lower than traditional wholesalers because:
   (a) They are paid cash for the goods so no overdraft is needed
   (b) They do not have to invest in delivery trucks
   (c) Less staff is required because of self-service

Cash and carry wholesalers act as supermarkets to retailers. Consumers are not permitted to shop in them.

RETAILING

A **retailer** is somebody (or an outlet) who sells finished goods to consumers.

A retailer buys goods in bulk from either a wholesaler or a manufacturer and then sells them in single units or small quantities to consumers.

Interestingly, some retailers, particularly in the food business, refer to themselves as **purveyors**. Originally purveyors were officials who supplied provisions to royal households. Today the term is usually restricted to specialist suppliers, e.g. *purveyor of fine wines*.

Types of retailers

There are many different types of retail outlets.

TYPES OF RETAILERS	
Unit or independent retailers	Small, privately owned shops that are usually located in or near a large number of houses
Voluntary groups	Independent retailers who contract to regularly buy a minimum amount of goods from a wholesaler. This means the wholesaler can buy a wide range of goods in bulk and pass on the discount to the retailer, e.g. Centra shops
Supermarkets	Large, self-service shops that sell a wide variety of grocery and household products
Chain stores	Large stores that sell a variety of goods and have many branches nationwide, e.g. Dunnes Stores
Multiple stores	Similar to chain stores but they tend to specialise in one good or a limited range of goods, e.g. Clarks (shoes) and Elverys (sportswear and equipment)
Department stores	Large stores that sell a variety of products in different sections (departments) of the one shop. They are really a number of shops under one roof! Examples are Clerys, Arnotts and Brown Thomas stores
Discount stores	Shops that sell a limited range of products at low prices. They tend to have long opening hours during weekdays and also open on bank holidays, e.g. Power City
Vending machines	Automated retail devices that can operate 24 hours a day selling convenience items such as drinks, chocolate bars and snack foods
Mail-order firms	Warehouses that advertise their goods on a national or international scale. Customers order the goods by phone, letter or email and the goods are delivered to their homes by post or courier
Direct selling organisations	Salespeople visit people's homes, demonstrate a product and take orders for the products that are then delivered to the consumers' homes, e.g. Tupperware (household) and Avon (cosmetics) products

Functions of retailers

1. Provide a wide range of goods to consumers in convenient locations
2. Sell goods to consumers in small quantities
3. Offer advice to consumers on products most suited to the consumers' needs
4. Offer advice to wholesalers/manufacturers on changes in consumer trends
5. Create demand for goods through their own advertising
6. Arrange finance for consumers to make it easier for them to purchase expensive consumer durable products
7. Some retailers will accept 'trade-ins' to make it easier for the consumer to buy new products. This is particularly important in the motor retail business.

Recent trends in retailing in Ireland

1. The arrival of international discount stores in the grocery and related products industry, e.g. Aldi and Lidl.
2. Major growth in the number of shopping centres and retail outlets throughout the country.
3. Greater use of e-commerce, i.e. selling goods and services over the Internet.
4. Growth of farmers' markets: many individual farmers are now selling their produce directly to the public at organised markets. They usually sell high-value products and organic or 'eco-friendly' products.
5. Many retailers of expensive consumer durable products are now providing or arranging low interest rate loans.
6. Recent research has shown a growth in the promotion and acceptance of 'own brand' labelled goods.

LEARN THE KEY TERMS

- The **chain of production** refers to the various production or processing stages that a good or service goes through before it is sold to the consumer.
- **Primary production (extractive industry)** refers to industries that take (extract) materials from the land or the sea.
- **Secondary production** is the manufacturing and construction sector of the economy.
- The **tertiary sector (services industry)** is made up of firms that provide services to other sectors of the economy.
- **Channels of distribution** are the methods used to transfer finished goods from manufacturers to consumers.

- A **wholesaler** is a company or person that buys large quantities of goods from many manufacturers and sells them in smaller quantities to retailers.
- A **retailer** is somebody (or an outlet) who sells finished goods to consumers.
- A **purveyor** is a specialist supplier of food, wines or meals.

QUESTIONS

1. Define the term **chain of production**.
2. Identify, in sequence, people involved in the extractive, production (secondary) and tertiary industries in the provision of envelopes to consumers.
3. Why is transport so important in the chain of production?
4. What is primary production? Give an example.
5. What is secondary production? Give an example.
6. What is the tertiary sector?
7. Classify the following types of workers as primary producers, secondary producers or service providers: *shop assistants* *miners* *factory workers*
8. What is meant by the term the **channels of distribution**?
9. Identify all the possible channels of distribution involved in getting a product from the maker to the final user.
10. What is a wholesaler?
11. What services are provided by a wholesaler to a manufacturer?
12. What services are provided by a wholesaler to a retailer?
13. What is a **cash and carry** wholesaler?
14. How does the role of the cash and carry wholesaler differ from that of the traditional wholesaler?
15. What is a retailer?
16. Outline any four functions of a retailer.
17. There are many different types of retail outlets. Describe any four of these.
18. Rewrite the following sentences to correct the deliberate mistakes.

    Manufacturers provide goods in small quantities to consumers.
    Wholesalers buy goods for their own personal use.
    Retailers make goods to be used by consumers.
    Consumers buy goods from manufacturers and sell goods to retailers.
19. How has the Internet changed the nature of retailing in recent times?
20. Describe any other two recent developments in retailing.

See workbook for more questions.

23 Delivery and transport systems

Delivery systems refer to the facilities used to transport people and goods from one place to another.

In the previous chapter we saw that transport is essential to get goods through each link in the chain of production.

A country's transport system is part of its infrastructure, i.e. capital that is not directly productive but is essential for efficient production.

A good transport and delivery system is essential to ensure:

1. Safe and timely delivery of raw materials to manufacturers.
2. Safe and timely delivery of finished goods to wholesalers, retailers and consumers.
3. Safe and efficient transportation of goods into and out of the country.
4. Easy access for all people to and from their place of work.

Many factors have to be considered when choosing a delivery system. Some systems may be fast, but expensive. Some systems may be cheap, but unreliable. And some systems, although expensive, may be the only way to transport a particular product.

Therefore a firm must weigh up all the following factors before deciding on the system best suited to its delivery requirements at any given time.

FACTORS TO CONSIDER WHEN CHOOSING A DELIVERY SYSTEM	
Cost	This is the first and most essential consideration. The cheapest delivery system will keep down both the cost of distribution and the selling price of the good.
Reliability	A firm's reputation can be destroyed if it does not deliver goods as promised. Therefore the firm must use a transport system that will guarantee delivery of goods when they are required.
Convenience	Many transport providers, such as trains and ships, operate to set timetables. These timetables may not be suitable for the needs of individual firms. Thus these firms will have to find transport providers that operate at suitable times.

FACTORS TO CONSIDER WHEN CHOOSING A DELIVERY SYSTEM (continued)	
Speed	The cost of the transport may not be a deciding factor when a product is required urgently. It may be more cost-effective to have a machine part delivered immediately by private aircraft from Galway to Dublin than to lose a day's production in a factory.
Type of goods being delivered	Some goods can only be delivered through the use of systems that are specifically designed for the product. This limits the choice of transport system. For example, oil and frozen foods need specialised modes of transport.
Destination	Some goods may require a combination of different forms of transport depending on the location of the buyer in relation to the location of the seller. If goods are being exported from Ireland a minimum of two different forms of transport must be used. Why?

COMMON DELIVERY SYSTEMS

ROAD TRANSPORT	
Advantages	Disadvantages
1. Fast over short distances.	1. Subject to traffic congestion.
2. Relatively cheap.	2. Bad weather may cause delays.
3. Goods loaded and unloaded once only, thus reducing handling and insurance costs.	3. Slow over very long distances.
4. Not subject to timetables.	4. Not suitable for bulky goods.

- **Tachographs** are devices installed on commercial vehicles that record the vehicle's speed and the length of time that it is moving or stationary to ensure that the driver complies with laws relating to speed and compulsory rest periods.

RAIL TRANSPORT	
Advantages	Disadvantages
1. Fast over long distances.	1. Usually subject to timetable.
2. Suitable and cheap for bulky goods.	2. Fixed routes only.
3. Not subject to traffic congestion.	3. Must be used in conjunction with another means of transport.
4. Reliable and safe.	4. Expensive over short distances.

SEA TRANSPORT	
Advantages	**Disadvantages**
Suitable for bulky goods.	Slow over long distances.
Cheap over long distances.	Must be used in conjunction with another means of transport.
Suitable for containers*.	Subject to weather conditions.
There are many specialised ships suitable for different goods.	Usually subject to timetable.

- ***Containers** are large metal boxes used to store goods that are to be transported. The containers are sealed after they have been filled. They are then loaded on trucks or ships for transportation.

Roll-on/roll-off (RO/RO) ferries are ships designed to allow cars and trucks to drive directly on to and off them.

Load on/load off (LO/LO) ferries are ships designed to allow goods to be lifted on to and off them, e.g. by cranes.

AIR TRANSPORT	
Advantages	**Disadvantages**
Fast over long distances.	Expensive, especially over short distances.
Suitable for small, expensive goods.	Subject to weather conditions.
Safe.	Not suitable for bulky goods.
	Must be used in conjunction with another means of transport.
	Additional handling of the goods can increase insurance costs.

PIPELINES	
Advantages	**Disadvantages**
Cheap to operate.	Expensive to set up.
Very good safety record.	Suitable only for gases and liquids.

- A **pipeline** is a system of inter-connected pipes that transports gases or liquids, usually over long distances.

COMMON CARRIERS

A common carrier is an individual or company that transports goods or people for a fee. Trucking companies, public airlines, railways and public bus companies are common carriers. These all operate under licence.

Use of own transport vehicles vs. use of common carrier

A business can purchase and use its own transport vehicles or it can use a common carrier. Whether or not a firm uses its own vehicles normally depends on the volume and frequency of its deliveries. There are advantages and disadvantages to a firm owning its transport fleet.

OWN TRANSPORT	
Advantages	**Disadvantages**
Transport is available when needed, 24 hours a day, 7 days a week.	The money required to purchase delivery vehicles may be better used in the business itself, i.e. there is an opportunity cost on the firm's finances.
Having the firm's name on the vehicles acts as a means of advertising.	Extra staff must be employed, e.g. drivers and maintenance staff.
The firm may be able to earn extra income by making vehicles available to others for return journeys.	Extra administration is required to keep track of delivery costs.
Deliveries are not affected by strikes in common carrier firms.	Transport vehicles tend to depreciate in value very quickly.

- The word **freight** is often used to describe the goods being transported by commercial transport companies.
- **Carriage** means the charge for transporting goods.

Couriers

A **courier** is a person or company used to deliver documents and small, valuable packages by hand. A courier service can operate on a local level, e.g. within a county, or on an international level. DHL and FedEx are two of the world's biggest courier services.

Pallets and forklifts

Goods are often stacked on pallets for transport and storing purposes.

- A **pallet** is a platform, usually wooden, onto which goods are loaded to make it easy to move them. There are slots at the base of the pallet that allow a forklift to lift it.
- A **forklift** is an easily manoeuvrable transport device with two protruding rigid steel bars that can be raised and lowered. It is used to load pallets on and off trucks and to stack pallets in warehouses.

Refrigerated transport

Many products need **refrigerated** modes of transport. This is any form of transport (e.g. trucks, vans and ships) that has a refrigerator incorporated into it.

CALCULATING DELIVERY TIMES

Transport managers and owner-drivers must be able to calculate the time required to make deliveries.

Traffic control regulations and defined working hours mean many businesses can take delivery of goods only at certain times, e.g. before 9.00 am (for traffic purposes) or between 6.00 and 7.00 pm (end of working day).

If a company cannot guarantee a delivery time then it will lose business.

To calculate the time required for a delivery, use the formula below.

$$\text{Time (in hours)} = \frac{\text{Distance}}{\text{Speed per hour}} + \text{time allowed for stoppages/rest periods}$$

Example

- A delivery company must deliver goods to a destination 300 kilometres from its base. Its delivery van travels at an average speed of 60 kilometres per hour.
- The van driver must take a half-hour rest after every four hours of driving.
- The delivery must be delivered before 9.00 am the following morning.
- Calculate the latest time that the delivery van driver must leave the base to ensure the delivery is made on time.

Show your answer and workings.

Solution

Journey time = distance divided by speed per hour, plus time allowed for stoppages/rest periods.

Therefore journey time is: distance of 300 divided by 60 (i.e. the speed per hour) = 5 hours.

Add a half hour for one rest period. Total time of journey is 5½ hours.

The delivery must be made by 9.00 am, so the latest time the delivery driver may leave the base is 5½ hours before 9.00 am, i.e. 3.30 am.

READING A DISTANCE TABLE

A distance table is a gridded table showing the distances between named towns; see table on next page.

Example

You are asked to find the distance from Tralee to Limerick.

To get the distance between two places on a distance table use a ruler to draw a line from the first named place (Tralee) to under the second named place (Limerick). Here, as you can see from the red line below, the distance is 105 kilometres.

Dundalk									
256	Ennis								
238	70	**Galway**							
240	37	105	**Limerick**						
92	16	144	148	Mullingar					
246	246	274	210	204	Rosslare				
168	195	138	232	135	326	Sligo			
346	94	162	**105**	254	290	288	**Tralee**		
242	164	220	130	170	82	292	210	Waterford	
118	228	254	190	185	19	306	275	62	Wexford

Likewise the distance from Dundalk to Galway is 238 kilometres as shown by the black line.

CALCULATING DISTANCE AND TIME

Worked example

Marian Jones, a courier based in Dundalk, picked up two packages from her base at 8.00 am one morning. She delivered the first one to a school in Mullingar and from there delivered the second one to an office in Sligo before returning home to Dundalk.

(a) Using the distance table below, calculate the total number of kilometres driven by Marian that day. Show all your calculations.

(b) Marian travelled at an average speed of 79 kilometres per hour. How many hours did she spend driving that day? Show all your calculations

Dundalk									
256	Ennis								
238	70	Galway							
240	37	105	Limerick						
92	16	144	148	**Mullingar**					
246	246	274	210	204	Rosslare				
168	195	138	232	**135**	326	**Sligo**			
346	94	162	105	254	290	288	Tralee		
242	164	220	130	170	82	292	210	Waterford	
118	228	254	190	185	19	306	275	62	Wexford

Solution

(a) Dundalk to Mullingar = 92 kilometres
Mullingar to Sligo = 135 kilometres
Sligo to Dundalk = 168 kilometres
Total miles driven = 395 kilometres

(b) Time = distance divided by average speed
$395 \div 79 = 5$ hours

CALCULATING TRANSPORT COSTS

If a business is to be profitable the selling price of its product should cover its total cost plus a mark-up for profit. The total cost of providing a product to a consumer must include the cost of transporting the product to the consumer.

Calculating daily transport costs

1. Divide the annual fixed costs by the number of days the business operates each year.
2. Add the daily cost of fuel, i.e. petrol or diesel.
3. Add other variable costs per day, e.g. driver's wages (including employer's PRSI/USC) and toll charges.

Example

from Junior Certificate Higher Level 2008

Calculate the cost of transport for one day from the following details provided by Fahy Ltd, a fruit distributor. (Show your workings.)

- FAHY Ltd operates 330 working days per year.
- The diesel van used can do 33 kilometres per litre.
- The distance travelled per day is 660 kilometres.
- The cost of diesel is €1.10 per litre.
- Gross wage of driver is €240 per day.
- Employer's PRSI (USC) is 12.5%.
- Annual motor tax is €1,320
- Annual motor insurance is €2,640.
- Annual motor repairs is €1,650.
- Toll charges are €30 per day.

PARTIALLY COMPLETED COMPARISON STATEMENT

FIXED COSTS	€	Daily cost €
Annual motor tax	1,320	
Annual motor insurance	2,640	
Annual motor repairs	1,650	
Total fixed cost	5,610	
Daily fixed cost	(5,610 ÷ 330)	**17**
COST OF FUEL		
Distance travelled per day	660 kilometres	
Divide by kilometres per litre	33 kilometres	
Daily fuel used	20 litres	
Cost per litre	1.10	
Daily cost of fuel	(20 × 1.10)	**22**
OTHER VARIABLE COSTS PER DAY		
Driver's wages	240	
Employer's PRSI (USC) (12.5 % of wages)	30	
Toll charges per day	30	
Total other variable costs per day		**300**
TOTAL COST FOR ONE DAY		**339**

PASSENGER TRANSPORT AND TIMETABLES

Public transport users need to read timetables accurately when planning journeys. This becomes doubly important when using one form of transport to link up with another, e.g. getting a bus or train to Dublin to connect with a flight departing from the airport.

Example

from Junior Certificate Ordinary Level 2005

Jean Campbell lives in Moate, Co. Westmeath. She has booked a flight to London on Wednesday 29 June 2005. The flight departs from Dublin Airport at 1340 (1.40 pm) but all passengers must check in at the airport at least one hour before the flight. Jean is taking the bus to Dublin Airport. Use the timetables below to answer the following questions.

AIR TIMETABLE: DUBLIN AIRPORT – LONDON AIRPORT

Flight no.	Dep	Arrival							
FR 202	0630	0745	Mon	Tue	Wed	Thur	Fri	Sat	Sun
FR 206	0825	0935	Mon	Tue	Wed	Thur	Fri	Sat	Sun
FR 212	1155	1305	Mon	—	—	—	Fri	—	—
FR 214	1230	1340	Mon	Tue	Wed	Thur	Fri	Sat	—
FR 216	1340	1450	Mon	Tue	Wed	Thur	Fri	Sat	—
FR 218	1430	1540	Mon	Tue	Wed	Thur	Fri	Sat	Sun
FR 226	1700	1810	—	—	—	—	—	—	Sun
FR 294	1835	1945	Mon	Tue	Wed	Thur	Fri	Sat	Sun
FR 224	2100	2210	Mon	Tue	Wed	Thur	Fri	—	Sun

BUS TIMETABLE: GALWAY – DUBLIN AIRPORT

	Everyday	Everyday	Everyday	Everyday	Sun Only
Galway	06:30	08:45	10:25	17:25	19:15
Loughrea	07:00	09:15	11:00	18:00	19:45
Ballinasloe	07:25	09:40	11:25	18:25	20:10
Athlone	07:50	10:05	11:50	18:50	20:30
Moate	08:00	10:20	12:10	19:00	20:45
Kinnegad	08:30	10:50	12:40	19:30	21:15
Enfield	09:00	11:20	13:00	20:00	21:45
Dublin Centre	09:30	11:50	13:35	20:40	22:15
Dublin Airport	10:00	12:20	14:15	21:10	22:45

Part A

(i) What is Jean's flight number?

(ii) What is the latest time that Jean should be at the bus stop in Moate in order to get to Dublin Airport in time for her flight?

(iii) What time will Jean's flight arrive in London Airport?

Part B

Calculate the total time taken by Jean to get from Moate bus stop to London Airport. Show your workings.

Solution

Part A

(i) FR 216. It is important to know the flight number because:
Departure gate information at the airport is displayed by flight number.
Changes to flight departure times are displayed by flight number.

(ii) 10:20. The next bus departing from Moate – the 12:10 bus – does not arrive at Dublin Airport until 14:15, which is too late for the 13:40 flight departure.

(iii) 14:50, as highlighted in the timetable on page 201.

Part B

Jean leaves Moate bus stop at 10:20 and arrives at London Airport at 14:50. Thus the total time taken from Moate to London Airport is 4 hours and 30 minutes.

Note: Most airlines insist that passengers check-in at the airport at least ninety minutes before the flight is due to depart. Allow for this when planning your arrival at the airport.

RECENT AND FUTURE TRANSPORT DEVELOPMENTS IN IRELAND

The Dublin Port Tunnel

Dublin Port Tunnel is an underground dual carriageway system linking the M1 and the M50 motorways to Dublin Port. The tunnel diverts heavy goods vehicles travelling to and from Dublin Port away from the city centre. This improves traffic flow in the city centre.

Terminal Two at Dublin Airport.

Work started on the second terminal (known as T2) in October 2007 and it was due to open in April 2010. This should ease the congestion at Dublin Airport.

Increased investment in motorways and toll roads

There has been a very big investment in Ireland's motorway system in recent years. The free-flow of traffic on these roads should speed up the delivery and distribution of goods throughout the country. Some of these motorways are toll roads, i.e. a fee is charged for using them. Although the toll is an additional transport cost, it may be offset by a reduction in fuel costs due to less traffic congestion.

An Luas

An Luas is a light rail tram system in Dublin connecting suburban areas to the city centre. Some commuters from the suburbs use this system rather than their private cars to access the city centre. *Luas* is the Irish word for speed.

Quality Bus Corridors

Quality Bus Corridors (QBCs) are parts of a public road that can be used only by buses and taxis.

Bypasses

Bypasses are roads built specifically to divert traffic away from villages, towns and cities.

Bicycle lanes

Bicycle lanes are parts of a public road that can be used only by cyclists.

Metro North

A new Metro North rail line is planned to run from St Stephen's Green in Dublin city centre via Dublin Airport to the north of Swords at Belinstown.

RECORDING THE PURCHASE OF A DELIVERY VAN BY CHEQUE

On 1/10/12 Murdel Ltd purchased a delivery van for €20,000 by cheque.

- A delivery van is an asset. Remember the rule? **Debit assets received.**
- The firm paid out money from its bank account. Therefore the Bank A/C must be credited. (**Credit things given.**)

Dr	DELIVERY VAN A/C				Cr
Date	Details	€	Date	Details	€
1/10/12	Bank	20,000			

Dr	BANK A/C				Cr
Date	Details	€	Date	Details	€
			1/10/12	Delivery van	20,000

LEARN THE KEY TERMS

- **Delivery systems** refer to the facilities used to transport people and goods from one place to another place.
- **Tachographs** are devices installed on commercial vehicles that record the vehicle's speed and the length of time that it is moving or stationary.
- **Roll-on/roll-off (RO/RO) ferries** are ships designed to allow cars and fully loaded trucks to drive directly on to and off them.
- **Load on/load off (LO/LO) ferries** are ships designed to allow goods to be lifted on to and off them, e.g. by cranes.
- **A pipeline** is a system of inter-connected pipes laid down to transport something over long distances.

- A **common carrier** is an individual or company that transports goods or people for a fee.
- A **courier** is a person or company that delivers documents and small, valuable packages by hand.
- **Freight** refers to goods being transported.
- **Carriage** is the cost of transporting goods.
- A **pallet** is a specially designed platform, usually wooden, on to which a large quantity of goods can be loaded to make it easy to move them.
- A **forklift** is an easily manoeuvrable transport device with two protruding rigid steel bars that can be raised and lowered. It is used to move pallets.
- **Distance tables** are gridded tables showing the distances between various places.
- **Containers** are large metal boxes used to store goods that are to be transported. The containers are sealed after the goods have been placed in them. They are then loaded on to trucks or ships for transportation.
- **Toll roads** are roads that can only be used on payment of a fee (toll).
- **Quality bus corridors** are parts of a public road that can only be used by buses and taxis.
- **Bypasses** are roads built specifically to divert traffic away from villages, towns and cities.
- **Bicycle lanes** are parts of a public road that can only be used by cyclists.
- A **refrigerated mode of transport** refers to any form of transport – e.g. trucks, vans and ships – that has a refrigerator incorporated into it.
- **An Luas** is a light rail passenger transport system in Dublin that connects suburban areas to the city centre.

QUESTIONS

1. Outline four reasons why it is necessary to have a good transport system.
2. Explain any four factors that must be taken into account when choosing a delivery system.
3. List and explain three advantages and three disadvantages of road transport.
4. List and explain three advantages and three disadvantages of rail transport.
5. List and explain three advantages and three disadvantages of sea transport.
6. List and explain three advantages and three disadvantages of air transport.
7. 'Pipelines are only suited to the transportation of a very limited number of goods'. Explain this statement.
8. Explain the difference between a common carrier and a courier.
9. What are the advantages and disadvantages to a business of owning its own transport fleet?
10. Explain the following terms used in transport: (a) pallets, (b) forklifts, (c) toll roads, (d) containers and (e) Quality Bus Corridors (QBCs).
11. Distinguish between RO/RO ferries and LO/LO ferries.

12. A delivery company must deliver goods to a destination 300 kilometres from its base.

    Its delivery van travels at an average speed of 50 kilometres per hour.
    The van driver must take a half-hour rest after every four hours of driving.
    The delivery must be made before 9.00 am.

    Calculate the latest time that the delivery van driver can leave the base to ensure that the delivery is made on time. Show your workings.

Use the distance table shown on page 199 to answer the following questions.

13. A courier, David O'Reilly, based in Tralee, picked up two packages from his base at 8.00 am one morning. He delivered the first one to a firm in Waterford and from there he drove to Rosslare to deliver the second package before returning home to Tralee.

    Calculate the total number of kilometres driven by David that day. Show all your calculations.

14. If, in question 13, David O'Reilly travelled at an average speed of 97 kilometres per hour and took two half-hour breaks, at what time would he get back to Tralee if he left there at 7.00 am? Show all your calculations

15. If David's fuel consumption was 29.1 kilometres per litre what was the total cost of fuel for that trip, assuming the fuel cost €1.15 per litre?

16. Calculate the cost of transport for one day from the following details provided by Murphy Ltd, a common carrier. Show your workings.

    Murphy Ltd operates 320 working days per year.
    The diesel van used can do 32 kilometres per litre.
    The distance travelled per day is 960 kilometres.
    The cost of diesel is €1.20 per litre.
    Gross wage of driver is €200 per day.
    Employer's PRSI (USC) is 12.5%.
    Annual motor tax is €1,000.
    Annual motor insurance is €3,000.
    Annual motor repairs is €1,000.
    Toll charges are €90 per day.

17. Calculate a firm's cost of transport for one day from the following details. Show your workings.

    The firm operates 325 working days per year.
    The diesel van used can do 37 kilometres per litre.
    The distance travelled per day is 740 kilometres.
    The cost of diesel is €1.05 per litre.
    Gross wage of driver is €200 per day.
    Employer's PRSI (USC) is 12.5%.
    Annual motor tax is €1,300.
    Annual motor insurance is €2,275.
    Annual motor repairs is €1,300.
    Toll charges are €20 per day.

See workbook for more questions.

24 Marketing

A **market** refers to all the people and institutions involved in the buying and selling of a product.

Marketing means identifying consumers' requirements and identifying how to supply these requirements at a profit.

THE MARKETING MIX

The marketing mix is the combination of marketing techniques that can be used to successfully satisfy consumers' requirements profitably. This combination of marketing techniques is often called the 'four Ps' of marketing.

The 'four Ps' of marketing (the marketing mix)

1. **Product.** Establish what product is to be produced and decide on its packaging.
2. **Price.** Establish the price to be charged for the product and decide whether there will be a fixed price or discounts for bulk purchases.

   The price charged for a product must take into account the production cost. If the price is less than the production cost then the business will not be able to supply consumers' requirements profitably. Look back at the definition of marketing. When a business is pricing a product it must be aware of the price that its competitors are charging for similar products.
3. **Promotion.** Establish the marketing, advertising, sales and after-sales service policy of the business.
4. **Place.** Establish the distribution policy, i.e. how to get the product from the manufacturer to the consumer. Are goods to be sold by the manufacturer to wholesalers, or to retail shops, or will the manufacturer sell the goods directly to the consumer? See Chapter 22, *Channels of distribution*.

Even the most successful firms continuously redesign or rename their products.

Product development is the process of creating a new product or altering an existing one.

Every now and then most of the major car manufacturers bring out new versions of their successful models. This is to encourage existing customers to purchase the new model and so increase sales.

Other firms rename their existing product to create a new image for it and benefit from the publicity surrounding the re-launch.

For example, 'Jif', one of Unilever's well-known household products, was renamed 'Cif' in 2001 and the publicity surrounding the renaming resulted in an increase in sales.

A **target market** is a group of consumers identified as being the people most likely to buy a particular product. Advertising and promotion is aimed at this group.

Market segmentation means subdividing the market for a product into specific groups of people who share common characteristics: e.g. young people, middle-aged people and senior citizens.

It is important to distinguish between different consumers of the same type of product because different forms of advertising and sales promotions may have to be used to appeal to each market segment. There may also have to be slight variations in the product to make it attractive to each section.

For example, an ice cream producer can undertake market research to establish the flavours preferred by different age groups. In this way the producer can increase sales by offering the relevant flavours and running separate advertising campaigns for each age group.

Sub-divisions of marketing

1. Market research
2. Advertising
3. Sales promotion
4. Distribution
5. After-sales service

1. MARKET RESEARCH

Market research is the collection and analysis of information about a product and the market for that product.

Aims of market research

1. To find out what products consumers require.
2. To establish a suitable name for the product.
3. To discover the best means of advertising and promoting the product.
4. To find the best means of distributing a product.
5. To establish a suitable selling price.
6. To find out the extent of the competition in the industry.

Market research techniques

Desk research

Desk research is the use of information that has already been collected or published, e.g. reports, newspaper articles, statistics and other information on file.

Field research

Field research is gathering new information through research.
It may involve the following:

FIELD RESEARCH	
Postal, telephone and on-the-spot questionnaires	Questionnaires should be made up of scientifically designed, non-leading questions. They should be worded in such a way that allows the researchers to present their findings in data form.
Interviewing potential consumers	Interviews can be done face-to-face or by telephone. They are aimed at getting people's opinions on a product but are not as scientific as questionnaires.
Test marketing	A small quantity of a new product is put on sale in one sample area. The manufacturer can assess reaction to the product before deciding to go into full production.
Observation	Researchers often observe customers' habits and reactions when shopping. This can give valuable information on product colouring and packaging and on the ideal physical location of the product in the shop.
Consumer panels	This is a group of consumers chosen to give a record of their consumption of goods and services over a period of time. This method is widely used to ascertain TV viewing patterns. These are known as TAM (Television Audience Measurement) ratings.

2. ADVERTISING

Advertising is the communication of information about a product or service to people in general or to a particular group of people that tries to persuade them to buy the product or service.

Aims of advertising

1. To give information
2. To increase sales
3. To maintain a given level of sales, i.e. to retain the firm's share of the market
4. To project a good image for a firm
5. To counteract bad publicity

Forms of advertising

1. Informative advertising

Informative advertising gives useful information to the general public. For example:

> **INFLUENZA VACCINE**
>
> **Get the vaccine – not the flu**
>
> If you're over 65, living with a long-term health condition or are a carer then remember to get this year's vaccine.
>
> Make an appointment now with your family doctor (GP).

2. Persuasive advertising

Persuasive advertising attempts to convince people that they need this product. It normally appeals to some basic emotion or sensitivity. For example, L'Oreal, the cosmetics manufacturer, uses this slogan:

> **'Because you're worth it'**

This is a subtle way of convincing people to spend money on luxury (*wants* as distinct from *needs*) goods.

3. Competitive advertising

Competitive advertising is used by firms to convince people that the firm's product is better than that of their competitors. For example,

> **Would you swap two packets of Brand 'X' for one of Ariel?**

4. Generic or industrial advertising

In generic advertising all the firms in an industry come together to fund the advertising in an attempt to persuade people to buy more of that type of product. For example:

> **Drink more milk**

Advertising media

The word **media** is the plural of *medium* which, in this context, refers to the means used to advertise the product. Today the word *media* is commonly used to describe the various forms of mass communication, e.g. radio, TV, Internet, newspapers and magazines.

The medium (or media in many cases) used will depend on the target market.

National media

National TV and national radio stations, combined with the national newspapers, are used to advertise goods or services of mass consumption. Notice how Dunne's Stores uses all of these media.

Local media

Local radio and local newspapers are used to advertise goods and services whose consumption is confined to a given geographical area. For example, a garage in Cavan may restrict its advertising to the local radio stations and newspapers that cover Cavan and its surrounding counties.

Specialist media

Specialist magazines or publications are used to advertise products that are used by a limited number of consumers. The main advantage of these publications is that all their readers have an interest in the topic covered by them.

Accountancy Ireland is published by The Institute of Chartered Accountants in Ireland and has an average net circulation per issue of roughly 26,500. Any business selling accounting software packages would find this an ideal publication for its advertising because all of its readers would have an interest in the product.

Likewise *The Farmer's Journal* would be an ideal medium for advertising agriculture-related products, and *Golf World Magazine* would be perfect for golf-related products.

MOST COMMON ADVERTISING MEDIA	
TV	Expensive, but very effective when dramatic or animated presentation is required.
Radio	Can be either local or national. Cheaper than TV but still relatively expensive because regular repetition of the advertisement is required to make it effective.
Press	Can be local or national. National full-page advertising is expensive but tends to be effective.
Outdoor	This can be on billboards or advertisements carried on delivery trucks. The cost of billboard advertising depends on its location. A city centre location is more expensive than a suburban location.
Point-of-sale	Advertising material displayed in the shops where goods are sold.
Internet	Either emailing people whose names are on relevant data bases, or full advertisements carried on various search engines. The major disadvantage is that Internet users can block many of these advertisements.

MOST COMMON ADVERTISING MEDIA (continued)	
Mobile phones	Similar to Internet advertising. Many new mobile phones are Internet-friendly, which means that people do not have to be using their desktop or laptop computers to see the advertisements.
Handbills	Leaflets promoting a product or service are distributed in public places or to letterboxes.
Merchandising	A form of point-of-sale advertising, i.e. advertising a product in the place (shop) where it is being sold. It normally takes the form of a prominent display of the product in a shop.

The AIDA concept of advertising

A good advertising campaign should:

- Firstly get the **Attention** of the potential customers
- Then create an **Interest** in the product
- This interest should then create a **Desire** to have the product
- This desire should lead to **Action**, i.e. the potential customers should then buy the product.

Just remember the girl's name '**Aida**'!

Branding means applying a specific name or logo to a company's products to distinguish them from similar products made by other manufacturers.

A successful brand creates an image in the public's mind of a certain quality associated with the company's range of products. Some well-known brands are:

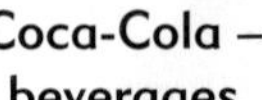

Coca-Cola – beverages

Google – Internet services

McDonald's – restaurants

Microsoft – computer software

Nokia – consumer electronic goods

A well-established brand becomes an asset of a business, i.e. it can acquire a money value and could be sold.

3. SALES PROMOTION

Sales promotion includes all activities, other than direct advertising, that firms use to promote their products and increase their sales.

SALES PROMOTION EXAMPLES	
Free samples	Normally distributed to households (or given out at point-of-sale) in the hope that consumers like the product and begin to purchase it
Coupons	Discount vouchers distributed to households to be used in shops
Competitions	Each time a consumer purchases a product he or she is entered into a draw for attractive prizes
Sponsorship	Ranges from jersey sponsorship for local football teams by local traders to the sponsorship of national events by national or multi-national companies

SALES PROMOTION EXAMPLES (continued)	
Bulk discounting	Often takes the form of 'Three for the price of two' offers
Joint selling	Offers such as a free packet of biscuits with a jar of coffee or a free carwash with every €60 worth of petrol purchased
Vouchers for next purchase	Given to customers when purchasing a product, allowing them a discount the next time they buy that same product

Public relations

Public relations (PR) is a sub-section of sales promotion. It involves establishing and maintaining a good company image in the mind of the public. It often involves giving information to the media that shows a positive image of the company.

4. DISTRIBUTION

Channels of distribution are the methods used to transfer finished goods from manufacturers to consumers.

Refer back to Chapter 22 for detailed explanation of the different systems used.

5. AFTER-SALES SERVICE

After-sales service is the support offered by manufacturers, distributors and retailers to consumers after they have purchased a product.

Consumers' image of a company is often determined by the quality of its after-sales service. Although the extent of manufacturers' warranties (guarantees) is extremely important, consumers also take account of the assistance available to them on the use of a product, e.g. training in its operation and solving problems. This is becoming very important for companies such as Internet and software providers.

Companies are becoming increasingly aware that their good-natured willingness to offer after-sales service is important to consumers and that their response time to problem solving should be as quick as possible.

Many companies now consider after-sales service so important that they promote it as strongly as they promote the product itself.

RECORDING ADVERTISING PAYMENTS

Money is paid out by a business for its advertising. As you will recall this is recorded on the credit side of the analysed cash book. (**Credit things given.**)

Advertising is an expense of running a business; therefore it will be recorded on the debit side of the expense (advertising) account.

Example

On 1/10/12 Murdel Ltd paid €5,000 by cheque to an advertising agency for its advertising campaign.

ANALYSED CASH BOOK (CREDIT SIDE)				
Date	Details	Chq no.	Bank	Advertising
1/10/12	Advertising agency	5054	5,000	5,000

Dr		ADVERTISING A/C			Cr
Date	Details	€	Date	Details	€
1/10/12	Bank	5,000			

LEARN THE KEY TERMS

- A **market** refers to all the people and institutions involved in the buying and selling of a product.
- **Marketing** means identifying consumers' requirements and identifying how to supply these requirements at a profit.
- **Product development** is the process of creating a new product or altering an existing one.
- A **target market** is a group of consumers identified as being the people most likely to buy a particular product. Advertising and promotion is aimed at this group.
- **Market segmentation** means subdividing the market for a product into specific groups of people who share common characteristics, e.g. young people, middle-aged people and senior citizens.
- **Market research** is the collection and analysis of information about a product and the market for that product.
- **Desk research** is using information that has already been collected.
- **Field research** is gathering new information through research.
- **Advertising** is the communication of information about a product or service to people in general or to a particular group of people that tries to persuade them to buy the product or service.
- **Informative advertising** is advertising that gives useful information to the general public.
- **Persuasive advertising** is advertising that attempts to convince people they need a product.
- **Competitive advertising** is used to convince people that the firm's product is better than that of their competitors.
- **Point-of-sale advertising** is advertising material in the place (shop) where a product is sold.
- **Merchandising** is a very prominent display of a product at the point-of-sale.
- **Branding** means applying a specific name or logo to a company's products to distinguish them from similar products made by other manufacturers.
- **Public relations (PR)** involves establishing and maintaining a good company image in the mind of the public.
- **After-sales service** is the support offered by manufacturers, distributors and retailers to consumers after they have purchased a product.

QUESTIONS

1. What is a market?
2. What is marketing?
3. The marketing mix is sometimes referred to as the 'four Ps'. Name and explain these four Ps.
4. Explain the factors a business must consider when deciding on the price it will charge for a product.
5. What is product development?
6. Name the five sub-divisions of marketing
7. What is market research?
8. What are the aims of market research?
9. What is meant by the term **the target market**?
10. What is market segmentation?
11. Distinguish between desk research and field research. Give two examples of each.
12. What is advertising?
13. What are the aims of advertising?
14. Distinguish between informative, persuasive and competitive advertising. Give an example of each.
15. What is branding?
16. What product(s) do you associate with each of the following logos?

17. What is meant by the term **sales promotion**?
18. Explain any four forms of sales promotion.
19. What is meant by the term **public relations**?
20. What is meant by the term **after-sales service**?

See workbook for more questions.

Work and employment

25

Have you ever noticed that the word **work** is often used to describe two different ideas.

- **Idea 1:** You decide to *work* harder at maths to improve your grade in that subject.
- **Idea 2:** You have a part-time job during the summer holidays and have to go to *work* each evening at 5 pm.

- In the first situation it means you intend to put in a greater effort at maths.
- In the second situation it means you must be at your place of employment by 5 pm.

In both situations you are undertaking some form of work. However, you receive payment in the second situation, but not in the first one.

SO WHAT IS WORK?

Work is *any* activity that requires effort.

It may be physical or mental effort.

WHAT IS EMPLOYMENT?

Employment is any work undertaken for payment.

If I cook a meal at home for my family the effort involved would be classified as work.

If, on the other hand, some naïve person gave me a job in a restaurant to cook a meal for the customers then the effort involved would be classified as employment.

- An employed person is known as an **employee**.
- An **employer** is the person who pays the employee for the work done.

THE LABOUR FORCE

The **labour force** is made up of those people who are working and who are available for work at the present wage rate.

Employment sectors

As economies develop, employment tends to be concentrated in the service sector. Ireland is no exception, as you can see from the following table. Although these are 2008 figures, the percentages do not tend to change much from year to year.

1. PRIMARY SECTOR	2. SECONDARY SECTOR	3. TERTIARY SECTOR
6%	24%	70%

1. The primary sector includes the extractive industries – farming, fishing and mining.
2. The secondary sector includes processing industries, manufacturing and construction.
3. The tertiary sector is made up of service industries (see page 188).

Employees' rights and responsibilites

All employees have both rights and responsibilities.

RIGHTS OF EMPLOYEES	RESPONSIBILITES OF EMPLOYEES
To receive a fair wage for work done.	To work to the best of their ability.
Not to be discriminated against on the basis of gender, religion or race.	To honour any company rules or regulations.
To be provided with a healthy and safe workplace.	Not to reveal confidential information to people outside the business.
To join a trade union.	To respect the property of the business.
To receive the statutory number of holidays.	To implement company policy at all times.

ORGANISATION OF A WORKPLACE

Every workplace must be organised so that each person's role in the organisation is clear. This is usually simple in a very small business where the owner manages the business and gives regular instructions to each of the small number of employees.

However, as a business expands, or in large limited companies, the organisation needs a more formal structure. This is normally depicted on a company's organisational chart.

A **company's organisational chart** outlines the division of the company into departments and shows the chain of command (who gives the orders!)

This organisational chart will vary from business to business, depending on the nature of the work carried out by it. The following example is for a large manufacturing firm.

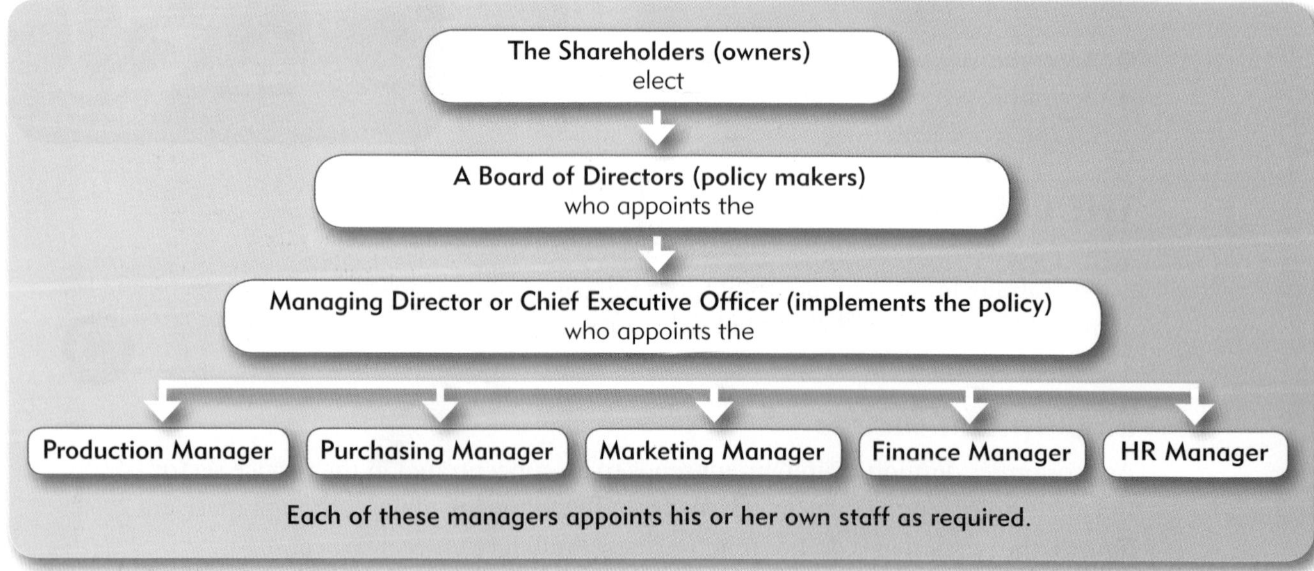

- The **production manager** ensures that the goods are produced to the required quality and in the quantity required at any given time.
- The **purchasing manager** ensures that there is always a sufficient supply of the materials needed by the production department and that these goods are purchased at the best possible price.
- The **marketing manager** undertakes marketing research and finds markets for the goods produced. Advertising and sales promotions are also the marketing manager's responsibility. The marketing manager should be in constant contact with the production manager to ensure that the firm can meet orders as they come in. A firm's reputation can suffer if it cannot deliver, on time, the goods ordered by its customers.
- The **finance manager** ensures that sales incomes are received on time, bills payable are paid at the appropriate time and financial transactions are properly recorded. The finance manager also draws up the final accounts of the business. (These will be dealt with in a later chapter.)
- The **human resources (HR) manager** hires new staff, trains the staff as per company policy and negotiates with trade unions and shop stewards (see Chapter 27) on pay and working conditions.

SELF EMPLOYMENT

Self employment refers to people who seek out paid work for themselves rather than be employed by somebody else.

Self-employed people are prepared to seek out paid work for themselves and invest some money in their own businesses.

ADVANTAGES OF SELF EMPLOYMENT	DISADVANTAGES OF SELF EMPLOYMENT
You make all the decisions concerning the running of the business.	You cannot be an expert in all aspects of a business so are likely to make some bad business decisions.
You can adapt your working hours to meet the needs of your customers.	You may lose all the money invested in your business.
You keep all the profits.	You may have to work long hours on the administration of the business. This extra work does not earn extra money.
Because you keep all the profits there is a great incentive to work hard.	You may find it difficult to take holidays because no money comes in if you are not working.
There can be great self-satisfaction if the business is a success.	If you have to borrow money for your business you may have to use your home as collateral for the loan.

UNEMPLOYMENT

People are regarded as being **unemployed** if they are out of work but available for work at the current wage rate.

Measurements of unemployment

1. The Quarterly National Household Survey (QNHS)

The official level of unemployment is measured by a national survey known as the Quarterly National Household Survey (QNHS).

The survey establishes the number of people in employment and the number of people actively seeking employment. Information is collected, every three months, from 39,000 households. Households are asked to take part in the survey for five consecutive quarters.

2. The Live Register

Because the Quarterly National Household Survey is published only four times a year, the Live Register is the best guide to the level of unemployment each week.

The Live Register is a list of all the people who sign a register each week to claim social welfare benefits. This register (list) includes part-time workers, seasonal and casual workers who are entitled to Jobseeker's Benefit or Allowance, as well as people who are signing on for credits for their old age contributory pension.

Therefore some people on the register are not officially unemployed. The majority of them *are*, however, unemployed.

The figures for the annual average unemployment rate in Ireland are shown below:

IRELAND – ANNUAL AVERAGE UNEMPLOYMENT RATE FOR YEARS ENDING							
2003	2004	2005	2006	2007	2008	2009	2010 (est.)
4.6%	4.4%	4.4%	4.4%	4.6%	6.3%	12.5%	13.5%

These figures show that Ireland had a very low rate of unemployment until 2007. The rate increased dramatically from 2008 onwards.

Causes of unemployment

1. **Structural unemployment:** This arises in situations where industries that were once major employers have gone into decline and there is no longer any demand for the skills of the ex-employees.
2. **Cyclical unemployment:** This a temporary form of unemployment associated with a general fall in demand during a downturn in the economy.
3. **Relocation of multi-national companies:** Multi-national companies, particularly manufacturing companies, tend to locate in countries that offer the lowest wage costs. When they move out of a country they cause unemployment in that country.
4. **Seasonal unemployment:** The demand for some goods and services is seasonal. Therefore little or no production takes place outside of that season. Thus the people working in that industry will have no employment for the off-season. This is evident in the tourist industry in Ireland.
5. **Technology-related unemployment:** This occurs when people are replaced by machines and computers in the workplace.

LEARN THE KEY TERMS

- **Work** is *any* activity that requires effort.
- **Employment** is any work undertaken for payment.
- The **labour force** is made up of those people who are working and who are available for work at the present wage rate.
- A **company's organisational chart** outlines the division of the company into various departments and shows the chain of command (who gives the orders!) throughout the business.
- **Unemployed people** are those people who are out of work but are available for work at the current wage rate.
- The Quarterly National Household Survey (QNHS) is a national survey of 39,000 households used to establish the number of people in employment and the number of people actively seeking employment.
- The **Live Register** is a list of all the people who sign a register each week to claim social welfare benefits.
- **Self employment** refers to people who seek out paid work for themselves rather than be employed by somebody else.

QUESTIONS

1. Distinguish between work and employment.
2. Distinguish between an employer and an employee.
3. What is the labour force?
4. Name any three rights of employees.
5. Name any three responsibilities of employees.
6. What is a company's organisational chart?
7. When is a person deemed to be unemployed?
8. What is the Quarterly National Household Survey?
9. What is the Live Register?
10. What do you understand by the term **self employment**?
11. Describe any three rewards of self employment.
12. Describe any three risks of self employment.

See workbook for more questions.

26 Employers

An **employer** is anybody who pays somebody else to do work.

An employer may be a small sole trader employing one or two people. Or an employer may be a large multi-national company employing thousands of people, such as Intel in Leixlip, Co Kildare, which employs approximately 4,500 people.

Over 360,000 people were employed in the public sector in 2009. This means that the government (both central and local government) is the single biggest employer in Ireland.

Employers, just like employees, have certain right and responsibilities

RIGHTS OF EMPLOYERS	RESPONSIBILITES OF EMPLOYERS
To decide the objectives of the business – remember the Memorandum of Association!	To give each employee, within one month of commencement of employment, a written statement of his/her terms of employment
To organise the business in any manner they want, provided it is done according to existing legislation	To provide a safe and healthy working environment
To expect a fair day's work from each of their employees in return for a fair wage	To provide each employee with a written statement of pay – a payslip. The payslip should show gross pay, deductions and net pay
To set the conditions of employment for their employees	To abide by employment laws, e.g. payment of minimum wage and giving minimum notice of dismissal
To dismiss an employee who has not honoured the terms of employment	Not to discriminate against employees on grounds of gender, religion or race*
To expect loyalty from their employees and expect that they respect the firm's property	To deduct and record PAYE and PRSI (USC) contributions from employees' wages and forward them to the Collector General of Taxes

*EQUAL OPPORTUNITY EMPLOYERS

The Employment Equality Act 2007 prohibits discrimination in employment and training on nine grounds: gender, marital status, family status, sexual orientation, religion, age, disability, race and membership of the Traveller community.

Employers who meet the requirements of the Act are called 'Equal Opportunity Employers'.

RECRUITMENT

Employers follow a certain procedure before they recruit a new employee. This is done to ensure that they recruit the person most suitable to their needs and that they follow all legal procedures concerning recruitment.

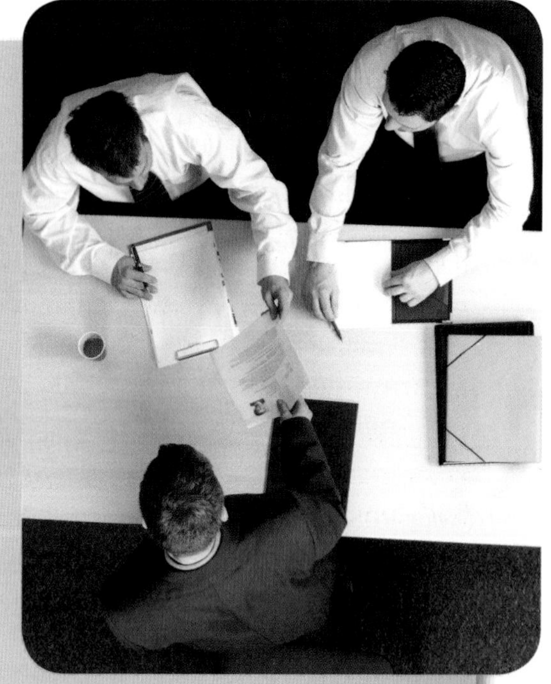

Procedure for employing staff

1. **Draw up a job description.** This would include the following:
   (a) the work the employee will be expected to do
   (b) the wages and other benefits which the employee will receive
   (c) the qualifications and experience required
   (d) commencement date
2. **Advertise the job.** This can be done:
   (a) within the firm
   (b) in local newspapers
   (c) in national newspapers
   (d) in trade magazines
   (e) in employment centres

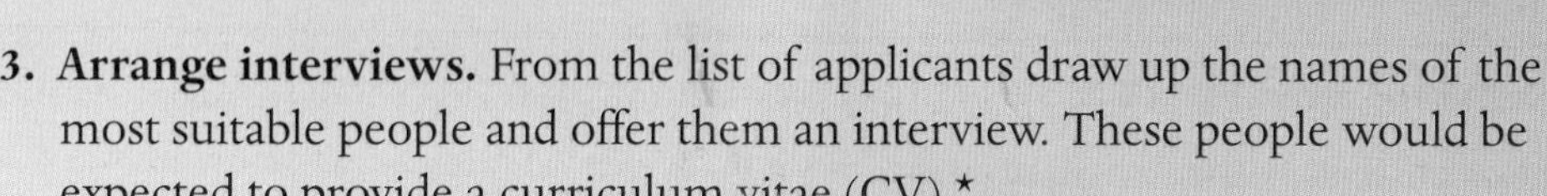

3. **Arrange interviews.** From the list of applicants draw up the names of the most suitable people and offer them an interview. These people would be expected to provide a curriculum vitae (CV).*
4. **Selection.** Having completed the interviews the company should now offer the job to the most suitable candidate. Sometimes it may take a number of interviews to establish this.
5. **Induction.** This means introducing the new employee to all aspects of company policy and also introducing the person to his or her new working colleagues.
6. **Give the new employee written terms of employment.** This is a written document setting out the new employee's terms and conditions of employment. It must be given to him or her within one month of commencing employment.

*A **curriculum vitae** (CV) is a document that outlines a job applicant's relevant work experience and education.

EMPLOYEE RECORDS

Employers are obliged to keep full records of their employees, including details of their income tax and PRSI (USC) contributions.

The **National Employment Rights Authority** (**NERA**), a body that ensures employers comply with employment rights legislation, can demand information on the following:

1. Full name, address and PPS number* for each employee (full-time and part-time)
2. Terms of employment for each employee
3. Payroll details (gross to net, rate per hour, overtime, deductions, shift and other premiums and allowances, commissions and bonuses, service charges, etc.)
4. Copies of payslips
5. Employees' job classification
6. Dates of commencement and, where relevant, termination of employment
7. Hours of work for each employee (including starting and finishing times, meal breaks and rest periods)
8. Register of employees under 18 years of age
9. Whether board and/or lodgings are provided and relevant details
10. Holidays and public holiday entitlements received by each employee
11. Any documentation necessary to demonstrate compliance with employment rights legislation.

Source: http://www.employmentrights.ie/en/aboutnera/

*Your **PPS number** is your Personal Public Service number. Every individual in the State is given a unique PPS number and it is used in all transactions between the individual and State Agencies such as The Revenue Commissioners, Social Welfare Services and Public Health Agencies. It is also used as your Student Identity number in your school and in the Department of Education and Science.

WAGES AND SALARIES

A **salary** is a payment made to an employee that is not dependent on the number of hours worked or the amount of goods produced or sold by the employee in a given period.

A **wage** is a payment made to an employee that is dependent on the number of hours worked or the amount of goods produced or sold by the employee in a given period.

CALCULATION OF WAGES

Wages can be calculated on a time rate, a piece rate or a commission rate.

Time rates

An employee on time rates is paid per hour worked. A higher hourly rate is usually paid for overtime (see Chapter 1).

Piece rates

An employee on piece rates is paid per unit of the good produced. A higher payment per unit produced is usually paid when production exceeds a stated number of units.

Example

Joe Smith, a block layer, is paid €0.50 per block laid. If he lays more than 3,000 blocks per week he receives an additional payment of €0.10 for each extra block. In a given week he laid 3,200 blocks. Calculate his gross pay for that week.

Solution

Production	Payment
3,000 blocks @ €0.50 per block	€1,500
200 blocks @ €0.60 per block	€120
GROSS WAGE	**€1,620**

Commission rates

An employee on commission rates is paid per unit of goods sold by the employee plus a small basic wage.

Example

Bríd Byrne is a salesperson for a company supplying a satellite TV service. She is paid a basic wage of €150 per week and receives €80 for every household who buys this service from her. In a given week she enlisted 7 households to buy this service. Calculate her gross wage for that week.

Solution

Basic wage	€150
7 enlisted households @ €80	€560
GROSS WAGE	**€710**

Calculation of PAYE

At the start of the tax year, the Revenue Commissioners send a Notice or Certificate to all employees showing the rates of tax that applies to the employee's income and the tax credits that reduce the tax payable. The size of the tax credit depends on the employee's circumstances, e.g. if he or she is married or single, if he or she has any incapacitated children or if he or she is paying third level college fees for a son or daughter.

Currently there are two tax rates in Ireland, the standard tax rate of 20% and the higher tax rate of 41%. **These rates can change from year to year.**

Once your income goes above a certain level (**the standard cut-off point**), the remainder of your income is taxed at the higher rate.

Example 1: Yearly tax

Joe Smith's income for the year is €60,000. The standard cut-off point is €36,000. The standard rate of tax is 20% and the higher rate is 41%. He has a tax credit of €1,200.

Workings

€36,000 @ 20%	€7,200
€24,000 (€60,000 less €36,000) @ 41%	€9,840
Gross tax	€17,040
Less tax credit	€1,200
Tax payable for the year	**€15,840**

Tax levies

A tax levy is an **addition** to the tax paid under the PAYE system and can be changed at any time. In the tax year 2009 a new 2% income tax levy was introduced on most incomes.

In the previous example this is 2% of the gross wage of €60,000 = €1,200, which brings the total tax payable to €17,040.

Example 2: Monthly tax

If Joe is paid monthly divide his annual income, the standard cut-off point and the tax credit by 12.This gives a monthly income of €5,000, a standard cut-off point of €3,000 and a tax credit of €100.

Workings	
€3,000 @ 20%	€600
€2,000@ 41% (€5,000 less €3,000)	€820
Gross tax	€1,420
Less tax credit	€100
Tax payable for the month	**€1,320**

If the income levy of 2% is applied to this example then an extra €100 would be paid in tax, i.e. 2% of the monthly income of €5,000.

If Joe was paid weekly you would divide his annual income, the standard cut-off point and the tax credit by 52 and then apply these figures in the same way.

Deductions

Below is an example of Joe Smith's monthly wages slip, taking account of his other deductions as explained in Chapter 1, i.e. the statutory and voluntary deductions.

You will recall that **statutory deductions** are the ones that, by law, must be taken from the gross wage. **Voluntary deductions** are those agreed between the employer and the employee.

22/10/2010		**WAGE SLIP – JOE SMITH**		**PERIOD 5**
Pay	€	Deductions	€	
Basic	€5,000	PAYE	€1,320	
		PRSI (USC)	€375	
		VHI	€150	
		Pension	€300	**Net pay**
Gross pay	€5,000	**Total deductions**	€1,845	€3,155

THE WAGES BOOK

Employers record all details of wages paid in a wages book. This records the basic pay, overtime where applicable, all deductions and the net pay of each employee **as well as** the employer's PRSI (USC) contribution.

The **total cost of wages to the employer** is the employee's gross wage plus the employer's PRSI (USC) contribution.

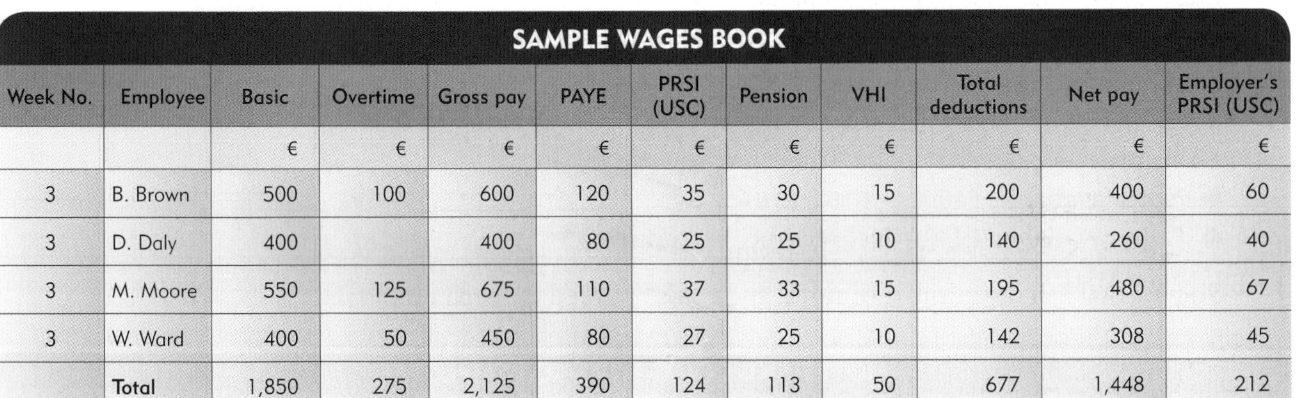

SAMPLE WAGES BOOK

Week No.	Employee	Basic	Overtime	Gross pay	PAYE	PRSI (USC)	Pension	VHI	Total deductions	Net pay	Employer's PRSI (USC)
		€	€	€	€	€	€	€	€	€	€
3	B. Brown	500	100	600	120	35	30	15	200	400	60
3	D. Daly	400		400	80	25	25	10	140	260	40
3	M. Moore	550	125	675	110	37	33	15	195	480	67
3	W. Ward	400	50	450	80	27	25	10	142	308	45
	Total	1,850	275	2,125	390	124	113	50	677	1,448	212

The total cost of wages to the employer is the gross pay of €2,125 plus employer's PRSI (USC) of €212 = €2,337.

Recording the payment of wages

Wages are an expense of running a business. Thus when wages are paid, the amount paid is credited in the analysed cash book (money given) and debited to the *Wages* account.

Example

Assume the wages paid total €10,000.

ANALYSED CASH BOOK (CREDIT SIDE)

Date	Details	Chq no.	Bank	Wages
1/1/12	Wages	234567	€10,000	€10,000

Dr — WAGES A/C — Cr

Date	Details	€	Date	Details	€
1/1/12	Bank	€10,000			

PAYMENT OF WAGES

Employees may be paid in cash, by cheque or by Paypath.

Payment by cash

When employees are paid in cash the employer has to make out a **wages cash analysis statement** to ensure that the correct amount of cash is collected from the bank for each employee and that each employee receives the minimum number of notes and coins in the wage packets.

Although our notes range in value from €500 to €5, employers rarely use notes higher in value than €50. Therefore in the following example we assume the following notes and coins are available.

Example

- **Notes available:** €50, €20, €10 and €5
- **Coins available:** €2, €1, 50c, 20c, 10c, 5c, 2c and 1c

Step1: Establish the number of notes and coins required for **each employee**.

NOTES AND COINS FOR EACH EMPLOYEE

		€	€	€	€	€	€	€	€	€	€	€	€
Employee	**Net wage**	50	20	10	5	2	1	0.50	0.20	0.10	0.05	0.02	0.01
B. Byrne	540.26	10	2						1		1		1
F. Flynn	488.25	9	1	1	1	1	1		1		1		
H. Horan	573.23	11	1			1	1		1			1	1
M. Moore	535.60	10	1	1	1	—	—	1	—	1	—	—	—
Total	**2,137.34**	**40**	**5**	**2**	**2**	**2**	**2**	**1**	**3**	**1**	**2**	**1**	**2**

Step 2: Make a list of the **total number** of notes and coins required. Ensure that the total value of these notes and coins equals the total net wages.

TOTAL NUMBER OF NOTES AND COINS

€50 × 40	€2,000.00
€20 × 5	€100.00
€10 × 2	€20.00
€5 × 2	€10.00
€2 × 2	€4.00
€1 × 2	€2.00
50c × 1	€0.50
20c × 3	€0.60
10c × 1	€0.10
5c × 2	€0.10
2c × 1	€0.02
1c × 2	€0.02
Total	**€2,137.34**

Step 3: Take the list to the bank and withdraw the required number of notes and coins from the employer's bank account.

Step 4: On returning from the bank fill a wage packet for each employee, inserting the number of notes and coins as indicated in the wages cash analysis statement. Insert a wage slip in each wage packet before handing them to the employees.

Employers who employ large numbers of employees dislike paying wages by cash for the following reasons:

1. the extra work involved in preparing the wages cash analysis statement
2. the danger to people collecting large sums of cash from the banks
3. the danger of having large sums of cash on the business premises at any given time
4. the possibility that employees could lose their wage packets

Payment by cheque

Payment of wages by cheque eliminates all the problems associated with payment by cash. On completion of the wages book, the employer simply makes out cheques for each employee for their net wages. The employees can lodge the cheques to their own bank accounts or can cash or sell the cheques (see Chapter 10) if they require cash.

Payment by Paypath

Paypath is becoming an increasingly popular method of paying wages. You should recall from Chapter 9 that Paypath is an electronic means of transferring an employee's wages from the employer's bank account to an employee's bank account. This has many advantages.

1. It eliminates all the problems associated with payment by cash.
2. The employer does not have to make out cheques for each individual employee.
3. The employees do not run the risk of losing their cash or cheques.
4. The employees do not have to go to a bank to lodge or cash their cheques.
5. The wages are lodged instantly to the employees' bank accounts, which could earn interest for them or reduce overdraft charges.
6. Employees can access the amount of cash they require at any ATM at any time.

The Paypath system is, of course, dependent on all the employees having bank accounts.

FLEXITIME

Flexitime is a system that allows employees, within limits, to choose when to work the required number of hours for their basic pay.

Example

An employee is required to work 40 hours a week for his or her basic wage. Assume a one-hour break each day.

- The employee may opt to work from 7 am to 4 pm on Monday and Tuesday (16 hours).
- On Wednesday the employee may opt to work from 10 am to 5 pm (6 hours).
- On Thursday the employee may opt to work from 7 am to 6 pm (10 hours).
- On Friday the employee may work from 9 am to 5 pm (8 hours).

This gives a total of 40 hours worked.

Some employers may insist that the employee attends work each day between set hours, e.g. 10 am to 3 pm, and can then work the remaining hours at times suitable to the employee.

LEARN THE KEY TERMS

- An **employer** is anybody who pays somebody else to do work.
- A **curriculum vitae (CV)** is a document sent by a person applying for a job to a potential employer that outlines the applicant's relevant work experience and education.
- The **National Employment Rights Authority (NERA)** is a body that ensures all employers comply with employment rights legislation.
- A **salary** is a payment made to an employee that ***is not*** dependent on the number of hours worked or the amount of goods produced or sold by the employee in a given period.
- A **wage** is a payment made to an employee that ***is*** dependent on the number of hours worked or the amount of goods produced or sold by the employee in a given period.
- A **time rate** means wages are calculated on a payment per hour worked by the employee.
- A **piece rate** means wages are calculated on a payment per unit of the good produced by the employee.
- A **commission rate** means wages are calculated on a payment per unit of the good sold by the employee (usually plus a small basic wage).
- A **wages cash analysis statement** is used to ensure that the correct amount of cash is collected from the bank for each employee and that each employee receives the minimum number of notes and coins in the wage packets.
- **Flexitime** is a system that allows employees, within limits, to choose when to work the required number of hours for their basic pay.

QUESTIONS

1. Explain three rights of employers.
2. Explain three responsibilities of employers.
3. Outline the six steps involved in the procedure for employing staff.
4. Name any five items of information about employees that must be recorded by employers.
5. What is the difference between a salary and a wage?
6. Name three different methods by which wages could be calculated.
7. What is a wages cash analysis statement?
8. Jenny Murphy worked 50 hours in a given week. She is paid €12 per hour for a standard 40-hour week and is paid at time-and-a-half for overtime. Calculate, showing all your calculations, her gross wage for that week.
9. Gerard Green is a fruit-picker. He receives a basic wage of €100 per week and is paid 50 cent for the first 200 punnets of strawberries he fills and 75 cent for every punnet in excess of 200. In a particular week he filled 400 punnets of strawberries. Calculate, showing all your calculations, his gross wage for that week.
10. Darach Dunne is a TV salesman who is paid on a commission basis only. Each week he is paid €40 for the first 5 TVs he sells and €50 for each extra TV after that. Darach sells an average of 10 TVs each week.
    - (a) Calculate, showing all your calculations, his average gross weekly income.
    - (b) Darach's employer offered to change his conditions of employment, offering a guaranteed minimum weekly wage of €250 and €15 for every TV he sold. Should Darach accept this offer, assuming his average sales remained at 10 TVs per week? Give a detailed explanation of your answer.
11. Juliet Jones's income for the year is €25,000. The standard cut-off point is €36,000. The standard rate of tax is 20% and the higher rate is 41%. She has a tax credit of €1,500. Calculate the amount of PAYE payable by Juliet in that year, assuming there is also a 1% tax levy on all income. Show all your calculations.
12. Joe Jevin's income for the year is €90,000. The standard cut-off point is €36,000. The standard rate of tax is 20% and the higher rate is 41%. He has a tax credit of €1,200. Calculate the amount of PAYE payable by Joe in that year. Show all your calculations.
13. Katie Cline has an annual income of €96,000 that is paid on a monthly basis. The annual standard cut-off point is €36,000. Calculate the gross **monthly** PAYE payable by Katie assuming the standard rate of tax is 20% and the higher rate of tax is 41%.

See workbook for more questions.

27 Industrial relations

Industrial relations is the term used to describe the relationship between management and workers in a firm.

It is important to have a good working relationship between management and workers in a firm because:

1. Workers know they can discuss and solve their problems with the management quickly and in a friendly manner.
2. Managers know they can outline the problems facing the company at any given time and get the cooperation of the workers to solve these problems.
3. Cooperation between workers and management normally leads to a high level of production in the firm.
4. The increase in productivity may lead to an increase in profits and wages.

A poor working relationship between management and workers leads to:

1. Suspicion and lack of cooperation between workers and management
2. A decrease in the rate of production
3. Industrial action, which may cause the closure of the firm
4. A poor public image of the firm, which could result in the loss of customers.

Workers are normally represented in industrial relations by a trade union. Management is usually represented by the human resources manager.

TRADE UNIONS

A **trade union** is an organisation of workers set up to protect and improve their conditions of employment.

Functions of a trade union

1. To protect the members' jobs
2. To improve members' working conditions
3. To secure pay increases for members
4. To represent workers in an industrial dispute

A **shop steward** is a worker elected by fellow workers to represent the trade union in the work place.

Functions of a shop steward

1. To recruit new members to the union
2. To organise the collection of union dues
3. To represent the workers in talks with management
4. To ensure that all agreements between management and unions are honoured

There are many trade unions in Ireland. However, for convenience purposes they are categorised under the following headings.

Different types of trade unions

1. **Craft trade unions** represent people of the same trade or skill, e.g. the National Union of Sheet Metal Workers of Ireland and the Technical Engineering and Electrical Union (TEEU).
2. **Industrial trade unions** represent all employees in a particular industry regardless of the nature of their employment, e.g. Electricity Supply Board's Officers' Association (ESBOA).
3. **General trade unions** represent all categories of workers in all industries, e.g. the Services, Industrial, Professional and Technical Union (SIPTU) and UNITE.
4. **White-collar trade unions** represent people who work in office jobs or work in the services industries, e.g. Irish Bank Officials' Association (IBOA), Association of Secondary Teachers, Ireland (ASTI) and Irish Nurses' Organisation (INO).

Irish Congress of Trade Unions (ICTU)

The Irish Congress of Trade Unions is a representative body for most trade unions in Ireland. There were 55 unions affiliated to Congress in 2008 with a total membership of 833,486, of whom 602,035 were in the Republic and 231,451 in Northern Ireland.

The role of ICTU in industrial relations is to:

1. Negotiate national wage agreements with the government and employers on behalf of trade unions
2. Help to resolve disputes between unions and employers
3. Help to resolve inter-union disputes.

IRISH BUSINESS AND EMPLOYERS CONFEDERATION (IBEC)

The Irish Business and Employers Confederation is a representative body that promotes the interests of businesses and employers in Ireland.

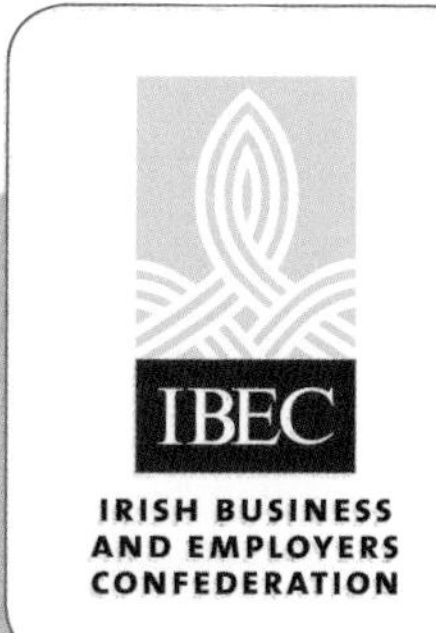

The role of IBEC in industrial relations is to:

1. Negotiate national wage agreements with the government and trade unions on behalf of employers
2. Give advice to employers concerning their rights and obligations in industrial disputes
3. Represent employers on Labour Court Committees

COMMON CAUSES OF INDUSTRIAL DISPUTES

1. **Disputes about wages and conditions of employment:** these arise if employees' demand for a wage increase or shorter working week is not met.
2. **Demarcation disputes:** these arise when there is disagreement between employees concerning the tasks to be performed by them. For instance, electricians may insist that no unqualified electrician may change a fuse in a plug and will not cooperate with these unqualified workers if they do so.
3. **Redundancies:** some employees may be made redundant (lose their jobs) when there is insufficient work for them. This often leads to disputes about redundancy payments or about which employees should be made redundant.
4. **Dismissal of workers:** these disputes may arise if the fellow-workers of a sacked employee feel that the person was unfairly sacked.
5. **Promotional procedures:** these disputes may arise if some workers feel that a particular worker was treated more favourably than others in the selection process for promotion.

Procedures for resolving disputes

If employees have a problem at work they try to resolve it by following the procedure laid out below. Remember that the procedure will only go from stage 1 to stage 2 if the problem has not been resolved at stage 1. Likewise the procedure will only go on to stage 3 if it has not been resolved at stage 2 and so on.

1. Workers discuss their problem with their supervisors.
2. Shop steward discusses problem with human resources manager.
3. Union official from the trade union discusses with management.
4. A third party provides a conciliation service, i.e. the two sides agree to discuss the issue with an unbiased third party. (See following notes on Equality Officers, Rights Commissioners, The Labour Court and The Employment Appeals Tribunal.)
5. Both sides agree to appoint an arbitrator from the Labour Court.
6. If all the above procedures do not resolve the dispute then it may result in industrial action.

Forms of industrial action

1. **An official strike**
   - Here the members of the union hold a secret ballot.
   - The union then gives the company notice of strike action.
   - The members may receive strike pay, i.e. a payment made from union funds to those on strike.
2. **All-out strike**
   - This is an official strike that is supported by other trade unions and approved by ICTU.
3. **An unofficial strike**
   - Here the workers go on strike without the approval of their trade union.
   - They do not receive any strike pay from the union.
4. **A wild-cat or lightning strike**
   - This is similar to an unofficial strike but no notice of strike is given.
5. **A work to rule**
   - This is a situation where workers remain in work but only carry out the essential elements of their employment. This slows down production and causes great inconvenience for the employer.

INSTITUTIONS INVOLVED IN INDUSTRIAL RELATIONS

The Labour Relations Commission (LRC)

The LRC was set up in 1990 under the Industrial Relations Act 1990 to improve industrial relations and to help settle industrial disputes. It provides a **conciliation** service during a dispute.

Conciliation means that an independent person works with the opposing parties in a dispute with the aim of helping them to reach an agreement, i.e. reconciling their differences.

Arbitration is the process of resolving disputes by referring the issue to a third party who makes a judgment on the dispute.

Equality Officers

Equality Officers are appointed by the Labour Relations Commission to provide a conciliation service for equality matters in employment, e.g. to ensure that employees are not discriminated against because of their race, religion or gender.

Rights Commissioners

Rights Commissioners are appointed by the Labour Relations Commission to provide an informal and quick resolution to disputes between individual (or small groups of) employees and employers on any issues other than equality.

The Labour Court

The **Labour Court** is a tribunal (a body that is set up to make a judgment) used to attempt to resolve disputes that could not be resolved by the Labour Relations Commission.

The Labour Court is a court of last resort, i.e. cases are referred to it only when all other efforts to resolve a dispute have failed. It listens to the arguments put forward by both sides to the dispute and makes a recommendation. This is known as **arbitration**.

The Employment Appeals Tribunal

The Employment Appeals Tribunal is an independent body that deals with disputes where employees think their employment rights have been infringed (ignored) in areas such as redundancies, alleged unfair dismissals and maternity leave.

LEARN THE KEY TERMS

- **Industrial relations** is the term used to describe the relationship between management and workers in a firm.
- A **trade union** is an organisation of workers set up to protect and improve their conditions of employment.
- A **shop steward** is a worker elected by fellow workers to represent the trade union in the actual place of work.
- **Craft trade unions** are unions that represent people of the same trade or skill.
- **Industrial trade unions** are unions that represent all employees in a particular industry regardless of the nature of their employment.
- **General trade unions** represent all categories of workers in all industries.
- **White-collar trade unions** represent people who work in either office jobs or service industries.
- The **Irish Congress of Trade Unions (ICTU)** is a representative body for most trade unions in Ireland.
- The **Irish Business and Employers Confederation (IBEC)** is a representative body that promotes the interests of businesses and employers in Ireland.
- **Conciliation** means that an independent person works with the opposing parties in a dispute with the aim of helping them to reach an agreement.
- **Arbitration** is the process of resolving disputes by referring the issue to a third party who makes a judgment on the dispute.
- The **Labour Relations Commission (LRC)** aims to improve industrial relations and to help settle industrial disputes.
- **Equality Officers** are appointed by the Labour Relations Commission to provide a conciliation service for equality matters in employment.
- **Rights Commissioners** provide an informal and quick resolution to disputes between individual (or small groups of) employees and employers on issues other than equality.
- The **Labour Court** is a tribunal used to attempt to resolve disputes that could not be resolved by the Labour Relations Commission.
- The **Employment Appeals Tribunal** is an independent body that deals with disputes where employees think their employment rights have been infringed.

QUESTIONS

1. What is meant by the term **industrial relations**?
2. Outline three advantages of a good working relationship between management and workers in a firm.
3. What is a trade union?
4. What are the functions of a trade union?
5. What is a shop steward?
6. What are the functions of a shop steward?
7. Describe four different types of trade unions in Ireland and name an example of each.
8. What is the role of the Irish Congress of Trade Unions (ICTU) in industrial relations?
9. What is the role of the Irish Business and Employers Conference (IBEC) in industrial relations?
10. Explain any three common causes of industrial disputes.
11. Outline the five normal stages in resolving disputes before industrial action is taken by employees.
12. Distinguish between an official strike and an unofficial strike.
13. What is a work to rule?
14. What is a wild-cat strike?
15. Distinguish between conciliation and arbitration.
16. What are the functions of the Labour Relations Commission?
17. What is an Equality Officer?
18. What is a Rights Commissioner?
19. What is the Labour Court?
20. What forms of dispute are dealt with by the Employment Appeals Tribunal?

See workbook for more questions.

28 Communication

When people communicate properly with each other, ideas, messages or facts can be exchanged clearly between them.

If I am speaking with another person on the telephone we will communicate properly only if that person is listening attentively and I am expressing myself clearly.

Communication is the transfer of ideas, messages or facts between people.

MEANS OF COMMUNICATION

There are two basic means by which we communicate with each other:

- Oral communication
- Written communication

These two means of communication can be enhanced with visual forms of communication such as graphs, bar charts, pictures and PowerPoint® presentations.

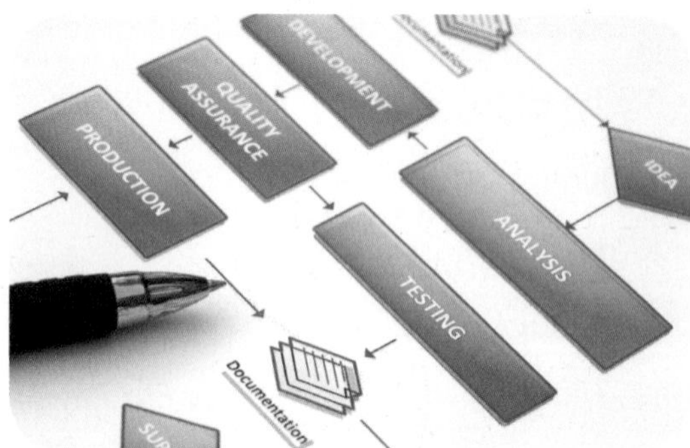

Examples of oral communication

1. **One-to-one (person-to-person) conversations**
2. **One-to-one telephone conversations**
3. **Intercom system:** allows people within a restricted area (e.g. within a factory or a stadium) to speak to each other or to make announcements that are heard within that area. (*Intercom* is an abbreviation for *internal communication*).
4. **Meetings:** a number of people gathering together in one place to discuss something.
5. **Videoconferences:** use audio and video links to allow people located in different places to see and speak to each other via the Internet.
6. **Teleconferences:** use audio links to allow people located in different places to speak to each other.

ORAL COMMUNICATION	
Advantages	**Disadvantages**
Speed: it is a quick and easy way to exchange information.	There is no record of the conversation or agreements reached (with the exception of the minutes of formal meetings).
Direct questions cannot be ignored.	People may make hasty decisions in order to save time.
Clarifications can be sought and given instantly.	People may easily forget essential details of a conversation and later disagree on the outcome.
It is relatively easy, when attending meetings, to judge other people's reactions to suggestions by observing their facial expressions (sometimes referred to as 'eyeballing').	

Examples of written communication

1. **Board notices**
2. **Memos:** short notes circulated to people within an organisation to act as reminders or instructions
3. **E-mail (electronic mail):** mail or letters that are sent and received via the Internet
4. **Facsimiles (fax):** documents are copied and sent via telephone networks or the Internet
5. **Text messaging**
6. **Letters:** see next page
7. **Business documents:** see Chapter 29
8. **Reports:** see page 242
9. **Newspapers and magazines:** for advertising and publicity purposes
10. **Websites**

WRITTEN COMMUNICATION	
Advantages	**Disadvantages**
There is a permanent record of views and opinions expressed.	Slows down decision-making as much time may be lost in exchanging correspondence.
People have time to give serious consideration to points raised before replying.	Correspondence received may be ignored.
	Confidential information that is kept on files may fall into the wrong hands.

Letter writing

Letters should always be as brief and clear as possible. They should be written in simple language (except, of course, in cases where technical information is being exchanged between people who understand that technical language).

A formal letter should contain the following:

1. Sender's contact details
2. Date
3. Full name (or title) and address of the addressee (the person to whom the letter is being sent)
4. Salutation, e.g. *Dear John* or *Dear Sir or Madam*
5. Introductory paragraph
6. Main body of letter, giving full details of the purpose of the letter
7. Brief paragraph outlining the expected response to the letter
8. A final paragraph giving any other relevant information
9. Closure: *Yours sincerely/Yours faithfully*

Example of a formal letter

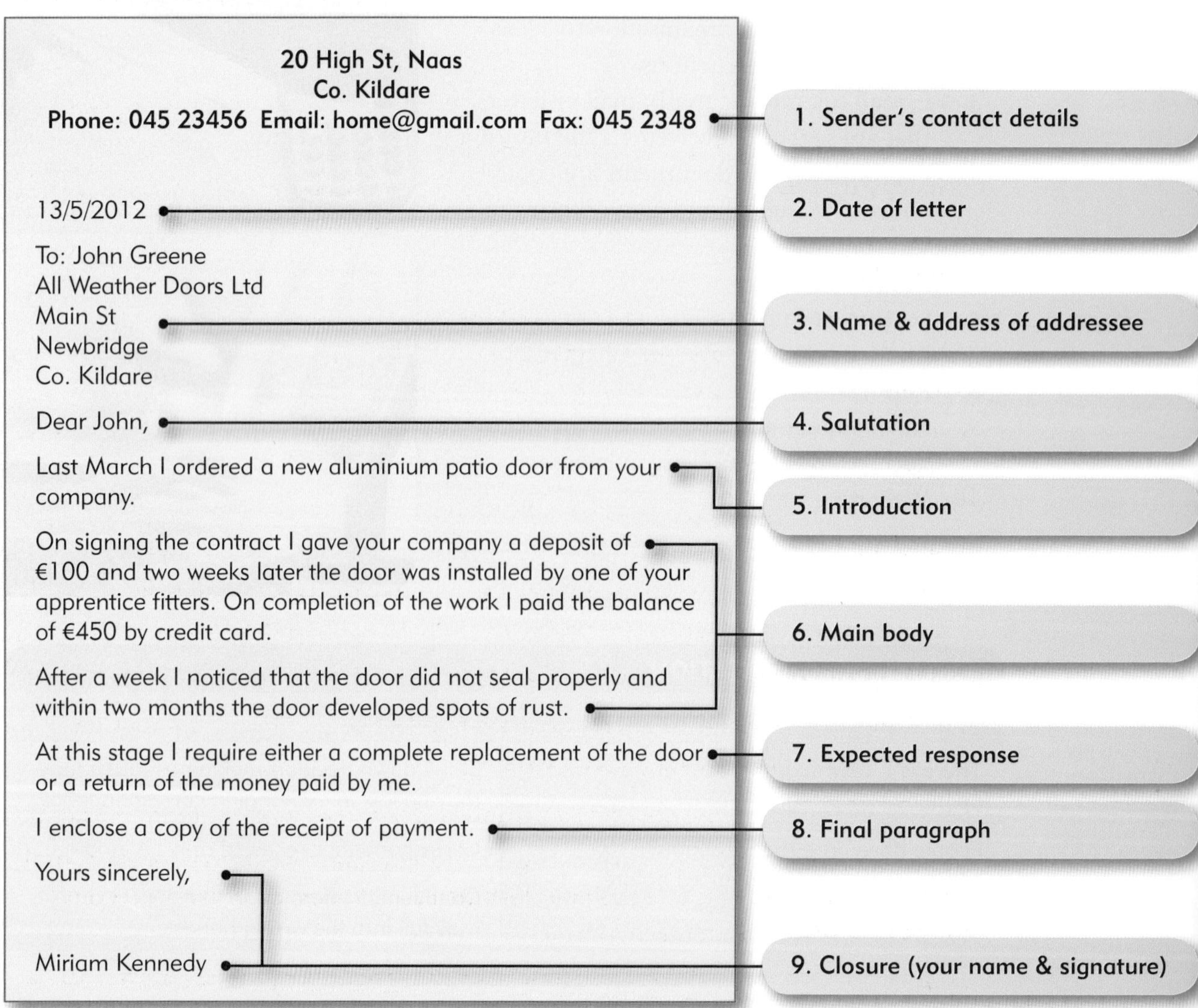

20 High St, Naas
Co. Kildare
Phone: 045 23456 Email: home@gmail.com Fax: 045 2348

13/5/2012

To: John Greene
All Weather Doors Ltd
Main St
Newbridge
Co. Kildare

Dear John,

Last March I ordered a new aluminium patio door from your company.

On signing the contract I gave your company a deposit of €100 and two weeks later the door was installed by one of your apprentice fitters. On completion of the work I paid the balance of €450 by credit card.

After a week I noticed that the door did not seal properly and within two months the door developed spots of rust.

At this stage I require either a complete replacement of the door or a return of the money paid by me.

I enclose a copy of the receipt of payment.

Yours sincerely,

Miriam Kennedy

INTERNAL AND EXTERNAL COMMUNICATION

- **Internal communication** is any form of communication that allows people *within* an organisation to communicate with each other.
- **External communication** is any form of communication that allows people in one organisation to communicate with people *outside* of that organisation.

Internal communication involves:

1. A **downward flow of information**, i.e. from the Board of Directors down to the general employees.
2. An **upward flow of information**, i.e. from the general employees up to the Board of Directors.
3. A **lateral flow of information**, i.e. the flow of information between people who are working at the same level within the firm. This could be between two people working in the accounts department, or between the managers of the production and the sales departments. This is sometimes called a sideways flow of information.

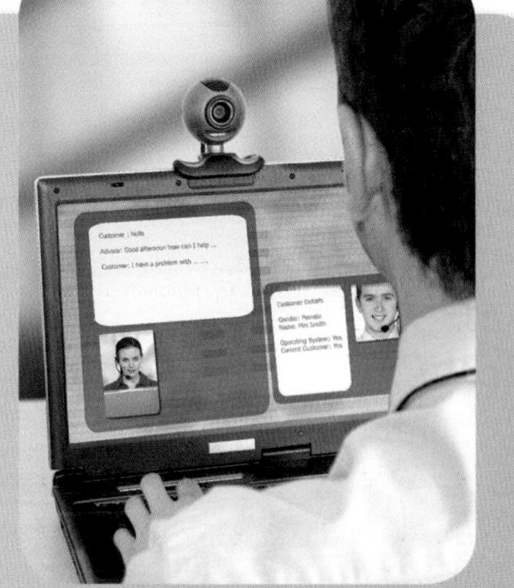

External communication involves:

1. The flow of information between a **firm and its customers**.
2. The flow of information between a **firm and its suppliers**.
3. The flow of information between a **firm and the government**, e.g. re taxes and grants.
4. The flow of information between a **firm and its shareholders**, e.g. AGMs and annual reports.
5. The flow of information between a **firm and its banks**.
6. The flow of information between a **firm and the general public**, e.g. by means of advertising, sales promotions or general sponsorship.

The oral and written forms of communication listed on pages 236 and 237 may be internal or external depending on their usage.

- Memos and noticeboards are exclusively **internal** forms of written communication.
- Videoconferences and teleconferences are almost exclusively **external** forms of **oral** communication. Letters and business documents are almost exclusively **external** forms of **written** communication.
- However, telephone and text communications may be either internal or external means of communication.

VISUAL AIDS TO COMMUNICATION

Line graphs

Line graphs are a convenient way to present summaries of trends in a visual form. When drawing graphs, always ensure that both axes are properly labelled and the graph has a title.

The following graph shows the trend in a firm's sales from the first to the last quarter of the year.

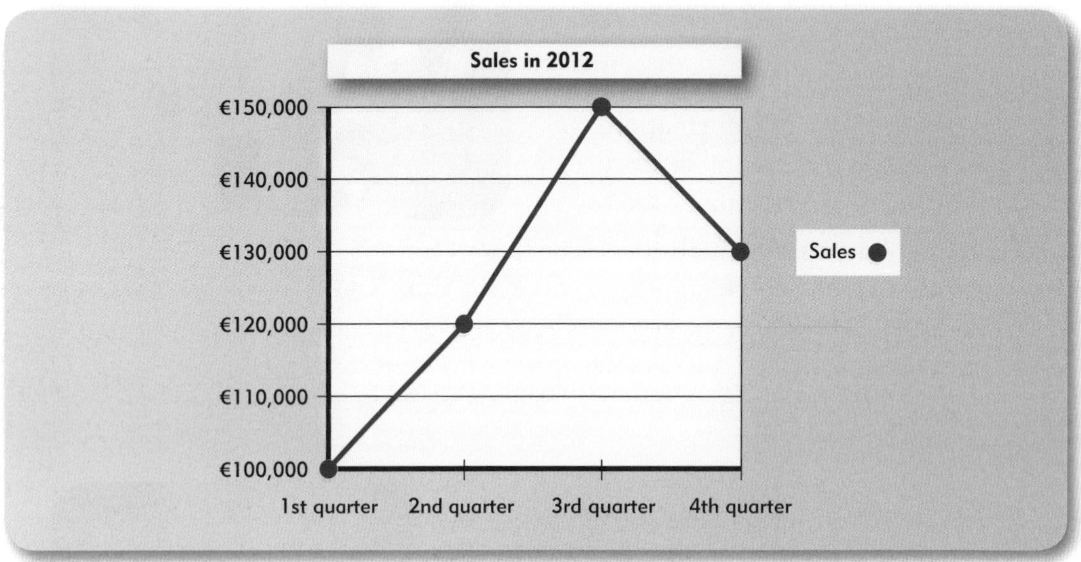

Bar charts

Bar charts are a convenient way to show comparisons.

The following bar chart shows the percentage sales achieved in each region in 2011 and 2012.

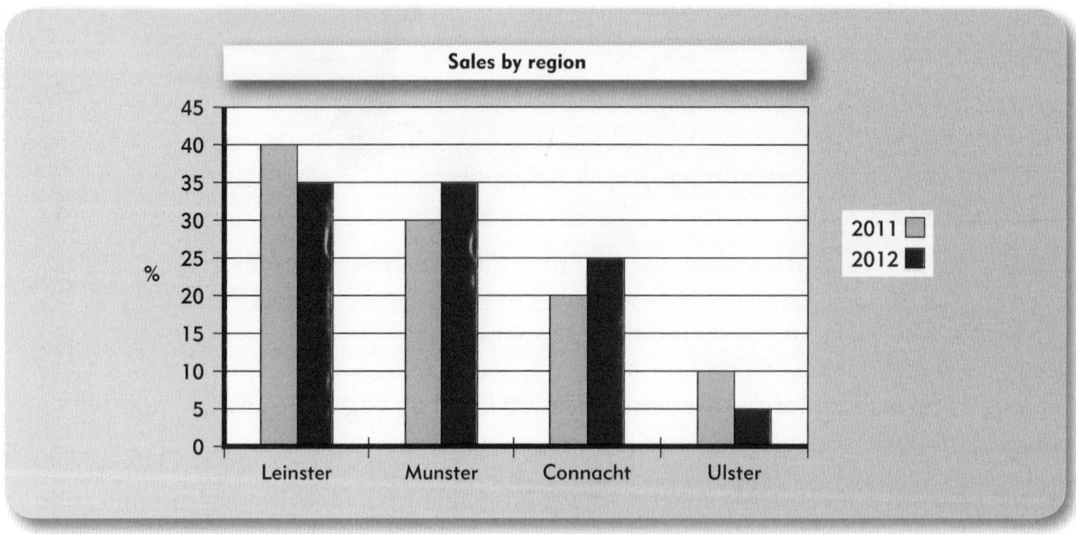

Pie charts

Pie charts are used to show the components of a total figure.

The following pie chart shows (for demonstration purposes only) the percentage of national income earned by each of the factors of production in Ireland in 2012.

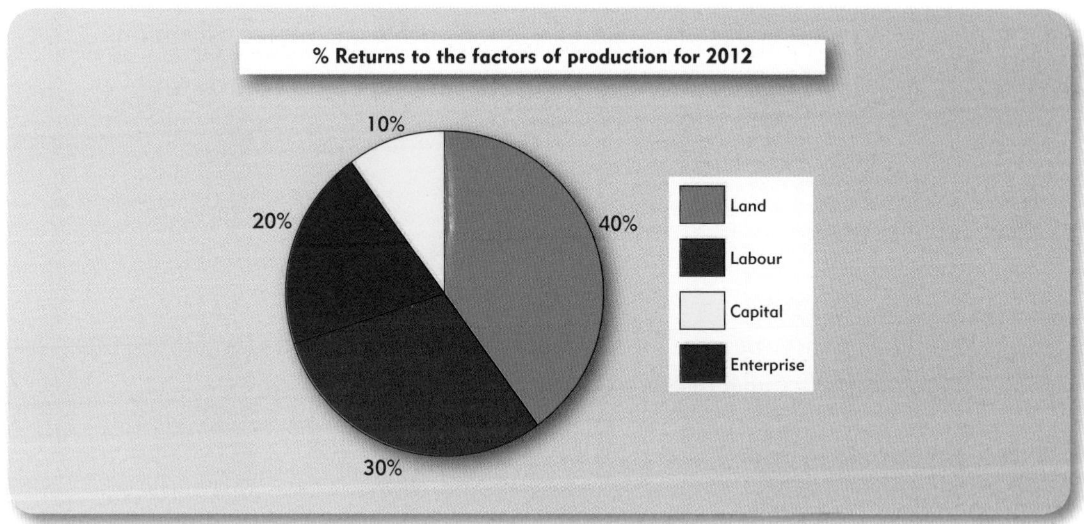

Pictograms

A pictogram is a chart or diagram that uses symbols or objects to represent a value.

Each car shown below represents sales of €10,000.

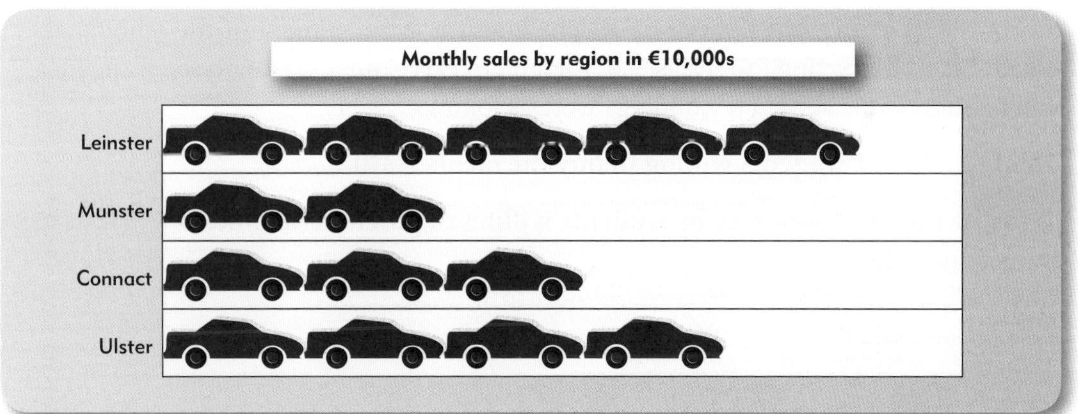

PowerPoint® presentations

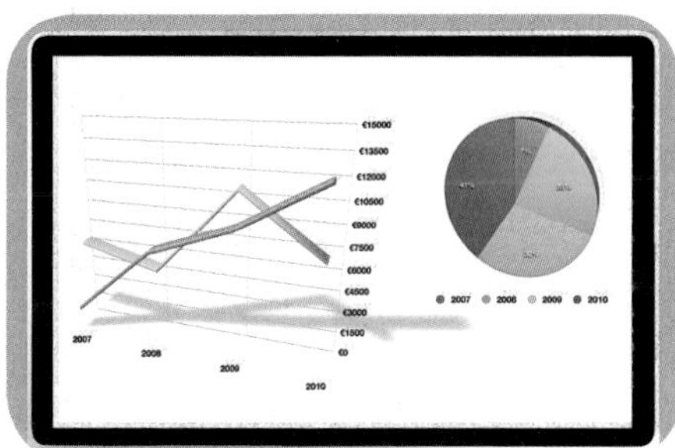

These are computer-generated slide shows that can contain one or a combination of the following: words, diagrams, animations and sound effects. They are particularly useful during meetings to break the monotony that could be created by one person speaking for a long time.

REPORT WRITING

A **report** is a written account of the outcome of an examination or analysis of a particular topic.

The content of a report is *similar* to that of a letter, with some minor exceptions. It should contain:

1. Sender's contact details
2. Date
3. Full name (or title) and address of the addressee
4. Title. In the example shown on page 243 this is *Report re: Viability of proposal to provide hot meals in school*
5. Terms of reference (purpose of the report). In the example this is *Arising from your instructions we undertook a survey of the pupils in your school*
6. Main body of report should outline the methodology followed and, where applicable, calculations used
7. Recommendations based on the report's contents
8. Formal closure

Example

from Junior Certificate 2001, Paper 2, Question 3

Oakfield Second Level School, situated three kilometres from the nearest town, has five hundred students. The school is considering providing students with hot meals at lunchtime, at a price of €1.50 per meal. The Board of Management of the school has asked P & M Marketing Ltd, Naas, Co. Kildare, to carry out a survey to see if the idea will be successful. The survey findings were as follows:

Total number of students willing to buy the meals 350

Types of hot food preferred by students willing to purchase the meals

Burger and chips	210
Chicken curry and rice	91
Lasagne and salad	49

Cost of meals

Food	€0.95 per meal
Other costs	€0.30 per meal

Assume you are Patricia Moore, Marketing Consultant, P & M Marketing Ltd. Prepare a **report on today's date**, for the Board of Management of Oakfield Second Level School. Your report should include:

(i) The percentage of students in the school willing to purchase hot meals
(ii) The percentage of students requiring the different types of meals
(iii) The daily profit to be made by the school if 350 meals are sold
(iv) **Three** suitable methods of promoting the hot meals in the school
(v) Recommendation, with reason, on whether or not to go ahead with the provision of hot meals.

Solution

1. Contact details

2. Date

3. Addressee

4. Report title

5. Terms of reference

6. Main body

Note: This report contains a **visual aid**. This form of aid should be used where it is convenient to do so. However, you do not have to include any such visual aids in a Junior Certificate examination question unless you are requested to do so.

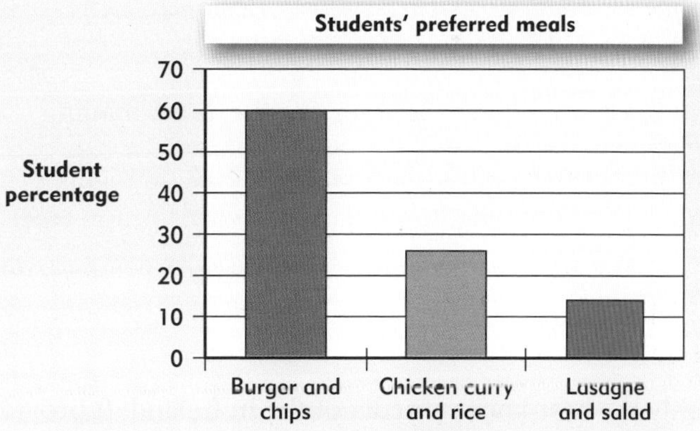

7. Recommendations

8. Formal closure

P & M Marketing Ltd
Naas, Co. Kildare

31/12/2012

To: The Board of Management
Oakfield Secondary School

Report re: Viability of proposal to provide hot meals in school

Arising from your instructions we undertook a survey of the pupils in your school and established the following facts:

RESEARCH FINDINGS

70% (350) of the pupils are willing to purchase hot meals.

Of these 60% (210 of the 350 pupils) preferred burger and chips.
26% preferred chicken curry and rice.
14% preferred lasagne and salad.

These figures are summarised on the bar chart below:

The daily total cost of providing these meals would be €437.50
(food @ €0.95 + other costs @ €0.30 per meal × 350)

Income per day from the meals, selling @ €1.50 each, would be €525.00

This would earn a daily profit for the school of €87.50

RECOMMENDATIONS

1. Methods of promoting the hot meals in the school

(a) Place advertisements around the school.
(b) Write to parents advising them of the convenience of purchasing these meals in preference to walking three kilometres to the nearest town.
(c) Actively encourage the pupils to purchase these meals by highlighting the benefits of the scheme to them and to the school in general.

2. Implement the scheme

Assuming meals are sold on 160 days per year, this would earn an annual profit for the school of €14,000. Your school could make good use of this extra €14,000 income, so we advise that you implement this scheme.

If you wish to discuss this report in any more details I can be contacted at the above address.

Signed: Patricia Moore
Marketing Consultant

ORGANISATIONS PROVIDING COMMUNICATIONS SERVICES

An Post

The following are some of the communications services provided by An Post:

1. **Registered post:** provides proof of posting and proof of delivery.
2. **Business response service:** allows a business to send mail to other businesses or customers who then do not have to pay postage for replying. The original sender pays An Post for any mail returned to it under this service.
3. **Publicity Post:** allows businesses to send unaddressed leaflets to all people in a stated geographical area with the regular postal delivery (the postman delivers the leaflets when making normal postal deliveries).
4. **Business Collection Service:** business customers can have their mail collected directly from their premises.
5. **Poste Restante** allows visitors to a town to have their mail posted to the local Post Office for collection using a 'Poste Restante' address. This service is provided free of charge.
6. **PostAim** is a special discounted service for direct mailing.
7. **Publication Services:** for publishers who post newspapers or periodicals to many readers nationwide. It reduces their distribution costs.

RTÉ

RTÉ is probably the best-known media outlet in Ireland. It provides an advertising outlet for all businesses and communities in the country as well as a wide range of programmes on its TV channels and radio stations.

RTÉ is a **Public Service Broadcaster**. This means that RTÉ must reflect the democratic, social and cultural values of Irish society.

TELECOMMUNICATIONS BODIES IN IRELAND

Today, in Ireland, there are many companies providing telecommunications services. These include:

- BT Ireland
- Cable & Wireless Services (Ireland) Ltd
- Eircom
- Meteor Mobile Communications
- O_2 Communications Ireland Limited
- Vodafone Ireland

LEARN THE KEY TERMS

- **Communication** is the transfer of ideas, messages or facts between people.
- **Internal communication** is any form of communication that allows people *within* an organisation to communicate with each other.
- **External communication** is any form of communication that allows people in one organisation to communicate with people *outside* of that organisation.
- **Memos** are short notes circulated to people within an organisation to act as reminders or instructions.
- A **fax** (facsimile) machine allows you to copy and send documents via telephone networks or the Internet.
- **E-mail** (electronic mail) is mail or letters that are sent and received via the Internet.
- A **report** is a written account of the outcome of an examination or analysis of a particular topic.

QUESTIONS

Note: Exercises on Report Writing are omitted from here as they are incorporated into future chapters. Suggestions for Written Reports on topics already studied are included in the Workbook.

1. What is meant by the term **communication**?
2. Explain three methods of oral communication in a workplace.
3. Explain any three advantages of oral communication.
4. Explain any three disadvantages of oral communication.
5. Give three methods of written communication in a workplace.
6. Explain any three advantages of written communication.
7. Explain any three disadvantages of written communication.
8. What is meant by the term **internal communication**?
9. Explain three methods of internal communication in a workplace.
10. Distinguish clearly between a downward flow of information, an upward flow of information and a lateral flow of information.
11. Present the following information on a line graph, a bar chart, a pie chart and a pictogram.

Month	January	February	March	April
Sales (€)	250,000	300,000	350,000	400,000

13. Name and explain any three services offered by An Post to businesses.
14. 'RTÉ is a Public Service Broadcaster.' What obligations does this statement place on RTÉ?

See workbook for more questions.

29 Record keeping and business documents

DAY BOOKS

When a business enters into a transaction it uses one of the **source documents** (see next page) to initially record this transaction in one of the **day books**. The day books are also known as the **books of original (first) entry**.

There are **seven day books**:

DAY BOOKS	
1. Purchases book	For recording the credit purchase of goods that the business normally trades in, i.e. goods purchased on credit that are for resale.
2. Purchases returns book	For recording the return of goods whose purchase had originally been recorded in the purchases book.
3. Sales book	For recording the credit sale of goods that the business normally trades in.
4. Sales returns book	For recording the return of goods whose sale had originally been recorded in the sales book.
5. Analysed cash book	For recording all cash transactions (receipts and payments).
6. Petty cash book	For recording small-value cash payments associated with the day-to-day expenses of running an office.
7. General journal	For recording any transaction that cannot be entered in any of the other day books, e.g. the credit purchase of an asset.

Notes

1. A **cash transaction** is one where money is exchanged. This may be in cash, by cheque, or by another means of bank transfer.
2. A **credit transaction** is one where goods are bought or sold at a given time but not paid for until some future date.
3. **Record Book No. 1** is used for the cash book and the petty cash book.
4. **Record Book No. 2** is used for the purchases, purchase returns, sales and sales returns books as well as the general journal.

The details of recording transactions in each of these day books will be covered separately in later chapters.

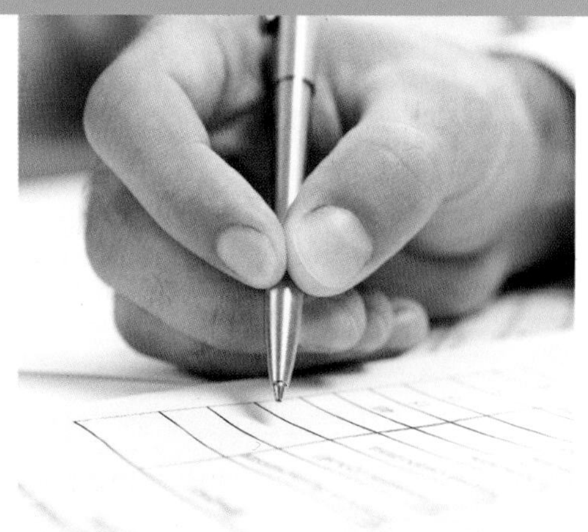

BUSINESS DOCUMENTS

Throughout the course of any business transaction many documents pass between the buyer and seller. The information contained in these documents is used to write up the day books. In these situations the documents are known as **source documents**.

Letters of enquiry

A firm wishing to purchase goods usually makes a number of **enquiries** from different suppliers.

An **enquiry** is a request from a buyer to a seller for the price and terms of sale of certain goods.

Such enquiries may take many different forms. The buyer may write a formal letter as below, send an email, or enquire over the phone.

Joe Soap Ltd
11 High St
Dingle
Co. Kerry

Telephone: 345876
Fax: 345967
email: soap@iol.ie
VAT No. IE 987654S

To: **Swift Products Ltd**
10 Main St
Cobh
Co. Cork

21/11/10

Dear Sir/Madam,

I wish to purchase the goods listed below and am seeking a quotation detailing your best prices and terms of sale for same.

10 23″ Colour TVs
20 DVD Players
30 Video Recorders

Your sincerely,

Joe Soap

Joe Soap
Purchasing Manager

When the enquiry is received, the seller checks the current price of the goods and whether or not they are in stock. The seller then prepares a **quotation**.

Quotations

A **quotation** is a document, sent by the seller to the buyer, that shows the price of the goods and the terms of sale.

QUOTATION

Tel 01 203498 Fax 01 203478 Email swift@iol.ie	**Swift Products Ltd** 10 Main St Cobh, Co. Cork	Vat Registration no. IE 1234567W

To: Joe Soap Ltd
11 High St
Dingle
Co. Kerry

23/11/10

Thank you for your enquiry. The following are the current prices for the goods referred to in your enquiry.

Please note that all goods are subject to a trade discount of 10%. A VAT rate of 10% currently applies to all goods.

Quantity	Description	Model No.	Price each (€)
10	23″ Colour TVs	TV 023	200.00
20	DVD Players	DV 345	150.00
30	Video Recorders	VR 567	90.00

Carriage paid. E & OE. Cash discount 5% for 10 days

Notes

1. **Carriage paid** means that the seller will pay for the delivery of the goods to the buyer.
2. **E&OE** stands for **Errors and omissions excepted**. This is a traditional addition to many business documents which attempts to absolve the sender from legal consequences arising from mistakes or omissions in the document. It does not have much legal significance today.
3. **Trade discount** is a reduction in the selling price given between people in the same line of business. It is always deducted before VAT is added.
4. **Cash discount** is an extra discount given to the buyer if the bill is paid within a stated period of time. It is given to encourage the quick payment of the amount owed.
5. **VAT** is a tax levied (placed) on the added value of a good or service as it goes through the channels of distribution, i.e. from the manufacturer to the consumer (see page 266).
6. **Other terms of sale are:**
   (a) **Ex works:** the buyer must pay for the transportation of the goods, or there is an extra charge for the transport.
   (b) **CWO (cash with order):** payment for the goods is required at the time of ordering the goods.
   (c) **COD (cash on delivery):** payment for the goods is required at the time of delivering the goods.

Orders

If the prices shown in the quotation are acceptable to the buyer he or she will place an order for the goods.

An **order** is a written request from a buyer to a seller to supply certain goods. The order must be signed by the buyer.

ORDER NO. 567

Joe Soap Ltd
11 High St
Dingle
Co. Kerry

Telephone: 345876
Fax: 345967
email: soap@iol.ie
VAT No. IE 987654S

25/11/10

To: **Swift Products Ltd**
10 Main St
Cobh
Co. Cork

Please supply the following goods:

Quantity	Description	Model No.	Price each (€)
10	23″ Colour TVs	TV 023	200.00
20	DVD Players	DV 345	150.00
30	Video Recorders	VR 567	90.00

Your sincerely,

Joe Soap

Joe Soap
Purchasing Manager E & OE

Note that the order is one of the few documents that **must be signed**.

The order number is very important because it may have to be referred to if there are queries concerning the order at some time in the future.

Credit worthiness

When a firm sells goods on credit it runs the risk of incurring bad debts, i.e. the buyers may not pay for the goods. Therefore before selling goods on credit to a new customer, the firm should take steps to reduce the risk of non-payment. This can be done by:

1. Asking the customer to supply a reference from other firms that had previously supplied goods on credit to the customer.
2. Asking the customer to supply a credit reference from his or her own bank.
3. Checking the customer's credit history with The Irish Credit Bureau. This is an organisation that holds information on the credit rating of individuals and companies based on their history of repaying loans.

Delivery notes (dockets)

On receipt of an order the seller will prepare the goods for delivery. A **delivery note** and an **invoice** will be made out. When the goods are being delivered the seller sends a delivery note with them.

A **delivery note** is a document, sent by the seller to the buyer, that lists the goods being delivered.

DELIVERY DOCKET NO. 34

Tel 01 203498
Fax 01 203478
Email swift@iol.ie

Swift Products Ltd
10 Main St
Cobh, Co. Cork

Vat Registration no.
IE 1234567W

To:
Joe Soap Ltd
11 High St
Dingle
Co. Kerry

28/11/10

Quantity	Description	Model No.
10	23″ Colour TVs	TV 023
20	DVD Players	DV 345
30	Video Recorders	VR 567

Received the above goods in good condition.

Signed: *Joe Soap* Purchasing Manager

Procedure to be followed when the goods are delivered

1. The buyer should examine the delivery note in detail to ensure:
   (a) The goods being delivered are the goods that were ordered.
   (b) The goods being delivered are the ones stated on the delivery note.
   (c) The goods being delivered are the goods the buyer was charged for on the invoice.
2. If everything is in order then the buyer should sign the delivery note and return it to the seller.
3. The buyer is given a copy of the signed delivery note.
   The seller can then use it to prove that the goods were delivered.

Invoices

An **invoice** is a document sent by the seller to the buyer giving details of the quantity, quality (usually with a catalogue number or description code) and price of the goods being sent, terms of sale and details about carriage.

The invoice is the source document for the seller's sales book and the buyer's purchase book.

The invoice acts as a bill for the goods being delivered.

INVOICE NO. 57

Tel 01 203498 Fax 01 203478 Email swift@iol.ie	**Swift Products Ltd** 10 Main St Cobh, Co. Cork	Vat Registration no. IE 1234567W

To:
Joe Soap Ltd
11 High St
Dingle
Co. Kerry

Date: 3/12/10
Your Order no. 567

Quantity	Description	Model No.	Price each (€)	Total (€)
10	23″ Colour TVs	TV 023	200.00	2,000.00
20	DVD Players	DV 345	150.00	3,000.00
30	Video Recorders	VR 567	90.00	2,700.00
			Total excluding VAT	7,700.00
			Trade discount 10%	770.00
Carriage paid			Subtotal (net)	6,930.00
Terms: 5% 10 days			VAT 10%	693.00
E & OE			Total including VAT	7,623.00

Note: When trade discount **and** VAT appear on a document the trade discount is always subtracted **before** the VAT is added.

Functions of the invoice

1. The seller uses the invoice details to write up the sales book and later posts the details to the debtor's ledger account.
2. The seller files a copy of the invoice to provide a permanent record of the transaction.
3. The buyer checks the invoice against the delivery note to ensure that the goods delivered are the goods charged for.
4. The buyer uses the invoice details to write up the purchases book and later posts the details to the creditor's ledger account.
5. The buyer files the invoice to provide a permanent record of the transaction.

Credit notes

A **credit note** is a document, sent by the seller to the buyer, that shows a reduction in the amount owed by the buyer.

The credit note is the source document for the seller's sales returns book and for the buyer's purchases returns book.

A credit note is sent:

1. In the event of an overcharge.
2. If some of the invoiced goods were not delivered.
3. If some of the goods were damaged or were of an inferior quality to the ones ordered.
4. If some of the goods were returned to the seller.

CREDIT NOTE NO. 57

Tel 01 203498
Fax 01 203478
Email swift@iol.ie

Swift Products Ltd
10 Main St
Cobh, Co. Cork

Vat Registration no.
IE 1234567W

To: Joe Soap Ltd
11 High St
Dingle
Co. Kerry

12/12/10

Ref: Invoice no. 57, being an allowance for:

Quantity	Description	Model No.	Price each (€)	Total (€)
5	23″ Colour TVs	TV 023	200.00	1,000.00
2	DVD Players	DV 345	150.00	300.00
10	Video Recorders	VR 567	90.00	900.00
			Total excluding VAT	2,200.00
			Trade discount 10%	220.00
			Subtotal (net)	1,980.00
			VAT 10%	198.00
			Total including VAT	2,178.00

Functions of a credit note

1. The **seller** uses the credit note details to write up the sales returns book and later posts the details to the debtor's ledger.
2. The **seller** files a copy of it to provide a permanent record of the transaction.
3. The **buyer** uses the credit note details to write up the purchases returns book and later posts the details to the creditor's ledger.
4. The **buyer** files it to provide a permanent record of the transaction.

Debit notes

A **debit note** is issued by the seller if the customer was undercharged for any goods delivered to him or her.

It is set out in the same way as the credit note, with the obvious exception of the title.

Statements

A **statement** is a copy of a debtor's ledger account sent periodically by the creditor.

A statement is sent by the seller to the buyer and shows the full amount owed by the buyer. It shows the opening balance (any money owed at the start of the period) plus details of all the transactions between the seller and the buyer during that period. It acts as a demand for payment of the amount owed.

STATEMENT NO. 96

Tel 01 203498
Fax 01 203478
Email swift@iol.ie

Swift Products Ltd
10 Main St
Cobh, Co. Cork

Vat Registration no.
IE 1234567W

To: **Joe Soap Ltd**
11 High St
Dingle
Co. Kerry

20/12/10

Date	Details	Debit (€)	Credit (€)	Balance (€)
1/12/10	Balance			5,000.00
3/12/10	Invoice no. 57	7,623.00		12,623.00
5/12/10	Credit Note no. 34		2,178.00	10,445.00

Terms: 5% 10 days

Note: This form of statement is known as a **continuous balancing ledger** and will be dealt with in more detail in Chapter 33.

Notes

1. The balance shown on the 1st of a month is the amount owed by the buyer at that date.
2. Any amount entered in the debit column is added to the previous balance to show the new balance.
3. Any amount entered in the credit column is subtracted from the previous balance to show the new balance.
4. The phrase **Terms 5% 10 days** means that a discount of 5% will be given if the buyer pays the full amount owed within 10 days of the date of the statement.

Before Joe Soap pays the €10,445 shown as being owed in the statement he should:

1. Check that the opening balance is correct.
2. Check to ensure that he has in fact received all the goods for which he has been charged.
3. Check that the amounts stated on the statement for the invoices and credit notes are correct.
4. Check the arithmetic on the invoice.

Remittance advice slips

The word **remittance** means **payment**. A **remittance advice slip** is often attached to a statement. The buyer returns the slip to the seller when paying the amount owed.

A **remittance advice slip** is a pre-printed document attached to a statement that is returned by the buyer when paying the amount owed. It shows the amount due and a reference number that makes it easy for the seller to identify the debtor's account.

REMITTANCE ADVICE SLIP NO. 54

To:
Joe Soap Ltd
11 High St
Dingle
Co. Kerry

Your Order No. **567**
Invoice No. **57**
Statement No. **96**

Payment due by: **31/12/10**

Total amount due: **€10,445.00**

Receipts

A **receipt** is a written acknowledgement of payment.
It is signed by the seller and given to the buyer.

The sole function of the receipt is to act as proof of payment by the buyer.

RECEIPT

Swift Products, 10 Main St, Cobh, Co. Cork

Date	12/1/11	
Received from	Joe Soap Ltd	
The sum of	Ten thousand, four hundred and forty-five euro only	€10,445.00
With thanks	*Suzanne Green* Suzanne Green, Accounts Manager	

Summary of business documents exchange

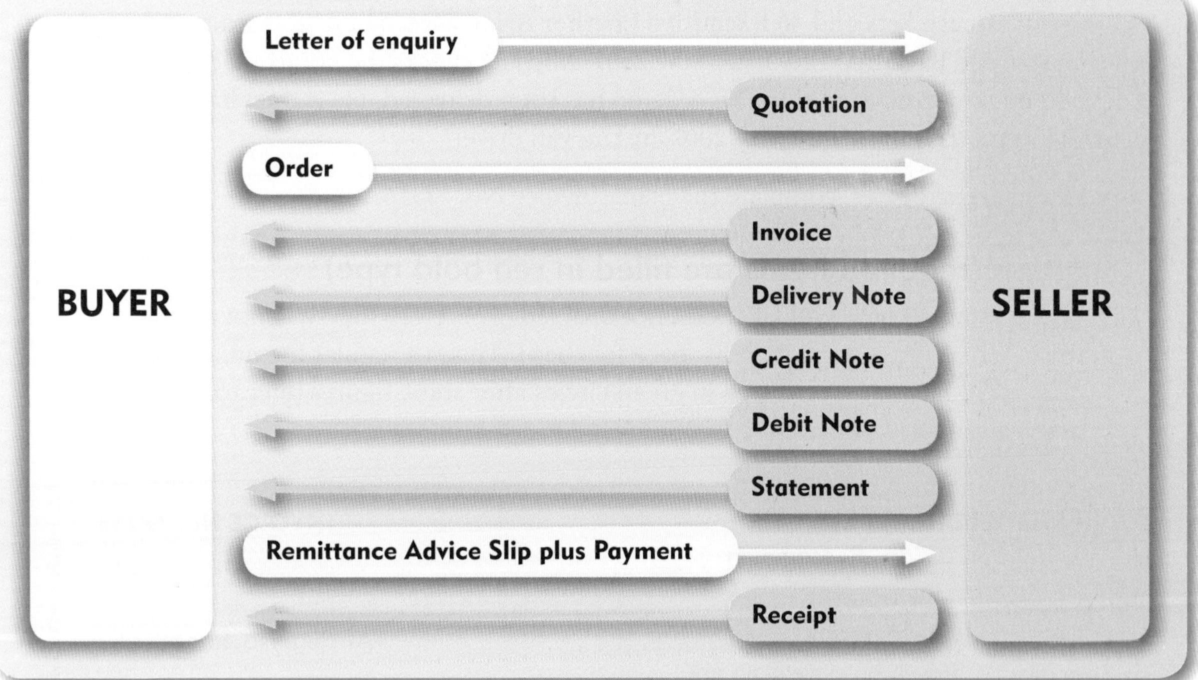

The format (layout) of these documents will vary from firm to firm but the basic information is the same.

Examination type question *from Junior Certificate Ordinary Level Paper 2007*

Michael Brady is the Purchasing Manager at The Bag Shop Ltd. On 22 May 2007, he received the following quotation:

Travel Wholesale Ltd **QUOTATION No. 137762**
Hyde Business Park, Roscommon

Telephone: 090-7661992
Fax: 090-7771995 VAT Reg. No. IE 8181552
e-mail: travelwholesale@alo.net

To: 21 May 2007
The Purchasing Manager
The Bag Shop Ltd
Park Road
Boyle
Co. Roscommon

Code no.	Description	Price each (€)	Delivery
CLS35	Carlton 5-piece Luggage Sets	125.00	Ready
PSS48	Crown 3-piece Suitcase Sets	55.00	Ready
HPL12	Puma Large Holdall	67.00	Ready
LBE76	Executive Leather Briefcases	85.00	Ready

Trade discount 25% on all goods
VAT 20% on all goods
Carriage paid
For acceptance within 30 days

Michael decides that the Puma Large Holdalls are too costly. He sends an Order (No. 31846) to Travel Wholesale Ltd for **20 Carlton 5-piece Luggage Sets, 80 Crown 3-piece Suitcase Sets and 40 Executive Leather Briefcases**. These goods are delivered by van to The Bag Shop Ltd on 24 May 2007. Michael checks the goods when they arrive and finds that everything he ordered has been delivered. He is then handed Invoice No. 72356, dated 24 May 2007, by the van driver.

From the above details, complete the blank Invoice No. 72356.

Solution (required items are filled in red bold type)

Note: The Puma Large Holdalls were not ordered. Therefore they will not appear on the invoice even though there is space for them. This is a regular feature of exam questions. The numbers 1 to 8 in green circles after some figures refer to explanatory notes given after the invoice.

Travel Wholesale Ltd **INVOICE No. 72356**
Hyde Business Park, Roscommon

Telephone: 090-7661992
Fax: 090-7771995
e-mail: travelwholesale@alo.net

VAT Reg. No. IE 8181552

Date: 24 May 2007
Your Order no. 31846

To:

The Purchasing Manager
The Bag Shop Ltd
Park Road
Boyle
Co. Roscommon

Quantity	Description	Code no.	Price each (€)	Total (€)	
20	Carlton 5-piece Luggage Sets	CLS35	125.00	2,500.00	1
80	Crown 3-piece Suitcase Sets	PSS48	55.00	4,400.00	2
40	Executive Leather Briefcases	LBE76	85.00	3,400.00	3
			Total (excluding VAT)	10,300.00	4
			Trade discount	2,575.00	5
Carriage paid			Subtotal	7,725.00	6
E & OE			VAT	1,545.00	7
			Total (including VAT)	9,270.00	8

Explanatory notes:

1. Quantity of 20 × €125.00
2. Quantity of 80 × €55.00
3. Quantity of 40 × €85.00
4. The sum of (1), (2) and (3)
5. 25% of €10,300
6. Trade discount subtracted from total (excluding VAT)
7. 20% of (6)
8. VAT plus subtotal

LEARN THE KEY TERMS

- **COD** stands for **cash on delivery**.
- **CWO** stands for **cash with order**.
- **Ex works** means that the cost of delivery is not included.
- **Carriage paid** means that the seller will pay for the delivery of the goods to the buyer.
- **E&OE** stands for **Errors and omissions excepted**.
- **Trade discount** is a reduction in the selling price given between people in the same line of business.
- **Cash discount** is an extra discount given to the buyer if the bill is paid within a stated period of time.
- An **enquiry** is a request from a buyer to a seller for the price and terms of sale of certain goods.
- A **quotation** is a document, sent by the seller to the buyer, that shows the price of the goods and the terms of sale.
- An **order** is a written request from a buyer to a seller to supply certain goods. The order must be signed by the buyer.
- An **invoice** is a document, sent by the seller to the buyer, that lists the items delivered (usually with a catalogue number or description code), the quantity, price, terms of sale and carriage details.
- A **delivery note** is a document, sent by the seller to the buyer, that lists the goods being delivered.
- A **credit note** is a document, sent by the seller to the buyer, that shows the reduction in the amount owed by the buyer.
- A **debit note** is issued by the seller if the customer was undercharged for any goods delivered to him or her.
- A **statement** is a copy of a debtor's ledger account sent periodically by the creditor.
- A **remittance advice slip** is a pre-printed document attached to a statement that is returned by the buyer when paying the amount owed. It shows the amount due and a reference number that makes it easy for the seller to identify the debtor's account.
- A **receipt** is a written acknowledgement of payment. It is signed by the seller and given to the buyer.

QUESTIONS

1. Explain the following terms of sale: CWO, COD, Ex works, Carriage paid.
2. Distinguish between **trade discount** and **cash discount**.
3. What is a quotation?
4. What is an order?
5. Describe three ways a seller can attempt to reduce the possibility of bad debts when goods are sold on credit.
6. What is an invoice?
7. What are the functions of an invoice?
8. What is a credit note?
9. Explain three occasions when a credit note would be used.
10. What is a delivery note (docket)?
11. What are the functions of a delivery note?
12. What is a statement?
13. What are the steps taken by a buyer before paying the amount shown to be due for payment on a statement?
14. Who prepares a remittance advice slip?
15. How is a remittance advice slip used?

See workbook for more questions.

Double-entry records and the trial balance 30

This chapter introduces ledger accounts and the theory of double-entry accounting. You will recall from Chapter 29 that business transactions are initially recorded in one of the **day books**.

LEDGERS (RECORD BOOK NO. 3)

The information in the day books is **posted to** (transferred to) the ledgers. Ledgers are books in which all individual **accounts** are recorded.

An account is used to bring together:

1. All the transactions involving a particular person or company; or
2. All the transactions involving a particular income or expense; or
3. All the transactions involving a particular object.

Thus we could have an account (A/C) for John Browne called *John Browne A/C*. Likewise we could have a *Sales A/C*, an *Electricity A/C*, and a *Premises A/C* and so forth.

Accounts can be classified as follows:

1. **Personal accounts:** used to record transactions with people and companies such as debtors, creditors and institutions from which money has been borrowed.
2. **Real accounts:** used to record transactions dealing with objects such as computers and buildings.
3. **Nominal accounts:** used to record all the expenses and gains involved in running a business, e.g. wages, insurance and rent received. They are regarded as temporary accounts; their value returns to zero at the end of each year (see Chapter 39).

When posting information from the day books to the ledgers we follow the basic rules of bookkeeping that have been mentioned throughout the book. Remember:

When we say **debit an account** we mean the transaction is to be recorded on the **debit side** of the account.

When we say **credit an account** we mean the transaction is to be entered on the **credit side** of the account.

Summary of basic bookkeeping rules

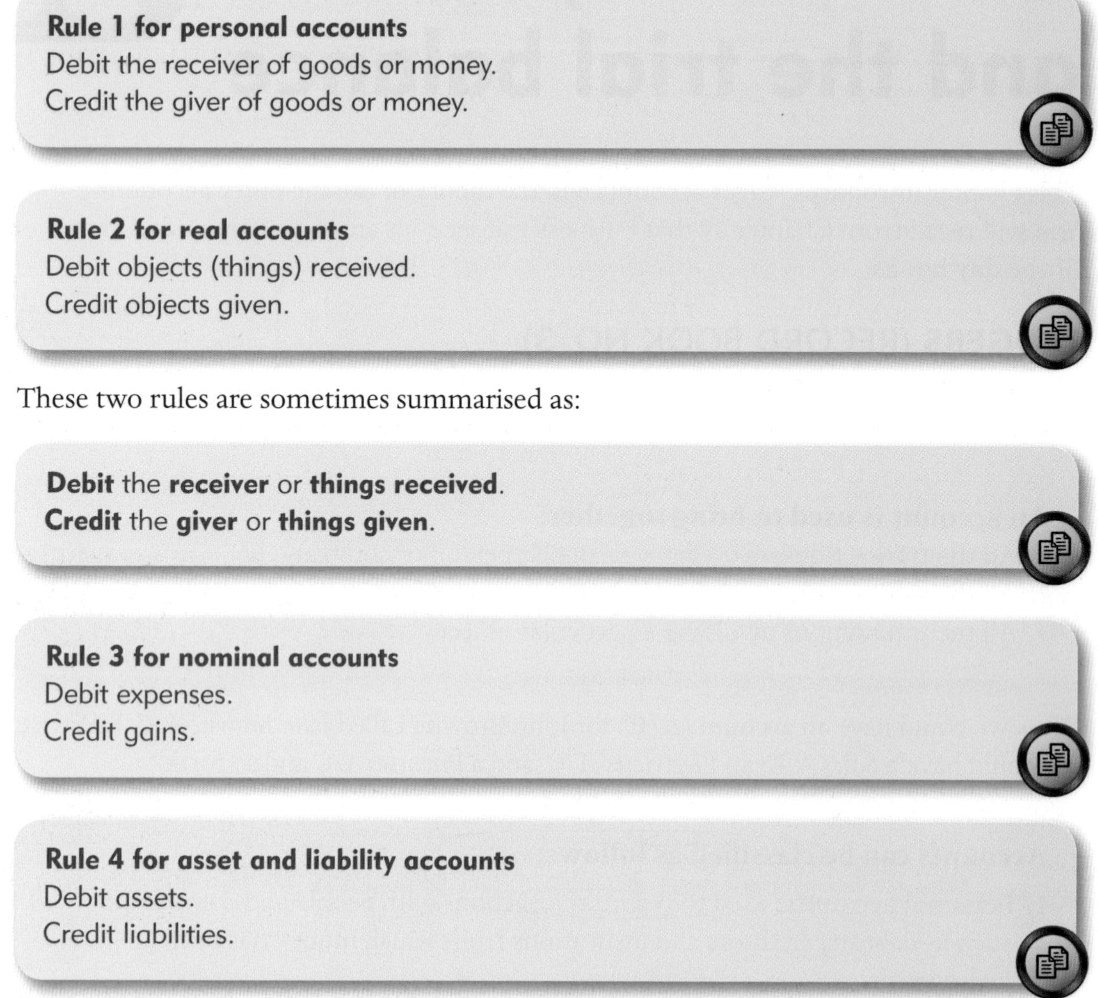

Rule 1 for personal accounts
Debit the receiver of goods or money.
Credit the giver of goods or money.

Rule 2 for real accounts
Debit objects (things) received.
Credit objects given.

These two rules are sometimes summarised as:

Debit the **receiver** or **things received**.
Credit the **giver** or **things given**.

Rule 3 for nominal accounts
Debit expenses.
Credit gains.

Rule 4 for asset and liability accounts
Debit assets.
Credit liabilities.

Ledger accounts in Record Book No. 3 take the format shown here:

Debit side				Credit side			
Date	Details	F	€	Date	Details	F	€

Note: The **folio column**, usually shown as '**F**', is used for reference purposes and we will deal with this later.

DOUBLE ENTRY

Every transaction posted from the day books is entered twice in the ledger accounts because there is both a **giving aspect** and a **receiving aspect** to each transaction. Thus we say:

For every debit entry there **must** be a corresponding credit entry.

Note: The following transactions assume that the day books have already been completed. The examples are used simply to illustrate the concept of double entry. The completion of the day books and posting from them to the ledgers will be dealt with in detail in following chapters.

Example 1

The following transaction was recorded in the general journal of D. Clarke.

On 1/3/2012, D. Clarke Ltd purchased a computer on credit from Compu Ltd costing €780. You are required to show the ledger entries in D. Clarke's books.

D. Clarke **received** something, i.e. the computer.
Compu Ltd was the **giver** of the computer.

- D. Clarke must debit the *Computer* A/C in her books.
  Remember: debit objects received.
- D. Clarke must credit *Compu Ltd* A/C in her books.
  Remember: credit the giver.

Enter, in the details column, the name of the company from whom you **received** the computer.

Debit side		**COMPUTER A/C**					**Credit side**
Date	Details	F	€	Date	Details	F	€
1/3/12	Compu Ltd	GJ	780				

Enter, in the details column, the item **given** by Compu Ltd.

Debit side		**COMPU LTD A/C**					**Credit side**
Date	Details	F	€	Date	Details	F	€
				1/3/12	Computer	GJ	780

From this you can see clearly that there is a corresponding credit entry for the debit entry.

Example 2

The following transaction was recorded in the sales book of D. Clarke.

On 3/3/12, D. Clarke sold, on credit, goods that she normally trades in to J. Jones Ltd for €1,000. Enter this transaction in the ledgers in D. Clarke's books.

- J. Jones is the **receiver** of the goods so his account must be debited.
- The items **given** were the goods sold by D. Clarke (called *Sales*); so the *Sales* A/C must be credited.

Debit side		**J. JONES A/C**					**Credit side**
Date	Details	F	€	Date	Details	F	€
3/3/12	Sales	SB	1,000				

Debit side		**SALES A/C**					**Credit side**
Date	Details	F	€	Date	Details	F	€
				3/3/12	J. Jones	SB	1,000

Again you can see that there is both a debit and a credit entry for this transaction.

Example 3

The following transaction was recorded in D. Clarke's sales returns book.

On 5/3/12, J. Jones returned goods to D. Clarke valued at €400.

This is the same J. Jones to whom D. Clarke sold goods on 3/12/12 and the entry for the sales transaction is already posted to J. Jones' account as shown above.

Use only one account for any one person, any one object or any one nominal transaction.

- J. Jones is the **giver** of the goods (he is giving them back to D. Clarke) so his account must be credited.
- The items **received** were the goods returned to D. Clarke (called *Sales returns*); so the *Sales returns* A/C must be credited.

The entries for this transaction are shown in blue print in the ledgers.

Debit side		J. JONES A/C					Credit side
Date	Details	F	€	Date	Details	F	€
3/3/12	Sales	SB	1,000	5/3/12	Sales returns	SRB	400

Debit side		SALES RETURNS A/C					Credit side
Date	Details	F	€	Date	Details	F	€
5/3/12	J. Jones	SRB	400				

Again you can see that there is a debit and a corresponding credit entry.

Look back at all the ledger accounts we have recorded so far.

1. You can see that the value of the computers owned by D. Clarke is €780. Thus we say that the balance on the *Computer* A/C is a debit of €780.
2. The amount owed to Compu Ltd is also €780. Thus we say that the balance on Compu Ltd's A/C is a credit of €780.
3. The value of the sales was €1,000, giving a credit balance of €1,000.
4. The value of the sales returns was €400, giving a debit balance of €400.
5. However, there are two transactions on J. Jones's A/C and the amount that he owes (the balance) must be calculated. The balance is calculated as follows.

BALANCING AN ACCOUNT

In the following procedure steps (a) to (c) should be done mentally, on a rough work page or on a calculator. Do not write anything in the ledger account until step (d).

(a) Add all the entries on the debit side of the account (€1,000).

(b) Add all the entries on the credit side of the account (€400).

(c) Subtract the smaller answer from the bigger answer (€1,000 – €400 = €600).

(d) On the last date of the month place the difference (the €600) on the smallest side (the credit side) of the account and call it *Balance.*

(e) Now total each side. The totals should be the same.

(f) Bring the balance down to the opposite side (the debit side) at the start of the next period.

(g) This now shows us a debit balance of €600 on J. Jones's account.

Debit side				J. JONES A/C			Credit side
Date	Details	F	€	Date	Details	F	€
3/3/12	Sales	SB	1,000	5/3/12	Sales returns	SRB	400
				31/3/12	Balance c/d		600
			1,000				1,000
1/4/12	Balance b/d		600				

Note: The *b/d* on the debit side stands for *brought down*. The *c/d* on the credit side stands for *carried down*. Some people write *b/f* (brought forward) and *c/f* (carried forward). They are traditional ways of showing the amount being transferred to the next month.

The debtors, creditors and general ledgers

Most businesses organise their accounts under three headings:

1. **The debtors ledger:** the accounts of all customers to whom the business has sold goods on credit.
2. **The creditors ledger:** the accounts of all customers from whom the business has purchased goods on credit.
3. **The general ledger:** all the nominal accounts.

Note: These ledgers are sometimes referred to as the *sales ledger*, the *purchases ledger* and the *nominal ledger* respectively.

The trial balance

When all the accounts have been written up and balanced, a test is conducted to ensure that the value of all debit balances equals the value of all credit balances. Remember that for every debit entry there must be a credit entry. It follows that the sum of the debit balances must equal the sum of all credit balances.

We say that we are **extracting** a trial balance when we carry out this procedure.

Procedure

Go through all the accounts, making a list of all the balances under two headings, *Debit balances* and *Credit balances*.

Nothing is entered in the trial balance where there is **no balance** on an account, i.e. where the amounts on the debit side of the account are equal to the amounts on the credit side of the account.

Now look again at all the accounts in D. Clarke's records and make out this list.

Debit side			COMPUTER A/C				Credit side
Date	Details	F	€	Date	Details	F	€
1/3/12	Compu Ltd	GJ	780				

Debit balance

Debit side			COMPU LTD A/C				Credit side
Date	Details	F	€	Date	Details	F	€
				1/3/12	Computer	GJ	780

Credit balance

Debit side			SALES A/C				Credit side
Date	Details	F	€	Date	Details	F	€
				3/3/12	J. Jones	SB	1,000

Credit balance

Debit side			SALES RETURNS A/C				Credit side
Date	Details	F	€	Date	Details	F	€
5/3/12	J. Jones	SRB	400				

Debit balance

Debit side			J. JONES A/C				Credit side
Date	Details	F	€	Date	Details	F	€
3/3/12	Sales	SB	1,000	5/3/12	Sales returns	SRB	400
				31/3/12	Balance c/d		600
			1,000				1,000
1/4/12	Balance b/d		600				

Debit balance

Note: Record Book No. 2 is probably the most suitable place to **extract** the trial balance, but your teacher will guide you on this.

TRIAL BALANCE AT 31/12/12 (always show the date)		
	Dr €	Cr €
Computer A/C	780	
Compu Ltd A/C		780
Sales A/C		1,000
Sales returns A/C	400	
J. Jones A/C	600	
	1,780	1,780

When the trial balance does not balance, it indicates a mistake or mistakes have been made in the business's records. This means that all the accounts have to be rechecked until the mistakes have been rectified.

LEARN THE KEY TERMS

- **Personal accounts** are used to record transactions with people and companies.
- **Real accounts** are used to record transactions dealing with objects.
- **Nominal accounts** are used to record all the expenses and gains involved in running a business and to record some forms of liabilities.
- The **debtors ledger (or sales ledger)** is used to keep together the accounts of all customers to whom the business has sold goods on credit.
- The **creditors ledger (or purchases ledger)** is used to keep together the accounts of all customers from whom the business has purchased goods on credit.
- The **general ledger (or nominal ledger)** is used to keep together all the nominal accounts.
- A **trial balance** is a test conducted to ensure that the value of all debit balances equals the value of all credit balances.

QUESTIONS

1. Distinguish between personal accounts, real accounts and nominal accounts.
2. Distinguish between the debtors, creditors and general ledgers.
3. What is a trial balance?

See workbook for more questions.

31 The purchases and purchases returns books

PURCHASING GOODS

Businesses purchase two distinct (different) types of goods. Take, for example, a grocer's business.

The grocer buys goods needed to run the business such as weighing scales, fridges, freezers and delivery vans. These goods are not purchased for resale purposes.

The grocer also buys items such as fruit, potatoes, cheese, milk, bread and biscuits. This group of goods is purchased with the intention of reselling them, hopefully, at a profit. These are the goods in which the grocer trades. You will recall from Chapter 7 that a trader is a person who buys goods to resell them.

The **purchases book** is used to record the credit purchase of goods that the business normally trades in, i.e. goods purchased on credit by the business that it intends to resell.

HOW THE VAT (VALUE ADDED TAX) SYSTEM OPERATES

Before we proceed any further it is important to understand our VAT system.

VAT is a tax on consumer spending.

To make it difficult for people to avoid paying VAT, the responsibility of collecting it is placed on the seller of the goods at all points on the chain of distribution from the manufacturer to the retailer. Thus each firm in the chain of distribution pays VAT on the value added by that firm.

Each firm can offset the amount of VAT paid by it against the amount collected by it. Therefore the final consumers bear the full burden of the VAT, because they cannot claim it against anybody else.

Example

COLLECTION OF 21% VAT		
Chain of distribution	Calculation of VAT paid	VAT
Manufacturer sells to wholesaler for €1,000 + 21% VAT	Manufacturer collects €210 from the wholesaler and pays this as VAT	€210
Wholesaler sells to retailer for €1,500 + 21% VAT	Wholesaler collects €315 from the retailer and pays (€315 – €210) = €105 as VAT	€105
Retailer sells to consumer for €2,000 plus 21% VAT	Retailer collects €420 from the consumer and pays (€420 – €315) = €105 as VAT	€105
	Total VAT paid	€420

The **consumer**, in reality, **pays the entire €420 VAT** because this is the amount collected by the retailer from the consumer. For this reason all firms must keep a record of the VAT they pay and the VAT they collect.

Each firm initially records the VAT in all their day books and later posts all the VAT to **one** VAT account in order to calculate the difference between the amount paid and the amount collected by that firm.

WRITING UP THE PURCHASES BOOK

The **source documents** used to record entries in the purchases book are **invoices received** by the buyer.

The layout of **your** purchases book in Record Book No. 2 is as shown below. VAT in this example is 21%.

PURCHASES BOOK

Date	Details	F	Net €	VAT €	Total €
1/1/13	M. Motors Ltd, Inv. no. 345	CL1	100	21	121
		GL1	100	21	121

Explanation

1. The *Date* column records the date on which the transaction took place.
2. The *Details* column gives the name of the person or company from whom the goods were purchased, plus the number of the invoice sent by the seller.
3. The *Folio* column indicates posting details, i.e. the ledger to which the item is posted.
4. The *Net*, *VAT* and *Total* columns show the information taken from the invoice.

You may see some purchases books in examination questions with an extra column for the invoice number, as shown below.

PURCHASES BOOK

Date	Details	Inv. no.	F	Net €	VAT €	Total €
1/1/13	M. Motors Ltd	345	CL1	100	21	121
			GL1	100	21	121

We will now look at an invoice received by a business and see how this is recorded in the purchases book. The following invoice was received by Joe Soap Ltd from Swift Products Ltd.

INVOICE NO. 57

Tel 01 203498 Fax 01 203478 Email swift@iol.ie	**Swift Products Ltd** 10 Main St Cobh, Co. Cork	Vat Registration no. IE 1234567W

To:
Joe Soap Ltd
11 High St
Dingle
Co. Kerry

Date: 3/12/12
Your Order no. 567

Quantity	Description	Model No.	Price each (€)	Total (€)
10	23″ Colour TVs	TV 023	200.00	2,000.00
20	DVD Players	DV 345	150.00	3,000.00
30	Video Recorders	VR 567	90.00	2,700.00
			Total excluding VAT	7,700.00
			Trade discount 10%	770.00
Carriage paid			Subtotal (net)	6,930.00
Terms: 5% 10 days			VAT 10%	693.00
E & OE			Total including VAT	7,623.00

PURCHASES BOOK

Date	Details	F	Net/ Purchases €	VAT €	Total €
3/12/12	Swift Products Ltd, Inv. no. 345	CL	6,930.00	693.00	7,623.00

1. The **true cost (net cost)** of the goods purchased is €6,930.00 (the amount after the trade discount has been subtracted). This is the amount charged by the seller. This is entered in the *Net* column.

   Note: It would be more convenient to call the *Net* column the *Purchases* column. So **initially** we will call the *Net* column the *Net/Purchases* column until you get used to the idea that the *Net* column represents the cost of the purchases.

2. The seller must add on and collect **VAT** of €693.00. This VAT will eventually go to the government. It is entered in the VAT column.
3. Therefore the **total amount** owed by Joe Soap Ltd to Swift Products Ltd is the *Net* amount (€6,930.00) plus the VAT (€693.00) = €7,623.00.

Folios

Day books

The entry in the folio column indicates the ledger and account number to which the item is being posted. Example: **DL1** indicates that the item is being posted to the **debtors ledger, account no. 1**.

Ledgers

The entry in the folio column indicates the day book from which the item has been posted. Example: **PB1** indicates that the item has been posted from **page 1** in the **purchases book**.

EXERCISE 1

Purchases book, ledgers and trial balance

Record the following credit transaction in the purchases book of Abbott Ltd, post them to the ledgers and extract a trial balance on the last day of the month.

All transactions are subject to VAT of 21%.

- 1/1/13 Purchased goods on credit from Lyons Ltd
  Invoice received no. 21 €15,000
- 3/1/13 Purchased goods on credit from Malone Ltd
  Invoice received no. 33 €10,000
- 5/1/13 Purchased goods on credit from Nolan Ltd
  Invoice received no. 44 €18,000

Step 1: Enter the transaction in the purchases book and show the total for each column.

PURCHASES BOOK (page 1)

Date	Details	F	Net/ Purchases €	VAT €	Total €
1/1/13	Lyons Ltd, Inv. no. 21	CL1	15,000.00	3,150.00	18,150.00
3/1/13	Malone Ltd, Inv. no. 33	CL2	10,000.00	2,100.00	12,100.00
5/1/13	Nolan Ltd, Inv. no. 44	CL3	18,000.00	3,780.00	21,780.00
		GL1, 2	43,000.00	9,030.00	52,030.00

Post to **debit side** of these accounts

Post to **credit side** of their accounts

Step 2: Post the **individual** amounts in the **third column** (the *Total* column) to the credit side of the respective personal accounts in the creditors ledger. *Remember:* **Credit the giver**. See below.

Step 3: Post the **totals** of the first two columns to the debit side of the *Purchases* and *VAT* accounts in the general ledger. The goods purchased by Abbott Ltd are items received by the firm. *Remember:* **Debit items received**. See below.

Creditors ledger

LYONS LTD A/C (1)

Debit side							Credit side
Date	Details	F	€	Date	Details	F	€
				1/1/13	Purchases	PB1	18,150.00

MALONE LTD A/C (2)

Date	Details	F	€	Date	Details	F	€
				3/1/13	Purchases	PB1	12,100.00

NOLAN LTD A/C (3)

Date	Details	F	€	Date	Details	F	€
				5/1/13	Purchases	PB1	21,780.00

General ledger

Debit side		PURCHASES A/C (1)					Credit side
Date	Details	F	€	Date	Details	F	€
31/1/13	Sundry creditors*	PB1	43,000.00				

		VAT A/C (2)					
Date	Details	F	€	Date	Details	F	€
31/1/13	Sundry creditors*	PB1	9,030.00				

*__Sundry creditors__ in this context means **various unnamed creditors**. It refers to all the creditors listed on page 1 of the purchases book. Hence the PB1 reference in the *Folio* column. This word *Sundry* is used when posting the total figure in the first two columns in all the day books.

Step 4: Extract the trial balance. *Remember:* a **debit in the ledger** is also a **debit in the trial balance** and a **credit in the ledger** is also a **credit in the trial balance**.

TRIAL BALANCE AT 31/1/13		
	Dr €	Cr €
Lyons Ltd A/C		18,150.00
Malone Ltd A/C		12,100.00
Nolan Ltd A/C		21,780.00
Purchases A/C	43,000.00	
VAT A/C	9,030.00	
	52,030.00	52,030.00

Summary

1. The purchases book is written up using the details shown in invoices received.
2. The **individual amounts** in the **Total column** are posted to the **credit side of the personal accounts** in the creditors ledger. *Remember:* Credit the giver.
3. The **total** of the **Net (purchases) column** is posted to the **debit side of the purchases account**. *Remember:* Debit items received.
4. The **total** of the **VAT column** is posted to the **debit side of the VAT account** (part of the cost of items *received*).
5. The **dates** in the **Purchases** and **VAT accounts** are usually the last day of the month.

THE PURCHASES RETURNS BOOK

In Chapter 29 we saw that a **credit note** is sent by the seller to the buyer in any of the following cases:

1. if some of the goods are returned to the seller
2. in the event of an overcharge
3. if some of the invoiced goods were not delivered
4. if some of the goods were damaged or were of an inferior quality to the ones ordered.

In all of these cases the **purchases returns book** is used to write up the information contained in the **credit note** received by the buyer.

Thus we can say that the **source documents** used to write up the purchases returns book are **credit notes received**.

You will recall that a credit note is a document sent by the seller to the buyer showing the reduction in the amount owed by the buyer. We will now look at a credit note received.

CREDIT NOTE NO. 57

Tel 01 203498 Fax 01 203478 Email swift@iol.ie	**Swift Products Ltd** 10 Main St Cobh, Co. Cork	Vat Registration no. IE 1234567W

To: Joe Soap Ltd
11 High St
Dingle
Co. Kerry

10/12/12

Quantity	Description	Model No.	Price each (€)	Total (€)
2	23″ Colour TVs	TV 023	200.00	400.00
3	DVD Players	DV 345	150.00	450.00
5	Video Recorders	VR 567	90.00	450.00
			Total excluding VAT	1,300.00
			Trade discount 10%	130.00
			Subtotal (net)	1,170.00
			VAT 10%	117.00
			Total including VAT	1,287.00

PURCHASES RETURNS BOOK

Date	Details	F	Net/ Purch. Ret. €	VAT €	Total €
10/12/12	Swift Products Ltd Cr. note no. 345	CL	1,170.00	117.00	1,287.00

From this you can see that the purchases returns book is written up in the same way as the purchases book, but the credit note received is the source document rather than the invoice received.

Note: We are calling the *Net* column the *Net/Purchases Returns* column until you get used to the idea that the net column is the value of the purchases returns.

EXERCISE 2
Purchases returns book, ledgers and trial balance

Record the following credit transaction in the purchases returns book of Abbott Ltd, post them to the ledgers and extract a trial balance on the last day of the month.

All transactions are subject to VAT of 21%.

- 4/1/13 Returned goods to Lyons Ltd
  Credit note received no. 88 €1,000
- 8/1/13 Returned goods to Malone Ltd
  Credit note received no. 56 €2,100
- 9/1/13 Returned goods to Nolan Ltd
  Credit note received no. 96 €3,000

Step 1: Enter the transaction in the purchases book and show the total for each column.

PURCHASES RETURNS BOOK (page 1)					
Date	Details	F	Net/ Purch. Ret. €	VAT €	Total €
4/1/13	Lyons Ltd, Cr. note no. 88	CL1	1,000.00	210.00	1,210.00
8/1/13	Malone Ltd, Cr. note no. 56	CL2	2,100.00	441.00	2,541.00
9/1/13	Nolan Ltd, Cr. note no. 96	CL3	3,000.00	630.00	3,630.00
		GL1, 2	6,100.00	1,281.00	7,381.00

Post to **credit** side of these accounts

Post to **debit** side of their A/Cs. **Debit the receiver**

Step 2: Post the **individual** amounts in the **third column** (the *Total* column) to the debit side of the respective personal accounts in the creditors ledger. *Remember:* **Debit the receiver**. When the buyer returns goods, the seller becomes the receiver of these goods. See below.

Step 3: Post the **totals** of the first two columns to the **credit side** of the **purchases returns** and **VAT accounts** in the general ledger. These are items **given** by the buyer to the seller. *Remember:* **Credit items given**. See below.

Creditors ledger

Debit side			LYONS LTD A/C (1)				Credit side
Date	Details	F	€	Date	Details	F	€
4/1/13	Purchase returns	PRB1	1,210.00				

MALONE LTD A/C (2)							
Date	Details	F	€	Date	Details	F	€
8/1/13	Purchase returns	PRB1	2,541.00				

NOLAN LTD A/C (3)							
Date	Details	F	€	Date	Details	F	€
9/1/13	Purchase returns	PRB1	3,630.00				

General ledger

Debit side		PURCHASES RETURNS A/C (1)					Credit side
Date	Details	F	€	Date	Details	F	€
				31/1/13	Sundry creditors	PRB1	6,100.00

VAT A/C (2)							
Date	Details	F	€	Date	Details	F	€
				31/1/13	Sundry creditors	PRB1	1,281.00

Step 4: Extract the trial balance. *Remember:* a **debit in the ledger** is also a **debit in the trial balance** and a **credit in the ledger** is also a **credit in the trial balance**.

TRIAL BALANCE AT 31/1/13		
	Dr €	Cr €
Lyons Ltd A/C	1,210.00	
Malone Ltd A/C	2,541.00	
Nolan Ltd A/C	3,630.00	
Purchases returns A/C		6,100.00
VAT A/C		1,281.00
	7,381.00	7381.00

Summary

1. The purchases returns book is written up using the details shown in credit notes received.
2. The **individual amounts** in the **Total column** are posted to the **debit side of the personal accounts** in the creditors ledger. *Remember:* Debit the receiver.
3. The **total** of the **Net (purchases returns) column** is posted to the **credit side of the purchases returns account** in the general ledger. *Remember:* Credit items given.
4. The **total** of the **VAT column** is posted to the **credit side of the VAT account** in the general ledger (part of the cost of **items given**).
5. The **dates** in the **Purchases returns** and **VAT accounts** are usually the last day of the month.

EXERCISE 3
Combined purchases and purchases returns books, ledgers and trial balance

This exercise involves posting both the purchases book and the purchases returns book to the ledgers and extracting a trial balance.

Remember: there is only **one account** for each person or company and only **one VAT account**.

All transactions are subject to 13½%. VAT.

Record the following transactions in the purchase and purchases returns books of J. Hayes Ltd, post them to the ledgers and extract a trial balance on the last day of the month.

- 1/4/13 Purchased goods on credit from S. Slater Ltd Invoice no. 76 €7,000
- 4/4/13 Purchased goods on credit from T. Tynan Ltd Invoice no. 64 €8,000
- 5/4/13 Returned goods to S. Slater Ltd Credit note no. 32 €1,500
- 7/4/13 Returned goods to T. Tynan Ltd Credit note no. 48 €2,000
- 9/4/13 Purchased goods on credit from U. Urney Ltd Invoice no. 87 €3,000
- 11/4/13 Returned goods to U. Urney Ltd Credit note no. 53 €1,000

PURCHASES BOOK (page 2)

Date	Details	F	Net/ Purchases €	VAT €	Total €
1/4/13	S. Slater Ltd, Inv. no. 76	CL1	7,000.00	945.00	**7,945.00**
4/4/13	T. Tynan Ltd, Inv. no. 64	CL2	8,000.00	1,080.00	**9,080.00**
9/4/13	U. Urney Ltd, Inv. no. 87	CL3	3,000.00	405.00	**3,405.00**
		GL1, 3	**18,000.00**	**2,430.00**	20,430.00

PURCHASES RETURNS BOOK (page 2)

Date	Details	F	Net/ Purch. Ret. €	VAT €	Total €
5/4/13	S. Slater Ltd, Cr. note no. 32	CL1	1,500.00	202.50	**1,702.50**
7/4/13	T. Tynan Ltd, Cr. note no. 48	CL2	2,000.00	270.00	**2,270.00**
11/4/13	U. Urney Ltd, Cr. note no. 53	CL3	1,000.00	135.00	**1,135.00**
		GL2, 3	**4,500.00**	**607.50**	5,107.50

Creditors ledger

Debit side — S. SLATER LTD A/C (1) — Credit side

Date	Details	F	€	Date	Details	F	€
5/4/13	Purchase returns	PRB2	1,702.50	1/4/13	Purchases	PB2	7,945.00
30/4/13	Balance c/d		6,242.50				
			7,945.00				7,945.00
				1/5/13	Balance b/d		6,242.50

T. TYNAN LTD A/C (2)

Date	Details	F	€	Date	Details	F	€
7/4/13	Purchase returns	PRB2	2,270.00	4/4/13	Purchases	PB2	9,080.00
30/4/13	Balance c/d		6,810.00				
			9,080.00				9,080.00
				1/5/13	Balance b/d		6,810.00

U. URNEY LTD A/C (3)

Date	Details	F	€	Date	Details	F	€
11/4/13	Purchase Returns	PRB2	1,135.00	9/4/13	Purchases	PB2	3,405.00
30/4/13	Balance c/d		2,270.00				
			3,405.00				3,405.00
				1/5/13	Balance b/d		2,270.00

General ledger

Debit side — PURCHASES A/C (1) — Credit side

Date	Details	F	€	Date	Details	F	€
30/4/13	Sundry creditors	PB2	18,000.00				

PURCHASES RETURNS A/C (2)

Date	Details	F	€	Date	Details	F	€
				30/4/13	Sundry creditors	PRB2	4,500.00

VAT A/C (3)

Date	Details	F	€	Date	Details	F	€
30/4/13	Sundry creditors	PB2	2,430.00	30/4/13	Sundry creditors	PRB2	607.50
				30/4/13	Balance c/d		1,822.50
			2,430.00				2,430.00
1/5/13	Balance b/d		1,822.50				

TRIAL BALANCE AT 30/4/13		
	Dr €	Cr €
S. Slater Ltd A/C		6,242.50
T. Tynan Ltd A/C		6,810.00
U. Urney Ltd A/C		2,270.00
Purchases A/C	18,000.00	
Purchases Returns A/C		4,500.00
VAT A/C	1,822.50	
	19,822.50	19,822.50

CASH PURCHASES FOR RESALE

Not all purchases for resale are credit purchases. Sometimes firms pay for the goods at the time of purchase. These are known as **cash purchases**, regardless of whether they are paid for by cash or by cheque.

Cash purchases are recorded in the cash book (credit side) and posted to the debit side of the purchases account in the general ledger.

Example

D. Deasy Ltd purchased goods by cheque (no. 400916) on 1/1/13.

ANALYSED CASH BOOK (credit side only)				
Date	Details	F	Bank €	Purchase €
1/1/13	Purchases, Chq. 400916	GL1	6,606.00	6,606.00

General ledger

Debit side		PURCHASES A/C (1)					Credit side
Date	Details	F	€	Date	Details	F	€
1/1/13	Bank	CB1	6,606.00				

SUMMARY

THE PURCHASES BOOK

The purchases book is used to record the credit purchase of goods in which the company normally deals.

Source documents

Invoices received by the buyer.

Posting from the purchases book

(a) The **individual amounts** in the **Total column** are posted to the **credit side of the personal accounts** in the creditors ledger. *Remember:* Credit the giver.

(b) The **total** of the **Net column** is posted to the **debit side of the purchases account**. *Remember:* Debit items received.

(c) The **total** of the **VAT column** is posted to the **debit side of the VAT account** (part of the cost of items received).

THE PURCHASES RETURNS BOOK

The purchases returns book is used to record the return of goods that had originally been recorded in the purchases book.

Source documents

Credit notes received by the buyer.

Posting from the purchases returns book

(a) The **individual amounts** in the **total column** are posted to the **debit side of the personal accounts** in the creditors ledger. *Remember:* Debit the receiver.

(b) The **total** of the **Net column** is posted to the **credit side of the purchases account** in the general ledger. *Remember:* Credit items given.

(c) The **total** of the **VAT column** is posted to the **credit side of the VAT account** in the general ledger (part of the cost of items given).

THE TRIAL BALANCE

(a) A **debit balance** in the **ledger** is entered as a **debit** in the **trial balance**.

(b) A **credit balance** in the **ledger** is entered as a **credit** in the **trial balance**.

QUESTIONS

Purchases book

In each of the following cases write up the firm's purchases book, post the relevant figures to the ledgers and extract a trial balance on the last day of the month.

1.	1/1/13	Purchased goods on credit from J. Jones Ltd	Invoice no. 21	€13,000	VAT 21%
	3/1/13	Purchased goods on credit from S. Smith Ltd	Invoice no. 67	€15,000	VAT 21%
	6/1/13	Purchased goods on credit from M. Mongey Ltd	Invoice no. 21	€13,000	VAT 21%
	9/1/13	Purchased goods on credit from N. Noonan Ltd	Invoice no. 43	€18,000	VAT 21%
2.	5/2/13	Purchased goods on credit from C. Cullen Ltd	Invoice no. 56	€12,000	VAT 21%
	6/2/13	Purchased goods on credit from D. Dunne Ltd	Invoice no. 87	€17,000	VAT 21%
	8/2/13	Purchased goods on credit from F. Flynn Ltd	Invoice no. 21	€16,000	VAT 21%
	9/2/13	Purchased goods on credit from G. Gunne Ltd	Invoice no. 45	€10,000	VAT 21%
3.	6/3/13	Purchased goods on credit from R. O'Reilly Ltd	Invoice no. 76	€13,000	VAT 13½%
	9/3/13	Purchased goods on credit from B. O'Brien Ltd	Invoice no. 56	€9,000	VAT 13½%
	10/3/13	Purchased goods on credit from D. O'Leary Ltd	Invoice no. 23	€22,000	VAT 13½%
	12/3/13	Purchased goods on credit from R. O'Gara Ltd	Invoice no. 67	€18,500	VAT 13½%
4.	3/4/13	Purchased goods on credit from G. McCarthy Ltd	Invoice no. 18	€26,500	VAT 21%
	5/4/13	Purchased goods on credit from S. O'Halpin Ltd	Invoice no. 16	€29,000	VAT 21%
	7/4/13	Purchased goods on credit from F. Murphy Ltd	Invoice no. 12	€12,500	VAT 21%
	9/4/13	Purchased goods on credit from B. O'Sullivan Ltd	Invoice no. 14	€13,500	VAT 21%
5.	3/5/13	Purchased goods on credit from D. Hyde Ltd	Invoice no. 73	€11,500	VAT 13½%
	6/5/13	Purchased goods on credit from S. O'Kelly Ltd	Invoice no. 93	€12,000	VAT 13½%
	8/5/13	Purchased goods on credit from E. de Valera Ltd	Invoice no. 56	€13,000	VAT 13½%
	10/5/13	Purchased goods on credit from E. Childers Ltd	Invoice no. 23	€14,000	VAT 13½%

Purchases returns book

In each of the following cases write up the firm's purchases returns book, post the relevant figures to the ledgers and extract a trial balance on the last day of the month.

6.	1/5/13	Returned goods to J. Giles Ltd	Credit note no. 21	€6,000	VAT 21%
	5/5/13	Returned goods to E. Dunphy Ltd	Credit note no. 98	€4,000	VAT 21%
	7/5/13	Returned goods to L. Brady Ltd	Credit note no. 52	€1,500	VAT 21%
	9/5/13	Returned goods to R. Whelan Ltd	Credit note no. 46	€4,500	VAT 21%
7.	2/6/13	Returned goods to G. O'Hara Ltd	Credit note no. 98	€4,000	VAT 21%
	4/6/13	Returned goods to G. Dwyer Ltd	Credit note no. 26	€6,500	VAT 21%
	6/6/13	Returned goods to P. Whelan Ltd	Credit note no. 86	€7,000	VAT 21%
	8/6/13	Returned goods to L. Hartigan Ltd	Credit note no. 76	€2,500	VAT 21%
8.	5/7/13	Returned goods to J. Lynch Ltd	Credit note no. 37	€6,400	VAT 21%
	7/7/13	Returned goods to C. Haughey Ltd	Credit note no. 31	€3,300	VAT 21%
	9/7/13	Returned goods to G. Fitzgerald Ltd	Credit note no. 42	€2,200	VAT 21%
	11/7/13	Returned goods to B. Ahern Ltd	Credit note no. 91	€6,400	VAT 21%
9.	1/8/13	Returned goods to E. Hand Ltd	Credit note no. 11	€7,700	VAT 21%
	3/8/13	Returned goods to J. Charlton Ltd	Credit note no. 22	€8,800	VAT 21%
	7/8/13	Returned goods to M. McCarthy Ltd	Credit note no. 33	€9,900	VAT 21%
	10/8/13	Returned goods to S. Staunton Ltd	Credit note no. 37	€6,600	VAT 21%

10.	1/9/13	Returned goods to P. Harrington Ltd	Credit note no. 88	€3,300	VAT 13½%
	5/9/13	Returned goods to R. McIlroy Ltd	Credit note no. 56	€5,700	VAT 13½%
	8/9/13	Returned goods to D. Clarke Ltd	Credit note no. 49	€6,400	VAT 13½%
	12/9/13	Returned goods to P. McGinley Ltd	Credit note no. 77	€8,100	VAT 13½%

Purchases and purchases returns book

In each of the following cases write up the firm's purchases and purchases returns book, post the relevant figures to the ledgers and extract a trial balance on the last day of the month.

11.	4/10/13	Purchased goods on credit from J. Devitt Ltd	Invoice no. 14	€15,600	VAT 21%
	7/10/13	Returned goods to J. Devitt Ltd	Credit note no. 77	€8,100	VAT 21%
	8/10/13	Purchased goods on credit from K. Smith Ltd	Invoice no. 61	€19,100	VAT 21%
	9/10/13	Returned goods to K. Smith Ltd	Credit note no. 11	€8,000	VAT 21%
	1/11/13	Purchased goods on credit from T. Matthews Ltd	Invoice no. 14	€20,000	VAT 21%
	5/11/13	Purchased goods on credit from P. Quinn Ltd	Invoice no. 49	€24,000	VAT 21%
	7/11/13	Returned goods to P. Quinn Ltd	Credit note no. 66	€1,100	VAT 21%
	7/11/13	Returned goods to T. Matthews Ltd	Credit note no. 11	€8,000	VAT 21%
13.	1/12/13	Purchased goods on credit from G. McCauley Ltd	Invoice no. 41	€40,000	VAT 21%
	2/12/13	Purchased goods on credit from G. McCauley Ltd	Invoice no. 56	€23,000	VAT 21%
	5/12/13	Purchased goods on credit from F. O'Connor Ltd	Invoice no. 76	€34,000	VAT 21%
	7/12/13	Returned goods to G. McCauley Ltd	Credit note no. 11	€3,100	VAT 21%
	9/12/13	Returned goods to F. O'Connor Ltd	Credit note no. 32	€1,100	VAT 21%
14.	1/1/12	Purchased goods on credit from M. Ryan Ltd	Invoice no. 47	€17,000	VAT 21%
	5/1/12	Returned goods to M. Ryan Ltd	Credit note no. 75	€4,400	VAT 21%
	7/1/12	Purchased goods on credit from E. Hurley Ltd	Invoice no. 65	€31,000	VAT 21%
	9/1/12	Returned goods to E. Hurley Ltd	Credit note no. 75	€2,200	VAT 21%
	11/1/12	Purchased goods on credit from M. Ryan Ltd	Invoice no. 53	€19,000	VAT 21%
	15/1/12	Returned goods to M. Ryan Ltd	Credit note no. 85	€3,500	VAT 21%
15.	1/2/12	Purchased goods on credit from B. Browne Ltd	Invoice no. 12	€14,500	VAT 21%
	5/2/12	Returned goods to B. Browne Ltd	Credit note no. 13	€14,500	VAT 21%
	9/2/12	Purchased goods on credit from W. White Ltd	Invoice no. 31	€28,000	VAT 21%
	12/2/12	Returned goods to W. White Ltd	Credit note no. 77	€8,500	VAT 21%
	15/2/12	Purchased goods on credit from G. Greene Ltd	Invoice no. 56	€16,900	VAT 21%
	19/2/12	Purchased goods on credit from G. Greene Ltd	Invoice no. 60	€17,000	VAT 21%
	22/2/12	Returned goods to G. Greene Ltd	Credit note no. 24	€8,500	VAT 21%

See workbook for more questions.

32 The sales and sales returns books

Just like its purchases, a firm has both credit and cash sales.

The Sales Book is used to record the credit sale of goods in which the business normally deals.

WRITING UP THE SALES BOOK

The **source documents** used to record entries in the sales book are **invoices sent** by the seller.

The layout of your sales book in Record Book No. 2 is as shown below:

SALES BOOK					
Date	Details	F	Net €	VAT €	Total €
1/1/13	M. Motors Ltd, Inv. no. 345	DL	100	21	121

Explanation

1. The *Date* column records the date on which the transaction took place.
2. The *Details* column gives the name of the person or company from whom the goods were purchased, plus the number of the invoice sent by the seller.
3. The *Folio* column indicates posting details, i.e. the ledger used for this account.
4. The *Net*, *VAT* and *Total* columns show the information taken from the invoice.

As mentioned in Chapter 31, you may also see some sales books in examination questions with an extra column for the invoice number as shown below.

SALES BOOK						
Date	Details	Inv. no.	F	Net €	VAT €	Total €
1/1/13	M. Motors Ltd	345	DL	100	21	121

We will now look at an invoice sent by a business and see how this is recorded in the sales book.

The following invoice was sent by Swift Products Ltd to Joe Soap Ltd. You may notice that this is the invoice that was received by Joe Soap Ltd in the previous chapter.

INVOICE NO. 57

Tel 01 203498 Fax 01 203478 Email swift@iol.ie	**Swift Products Ltd** 10 Main St Cobh, Co. Cork	Vat Registration no. IE 1234567W

To:
Joe Soap Ltd
11 High St
Dingle
Co. Kerry

Date: 3/12/12
Your Order no. 567

Quantity	Description	Model No.	Price each (€)	Total (€)
10	23″ Colour TVs	TV 023	200.00	2,000.00
20	DVD Players	DV 345	150.00	3,000.00
30	Video Recorders	VR 567	90.00	2,700.00
			Total excluding VAT	7,700.00
			Trade discount 10%	770.00
Carriage paid			Subtotal (net)	6,930.00
Terms: 5% 10 days			VAT 10%	693.00
E & OE			Total including VAT	7,623.00

SALES BOOK

Date	Details	F	Net/ Sales €	VAT €	Total €
3/12/12	Joe Soap Ltd, Inv. no. 345	CL	6,930.00	693.00	7,623.00

1. The **true price (net)** of the goods sold is €6,930.00 (the amount after the trade discount has been subtracted). This is the amount kept by the seller. This is entered in the *Net* column.

   Note: Again it would be more convenient to call the *Net* column the *Sales* column. So **initially** we will call the *Net* column the *Net/Sales* column until you get used to the idea that the *Net* column represents the cost of the *Sales*.

2. The seller must add on and collect **VAT** of €693.00. This VAT will eventually go to the government. It is entered in the VAT column.

3. Therefore the **total amount** owed by Joe Soap Ltd to Swift Products Ltd is the *Net* amount (€6,930.00) plus the VAT (€693.00) = €7,623.00.

EXERCISE 1

Sales book, ledgers and trial balance

Record the following credit transactions in the sales book of Abbott Ltd, post them to the ledgers and extract a trial balance on the last day of the month.

All transactions are subject to VAT of 21%.

- 1/1/13 Sold goods on credit to Dunne Ltd
Invoice sent no. 21 €10,000
- 3/1/13 Sold goods on credit to Flynn Ltd
Invoice sent no. 22 €15,000
- 5/1/13 Sold goods on credit to Healy Ltd
Invoice sent no. 23 €30,000

SALES BOOK (page 1)

Date	Details	F	Net/ Sales €	VAT €	Total €
1/1/13	Dunne Ltd, Inv. no. 21	DL1	10,000.00	2,100.00	12,100.00
3/1/13	Flynn Ltd, Inv. no. 22	DL2	15,000.00	3,150.00	18,150.00
5/1/13	Healy Ltd, Inv. no. 23	DL3	30,000.00	6,300.00	36,300.00
		GL1, 2	55,000.00	11,550.00	66,550.00

Post to **credit** side of these accounts. **Credit items given.**

Post to **debit** side of their accounts. **Debit the receiver.**

Step 1: Enter the transaction in the sales book and show the total for each column.

Step 2: Post the **individual amounts** in the **third column** (the *Total* column) to the debit side of the respective personal accounts in the debtors ledger. *Remember:* **Debit the receiver.** See below.

Step 3: Post the **totals** of the first two columns to the credit side of the *Sales* and *VAT* accounts in the general ledger. The goods sold by Abbott Ltd are items given by the firm. *Remember:* **Credit items given.** See below.

Debtors ledger

Debit side — **DUNNE LTD A/C (1)** — Credit side

Date	Details	F	€	Date	Details	F	€
1/1/13	Sales	SB1	12,100.00				

FLYNN LTD A/C (2)

Date	Details	F	€	Date	Details	F	€
3/1/13	Sales	SB1	18,150.00				

HEALY LTD A/C (3)

Date	Details	F	€	Date	Details	F	€
5/1/13	Sales	SB1	36,300.00				

General ledger

Debit side		SALES A/C (1)					Credit side
Date	Details	F	€	Date	Details	F	€
				31/1/13	Sundry debtors	SB1	55,000.00

		VAT A/C (2)					
Date	Details	F	€	Date	Details	F	€
				31/1/13	Sundry debtors	SB1	11,550.00

Step 4: Extract the trial balance. *Remember:* a **debit in the ledger** is also a **debit in the trial balance** and a **credit in the ledger** is also a **credit in the trial balance**.

TRIAL BALANCE AT 31/1/13		
	Dr €	Cr €
Dunne Ltd A/C	12,100.00	
Flynn Ltd A/C	18,150.00	
Healy Ltd A/C	36,300.00	
Sales A/C		55,000.00
VAT A/C		11,550.00
	66,550.00	66,550.00

Summary

1. The sales book is written up using the details shown in invoices sent: 's' for **sent** and 's' for **sales**.
2. The **individual amounts** in the **Total column** are posted to the **debit side of the personal accounts**. *Remember:* **Debit the receiver**.
3. The **total** of the **Net (sales) column** is posted to the **credit side of the sales account**. *Remember:* **Credit items given**.
4. The **total** of the **VAT column** is posted to the **credit side of the VAT account** (part of the price of items given).
5. The **dates** in the **Sales** and **VAT accounts** are usually the last day of the month.

THE SALES RETURNS BOOK

In Chapter 29 we saw that a credit note is sent by the seller to the buyer in any of the following cases:

1. if some of the goods are returned to the seller
2. in the event of an overcharge
3. if some of the invoiced goods were not delivered
4. if some of the goods were damaged or were of an inferior quality to those ordered.

In all of these cases the **sales returns book** is used to write up the information contained in the **credit note** sent by the seller.

Thus we can say that the **source documents** used to write up the sales returns book are **credit notes sent**.

You will recall that a credit note is a document sent by the seller to the buyer showing the reduction in the amount owed by the buyer. We will now look at a credit note sent by a seller.

CREDIT NOTE NO. 57

Tel 01 203498
Fax 01 203478
Email swift@iol.ie

Swift Products Ltd
10 Main St
Cobh, Co. Cork

Vat Registration no.
IE 1234567W

To: **Joe Soap Ltd**
11 High St
Dingle
Co. Kerry

10/12/12

Quantity	Description	Model No.	Price each (€)	Total (€)
2	23″ Colour TVs	TV 023	200.00	400.00
3	DVD Players	DV 345	150.00	450.00
5	Video Recorders	VR 567	90.00	450.00
			Total excluding VAT	1,300.00
			Trade discount 10%	130.00
			Subtotal (net)	1,170.00
			VAT 10%	117.00
			Total including VAT	1,287.00

SALES RETURNS BOOK

Date	Details	F	Net/ Sales Ret. €	VAT €	Total €
10/12/12	Swift Products Ltd, Credit note no. 345	CL	1,170.00	117.00	1,287.00

From this you can see that the sales returns book is written up in the same way as the sales book, but the credit note sent is the source document rather than the invoice sent.

Note: We are calling the *Net* column the *Net/Sales Returns* column until you get used to the idea that the *Net* column is the value of the sales returns.

EXERCISE 2

Sales returns book, ledgers and trial balance

Record the following credit transaction in the sales returns book of Abbott Ltd, post them to the ledgers and extract a trial balance on the last day of the month.

All transactions are subject to VAT of 21%.

- 4/1/13 Dunne Ltd returned goods Credit note sent no. 88 €2,000
- 8/1/13 Flynn Ltd returned goods Credit note sent no. 89 €2,100
- 9/1/13 Healy Ltd returned goods Credit note sent no. 90 €3,000

Step 1: Enter the transaction in the sales returns book and show the total for each column.

SALES RETURNS BOOK (page 1)

Date	Details	F	Net/ Sales Ret. €	VAT €	Total €
4/1/13	Dunne Ltd, Credit note no. 88	DL1	2,000.00	420.00	2,420.00
8/1/13	Flynn Ltd, Credit note no. 89	DL2	2,100.00	441.00	2,541.00
9/1/13	Healy Ltd, Credit note no. 90	DL3	3,000.00	630.00	3,630.00
		GL1, 2	7,100.00	1,491.00	8,591.00

Post to **debit** side of these accounts. **Debit items received.**

Post to **credit** side of their accounts. **Credit the giver.**

Step 2: Post the **individual amounts** in the **third column** (the *Total* column) to the credit side of the respective personal accounts in the debtors ledger. *Remember:* **Credit the giver**. When the buyer returns goods, the seller becomes the receiver of these goods. See below.

Step 3: Post the **totals** of the first two columns to the debit side of the **sales returns** and **VAT accounts** in the general ledger. These are items **received back** by the seller *Remember:* **Debit items received**. See below.

Creditors ledger

DUNNE LTD A/C (1) (Debit side | Credit side)

Date	Details	F	€	Date	Details	F	€
				4/1/13	Sales returns	SRB1	2,420.00

FLYNN LTD A/C (2)

Date	Details	F	€	Date	Details	F	€
				8/1/13	Sales returns	SRB1	2,541.00

HEALY LTD A/C (3)

Date	Details	F	€	Date	Details	F	€
				9/1/13	Sales returns	SRB1	3,630.00

General ledger

Debit side		SALES RETURNS A/C (1)					Credit side
Date	Details	F	€	Date	Details	F	€
31/1/13	Sundry debtors	SRB1	7,100.00				

		VAT A/C (2)					
Date	Details	F	€	Date	Details	F	€
31/1/13	Sundry debtors	SRB1	1,491.00				

Step 4: Extract the trial balance. *Remember:* a **debit in the ledger** is also a **debit in the trial balance** and a **credit in the ledger** is also a **credit in the trial balance**.

TRIAL BALANCE AT 31/1/13		
	Dr €	Cr €
Dunne Ltd A/C		2,420.00
Flynn Ltd A/C		2,541.00
Healy Ltd A/C		3,630.00
Sales returns A/C	7,100.00	
VAT A/C	1,491.00	
	8,591.00	8,591.00

Summary

1. The sales returns book is written up using the details shown in credit notes sent.
2. The **individual amounts** in the **Total column** are posted to the **credit side of the personal accounts**. *Remember:* Credit the giver.
3. The **total** of the **Net (sales returns) column** is posted to the **debit side of the sales returns account**. *Remember:* Debit items received.
4. The **total** of the **VAT column** is posted to the **debit side of the VAT account** (part of the price of **items received**).
5. The **dates** in the **Sales returns** and **VAT accounts** are usually the last day of the month.

EXERCISE 3

Combined sales and sales returns books, ledgers and trial balance

This exercise involves posting both the sales book and the sales returns book to the ledgers and extracting a trial balance.

Remember: there is only **one account** for each person or company and only **one VAT account**.

All transactions are subject to 13½% VAT.

Record the following transactions in the sales and sales returns books of J. Hayes Ltd, post them to the ledgers and extract a trial balance on the last day of the month.

- 1/4/13 Sold goods on credit to Fox Ltd Invoice no. 76 €7,000
- 4/4/13 Sold goods on credit to Badger Ltd Invoice no. 77 €8,000
- 5/4/13 Fox Ltd returned goods Credit note no. 32 €1,500
- 7/4/13 Badger Ltd returned goods Credit note no. 33 €2,000
- 9/4/13 Sold goods on credit to Hare Ltd Invoice no. 78 €3,000
- 11/4/13 Hare Ltd returned goods Credit note no. 34 €1,000

SALES BOOK (page 2)

Date	Details	F	Net/ Sales €	VAT €	Total €
1/4/13	Fox Ltd, Inv. no. 76	DL1	7,000.00	945.00	**7,945.00**
4/4/13	Badger Ltd, Inv. no. 77	DL2	8,000.00	1,080.00	**9,080.00**
9/4/13	Hare Ltd, Inv. no. 78	DL3	3,000.00	405.00	**3,405.00**
		GL1, 3	**18,000.00**	**2,430.00**	20,430.00

SALES RETURNS BOOK (page 2)

Date	Details	F	Net/ Sales Ret. €	VAT €	Total €
5/4/13	Fox Ltd, Credit note no. 32	DL1	1,500.00	202.50	**1,702.50**
7/4/13	Badger Ltd, Credit note no. 33	DL2	2,000.00	270.00	**2,270.00**
11/4/13	Hare Ltd, Credit note no. 34	DL3	1,000.00	135.00	**1,135.00**
		GL2, 3	**4,500.00**	**607.50**	5,107.50

Debtors ledger

Debit side				FOX LTD A/C (1)			Credit side
Date	Details	F	€	Date	Details	F	€
1/4/13	Sales	SB2	7,945.00	5/4/13	Sales returns	SRB2	1,702.50
				30/4/13	Balance c/d		6,242.50
			7,945.00				7,945.00
1/5/13	Balance b/d		6,242.50				

				BADGER LTD A/C (2)			
Date	Details	F	€	Date	Details	F	€
4/4/13	Sales	SB2	9,080.00	7/4/13	Sales Returns	SRB2	2,270.00
				30/4/13	Balance c/d		6,810.00
			9,080.00				9,080.00
1/5/13	Balance b/d		6,810.00				

				HARE LTD A/C (3)			
Date	Details	F	€	Date	Details	F	€
9/4/13	Sales	SB2	3,405.00	11/4/13	Sales Returns	SRB2	1,135.00
				30/4/13	Balance c/d		2,270.00
			3,405.00				3,405.00
1/5/13	Balance b/d		2,270.00				

General ledger

Debit side				SALES A/C (1)			Credit side
Date	Details	F	€	Date	Details	F	€
				30/4/13	Sundry debtors	SB2	18,000.00

				SALES RETURNS A/C (2)			
Date	Details	F	€	Date	Details	F	€
30/4/13	Sundry debtors	SRB2	4,500.00				

				VAT A/C (3)			
Date	Details	F	€	Date	Details	F	€
30/4/13	Sundry debtors	SRB2	607.50	30/4/13	Sundry debtors	SB2	2,430.00
30/4/13	Balance c/d		1,822.50				
			2,430.00				2,430.00
				1/5/13	Balance b/d		1,822.50

TRIAL BALANCE AT 30/4/13		
	Dr €	Cr €
Fox Ltd A/C	6,242.50	
Badger Ltd A/C	6,810.00	
Hare Ltd A/C	2,270.00	
Sales A/C		18,000.00
Sales Returns A/C	4,500.00	
VAT A/C		1,822.50
	19,822.50	19,822.50

SUMMARY

THE SALES BOOK

The sales book is used to record the credit sale of goods in which the company normally deals.

Source documents

Invoices sent by the seller.

Posting from the sales book

(a) The **individual amounts** in the **total column** are posted to the **debit side of the personal accounts** in the debtors ledger. *Remember:* Debit the receiver.

(b) The **total** of the **Net column** is posted to the **credit side of the sales account** in the general ledger. *Remember:* Credit items given.

(c) The **total** of the **VAT column** is posted to the **credit side of the VAT account** in the general ledger (part of the price of items given).

THE SALES RETURNS BOOK

The sales returns book is used to record the return of goods that had originally been recorded in the sales book.

Source documents

Credit notes sent by the seller.

Posting from the sales returns book

(a) The **individual amounts** in the **total column** are posted to the **credit side of the personal accounts** in the debtors ledger. *Remember:* Credit the giver.

(b) The **total** of the **Net column** is posted to the **debit side of the sales returns account** in the general ledger. *Remember:* Debit items received.

(c) The **total** of the **VAT column** is posted to the **debit side of the VAT account** in the general ledger (part of the price of items received).

THE TRIAL BALANCE

(a) A **debit balance** in the ledger is entered as a **debit** in the **trial balance**.

(b) A **credit balance** in the ledger is entered as a **credit** in the **trial balance**.

QUESTIONS

Sales book

In each of the following cases write up the firm's sales book, post the relevant figures to the ledgers and extract a trial balance on the last day of the month.

	Date	Details	Invoice	Amount	VAT
1.	1/1/13	Sold goods on credit to R. Roberts Ltd	Invoice no. 21	€8,000	VAT 21%
	3/1/13	Sold goods on credit to P. Power Ltd	Invoice no. 22	€9,000	VAT 21%
	6/1/13	Sold goods on credit to D. Dunne Ltd	Invoice no. 23	€10,000	VAT 21%
	9/1/13	Sold goods on credit to C. Cooney Ltd	Invoice no. 24	€12,000	VAT 21%
2.	5/2/13	Sold goods on credit to G. Grogan Ltd	Invoice no. 56	€15,000	VAT 21%
	6/2/13	Sold goods on credit to F. Feeney Ltd	Invoice no. 57	€18,000	VAT 21%
	8/2/13	Sold goods on credit to M. Moore Ltd	Invoice no. 58	€19,000	VAT 21%
	9/2/13	Sold goods on credit to T. Timmons Ltd	Invoice no. 59	€22,000	VAT 21%
3.	6/3/13	Sold goods on credit to R. O'Reilly Ltd	Invoice no. 76	€11,000	VAT 13½%
	9/3/13	Sold goods on credit to B. O'Brien Ltd	Invoice no. 77	€6,000	VAT 13½%
	10/3/13	Sold goods on credit to D. O'Leary Ltd	Invoice no. 78	€14,000	VAT 13½%
	12/3/13	Sold goods on credit to R. O'Gara Ltd	Invoice no. 79	€17,000	VAT 13½%
4.	3/4/13	Sold goods on credit to K. Keogh Ltd	Invoice no. 18	€6,500	VAT 21%
	5/4/13	Sold goods on credit to Q. Quinn Ltd	Invoice no. 19	€9,500	VAT 21%
	7/4/13	Sold goods on credit to V. Vaughan Ltd	Invoice no. 20	€8,500	VAT 21%
	9/4/13	Sold goods on credit to W. Walsh Ltd	Invoice no. 21	€10,500	VAT 21%

Sales returns book

In each of the following cases write up the firm's sales returns book, post the relevant figures to the ledgers and extract a trial balance on the last day of the month.

5.	1/5/13	S. Smith Ltd returned goods	Credit note no. 21	€6,000	VAT 21%
	3/5/13	H. Healy Ltd returned goods	Credit note no. 22	€7,500	VAT 21%
	5/5/13	M. Malone Ltd returned goods	Credit note no. 23	€4,500	VAT 21%
	7/5/13	W. Whelan Ltd returned goods	Credit note no. 24	€8,500	VAT 21%
6.	5/6/13	L. Kelly Ltd returned goods	Credit note no. 92	€4,000	VAT 21%
	7/6/13	R. Drew Ltd returned goods	Credit note no. 93	€2,500	VAT 21%
	9/6/13	B. McKenna returned goods	Credit note no. 94	€1,500	VAT 21%
	11 /6/13	J. Sheehan Ltd returned goods	Credit note no. 95	€9,500	VAT 21%
7.	5/7/13	Beano Ltd returned goods	Credit note no. 37	€3,500	VAT 21%
	7/7/13	Dandy Ltd returned goods	Credit note no. 38	€2,700	VAT 21%
	9/7/13	Handy Ltd returned goods	Credit note no. 39	€8,300	VAT 21%
	11/7/13	Tidy Ltd returned goods	Credit note no. 40	€4,600	VAT 21%
8.	1/8/13	Deco Ltd returned goods	Credit note no. 11	€1,600	VAT 21%
	3/8/13	Redco Ltd returned goods	Credit note no. 12	€2,700	VAT 21%
	7/8/13	Medico Ltd returned goods	Credit note no. 13	€3,800	VAT 21%
	10/8/13	Henco Ltd returned goods	Credit note no. 14	€4,900	VAT 21%

Sales and sales returns book

In each of the following cases write up the firm's sales and sales returns book, post the relevant figures to the ledgers, balance the accounts where necessary and extract a trial balance on the last day of the month.

9.	4/10/13	Sold goods on credit to Awl Rite Ltd	Invoice no. 14	€15,000	VAT 21%
	7/10/13	Awl Rite Ltd returned goods	Credit note no. 77	€8,000	VAT 21%
	8/10/13	Sold goods on credit to Awl Rite Ltd	Invoice no. 15	€19,000	VAT 21%
	9/10/13	Awl Rite Ltd returned goods	Credit note no. 78	€5,000	VAT 21%
10.	1/11/13	Sold goods on credit to Hi-Jump Ltd	Invoice no. 14	€25,000	VAT 21%
	5/11/13	Sold goods on credit to Low Lites Ltd	Invoice no. 15	€30,000	VAT 21%
	7/11/13	Hi-Jump Ltd returned goods	Credit note no. 66	€8,800	VAT 21%
	7/11/13	Low Lites Ltd returned goods	Credit note no. 67	€8,000	VAT 21%
11.	1/12/13	Sold goods on credit to J. Joyce Ltd	Invoice no. 41	€40,500	VAT 21%
	2/12/13	Sold goods on credit to S. O'Casey Ltd	Invoice no. 44	€20,600	VAT 21%
	5/12/13	Sold goods on credit to J. Joyce Ltd	Invoice no. 45	€34,000	VAT 21%
	7/12/13	J. Joyce Ltd returned goods	Credit note no. 11	€3,100	VAT 21%
	9/12/13	S. O'Casey Ltd returned goods	Credit note no. 12	€1,100	VAT 21%
12.	1/1/12	Sold goods on credit to Bee Good Ltd	Invoice no. 47	€17,000	VAT 21%
	5/1/12	Bee Good Ltd returned goods	Credit note no. 75	€4,400	VAT 21%
	7/1/12	Sold goods on credit to Bee Rite Ltd	Invoice no. 48	€31,000	VAT 21%
	9/1/12	Bee Rite Ltd returned goods	Credit note no. 76	€2,200	VAT 21%
	11/1/12	Sold goods on credit to C. Ray Ltd	Invoice no. 49	€19,000	VAT 21%
	15/1/12	C. Ray Ltd returned goods	Credit note no. 77	€3,500	VAT 21%

In each of the following exercises record the credit transactions undertaken by a firm in its purchases, sales, purchases returns and sales returns books, post the relevant figures to the ledgers, balance the accounts where necessary and extract a trial balance on the last day of the month. The first exercise includes the initials of the day books to be used.

VAT of 21% applies in all cases.

13.	1/5/10	Sold goods on credit to Yeates Ltd, €10,000, Invoice no. 32
	3/5/10	Sent Invoice no. 33 for €26,000 to Dempsey Ltd
	5/5/10	Received Invoice no. 21 from McCauley Ltd for €15,000
	7/5/10	Purchased goods on credit from McLaughlin Ltd for €28,000, Invoice no. 32
	9/5/10	Received Credit note no. 41 from McCauley Ltd, €2,000
	11/5/10	Sent Credit note no. 56 to Yeates Ltd for €3,700
	15/5/10	Returned goods to McLaughlin Ltd, €35,000, Credit note no. 75
	18/5/10	Dempsey Ltd returned goods, €6,000. Credit note no. 57
14.	1/6/10	Sent Invoice no. 1 to Hughes Ltd, €30,000
	3/6/10	Sent Invoice no. 2 to O'Connor Ltd, €45,000
	6/6/10	Received Invoice no. 21 from Cummins Ltd for €15,000
	8/6/10	Received Invoice no. 21 from Altman Ltd for €35,000
	9/6/10	Sent Credit note no. 2 to Hughes Ltd, €12,000
	10/6/10	Sent Credit note no. 3 to O'Connor Ltd for €13,000
	13/6/10	Received Credit note no. 41 from Cummins Ltd, €2,000
	18/6/10	Received Credit note no. 84 from Altman Ltd, €22,000

15. 1/7/10 Sold goods on credit to O'Neill Ltd, Invoice no. 12, €5,000
4/7/10 Sent Invoice no. 13 to O'Hara Ltd, €6,000
6/7/10 Sold goods on credit to O'Neill Ltd, Invoice no. 14, €7,000
7/7/10 Sent Invoice no. 15 to O'Hara Ltd, €8,000
10/7/10 Purchased goods on credit from O' Brien Ltd, Invoice no. 25, €9,000
11/7/10 Sent Credit note no. 76 to O'Neill Ltd, €1,000
14/7/10 Sent Credit note no. 77 to O'Hara Ltd, €2,000

16. 1/8/10 Purchased goods on credit from Gilroy Ltd, Invoice no. 45, €56,000
3/8/10 Sent Invoice no. 21 to Fagan Ltd, €26,000
7/8/10 Sold goods on credit to Govan Ltd, Invoice no. 22, €37,000
9/8/10 Purchased goods on credit from Looney Ltd, Invoice no. 99, €65,000
10/8/10 Sent Credit note no. 76 to Fagan Ltd, €11,000
11/8/10 Received Credit note no. 86 from Gilroy Ltd, €11,000
14/8/10 Sent Credit note no. 77 to Govan Ltd, €2,000
15/8/10 Received Credit note no. 84 from Looney Ltd, €11,000

17. 1/1/10 Purchased goods on credit from O'Reilly Ltd, €20,000, Invoice no. 45
2/1/10 Received Invoice no. 56 from Grogan Ltd, €18,000
4/1/10 Sold goods on credit to Murphy Ltd, €37,000, Invoice no. 70
6/1/10 Returned goods to O'Reilly Ltd, €1,500, Credit note no. 54
9/1/10 Sent Invoice no. 71 to Foley Ltd, €23,000
10/1/10 Sent Credit note no. 66 to Murphy Ltd €1,600
11/1/10 Received a Credit note, no. 56, from Grogan Ltd, €6,500
15/1/10 Foley Ltd returned goods, €2,300, Credit note no. 67

18. 1/2/10 Sold goods on credit to Noonan Ltd, €6,700, Invoice no. 23
3/2/10 Sent Invoice no. 24 for €56,000 to Cooney Ltd
5/2/10 Received Invoice no. 93 from Hurley Ltd for €35,000
7/2/10 Purchased goods on credit from Flanagan Ltd for €38,000, Invoice no. 32
9/2/10 Received Credit note no. 65 from Flanagan Ltd, €12,000
11/2/10 Sent credit note no. 65 to Noonan Ltd for €6,700
15/2/10 Returned goods to Hurley Ltd, €35,000, Credit note no. 32
18/2/10 Cooney Ltd returned goods, €6,000, Credit note no. 66

19. 1/4/10 Purchased goods on credit from Haughey Ltd for €76,000, Invoice no. 34
3/4/10 Sold goods on credit to Fitzgerald Ltd, Invoice no. 45, €13,000
6/4/10 Received Credit note no. 64 from Haughey Ltd, €35,000
8/4/10 Fitzgerald Ltd returned goods, €11,000, Credit note no. 12
10/4/10 Received Invoice no. 81 from Bruton Ltd, €14,500
15/4/10 Sent Invoice no. 46 to Aherne Ltd, €23,500
18/4/10 Received Credit note no. 21 from Bruton Ltd, €1,500
20/4/10 Sent Credit note no. 13 to Aherne Ltd, €3,500

20. The following trial balance was extracted on 31/1/10. However, as you can see, it failed to balance. Spot the obvious errors in it and redraw it.

TRIAL BALANCE AT 31/1/10		
	Dr €	Cr €
Dunphy Ltd (creditor)		10,000.00
Spillane Ltd (creditor)		30,000.00
Hook Ltd (debtor)	40,000.00	
Pope Ltd (debtor)	20,000.00	
Purchases		55,000.00
Purchases returns	25,000.00	
Sales	55,000.00	
Sales returns		8,000.00
VAT (correct balance)		3,000.00
	140,000.00	106,000.00

See workbook for more questions.

33 Continuous balance ledger accounts

The ledger format that we have used so far is known as a **T-ledger** because all debit transactions are recorded to the left of the centre and all credit transactions are recorded to the right of the centre, as shown below.

X LTD A/C	
Debits	Credits

The major disadvantage of the T-format is that the balance is calculated only at the end of a given period of time.

A **continuous balance ledger account** is an account that records the debit and credit elements of transactions, and also shows the balance after each transaction.

The layout is the same as for the statement in Chapter 29 (page 253) and in the bank statements in Chapter 11 (page 106), with the addition of a *Folio* column. Thus it has six columns, as shown here:

CONTINUOUS BALANCE LEDGER					
Date	Details	F	Debit €	Credit €	Balance €

CONVERTING FROM A T-LEDGER TO A CONTINUOUS BALANCE LEDGER

EXAMPLE 1

Creditors ledger

The following is a T-ledger for TV Suppliers Ltd.

Creditors ledger

Debit side			TV SUPPLIERS LTD A/C (1)				Credit side
Date	Details	F	€	Date	Details	F	€
6/1/12	Purchases returns	PRB1	3,610	2/1/12	Purchases	PB1	12,100
31/1/12	Balance c/d		8,490				
			12,100				12,100
				2/2/12	Balance b/d		8,490

The same rules apply to both ledger formats:
Debit the receiver or items received *and* **Credit** the giver or items given.

Now we will convert this to a continuous balance ledger.

Creditors ledger

TV SUPPLIERS LTD A/C (1)					
Date	Details	F	Debit €	Credit €	Balance €
2/1/12	Purchases	PB1		12,100	12,100
6/1/12	Purchases returns	PRB1	3,610		8,490

Explanation

1. On 2/1/12 goods were purchased on credit from TV Suppliers Ltd. Therefore the A/C of TV Suppliers Ltd has to be credited (credit the giver). This is shown in the *Credit* column above. However, the *Balance* column is also used to show that TV Suppliers Ltd is now owed €12,100.00.
2. On 6/1/12 goods were returned to TV Suppliers Ltd. Therefore the A/C of TV Suppliers Ltd has to be debited (debit the receiver). This is shown in the *Debit* column above. However, the *Balance* column is also used to show that TV Suppliers Ltd is now owed only €8,490.00.

Now we will do the same for an account in the debtors ledger.

EXAMPLE 2

Debtors ledger

The following is a T-ledger for Home Suppliers Ltd.

Debtors ledger

Debit side	HOME SUPPLIERS LTD A/C (1)						Credit side
Date	Details	F	€	Date	Details	F	€
4/1/12	Sales	SB1	44,770	10/1/12	Sales returns	SRB1	6,776
				31/1/12	Balance c/d		37,994
			44,770				44,770
1/5/12	Balance b/d		37,994				

Converting this to a continuous balance format gives us the following:

Debtors ledger

HOME SUPPLIERS LTD A/C (1)					
Date	Details	F	Debit €	Credit €	Balance €
4/1/12	Sales	SB1	44,770		44,770
10/1/12	Sales returns	SRB1		6,776	37,994

Explanation

1. On 4/1/12 goods were sold on credit to Home Suppliers Ltd. Therefore the A/C of Home Suppliers Ltd has to be debited (debit the receiver). This is shown in the *Debit* column above. However, the *Balance* column is also used to show that Home Suppliers Ltd now owes €44,770.
2. On 10/1/12 Home Suppliers Ltd returned goods. Therefore the A/C of Home Suppliers Ltd has to be credited (credit the giver). This is shown in the *Credit* column above. However, the *Balance* column is also used to show that Home Suppliers Ltd now only owes €37,994.00.

Note:

In the **creditors** ledger, **credit** entries **increase** the balance; debit entries decrease the balance.

In the **debtors** ledger, **debit** entries **increase** the balance; credit entries decrease the balance.

Accounts with opening balances

In the following T-ledger in a debtor's account, there is an opening debit balance indicating that the debtor owes this amount from the previous period.

Debtors ledger

Debit side			JONES LTD A/C (1)				Credit side
Date	Details	F	€	Date	Details	F	€
1/1/12	Balance b/d		20,000.00	10/1/12	Sales returns	SRB1	6,000.00
4/1/12	Sales	SB1	40,000.00	13/1/12	Sales returns	SRB1	4,000.00
11/1/12	Sales	SB1	15,000.00	31/1/12	Balance c/d		65,000.00
			75,000.00				75,000.00
1/2/12	Balance b/d		65,000.00				

When converting this to a continuous balance format we start by **entering the opening balance in the balance column only**. We then continue as shown in the previous debtor's ledger.

Debtors ledger

JONES LTD A/C (1)					
Date	Details	F	Debit €	Credit €	Balance €
1/1/12	Balance b/d				20,000.00
4/1/12	Sales	SB1	40,000.00		60,000.00
10/1/12	Sales returns	SRB1		6,000.00	54,000.00
11/1/12	Sales	SB1	15,000.00		69,000.00
13/1/12	Sales returns	SRB1		4,000.00	65,000.00

Note: When converting items from a T-ledger to a continuous balance ledger **ensure that the transactions are entered in date order**.

REVERSING THE PROCESS

In an exam question you could be asked to convert a continuous balance ledger to a T-ledger. This is straightforward if you follow the basic rules on the giving and receiving aspect of a transaction.

However, be careful about opening balances.

If the ledger is a **creditor's ledger**, then the opening balance will be entered on the **credit side**.

If the ledger is a **debtor's ledger**, then the opening balance will be entered on the **debit side**.

Example 1

Debtors ledger

FOX LTD A/C (1)					
Date	Details	F	Debit €	Credit €	Balance €
1/4/13	Balance b/d				10,000.00
2/4/13	Sales	SB2	7,945.00		17,945.00
5/4/12	Sales returns	SRB1		1,702.50	16,242.50

This converts as follows:

Debtors ledger

Debit side		FOX LTD A/C (1)					Credit side
Date	Details	F	€	Date	Details	F	€
1/4/13	Balance b/d		10,000.00	5/4/13	Sales returns	SRB2	1,702.50
2/4/13	Sales	SB2	7,945.00	30/4/13	Balance c/d		16,242.50
			17,945.00				17,945.00
1/5/13	Balance b/d		16,242.50				

Note that the opening balance is entered on the debit side because this is a debtor's ledger account.

Example 2

Creditors ledger

HARE LTD A/C (1)					
Date	Details	F	Debit €	Credit €	Balance €
1/4/13	Balance b/d				10,000.00
2/4/13	Purchases	PB2		15,000.00	25,000.00
5/4/12	Purchases returns	PRB2	6,000.00		19,000.00

This converts as follows:

Creditors ledger

Debit side			HARE LTD A/C (1)				Credit side
Date	Details	F	€	Date	Details	F	€
5/4/12	Purchases returns	PRB2	6,000.00	1/4/13	Balance b/d		10,000.00
30/4/12	Balance c/d		19,000.00	2/4/13	Purchases	PB2	15,000.00
			25,000.00				25,000.00
				1/5/12	Balance b/d		19,000.00

Note that the opening balance is entered on the credit side because this is a creditor's ledger account.

THE GENERAL LEDGER

Continuous balance accounts are also used for non-personal accounts in the general ledger. Here are a few examples showing both the T-ledger presentation and the continuous balance presentation in each case.

Example 1

A *Wages* account

Record the following in the *Wages* account using both the 'T' and continuous balance presentations, showing the balance on the account on 14/2/12.

- 7/2/12 Balance (Dr) €980
- 14/2/12 Paid wages by cash €800

T-presentation

Debit side			WAGES A/C				Credit side
Date	Details	F	€	Date	Details	F	€
7/2/12	Balance b/d		980.00	14/2/12	Balance c/d		1,780.00
14/2/12	Cash	CB2	800.00				
			1,780.00				1,780.00
14/2/12	Balance b/d		1,780.00				

Continuous balance presentation

WAGES A/C					
Date	Details	F	Debit €	Credit €	Balance €
7/2/12	Balance				980.00
14/2/12	Cash	CB2	800.00		1,780.00

Example 2

A *Machinery* account

Record the following in the *Machinery* account using both the 'T' and continuous balance presentations, showing the balance on the account on 15/3/12.

- 1/3/12 Balance (Dr) €20,000
- 15/3/12 Sold an old machine for cash €6,000

T-presentation

Debit side			MACHINERY A/C				Credit side
Date	Details	F	€	Date	Details	F	€
1/3/12	Balance b/d		20,000.00	15/3/12	Cash	CB1	6,000.00
				15/3/12	Balance c/d		14,000.00
			20,000.00				20,000.00
15/3/12	Balance b/d		14,000.00				

Continuous balance presentation

MACHINERY A/C					
Date	Details	F	Debit €	Credit €	Balance €
1/3/12	Balance b/d				20,000.00
15/3/12	Cash	CB2		6,000.00	14,000.00

Example 3

A *Rent received* account

This is an account used to record the rent received by a firm from letting a portion of its premises to a tenant; the rent received is a **gain** to the business. *Remember:* **Credit gains**.

Record the following in the *Rent received* account using both the 'T' and continuous balance presentations, showing the balance on the account on 8/1/12.

- 1/1/12 Balance (Cr) €16,000
- 8/1/12 Received rent in cash €2,000

T-presentation

Debit side		RENT RECEIVED A/C					Credit side
Date	Details	F	€	Date	Details	F	€
8/1/12	Balance c/d		18,000.00	1/1/12	Balance b/d		16,000.00
				8/1/12	Cash	CB1	2,000.00
			18,000.00				18,000.00
				8/1/12	Balance b/d		18,000.00

Continuous balance presentation

RENT RECEIVED A/C					
Date	Details	F	Debit €	Credit €	Balance €
1/1/12	Balance b/d				16,000.00
8/1/12	Cash	CB2		2,000.00	18,000.00

Example 4

A *Bank* account

Some firms may keep their *Bank* A/C in the general ledger rather than in the analysed cash book (see next chapter).

Record the following in the *Bank* Account using both the 'T' and continuous balance presentations, showing the balance on the account on 15/4/12.

- 1/4/12 Balance (Dr) €10,000
- 5/4/12 Cash sales lodged €1,500
- 9/4/12 Cash purchases, Cheque no. 1 €2,000
- 12/4/12 Paid wages, Cheque no. 2 €1,200
- 15/4/12 Rent received, lodged €2,000

T-presentation

Debit side		BANK A/C					Credit side
Date	Details	F	€	Date	Details	F	€
1/4/12	Balance b/d		10,000.00	9/4/12	Purchases Chq. 1	GL2	2,000.00
5/4/12	Sales	GL1	1,500.00	12/4/12	Wages Chq. 2	GL3	1,200.00
15/4/12	Rent received	GL4	2,000.00	15/4/12	Balance c/d		10,300.00
			13,500.00				13,500.00
15/4/12	Balance b/d		10,300.00				

Continuous balance presentation

BANK A/C					
Date	Details	F	Debit €	Credit €	Balance €
1/4/12	Balance b/d				10,000.00
5/4/12	Sales	GL1	1,500.00		11,500.00
9/4/12	Purchases Chq. 1	GL2		2,000.00	9,500.00
12/4/12	Wages Chq. 2	GL3		1,200.00	8,300.00
15/4/12	Rent received	GL4	2,000.00		10,300.00

LEARN THE KEY TERMS

- A **continuous balance ledger account** is an account that records the debit and credit elements of transactions, and also shows the balance after each transaction.

QUESTIONS

1. Using both ledger formats, enter the following bank transactions in the bank A/C of a firm. Use your own copy for this exercise.

   1/1/10 Balance (Dr) €15,000; 3/1/10 Paid wages, Cheque no. 1 €800; 7/1/1/10 Cash sales lodged €14,500; 9/1/10 Cash purchases, Cheque no. 2 €10, 000; 11/1/10 Rent received lodged €1,700.

2. Using both ledger formats, enter the following transactions in the Debtors Ledger for Murphy Ltd.

   1/2/11 Balance due by Murphy Ltd, €10,000; 3/1/11 Sold goods on credit to Murphy Ltd, €25,000; 13/2/11 Murphy Ltd returned goods, €6,000; 15/2/11 Murphy Ltd paid €12,000 by cheque.

3. Using both ledger formats, enter the following transactions in the Creditors Ledger for Kelly Ltd.

   1/3/11 Balance due to Kelly, €15,000; Purchased goods on credit from Kelly Ltd, €24,000; Returned goods to Kelly Ltd, €2,500; Paid Kelly Ltd by cheque, €10,000.

See workbook for more questions.

34 Business accounts: **The analysed cash book**

Businesses cannot operate effectively without sufficient amounts of money. It is, therefore, essential that they keep an accurate record of all money received by them and all money paid out by them. This gives them a clear picture of their financial position at any given time, and allows them to analyse the main sources of their income and the major areas of their expenditure.

The **analysed cash book** is used to record, under appropriate headings, all income received and all payments made by a business.

Most businesses lodge all money received to their bank accounts and make *all* payments through their bank accounts by using cheques, direct debits, credit transfers and standing orders.

However, *some* small regular payments are made in cash and are recorded separately in a **petty cash book**. This will be dealt with in Chapter 35.

The most commonly used source documents for the cash book

Income

1. **Receipts** issued by the business
2. **Bank statements:** these are used to obtain information concerning credit transfers paid directly into the business's bank account
3. **Cash register print-outs:** these are used to obtain the value of cash sales, as distinct from credit sales

Expenditure

4. **Cheque counterfoils** (see Chapter 10)
5. **Receipts** received by the business
6. **Bank statements:** these are used to obtain information concerning direct debits, standing orders, credit transfers to other firms' accounts and all forms of bank charges

The analysed cash book can be written in one of two formats (layouts):

1. A **double-page layout** using **one page as the debit side** (for money received) and **one page as the credit side** (for money paid out).

   This is the same format as used in Chapter 5 for recording household accounts

   or

2. **Two separate books:** an **analysed cash receipts and lodgement book** and an **analysed cheque payments book**.

   This format requires an additional summarised *Bank* A/C in the general ledger.

FORMAT 1
The double-page layout

The **analysed cash book** is one of the books of original (first) entry. Money received is recorded on the debit side and money paid out is recorded on the credit side. This format also acts as a ledger account for the bank account and so records one element of the double entry system.

When, for example, wages are paid by cheque they are recorded on the credit side of the analysed cash book and later posted to the debit side of the wages account in the general ledger.

This format also records the opening and closing bank balances, just like any other ledger account.

FORMAT 2
Two separate books

In this format the **analysed cash receipts and lodgement book** (for income) and the **analysed cheque payments book** (for payments) act as two separate books of first entry listing the incomes and payments under relevant headings.

They **do not** act as a ledger. Opening and closing bank balances are **not** recorded. A separate summarised *Bank* A/C has to be used in conjunction with them.

Example 1: no opening balance

Horgan Ltd had the following bank transactions. You are required to enter these in both formats of the analysed cash book, post to the ledgers and extract a trial balance at 31/11/09 using the following analysis columns.

- **Receipts:** *Bank* *Sales* *VAT* *Debtors* *Capital*
- **Payments:** *Bank* *Purchases* *VAT* *Creditors* *Electricity* *Rent*

- 1/11/09 Cash sales, lodged, €25,000 **plus** 10% VAT
- 3/11/09 Cash purchases, Cheque no. 1, €11,000 **including** €1,000 VAT
- 5/11/09 Received €5,000 from M. Martin, a debtor. Receipt no. 1. This was lodged.
- 8/11/09 Shareholders invested €20,000 in the business that was lodged.
- 10/11/09 Paid P. Power, a creditor, €2,500. Cheque no. 2
- 13/11/09 Paid ESB account, €350, with Cheque no. 3
- 15/11/09 Paid rent by Cheque no. 4, €1,000

Format 1

Dr side (money received)									**ANALYSED CASH BOOK**									**Cr side (money paid out)**
Date	Details	Rcpt	F	Bank	Sales	VAT	Debtors	Capital	Date	Details	Chq	F	Bank	Purchases	VAT	Creditors	Electricity	Rent
2009			€	€	€	€	€	€	2009			€	€	€	€	€	€	
1/11	Sales		GL1, 2	27,500	25,000	2,500			3/11	Purchases	1	GL1, 4	11,000	10,000	1,000			
5/11	M. Martin	1	DL1	5,000			5,000		10/11	P. Power	2	CL1	2,500			2,500		
8/11	Shareholders		GL3	20,000				20,000	13/11	ESB	3	GL5	350				350	
									15/11	Rent	4	GL6	1,000					1,000
									30/11	Balance c/d			37,650					
				52,500	25,000	2,500	5,000	20,000					52,500	10,000	1,000	2,500	350	1,000
1/12	Balance b/d			37,650														

Summary of procedure for Format 1

1. **Enter the opening bank balance** (when given): this is normally on the debit side, but will be entered on the credit side if the bank account is overdrawn.
2. **Enter all receipts (incomes) on the debit side:** once in the bank column and once in one of the analysed columns.
3. **Enter all payments on the credit side:** once in the bank column and once in one of the analysed columns.
4. **Calculate and enter the closing bank balance.**
5. **Enter the totals of all columns.**
6. **Bring down the closing balance** as the opening balance for the next period.
7. **Post the totals of each of the analysed columns** (with the exception of the debtors and creditors columns) to the relevant account in the general ledger. Remember that the analysed cash book is part of the double entry system, so:
   - Items on the debit side of the analysed cash book are posted to the credit side of the relevant ledger account, and
   - Items on the debit credit of the analysed cash book are posted to the debit side of the relevant ledger account
8. **Post the individual entries in the debtors and creditors columns** to the relevant **ledger accounts** in the debtors and creditors ledgers, again applying the above principle, i.e. debit in cash book = credit in the ledger and vice versa.

Format 2

ANALYSED CASH RECEIPTS AND LODGEMENT BOOK (page 1)

Date	Details	Receipt no.	F	Bank	Sales	VAT	Debtors	Capital
2009				€	€	€	€	€
1/11	Sales			27,500	25,000	2,500		
5/11	M. Martin	1	DL1	5,000			5,000	
8/11	Shareholders			20,000				20,000
				52,500	25,000	2,500	5,000	20,000

ANALYSED CHEQUE PAYMENTS BOOK (page 1)

Date	Details	Cheque no.	F	Bank	Purchases	VAT	Creditors	Electricity	Rent
2009				€	€	€	€	€	
3/11	Purchases	1		11,000	10,000	1,000			
10/11	P. Power	2	CL1	2,500			2,500		
13/11	ESB	3		350				350	
15/11	Rent	4		1,000					1,000
				14,850	10,000	1,000	2,500	350	1,000

Summary of procedure for Format 2

1. **Enter all receipts** in the **analysed cash receipts and lodgement book**: once in the bank column and once in one of the analysed columns.
2. **Enter all payments** in the **analysed cheque payments book**: once in the bank column and once in one of the analysed columns.
3. **Enter the totals of all columns.**
4. **Post the totals of each of the analysed columns** (with the exception of the debtors and creditors columns) to the relevant accounts in the general ledger.
   - The items in the analysed cash receipts and lodgement book go to the credit side of the relevant ledgers.
   - The items in the analysed cheque payments book go the debit side of the relevant ledger.
5. **Post the individual entries in the debtors and creditors columns** to the relevant ledger accounts in the debtors and creditors ledgers, applying these basic principles: debit the receiver and credit the giver.
6. **Open a *Bank* A/C in the general ledger.**
   (a) **Enter the opening balance** (when given) on the **debit** side (or on the credit side, if it is an overdraft).
   (b) **Enter the total of the bank column** from the analysed cash receipts and lodgement book on the **debit** side.
   (c) **Enter the total of the bank column** from the analysed cheque payments book on the **credit** side.
   (d) **Balance the account.**

LEDGER ACCOUNTS (common to both formats)

General ledger

Debit side		SALES A/C (1)					Credit side
Date	Details	F	€	Date	Details	F	€
				30/11/09	Bank	CB1	25,000

VAT A/C (2)

Date	Details	F	€	Date	Details	F	€
30/11/09	Cash book	CB1	1,000	30/11/09	Cash book	CB1	2,500
30/11/09	Balance c/d		1,500				
			2,500				2,500
				1/12/09	Balance b/d		1,500

CAPITAL A/C (3)

Date	Details	F	€	Date	Details	F	€
				30/11/09	Bank	CB1	20,000

PURCHASES A/C (4)

Date	Details	F	€	Date	Details	F	€
30/11/09	Bank	CB1	10,000				

ELECTRICITY A/C (5)

Date	Details	F	€	Date	Details	F	€
30/11/09	Bank	CB1	350				

RENT A/C (6)

Date	Details	F	€	Date	Details	F	€
30/11/09	Bank	CB1	1,000				

The following ledger account appears in Format 2 only.

BANK A/C (7)

Date	Details	F	€	Date	Details	F	€
30/11/09	Receipts	ACLB	52,500	30/11/09	Payments	ACPB	14,850
				30/11/09	Balance c/d		37,650
			52,500				52,500
1/12/09	Balance b/d		37,650				

Notice that this balance is the same as that in the analysed cash book Format 1.

Debtors ledger

Debit side		M. MARTIN A/C (1)					Credit side
Date	Details	F	€	Date	Details	F	€
				5/11/09	Bank	CB1	5,000

Creditors ledger

		P. POWER A/C (2)					
Date	Details	F	€	Date	Details	F	€
10/11/09	Bank	CB1	2,500				

TRIAL BALANCE AT 31/11/09		
	Dr €	Cr €
Bank A/C	37,650	
Sales A/C		25,000
VAT A/C		1,500
Capital A/C		20,000
Purchases A/C	10,000	
Electricity A/C	350	
Rent A/C	1,000	
M. Martin A/C		5,000
P. Power A/C	2,500	
	51,500	51,500

Remember, in Format 1 the cash book is also the bank ledger A/C. Therefore its closing balance must be included in the trial balance.

Example 2: with an opening bank balance

Jones Ltd had the following bank transactions. You are required to enter these in the analysed cash book, post to the ledgers and extract a trial balance at 31/12/10 using the following analysis columns.

- **Receipts:** *Bank* *Sales* *VAT* *Debtors* *Capital*
- **Payments:** *Bank* *Purchases* *VAT* *Creditors* *Wages* *Insurance*

- 1/12/10 Opening balance €5,000 (Dr)
- 5/12/10 Cash sales lodged, €20,000 plus 10% VAT
- 8/12/10 Cash purchases, Cheque no. 1, €6,000 including €500 VAT
- 12/12/10 Lodged a payment received from a debtor, B. Burke, €8,000. Receipt no. 1
- 14/12/10 Paid G. Greene, a creditor, €1,500 with Cheque no. 2
- 15/12/10 Paid wages, €900, with Cheque no. 3
- 18/12/10 Shareholders invested €60,000. This was lodged.
- 20/12/10 Paid insurance, Cheque no. 4, €400

Format 1

Dr side (money received)									ANALYSED CASH BOOK (page 1)									Cr side (money paid out)
Date	Details	Rcpt	F	Bank	Sales	VAT	Debtors	Capital	Date	Details	Chq	F	Bank	Purchases	VAT	Creditors	Wages	Insurance
2010			€	€	€	€	€	€	2010			€	€	€	€	€	€	€
1/12	Balance b/d		GL1	5,000					8/12	Purchases	1	GL4, 3	6,000	5,500	500			
5/12	Sales		GL2, 3	22,000	20,000	2,000			14/12	G. Greene	2	CL1	1,500			1,500		
12/12	B. Burke	1	DL1	8,000			8,000		15/12	Wages	3	GL4	900				900	
18/12	Shareholders		GL1	60,000				60,000	20/12	Insurance	4	GL5	400					400
									31/12	Balance c/d			86,200					
				95,000	20,000	2,000	8,000	60,000					95,000	5,000	500	1,500	900	400
1/1/11	Balance b/d			86,200														

Opening balance in Format 1

The **capital** of a business, **at any time**, is calculated by subtracting its liabilities from its assets.

The opening balance in the cash book is an asset of the business, i.e. something owned by the business. As there are no other assets or liabilities listed in the question, at this date, this opening balance in the cash book is also the opening balance in the *Capital* A/C. It is, therefore, posted to the credit side of the *Capital* A/C.

If the opening balance in the cash book is on the credit side then it is posted to the debit side of the *Capital* A/C.

Format 2

ANALYSED CASH RECEIPTS AND LODGEMENT BOOK (page 1)

Date	Details	Receipt no.	F	Bank	Sales	VAT	Debtors	Capital
2010				€	€	€	€	€
5/12	Sales		GL2, 3	22,000	20,000	2,000		
12/12	B. Burke	1	DL1	8,000			8,000	
18/12	Shareholders		GL1	60,000				60,000
				90,000	20,000	2,000	8,000	60,000

ANALYSED CHEQUE PAYMENTS BOOK (page 1)

Date	Details	Cheque no.	F	Bank	Purchases	VAT	Creditors	Wages	Insurance
2010				€	€	€	€	€	
8/12	Purchases	1	GL4, 3	6,000	5,500	500			
14/12	G. Greene	2	CL1	1,500			1,500		
15/12	Wages	3	GL4	900				900	
20/12	Insurance	4	GL5	400					400
				8,800	5,500	500	1,500	900	400

Opening balance in Format 2

The opening balance is **not** recorded in either the **analysed cash receipts and lodgement book** (ACLB) or in the **analysed cheque payments book** (ACPB). This is entered on the credit side of the *Capital* A/C in the general ledger and its corresponding debit is the opening balance in the bank account in the general ledger for the reasons mentioned in the *Note* to Format 1.

continued overleaf

LEDGER ACCOUNTS (common to both formats)

General ledger

Debit side — CAPITAL A/C (1) — Credit side

Date	Details	F	€	Date	Details	F	€
31/12/10	Balance c/d		65,000	1/12/10	Opening balance	GL7	5,000
				31/12/10	Bank	CB1	60,000
			65,000				65,000
				1/1/11	Balance b/d		65,000

SALES A/C (2)

Date	Details	F	€	Date	Details	F	€
				31/12/10	Bank	CB1	20,000

VAT A/C (3)

Date	Details	F	€	Date	Details	F	€
31/12/10	Cash book	CB1	500	31/12/10	Cash book	CB1	2,000
31/12/10	Balance c/d		1,500				
			2,000				2,000
				1/1/11	Balance b/d		1,500

PURCHASES A/C (4)

Date	Details	F	€	Date	Details	F	€
31/12/10	Bank	CB1	5,500				

WAGES A/C (5)

Date	Details	F	€	Date	Details	F	€
31/12/10	Bank	CB1	900				

INSURANCE A/C (6)

Date	Details	F	€	Date	Details	F	€
31/12/10	Bank	CB1	400				

This bank ledger account appears in Format 2 only.

BANK A/C (7)							
Date	Details	F	€	Date	Details	F	€
1/12/10	Opening balance		5,000	31/12/10	Payments	ACPB	8,800
31/12/10	Receipts	ACLB	90,000	31/12/10	Balance c/d		86,200
			95,000				95,000
1/1/11	Balance b/d		86,200				

Notice that this balance is the same as that in the analysed cash book Format 1.

Debtors ledger

Debit side			B. BURKE A/C (1)				Credit side
Date	Details	F	€	Date	Details	F	€
				12/12/10	Bank	CB1	8,000

Creditors ledger

G. GREEN A/C (2)							
Date	Details	F	€	Date	Details	F	€
14/12/10	Bank	CB1	1,500				

TRIAL BALANCE AT 31/12/10		
	Dr €	Cr €
Bank A/C	86,200	
Sales A/C		20,000
VAT A/C		1,500
Capital A/C		65,000
Purchases A/C	5,500	
Wages A/ C	900	
Insurance A/C	400	
B. Burke A/C		8,000
G. Greene A/C	1,500	
	94,500	94,500

Remember, in Format 1 the cash book is also the bank ledger A/C. Therefore its closing balance must be included in the trial balance.

Note: Some exercises will include an *Others* analysed column or a *Sundries* column on the payments side. These are used to record any transactions that do not match the other analysed columns you are told to use. Post the total of these columns to the *Other expenses* A/C or *Sundry expenses* A/C in the general ledger, unless instructed otherwise.

QUESTIONS

In each of the following exercises you are required to enter the transactions in the cash book using either Format 1 or Format 2, post to the ledgers and extract a trial balance on the final date. Use the analysed columns listed in each exercise. (See workbook for ordinary level format questions.)

Cash books without opening bank balances

1. **Receipts:** *Bank Sales VAT Debtors Capital*
   Payments: *Bank Purchases VAT Creditors Wages Insurance*
   5/2/10 Cash sales lodged, €25,000 plus 21% VAT
   7/2/10 Paid wages, €900, Cheque no. 1
   8/2/10 Cash purchases, Cheque no. 2, €7,260 (purchases €6,000, VAT €1,260)
   12/2/10 Lodged a payment received from a debtor, C. Clancy, €6,000. Receipt no. 1
   14/2/10 Paid H. Roche, a creditor, €1,500, Cheque no. 3
   15/2/10 Paid wages, €900, Cheque no. 4
   18/2/10 Shareholders invested €60,000. This was lodged.
   20/2/10 Paid insurance, Cheque no. 5, €800
   22/2/10 Paid wages, €900, Cheque no. 5

2. **Receipts:** *Bank Sales VAT Debtors Capital*
   Payments: *Bank Purchases VAT Creditors Rent Electricity*
   1/3/10 Cash sales lodged, €121,000 (sales €100,000, VAT €21,000)
   2/3/10 Paid rent, €800, Cheque no. 1
   8/3/10 Cash purchases, Cheque no. 2, €6,000 plus 21% VAT
   9/3/10 Paid rent, €500, Cheque no. 3
   10/3/10 Lodged a payment received from a debtor, F. Fagan, €18,000. Receipt no. 1
   11/3/10 Paid ESB bill, €300, Cheque no. 4
   14/3/10 Paid G. Gormley, a creditor, €2,000, Cheque no. 5
   15/3/10 Shareholders invested €80,000. This was lodged.
   16/3/10 Paid rent, €800, Cheque no. 6

Cash books with opening bank balances

3. **Receipts:** *Bank Sales VAT Debtors Capital*
   Payments: *Bank Purchases VAT Creditors Insurance Others*
   1/4/10 Opening bank (Dr) €5,000
   3/4/10 Shareholders invested €50,000. This was lodged.
   5/4/10 Paid insurance premium for the buildings, €580, Cheque no. 23
   7/4/10 A debtor, E. Ennis, paid €2,000, Receipt no. 21. This was lodged.
   10/4/10 Paid for heating oil, €800, Cheque no. 24
   12/4/10 Paid a creditor, J. Last, €6,000, Cheque no. 25
   15/4/10 Paid motor insurance premium, €800, Cheque no. 26
   18/4/10 Cash purchases, Cheque no. 27, €4,000 plus 21% VAT
   20/4/10 Cash sales lodged, €9,680 (sales €8,000 VAT €1,680)

4. **Receipts:** *Bank Sales VAT Debtors Capital*
   Payments: *Bank Purchases VAT Creditors Repairs Others*
   1/5/10 Opening bank €5,000 Cr (i.e. overdraft)
   3/5/10 Cash sales lodged, €7,260 (sales €6,000, VAT €1,260)
   8/5/10 Paid for repairs to roof, €500, Cheque no. 40
   10/5/10 Shareholders invested €12,000. This was lodged.
   12/5/10 Cash purchases, Cheque no. 41, €45,000 plus 21% VAT
   14/5/10 Received a cheque for €6,500 from a debtor, D. Dunne. Receipt no. 43
   18/5/10 Paid for motor van repairs, €359, Cheque no. 42
   19/5/10 Paid a creditor, P. Palmer, €500, Cheque no. 43
   20/5/10 Paid for advertising, €7,000, Cheque no. 44

5. **Receipts:** *Bank Sales VAT Debtors Capital*
   Payments: *Bank Purchases VAT Creditors Insurance Others*
   1/4/10 Opening bank (Dr) €26,000
   3/4/10 Cash purchases, Cheque no. 40, €4,000 plus 21% VAT
   4/4/10 Paid for stationery, Cheque no. 41, €560
   5/4/10 Cash sales lodged, €12,100 (sales €10,000, VAT €2,100)
   6/4/10 Shareholders invested €35,000, Receipt no. 64. This was lodged.
   5/4/10 Paid insurance premium for the buildings, €340, Cheque no. 42
   7/4/10 A debtor, F. Flynn paid €1,500, Receipt no. 65. This was lodged.
   10/4/10 Paid insurance on delivery van, €1,200, Cheque no. 43
   12/4/10 Paid a creditor, T. Twamley, €3,000, Cheque no. 44
   15/4/10 Cash purchases, Cheque no. 45, €4,000 plus 21% VAT
   20/4/10 Cash sales lodged, €14,520 (sales €12,000, VAT €2,520)

6. **Receipts:** *Bank Sales VAT Debtors Capital*
   Payments: *Bank Purchases VAT Creditors Repairs Others*
   1/5/11 Opening bank €2,000 Cr
   3/5/11 Cash sales lodged, €7,260 (sales €6,000, VAT €1,260)
   8/5/11 Paid for repairs to office equipment, €320, Cheque no. 80
   10/5/11 Shareholders invested €60,000. This was lodged. Receipt no. 33
   12/5/11 Cash purchases, Cheque no. 82, €32,000 plus 21% VAT
   14/5/11 Received a cheque for €6,500 from a debtor, Q. Quinn. Receipt no. 34
   18/5/11 Paid for motor van repairs, €359, Cheque no. 83
   19/5/11 Paid a creditor, S. Slater, €500, Cheque no. 84
   20/5/11 Paid for advertising, €2,500, Cheque no. 85
   22/5/11 Paid for printing, €570, Cheque no. 86
   23/5/11 Cash purchases, Cheque no. 87, €12,000 plus 21% VAT

See workbook for more questions.

35 The petty cash book and monitoring overheads

In Chapter 34 we saw that *most* businesses make *all* payments through their bank accounts. But many businesses also need to pay for small-value day-to-day expenses. These include postage stamps, milk and tea, occasional window cleaning and courier fees, and small travel expenses. It is inconvenient and expensive to pay such small amounts by cheque.

These payments are made out of a sum of cash that is kept in the office,usually in a small cash box known as a **petty cash box**. The person in charge of this cash, the **petty cashier**, records all the payments in a petty cash book using analysed columns similar to those used in the analysed cash book.

PETTY CASH VOUCHERS

A **petty cash voucher** is a form, authorising payment, which must be filled out at the time a petty cash payment is being paid. The vouchers are usually pre-printed and pre-numbered. Each must show the following items:

(a) voucher number
(b) date of the payment
(c) amount of the payment
(d) purpose of the payment
(e) name and/or signature of the person receiving the payment
(f) signature of the person approving the payment, usually the petty cashier

PETTY CASH VOUCHER		**No.** 234	
Date:	*23/11/09*	**Purpose of payment:**	*Travel expenses*
Amount paid:	*€25.50*		
Received by:	*Joe Dunne*	**Approved by:**	*Joan Rivers*

THE IMPREST SYSTEM

Most offices use an **imprest** system for their petty cash. An imprest is a fixed sum of money given (by the accountant or chief cashier) to the petty cashier in advance of payments being made. At the end of a period of time (e.g. a week or a month) and on production of the vouchers for the money spent, the petty cashier is again given a sum of money to bring the imprest back up to its original value.

Procedure

1. Enter the imprest (opening balance) on the first date in the *Total* column on the debit side.
2. Enter all the payments, and the dates of the payments, on the credit side: once in the total column and once in one of the analysed columns.
3. Show the totals for **all** columns at the end of the period. Place a double line under the totals of the analysed columns only.
4. Balance the **two *Total* columns** against each other, placing the balance on the credit side.
5. Show the totals in both *Total* columns, placing a double line under each.
6. Bring the balance down on the debit side on the first date of the next period.
7. Enter the sum of money received from the chief cashier to bring the imprest back to its original value. Note that this should equal the total amount spent during the previous period, as highlighted in the example.
8. Post the totals of the analysed columns to the debit side of the relevant ledger accounts in the general ledger.

Example

Adapted from JC Ordinary Level Paper 2005, Question 5

Michael Dillon is the office manager in Cubes Ltd. He uses a petty cash book to keep an account of small office expenses. He begins each month with an imprest of €400. The following were his petty cash transactions during May 2005:

- May 1 Balance (imprest) on hand €400.
- 3 Paid €18 for postage – Petty cash voucher no. 51.
- 5 Bought writing paper (stationery) for €32 – Petty cash voucher no. 52.
- 9 Paid €30 to a local charity for a sponsored walk – Petty cash voucher no. 53.
- 11 Bought envelopes (stationery) for €27 – Petty cash voucher no. 54.
- 12 Paid €57 for repairs to computer desk – Petty cash voucher no. 55.
- 17 Paid €26 to SPD Couriers Ltd to deliver a parcel (postage) – Petty cash voucher no. 56.
- 19 Paid €15 for a taxi to collect a customer at the station – Petty cash voucher no. 57.
- 20 Paid €35 for cleaning of office – Petty cash voucher no. 58.
- 23 Paid €30 for repairs to a printer – Petty cash voucher no. 59.
- 26 Purchased copying paper (stationery) for €54 – Petty cash voucher no. 60.
- 27 Paid train fare €40 for sales manager – Petty cash voucher no. 61.
- 31 Paid €24 for postage – Petty cash voucher no. 62.
- June 1 Received a cheque from the chief cashier to bring the balance up to the original imprest.

Write up the petty cash book for the month of May using the following analysis columns:

- **Dr side:** *Total*
- **Cr side:** *Total Postage Stationery Repairs Travel Sundries*

Total each analysis column and balance the petty cash book at the end of May.

Note: Use a *Sundries* column for entries that cannot be entered in the named analysis columns.

Solution

PETTY CASH BOOK (page 1)

Date	Details	Total	Date	Details	Voucher no.	Total	Postage	Stationery	Repairs	Travel	Sundries
2005		€				€	€	€	€	€	€
1/5	Balance (imprest)	400	3/5	Postage	51	18	18				
			5/5	Writing paper	52	32		32			
			9/5	Sponsored walk	53	30					30
			11/5	Envelopes	54	27		27			
			12/5	Desk repairs	55	57					57
			17/5	SPD Couriers Ltd	56	20	20				
			19/5	Taxi	57	15				15	
			20/5	Office cleaning	58	35					35
			23/5	Printer repairs	59	30			30		
			26/5	Copying paper	60	54		54			
			27/5	Train fare	61	40				40	
			31/5	Postage	62	24	24				
				Total spent		**382**	62	113	30	55	122
			31/5	Balance c/d		18	GL8	GL9	GL10	GL11	GL12
		400				400					
1/6	Balance b/d	18									
1/6	Cheque	**382**									

Notes

1. The posting references are inserted under the total of each analysed column.
2. The general ledger reference does not start at GL1 because these postings are included in the main general ledger.

General ledger

Debit side		POSTAGE A/C (8)					Credit side
Date	Details	F	€	Date	Details	F	€
31/5/05	Petty cash	PCB1	62				

STATIONERY A/C (9)							
Date	Details	F	€	Date	Details	F	€
31/5/05	Petty cash	PCB1	113				

REPAIRS A/C (10)							
Date	Details	F	€	Date	Details	F	€
31/5/05	Petty cash	PCB1	30				

TRAVEL A/C (11)							
Date	Details	F	€	Date	Details	F	€
31/5/05	Petty cash	PCB1	55				

SUNDRIES A/C (12)							
Date	Details	F	€	Date	Details	F	€
31/5/05	Petty cash	PCB1	122				

OVERHEADS

Overheads are the ongoing (frequently recurring) costs of running a business, excluding the costs of materials and direct labour involved in producing the business's products.

Overheads include such items as: rent, insurance, electricity, office expenses, telephone, maintenance and heating.

It is important to monitor (check regularly) the cost of overheads. These are indirect costs of production. Anything that increases the cost of producing a product or providing a service has the effect of decreasing profit. Therefore it is essential to keep costs as low as possible. If they are not checked regularly they can run out of control very quickly.

Some reasons why overhead costs may rise unnecessarily:

- Forgetting to turn off lights
- Over-use of central heating or air conditioning
- Employees over-using the telephone and Internet for private purposes
- Not obtaining new or regular quotations for items such as insurance and maintenance of office equipment
- Unnecessary photocopying
- Over-spending on ineffective advertising

Overheads are sometimes sub-divided under three headings:

1. **Selling expenses**, e.g. advertising
2. **Distribution expenses**, e.g. carriage outwards
3. **Administrative expenses**, e.g. wages of office staff

Monitoring overheads

1. A realistic annual budget should be set for each overhead. This can be done on the basis of previous years' figures.
2. Regular comparisons should be made between the budgeted figures and the actual money spent during the year. This can be done with a **budget comparison statement** (see Chapter 6). The figures for the actual money spent are taken from the **analysed cash book** and from the **petty cash book**.
3. If the actual money spent on the overheads is greater than the budgeted figures, then the firm needs to find out why.
4. Corrective action should be taken to bring the spending back to the budgeted figures.

BUDGET COMPARISON STATEMENT FOR JANUARY–JUNE 2012			
Overhead	Budgeted cost	Actual cost	Difference + or –
	€	€	€
Electricity	5,000	7,000	+ 2,000
Telephone	8,500	10,300	+ 1,800
Stationery	1,700	1,900	+ 200
Maintenance	6,000	4,800	– 1,200

In this situation the firm should investigate the over-spending on its electricity, telephone and stationery costs. There *may* be a good reason for the extra spending, e.g. an unforeseen increase in prices, but on the other hand there *may* be unnecessary over-use of these items.

It is equally important to investigate the under-spending on maintenance. There may be negligence in the upkeep of items such as machines or computers that could be much more costly in the long run.

LEARN THE KEY TERMS

- A **petty cash voucher** is a form, authorising payment, which must be filled out at the time a petty cash payment is being paid.
- An **imprest** is a fixed sum of money given to the petty cashier in advance of payments being made for petty cash purposes.
- **Overheads** are the ongoing (frequently recurring) costs of running a business, excluding the costs of materials and direct labour involved in producing the business's products.

QUESTIONS

1. What is the title of the person who is in charge of the petty cash?
2. What is an imprest?
3. What is a petty cash voucher?
4. What information should be listed on a petty cash voucher?

In **Questions 5 to 8**, Ordinary Level students are required to write up the petty cash book, total each of the analysed columns and balance the petty cash book at the end of the month.

Higher Level students are also required to post the totals of each of the analysed columns to the relevant ledger accounts.

5. Mary Maloney recorded the following transactions in the petty cash book.

   July 2010

   1 Balance (imprest) on hand €400.
   1 She bought writing paper (stationery) for €32, Petty cash voucher no. 1.
   3 She paid for window cleaning, €25, Petty cash voucher no. 2.
   6 She paid €22 for postage, Petty cash voucher no. 3.
   8 She paid €29 courier charges (postage), Petty cash voucher no. 4.
   9 She paid €12 bus fare into town for office clerk, Petty cash voucher no. 5.
   12 She paid €45 for writing paper, Petty cash voucher no. 6.
   18 She paid deposit for an airline ticket, €50, Petty cash voucher no. 7.
   19 She paid €20 for repairs to furniture, Petty cash voucher no. 8.
   22 She paid €15 courier charges, Petty cash voucher no. 9.
   31 She received a cheque from the chief cashier to bring the balance up to the original imprest.

   Use the following analysed columns on the credit side:
   Postage Stationery Travel Cleaning Sundries

6. Joe Jones recorded the following transaction in the petty cash book.

   September 2010

   1 Balance (imprest) on hand €300
   3 Paid courier charges (postage), €12, Petty cash voucher no. 19
   4 Paid bus fares, €10, Petty cash voucher no. 20
   5 Paid for printing paper (stationery), €15, Petty cash voucher no. 21
   8 Paid office cleaner, €30, Petty cash voucher no. 22
   10 Paid for repairs to computer, €30, Petty cash voucher no. 23
   14 Paid for tea and milk for the office, €12, Petty cash voucher no. 24
   16 Paid for stationery, €10, Petty cash voucher no. 25
   21 Paid train fares, €30, Petty cash voucher no. 26
   24 Paid donation to local charity, €50, Petty cash voucher no. 27
   26 Paid office cleaner, €25, Petty cash voucher no. 28
   27 Paid for postage stamps, €15, Petty cash voucher no. 29
   30 Received a cheque from the chief cashier to bring the balance up to the original imprest

   Use the following analysed columns on the credit side:
   Postage Stationery Travel Cleaning Others

7. Joan Rivers recorded the following transaction in the petty cash book.

November 2010

1 Balance (imprest) on hand €300
3 Paid for envelopes, €11, Petty cash voucher no. 70
5 Paid for postage, €20, Petty cash voucher no. 71
7 Paid for cleaning materials, €18, Petty cash voucher no. 72
10 Paid courier charges, (postage), €20, Petty cash voucher no. 73
12 Paid office cleaner, €35, Petty cash voucher no. 74
14 Paid for repairs to office door locks, €22, Petty cash voucher no. 75
17 Paid for writing paper, €18, Petty cash voucher no. 76
20 Paid bus fares, €10, Petty cash voucher no. 77
23 Paid for raffle tickets, €40, Petty cash voucher no. 78
27 Paid for postage, €35, Petty cash voucher no. 79
28 Paid for repairs to central heating system, €40, Petty cash voucher no. 80
30 Received a cheque from the chief cashier to bring the balance up to the original imprest

Use the following analysed columns on the credit side:
Postage Stationery Cleaning Repairs Others

8. Seán Howard recorded the following transaction in the petty cash book.

December 2010

1 Balance (imprest) on hand €300
3 Paid parcel post, €14, Petty cash voucher no. 90
5 Paid for writing paper, €18, Petty cash voucher no. 91
7 Paid office cleaner, €45, Petty cash voucher no. 92
8 Paid for tea and milk for the office, €18, Petty cash voucher no. 93
12 Paid for train fares, €25, Petty cash voucher no. 94
13 Paid for taxi fare, €17, Petty cash voucher no. 95
15 Paid for office Christmas decorations, €50. Petty cash voucher no. 96
17 Paid for postage stamps, €20, Petty cash voucher no. 97
19 Paid for envelopes, €15, Petty cash voucher no. 97
20 Paid for cleaning material, €26, Petty cash voucher no. 98
21 Paid for food for Christmas office party, €50, Petty cash voucher no. 99
30 Received a cheque from the chief cashier to bring the balance up to the original imprest

Use the following analysed columns on the credit side:
Postage Stationery Cleaning Office expenses Others

9. What is meant by 'the overheads' of a business?

10. Name the three subdivisions of overheads and give one example of each.

11. Outline four steps that should be followed in the process of monitoring overheads.

See workbook for more questions.

The general journal 36

We saw in Chapter 29 that there are seven books of first entry. So far we have dealt with six of these and seen that **each one** is used for a **specific purpose only**. Here is a reminder:

DAY BOOKS	
1. Purchases book	For recording the credit purchase of goods that the business normally trades in, i.e. goods purchased on credit that are for resale
2. Purchases returns book	For recording the return of goods whose purchase had originally been recorded in the purchases book
3. Sales book	For recording the credit sale of goods that the business normally trades in
4. Sales returns book	For recording the return of goods whose sale had originally been recorded in the sales book
5. Analysed cash book	For recording all cash transactions (receipts and payments)
6. Petty cash book	For recording small-value cash payments associated with the day-to-day expenses of running an office

THE GENERAL JOURNAL

The **general journal**, the seventh book of first entry, is used to record any transaction that cannot be recorded in any of the other books of first entry.

Use of the general journal

In the Junior Certificate course the general journal is used to record:

1. **Opening entries:** the values of the assets, liabilities and capital at the start of a financial period
2. **Credit purchases** and **credit sales of fixed assets**
3. **Bad debts being written off:** a bad debt arises when a debtor (a person who owes you money) cannot pay some or all the money owed to you

Note: The general journal is also used as the day book for recording **depreciation**. This will be dealt with in Chapter 43, *Final accounts with adjustments*.

The layout of the general journal is identical to that of the trial balance. Therefore it is convenient to use Record Book No. 2 as your general journal.

GENERAL JOURNAL				
Date	Details	F	Dr €	Cr €
9/1/09	Computer A/C	GL1	1,000	
	Computer Suppliers Ltd	CL1		1,000
Narration	**Being the credit purchase of a computer**			

The general journal, as a book of first entry, is used to show the accounts to be debited and credited for any given transaction. The value of debits must equal the value of credits. Every general journal entry requires a **narration**, which is a brief description of the transaction.

1. RECORDING OPENING ENTRIES

At the start of a new financial period, e.g. a new year, a business will have certain assets and liabilities carried over from the previous period.

- **Assets** are any things owned by the business and any debts owed **to** it.
- **Liabilities** are any debts owed **by** the business.

Basic rule:
Debit assets. Credit liabilities.

As explained in Chapter 34, the capital (or ordinary share capital) of a business is the difference between the value of its assets and liabilities at any given time.

To calculate the opening capital:
Subtract the opening liabilities from the opening assets.

Procedure:

1. **Record the assets in the debit column.** (*Remember:* Debit assets.)
2. **Record the liabilities in the credit column.** (*Remember:* Credit liabilities.)
3. **Record the ordinary share capital, in the credit column, as the difference between the value of the assets and liabilities.** (It goes on the credit side because the capital is *owed to* the shareholders or owners.)
4. **Insert a narration:** *Being the assets, liabilities and capital at that date.*
5. **Post the entries, as the opening balances, to the ledgers** using this guideline:
   - A debit in the general journal is also a debit in the ledger.
   - A credit in the general journal is also a credit in the ledger.

Example

On 1/1/10 Jones Ltd had the following opening assets and liabilities:
Buildings, €400,000; Machinery, €300,000; Debtor, N. Flynn, €3,500; Bank overdraft, €2,000 and Creditor, J. Morris, €6,000.

Record the opening balances in the general journal and post them to the ledgers.

Solution

GENERAL JOURNAL (page 1)				
Date	Details	F	Dr €	Cr €
1/1/10	Buildings	GL1	400,000	
	Machinery	GL2	300,000	
	Debtor: N. Flynn	DL1	3,500	
	Bank overdraft	CB1		2,000
	Creditor: J. Morris	CL1		6,000
	Ordinary share capital	GL3		695,500
			703,500	703,500
	Being the assets, liabilities and capital at 1/1/10			

General ledger

Debit side		BUILDINGS A/C (1)					Credit side
Date	Details	F	€	Date	Details	F	€
1/1/10	Balance	GJ1	400,000				

MACHINERY A/C (2)							
Date	Details	F	€	Date	Details	F	€
1/1/10	Balance	GJ1	300,000				

ORDINARY SHARE CAPITAL A/C (3)							
Date	Details	F	€	Date	Details	F	€
				1/1/10	Balance	GJ1	695,500

Debtors ledger

Debit side		N. FLYNN A/C (1)					Credit side
Date	Details	F	€	Date	Details	F	€
1/1/10	Balance	GJ1	3,500				

Creditors ledger

Debit side		J. MORRIS A/C (2)					Credit side
Date	Details	F	€	Date	Details	F	€
1/1/10	Balance	GJ1	2,000				

Dr side (money received)			ANALYSED CASH BOOK											Cr side (money received)	
Date	Details	F	Bank	1	2	3	4	Date	Details	F	Bank	1	2	3	4
2010			€	€	€	€	€	2010			€	€	€	€	€
								1/1/10	Balance	GJ1	2,000				

2. RECORDING CREDIT PURCHASES AND CREDIT SALES OF FIXED ASSETS

The credit purchase of a fixed asset

When an asset is purchased on credit it cannot be recorded in the purchases book because it is not an item in which the business normally deals. Neither can it be entered in the cash book because no money is paid at that time. Therefore it must be recorded in the general journal.

Basic rule:
Debit the receiver or items received.
Credit the giver or items given.

Example

On 5/6/10 T. Ryan, a grocer, purchased a delivery van on credit from Brady Ltd for €50,000. Record this in the general journal and post the items to the ledgers.

Solution

GENERAL JOURNAL (page 2)

Date	Details	F	Dr €	Cr €
5/6/10	Delivery van A/C	GL1	50,000	
	Brady Ltd A/C	CL1		50,000
	Being the credit purchase of a delivery van			

General ledger

DELIVERY VAN A/C (1) — Debit side / Credit side

Date	Details	F	€	Date	Details	F	€
5/6/10	Brady Ltd	GJ2	50,000				

Creditors ledger

BRADY LTD A/C (1) — Debit side / Credit side

Date	Details	F	€	Date	Details	F	€
				5/6/10	Delivery van	GJ2	50,000

The credit sale of a fixed asset

When an asset is sold on credit it cannot be recorded in the sales book because it is not an item in which the business normally deals. Neither can it be entered in the cash book because no money is paid at that time. Therefore it must be recorded in the general journal.

Basic rule:
Debit the receiver or items received.
Credit the giver or items given.

Example

On 8/9/10 T. Ryan, a grocer, sold an old computer on credit to P. Power Ltd for €200. Record this in the general journal and post the items to the ledgers.

Solution

GENERAL JOURNAL (page 3)				
Date	Details	F	Dr €	Cr €
8/9/10	P. Power Ltd A/C	DL1	200	
	Computer A/C	GL2		200
	Being the credit sale of a computer			

Debtors Ledger

Debit side		P. POWER A/C (1)					Credit side
Date	Details	F	€	Date	Details	F	€
8/9/10	Computer	GJ3	200				

General ledger

Debit side		COMPUTER A/C (1)					Credit side
Date	Details	F	€	Date	Details	F	€
				8/9/10	P. Power Ltd	GJ3	200

3. RECORDING A BAD DEBT WRITTEN OFF

Example 1: a full bad debt written off

Unfortunately, from time to time, some limited companies lose so much money they cannot keep on trading and cannot pay any of the debts owed by them. These companies are declared to be **bankrupt**. Bankruptcy occurs when a firm is deemed, legally, to be unable to pay off its debts.

If you are owed money by such a business then you will not receive the payment due to you. This is known as a **bad debt**. This bad debt is an **expense** to your business because you bought the goods for resale but did not get paid.

On the other hand it is a **gain** to the debtor because this business received goods from you that it did not pay for.

Look at the ledger account in your books of H. Times Ltd, a debtor.

Debtors ledger

Debit side		H. TIMES LTD A/C (1)					Credit side
Date	Details	F	€	Date	Details	F	€
1/1/10	Balance b/d	SB3	2,000				

This shows that H. Times Ltd owes you €2,000. Assume that H. Times Ltd, on 1/2/10, is declared bankrupt and cannot pay any of its debts. You must write off this bad debt because you can no longer expect payment. This can only be recorded in the general journal because it cannot be entered in any of the other books of first entry.

Basic rule: **Debit expenses. Credit gains.**

Solution

GENERAL JOURNAL (page 4)				
Date	Details	F	Dr €	Cr €
1/2/10	Bad debts A/C	GL5	2,000	
	H. Times Ltd A/C	DL1		2,000
	Being a bad debt written off			

Debtors ledger

Debit side			H. TIMES LTD A/C (1)				Credit side
Date	Details	F	€	Date	Details	F	€
1/1/10	Balance b/d	SB3	2,000	1/2/10	Bad debts	GJ4	2,000

General ledger

Debit side			BAD DEBTS A/C (1)				Credit side
Date	Details	F	€	Date	Details	F	€
1/2/10	H. Times Ltd	GJ4	2,000				

It is clear from these ledger accounts that there is no longer any balance on H. Times' account; but a new expense, bad debts, has been created.

Example 2: part of a debt is written off as a bad debt

Sometimes a bankrupt firm can pay some of the debt it owes. Assume H. Times Ltd is declared bankrupt. All its assets are sold for, say, €100,000. However, its total debts are €400,000, which means it can pay only ¼ of its debts. Each debtor will be paid ¼ of the debt owed to it.

Such an arrangement is usually described as *each debtor receives 25c in the €* owed to it. Likewise if it can pay ½ of its debt, each debtor receives 50c in the €, and so on.

Let us return to H. Times Ltd. Assume, again, that on 1/2/10 this firm is declared bankrupt, but can pay 25c in the €. You will receive ¼ of the debt owed to you by H. Times Ltd, i.e. €500. We will now record this in the general journal and ledger accounts.

Basic rule:
Debit bad debts A/C with the amount written off.
Debit the bank with the amount received.
Credit the debtor with the total amount.

GENERAL JOURNAL (page 4)				
Date	Details	F	Dr €	Cr €
1/2/10	Bad debts A/C	GL5	1,500	
	Bank A/C	CB1	500	
	H. Times Ltd A/C	DL1		2,000
	Being a bad debt written off			

Here the bad debt is €1,500. However, you also **received** €500 that must be debited to your *Bank* account. H. Times Ltd is credited with €2,000 (i.e. the gain of €1,500 bad debt written off and we must credit H. Times Ltd as the giver of €500).

Debtors ledger

Debit side				H. TIMES LTD A/C (1)			Credit side
Date	Details	F	€	Date	Details	F	€
1/1/10	Balance b/d	SB3	2,000	1/2/10	Bad debts	GJ4	1,500
				1/2/10	Bank	GJ4	500
			2,000				2,000

General ledger

Debit side				BAD DEBTS A/C (1)			Credit side
Date	Details	F	€	Date	Details	F	€
1/2/10	H. Times Ltd	GJ4	1,500				

Dr side (money received)					ANALYSED CASH BOOK									Cr side (money received)	
Date	Details	F	Bank	1	2	3	4	Date	Details	F	Bank	1	2	3	4
2010			€	€	€	€	€	2010			€	€	€	€	€
1/2/10	H. Times Ltd	GJ4	500												

Summary

Entire debt written off with the total amount

(a) Debit *Bad debts* A/C with the total amount.
(b) Credit the debtor's account with the total amount.

Partial debt written off

(a) Debit *Bad debts* A/C with amount written off.
(b) Debit the *Bank* A/C with the amount received.
(c) Credit the debtor's account with the total amount.

QUESTIONS

Credit purchase and sale of assets

1. Record the following transactions in the general journal of Maddock Ltd and post the figures to the ledgers. Balance the *Computer* account.

   1/1/10 Purchased a new computer on credit from J. Jones Ltd, €800
   5/1/10 Sold old computer on credit to S. Smith Ltd, €1,000

2. Record the following transactions in the general journal of Ryan Ltd and post the figures to the ledgers. Balance the *Machinery* account.

   1/2/10 Purchased machinery on credit from M. Chines Ltd, €15,000
   8/2/10 Sold old machinery on credit to D. Dump Ltd, €3,000

3. Record the following transactions in the general journal of Hartigan Ltd and post the figures to the ledgers. Balance the *Office Furniture* account.

   1/3/10 Sold old office furniture on credit to Flynn Ltd, €6,000
   8/3/10 Purchased new office furniture on credit from Geraghty Ltd, €10,000
   11/3/10 Purchased new office furniture on credit from Geraghty Ltd, €15,000

4. Record the following transactions in the general journal of Maloney Ltd and post the figures to the ledgers. Balance the *Equipment* account.

   1/4/10 Sold old equipment on credit to L. Lawler Ltd, €2,500
   5/4/10 Purchased equipment on credit from Equipit Ltd, €8,500
   8/4/10 Purchased equipment on credit from S. Slone Ltd, €7,800
   9/4/10 Sold old equipment on credit to Dumpit Ltd, €1,000

5. Record the following transactions in the general journal of Snappy Ltd and post the figures to the ledgers. Balance the *Motor vehicles* account.

   1/5/10 Purchased a new motor vehicle on credit from Motor Suppliers Ltd, €45,000
   5/5/10 Sold an old motor vehicle on credit to D. Dump Ltd, €500
   9/5/10 Purchased a new motor vehicle on credit from Trucks Ltd, €60,000
   9/5/10 Sold an old motor vehicle on credit to Dumpit Ltd, €800

Recording opening balances

6. Record the following opening balances in the general journal and calculate the ordinary share capital on 1/1/11. Post the figures to the ledgers.

   Assets
   Equipment €35,000; Land €100,000; Debtor D. Dunne Ltd €40,000; Bank €12,000

   Liabilities
   Creditor C. Clarke, €35,000

7. Record the following opening balances in the general journal and calculate the ordinary share capital on 1/2/11. Post the figures to the ledgers.

   Assets
   Buildings €400,000; Machinery €250,000; Land €500,000; Debtor G. Greene €25,000

   Liabilities
   Creditor F. Flynn €50,000; Bank overdraft €78,000

8. Record the following opening balances in the general journal and calculate the ordinary share capital on 1/3/11. Post the figures to the ledgers.

   Assets
   Motor vehicles €50,000; Computers €55,000; Office equipment 36,000; Debtor A. Armstrong €25,000; Bank €40,000

   Liabilities
   Bank term loan €500,000; Creditor T. Timmons €30,000

9. Record the following opening balances in the general journal and calculate the ordinary share capital on 1/4/11. Post the figures to the ledgers.

   Assets
   Equipment €50,000; Stock €60,000*; Buildings €200,000; Debtor P. Power €10,000

   Liabilities
   Bank overdraft €20,000; Creditor L. Lynn €50,000; Bank term loan €35,000

   *This refers to the value of the stock of goods held by the business for resale

10. Record the following opening balances in the general journal and calculate the ordinary share capital on 1/5/11. Post the figures to the ledgers.

    Assets
    Computers €80,000; Land €150,000; Buildings €250,000; Debtor H. Holland €50,000; Bank €80,000

    Liabilities
    Creditor B. Byrne €40,000; Bank term loan €100,000

Bad debts written off

Record the following transactions in the general journal of X Ltd and post to the ledgers. Include, in each case, the opening balance in the debtor's ledger.

11. On 1/1/10, J. James Ltd, a debtor, had an opening balance of €600. On 15/1/10, J. James Ltd was declared bankrupt and the entire balance was written off as a bad debt.

12. On 1/2/10, K. Kehoe Ltd, a debtor, had an opening balance of €800. On 16/2/10, K. Kehoe Ltd was declared bankrupt and paid each creditor 20c in the €. This was lodged by X Ltd to its bank. The balance was written off as a bad debt.

13. M. Murray, a debtor, owed €1,500 on 1/3/10. Murray was declared bankrupt on 5/3/10 and paid all creditors 50c in the €. X Ltd lodged the amount received and wrote off the balance as a bad debt.

14. R. Roberts, a debtor, was declared bankrupt on 8/4/10. He paid X Ltd €500, which represented a payment of 25c in the €. This was lodged to X Ltd's bank account and the amount outstanding was written off as a bad debt.

15. M. Myles, a debtor, was declared bankrupt on 10/5/10. He paid X Ltd €400, which represented a payment of 10c in the €. This was lodged to X Ltd's bank account and the outstanding balance was written off as a bad debt.

See workbook for more questions.

37 Debtors and creditors control accounts

Firms continuously check the accuracy of their accounts. The trial balance is used to ensure the system of double entry is adhered to, i.e. that there is a corresponding debit for every credit.

Likewise we use bank reconciliation statements to ensure the accuracy of the firm's record of its bank accounts, i.e. checking it financial situation.

You have seen that firms sell and buy goods on credit. Therefore it is important that the records in the debtors and creditors ledgers are accurate.

Debtors and **creditors control accounts** are used to check the accuracy of accounts in each of these respective ledgers.

DEBTORS CONTROL ACCOUNTS

Question

- From your sales book you know you sold €6,000 worth of goods (including VAT) on credit to three debtors during July 2010.
- From your sales returns book you know they returned €600 worth of goods (including VAT) during that month.
- From your cash book you know these debtors paid you €3,300 during July.

What is the total owed to you by these debtors at the end of the month?

Solution

	€	€
Total sales to debtors		6,000
Less		
Sales returns from debtors	600	
Payments received from debtors	3,300	3,900
Total owed by debtors		2,100

Now look at the ledger accounts of these three debtors.

Debtors ledger

Debit side				P. POWER A/C (1)			Credit side
Date	Details	F	€	Date	Details	F	€
2/7/10	Sales	SB1	3,000	5/7/10	Returns	SRB1	300
				8/7/10	Bank	CB1	2,000
				31/7/10	Balance c/d		700
			3,000				3,000
1/8/10	Balance b/d		700				

Debit side				G. GROGAN A/C (2)			Credit side
Date	Details	F	€	Date	Details	F	€
4/7/10	Sales	SB1	2,000	8/7/10	Returns	SRB1	200
				11/7/10	Bank	CB1	500
				31/7/10	Balance c/d		1,300
			2,000				2,000
1/8/10	Balance b/d		1,300				

Debit side				H. HEALY A/C (3)			Credit side
Date	Details	F	€	Date	Details	F	€
8/7/10	Sales	SB1	1,000	11/7/10	Returns		100
				18/7/10	Bank		800
				31/7/10	Balance c/d		100
			1,000				1,000
1/8/10	Balance b/d		100				

Add these three balances together (€700 + €1,300 + €100) to get the total owed to you by these debtors, **€2,100**.

This is, and should be, equal to the answer to the above question.

Therefore we can conclude that:

A **debtors control account** is a general account used to ensure that the sum of the combined balances in the individual **debtors ledger accounts** is equal to the totals recorded in the **sales**, **sales returns** and **analysed cash books**.

Drawing up a debtors control account – formal procedure

Step 1: Balance each ledger account in the debtors ledger. Make a list of these balances and get the total of this list.

Step 2: Prepare a **debtors control A/C** from information in the sales book, sales returns book and analysed cash book. Enter the totals from these books in the **debtors control A/C** and balance it.

Step 3: The total at Step 1 should equal the balance in the control account.

Step 1

Debtors ledger

Debit side				P. POWER A/C (1)			Credit side
Date	Details	F	€	Date	Details	F	€
2/7/10	Sales	SB1	3,000	5/7/10	Returns	SRB1	300
				8/7/10	Bank	CB1	2,000
				31/7/10	Balance c/d		700
			3,000				3,000
1/8/10	Balance b/d		700				

Debit side				G. GROGAN A/C (2)			Credit side
Date	Details	F	€	Date	Details	F	€
4/7/10	Sales	SB1	2,000	8/7/10	Returns	SRB1	200
				11/7/10	Bank	CB1	500
				31/7/10	Balance c/d		1,300
			2,000				2,000
1/8/10	Balance b/d		1,300				

Debit side				H. HEALY A/C (3)			Credit side
Date	Details	F	€	Date	Details	F	€
8/7/10	Sales	SB1	1,000	11/7/10	Returns		100
				18/7/10	Bank		800
				31/7/10	Balance c/d		100
			1,000				1,000
1/8/10	Balance b/d		100				

List:

Power	€700
Grogan	€1,300
Healy	€100
Total	**€2,100**

Step 2

SALES BOOK (page 1)

Date	Details	F	Net €	VAT €	Total €
2/7/10	P. Power, Inv. no. 21	DL1	2,250	750	3,000
4/7/10	G. Grogan, Inv. no. 22	DL2	1,600	400	2,000
8/7/10	Healy Ltd, Inv. no. 23	DL3	800	200	1,000
			4,650	1,350	6,000

To **debit side** of control account

SALES RETURNS BOOK (page 1)

Date	Details	F	Net €	VAT €	Total €
5/7/10	P. Power, Credit note no. 3	DL1	225	75	300
8/7/10	G. Grogan, Credit note no. 4	DL2	150	50	200
8/7/10	H. Healy, Credit note no. 5	DL3	75	25	100
			450	150	600

To **credit side** of control account

Dr side (money received) — ANALYSED CASH BOOK (page 1) — Cr side (money received)

Date	Details	F	Bank	Debtors		Date	Details	F	Bank	2	
2010			€	€	€				€	€	€
8/7/10	P. Power	DL1	2,000	2,000							
11/7/10	G. Grogan	DL2	500	500							
18/7/10	H. Healy	DL3	800	800							
				3,300							

To **credit side** of control account

The debtors control account for the above transactions is as shown here.

Debit side — DEBTORS CONTROL A/C AT 31/7/10 (T-format) — Credit side

Date	Details	F	€	Date	Details	F	€
31/7/10	Sales	SB1	6,000	31/7/10	Returns	SRB1	600
				31/7/10	Bank	CB1	3,300
				31/7/10	Balance c/d		2,100
			3,000				3,000
	Balance b/d		2,100				

This can also be laid out using a continuous balance format as shown overleaf:

DEBTORS CONTROL A/C AT 31/7/10 (continuous balance format)					
Date	Details	F	Debit €	Credit €	Balance €
31/7/10	Sales	SB1	6,000		6,000
31/7/10	Returns	SRB1		600	5,400
31/7/10	Bank	CB1		3,300	2,100

Step 3

Total at Step 1 of €2,100 = **balance on debtors control A/C** of €2,100.

There were no opening balances (amounts owed from a previous period) in any of the debtors' ledgers featured in this example. However, if there were opening balances they would obviously *increase* the amounts owed by the debtors. The **total** combined value of these opening balances would have to be entered on the debit side of the debtors control account. These will be shown in the next example.

Debtors control accounts summary

1. Enter the total value of opening balances on the debit side of the control account.
2. The debtors *received* the goods sold to them, so *debit* the control account with the total value of sales.
3. The debtors are the *givers* of the goods returned, so *credit* the control account with the total value of sales returns.
4. The debtors are the *givers* of the payments received, so *credit* the control account with the total value of debtors in the analysed cash book.

Debtors control accounts: examination question

The following figures were extracted from the accounts of Holmes Ltd on 31/11/11:

- 1/11/11 Opening balances on debtors accounts €5,000
- Total credit sales during November €55,000
- Total receipts during November from debtors €25,000
- Sales returns during November €11,000

Prepare a debtors control account for the month of November using both:
(**a**) the T-ledger format, and
(**b**) the continuous balance ledger format.

Solution

(a)

Debit side		DEBTORS CONTROL A/C AT 31/11/11 (T-format)					Credit side
Date	Details	F	€	Date	Details	F	€
1/11/11	Opening balance		5,000	31/11/11	Bank	CB1	25,000
31/11/11	Sales	SB1	55,000	31/11/11	Returns	SRB1	11,000
				31/11/11	Balance c/d		24,000
			60,000				60,000
	Balance b/d		24,000				

(b)

DEBTORS CONTROL A/C AT 31/11/11 (continuous balance format)					
Date	Details	F	Debit €	Credit €	Balance €
1/11/11	Opening balance				5,000
31/11/11	Sales	SB1	55,000		60,000
31/11/11	Bank	CB1		25,000	35,000
31/11/11	Returns	SRB1		11,000	24,000

Note: In **debtors control accounts** *debit* entries *increase* the balance in the continuous balance format, whereas *credit* entries *decrease* the balance.

CREDITORS CONTROL ACCOUNTS

The principle governing debtors control accounts also applies to creditors control accounts, i.e. the *total is equal to the sum of its parts.*

A **creditors control account** is a general account used to ensure that the sum of the combined balances in the individual **creditors ledger accounts** is equal to the totals recorded in the **purchases, purchases returns** and **analysed cash books.**

Drawing up a creditors control account – formal procedure

Step 1: Balance each ledger account in the creditors ledger. Make a list of these balances and get the total of this list.

Step 2: Prepare a creditors control a/c from information in the purchases book, purchases returns book and the analysed cash book. Enter the totals from these books in the creditors control A/C and balance it.

Step 3: The total at Step 1 should equal the balance in the control account.

Step 1

Creditors ledger

Debit side				S. SLATER LTD A/C (1)			Credit side
Date	Details	F	€	Date	Details	F	€
5/4/10	Purchases returns	PRB2	1,702.50	1/4/10	Purchases	PB2	7,945.00
7/4/10	Bank	CB2	1,000.00				
30/4/10	Balance c/d		5,242.50				
			7,945.00				7,945.00
				1/5/10	Balance b/d		5,242.50

Debit side				T. TYNAN LTD A/C (2)			Credit side
Date	Details	F	€	Date	Details	F	€
7/4/10	Purchases returns	PRB2	2,270.00	4/4/10	Purchases	PB2	9,080.00
8/4/10	Bank	CB2	2,000.00				
30/4/10	Balance c/d		4,810.00				
			9,080.00				9,080.00
				1/5/10	Balance b/d		4,810.00

Debit side				U. URNEY LTD A/C (3)			Credit side
Date	Details	F	€	Date	Details	F	€
11/4/10	Purchases returns	PRB2	1,135.00	9/4/10	Purchases	PB2	3,405.00
15/4/10	Bank	CB2	1,000.00				
30/4/10	Balance c/d		1,270.00				
			3,405.00				3,405.00
				1/5/10	Balance b/d		1,270.00

List:

S. Slater	€5,242.50
T. Tynan	€4,810.00
U. Urney	€1,270.00
Total	**€11,322.50**

Step 2

PURCHASES BOOK (page 2)

Date	Details	F	Net €	VAT €	Total €
1/4/10	S. Slater Ltd, Inv. no. 76	CL1	7,000.00	945.00	7,945.00
4/4/10	T. Tynan Ltd, Inv. no. 64	CL2	8,000.00	1,080.00	9,080.00
9/4/10	U. Urney Ltd, Inv. no. 87	CL3	3,000.00	405.00	3,405.00
		GL1,3	18,000.00	2,430.00	20,430.00

To **credit side** of control account

PURCHASES RETURNS BOOK (page 2)

Date	Details	F	Net €	VAT €	Total €
5/4/10	S. Slater Ltd, Credit note no. 32	CL1	1,500.00	202.50	1,702.50
7/4/10	T. Tynan Ltd, Credit note no. 48	CL2	2,000.00	270.00	2,270.00
11/4/10	U. Urney Ltd, Credit note no. 53	CL3	1,000.00	135.00	1,135.00
		GL2,3	4,500.00	607.50	5,107.50

To **debit side** of control account

Dr side (money received) — ANALYSED CASH BOOK (page 2) — Cr side (money received)

Date	Details	F	Bank	Debtors		Date	Details	F	Bank	Creditors	
			€	€	€	2010			€	€	€
						7/4/10	S. Slater	CL1	1,000.00	1,000.00	
						8/4/10	T. Tynan	CL2	2,000.00	2,000.00	
						15/4/10	U. Urney	CL3	1,000.00	1,000.00	
										4,000.00	

To **debit side** of control account

Debit side — CREDITORS CONTROL A/C AT 30/4/10 (T-format) — Credit side

Date	Details	F	€	Date	Details	F	€
30/4/10	Purchases returns	PRB2	5,107.50	30/4/10	Purchases	PB2	20,430.00
30/4/10	Bank	CB2	4,000.00				
30/4/10	Balance c/d		11,322.50				
			20,430.00				20,430.00
				1/5/10	Balance b/d		11,322.50

CREDITORS CONTROL A/C AT 30/4/10 (continuous balance format)

Date	Details	F	Debit €	Credit €	Balance €
30/4/10	Purchases	PB2		20,430.00	20,430.00
30/4/10	Purchases returns	PRB2	5,107.50		15,322.50
30/4/10	Bank	CB2	4,000.00		11,322.50

Step 3

Total at Step 1 of €11,322.50 = **balance on creditors control A/C** of €11,322.50

There were no opening balances (amounts owed from a previous period) in any of the creditors' ledgers featured in this example. However, if there were opening balances they would obviously *increase* the amounts owed to the creditors. The **total** combined value of these opening balances would have to be entered on the credit side of the creditors control account. These will be shown in the next example.

Creditors control accounts summary

1. Enter the total value of opening balances on the credit side of the control account.
2. The creditors are the *givers* of goods purchased from them, so *credit* the control account with the total value of credit purchases.
3. The creditors are the *receivers* of the goods returned, so *debit* the control account with the total value of purchases returns.
4. The creditors are the *receivers* of the payments made, so *debit* the control account with the total value of creditors in the analysed cash book.

Creditors control accounts: examination question

The following figures were extracted from the accounts of Decos Ltd on 31/5/11:

- 1/5/11 Opening balances on creditors accounts €4,500
- Total credit purchases during May €35,000
- Total payments to creditors during May €25,000
- Total purchases returns during May €11,000

Prepare a creditors control account for the month of May using both:
(**a**) the T-ledger format, and
(**b**) the continuous balance ledger format.

Solution

(a)

Debit side		CREDITORS CONTROL A/C AT 31/5/11 (T-format)					Credit side
Date	**Details**	**F**	**€**	**Date**	**Details**	**F**	**€**
31/5/11	Bank	CB	25,000	1/5/11	Opening balance		4,500
31/5/11	Purchases returns	PRB	11,000	31/5/11	Purchases	PB	35,000
31/5/11	Balance		3,500				
			39,500				39,500
				1/6/11	Balance b/d		3,500

(b)

CREDITORS CONTROL A/C AT 31/5/11 (continuous balance format)

Date	Details	F	Debit €	Credit €	Balance €
1/5/11	Opening balance				4,500
31/5/11	Purchases	PB		35,000	39,500
31/5/11	Bank	CB	25,000		14,500
31/5/11	Purchases returns	PRB	11,000		3,500

Note: In **creditors control accounts**, *credit* entries *increase* the balance in the continuous balance format, whereas *debit* entries *decrease* the balance.

LEARN THE KEY TERMS

- **A debtors control account is a general account used to ensure that the sum of the combined balances in the individual debtors ledger accounts is equal to the totals recorded in the sales, sales returns and analysed cash books.**
- **A creditors control account is a general account used to ensure that the sum of the combined balances in the individual creditors ledger accounts is equal to the totals recorded in the purchases, purchases returns and analysed cash books.**

QUESTIONS

Debtors control accounts

In Questions 1 to 4 prepare a debtors control account at the end of the stated month. You may use either a T-format or a continuous balance format.

1. Credit sales during August 2011 totalled €54,000
   Sales returns during the month totalled €5,400
   Payments received from debtors during August totalled €39,400
2. Debtors' balances at 1/9/11 totalled €50,000
   Credit sales for the month totalled €60,000
   Payments received from debtors during the month totalled €90,000
3. The combined balances on the debtors' accounts on 1/10/11 was €60,000
   Credit sales for the month totalled €90,000
   Sales returns during the month totalled €20,000
   Payments received from debtors during the month totalled €100,000
4. The opening combined balances in the individual debtors' ledgers on 1/11/11was €80,000
   Total credit sales for the month were €70,000
   Sales returns during the month totalled €20,000
   Total payments received from debtors during the month were €90,000

Creditors control accounts

In questions 5 to 8 prepare a creditors control account at the end of the stated month. You may use either a T-format or a continuous balance format.

5. Credit purchases during March 2011 totalled €100,000
   Purchase returns during the month totalled €6,000
   Payments made to creditors during March totalled €90,000

6. Creditors' balances at 1/4/11 totalled €50,000
   Credit purchases for the month totalled €60,000
   Payments made to creditors during April totalled €80,000

7. The combined balances on the creditors' accounts on 1/5/11 was €80,000
   Credit purchases for the month totalled €60,000
   Purchase returns during the month totalled €15,000
   Payments made to creditors during May totalled €55,000

8. The opening combined balances in the individual creditors' ledgers on 1/6/11 was €80,000
   Total credit purchases for the month were €60,000
   Purchase returns during the month totalled €20,000
   Total payments made to creditors during the month were €40,000

See workbook for more questions.

Revision: Combining day books, ledgers & trial balances (HL) 38

This revision chapter undertakes exercises that involve:

- Writing up some or all of the following: the sales book, the sales returns book, the purchases book, the purchases returns book and the general journal.
- Writing up the analysed cash book
- Posting to the ledgers
- Extracting a trial balance

At this stage you should be familiar with writing up all the day books and posting them to the ledgers.

EXAMPLE 1: INCLUDES AN OPENING GENERAL JOURNAL

Question

X Ltd had the following **opening balances** at 1/5/10:

- Bank (Dr) €55,000
- Debtor, P. Power €45,000
- Creditor, S. Smith €35,000
- Machinery €15,000

Enter the above balances in the general journal, calculate the issued share capital and post all figures to the ledgers.

X Ltd had the following entries in its **sales** and **sales returns books**:

SALES BOOK

Date	Details	F	Net €	VAT €	Total €
2/5/10	P. Power, Invoice no. 1	DL1	20,000	2,000	22,000
			20,000	2,000	22,000
			GL3	GL6	

SALES RETURNS BOOK

Date	Details	F	Net €	VAT €	Total €
5/5/10	P. Power, Credit note no. 2	DL1	10,000	1,000	11,000
			10,000	1,000	11,000
			GL4	GL6	

Post the figures from the sales and sales returns books to the **ledgers**.

The following **bank transactions** took place during May:

- 2/5 Cash sales, €22,000 (€20,000 Sales + €2,000 VAT)
- 4/5 Paid wages, Cheque no. 1, €5,000
- 6/5 Shareholders invested capital of €60,000
- 9/5 Received a cheque from P. Power for €56,000
- 11/5 Purchased a new machine, Cheque no. 2, €25,000
- 12/5 Paid S. Smith, Cheque no. 3, €15,000
- 13/5 Purchased goods for resale, Cheque no. 4, €20,000 + 21% VAT

Enter these in the **cash book** using the following headings:
Receipts (debit) side: *Bank Sales VAT Debtors Capital*
Payments (credit) side: *Bank Purchases VAT Wages Machinery Creditors*

Post all transactions to the **ledgers** and extract a **trial balance** at 31/5/10.

Solution

Step 1: Write up the required day books

In this case you are asked to write up the **general journal** and the **analysed cash book**.

GENERAL JOURNAL AT 1/5/10

Date	Details	F	Dr €	Cr €
1/5/10	Bank	CB1	55,000	
	Debtor, P. Power	DL1	45,000	
	Machinery	GL1	15,000	
	Creditor, S. Smith	CL1		35,000
	Issued share capital			80,000
			115,000	115,000
	Being assets, liabilities and capital at 1/5/10			

Remember that the **opening bank balance** in the general journal must be entered in the **analysed cash book**. If it is a *debit* in the general journal it is entered on the *debit side* of the cash book. If it is a *credit* (overdraft) in the general journal then it is entered on the *credit side* of the cash book.

Dr side (money received) — ANALYSED CASH BOOK (page 1) — Cr side (money paid out)

Date	Details	F	Bank	Sales	VAT	Debtors	Capital	Date	Details	F	Bank	Purchases	VAT	Wages	Machinery	Creditors
2010		€	€	€	€	€	€	2010		€	€	€	€	€	€	
1/5	Balance	GJ1	55,000					4/5	Wages, Chq. 1		5,000			5,000		
2/5	Cash sales		22,000	20,000	2,000			11/5	Machinery, Chq. 2	GL1	25,000				25,000	
6/5	Shareholders	GL2	60,000				60,000	12/5	S. Smith, Chq. 3	CL1	15,000					15,000
9/5	P. Power	DL1	56,000			56,000		13/5	Purchases, Chq. 4		24,200	20,000	4,200			
								31/5	Balance		123,800					
			193,000	20,000	2,000	56,000	60,000				193,000	20,000	4,200	5,000	25,000	15,000
1/6	Balance b/d		123,800	GL3	GL6		GL2					GL5	GL6	GL7	GL1	

Step 2: Write up the ledgers

It is important to do this systematically to ensure no figure remains unposted. *Here is one suggested system.*

The general ledger

1. Start with the general journal. Take the first non-personal account named in it (not the bank) and start posting all transactions from all the day books for that account. In this case it is the *Machinery* A/C. Make sure you enter the folio reference in the day book to show it has been posted (see *Machinery* A/C GL1 below). Follow the same procedure for all other non-personal accounts mentioned in the general journal. In this case there is only the issued share capital (see *Capital* A/C GL2 below).
2. Next do the sales, sales returns, purchases and purchases returns accounts, where necessary. In this case there is no purchases returns account. Ensure you enter the cash sales and the cash purchases in the respective accounts.
3. Now move on to the *VAT* A/C and do this as shown previously.
4. Finally make sure to post any other non-personal item that remains unposted from the cash book.

Remember to balance each account where appropriate.

The debtors ledger

1. Start with the debtor, if any, recorded in the general journal. The item in the general journal is entered as the opening balance on the debit side. Next, start posting all transactions from all the day books for that person's account. Again remember to enter the folio references.
2. Next go to the sales book and write up any other person's account recorded there, ensuring you take information from all the day books.

Remember to balance each account where appropriate.

The creditors ledger

1. Start with the creditor, if any, recorded in the general journal. The item in the general journal is entered as the opening balance on the credit side. Next, start posting all transactions from all the day books for that person's account. Don't forget the folio references!
2. Next go to the purchases book and write up any other person's account recorded there, ensuring you take information from all the day books.

Remember to balance each account where appropriate.

The general ledger

Debit side — **MACHINERY A/C (1)** — Credit side

Date	Details	F	€	Date	Details	F	€
1/5/10	Balance	GJ1	15,000	31/5/10	Balance c/d		40,000
11/5/10	Bank	CB1	25,000				
			40,000				40,000
1/6/10	Balance b/d		40,000				

CAPITAL A/C (2)

Date	Details	F	€	Date	Details	F	€
31/5/10	Balance c/d		140,000	1/5/10	Balance	GJ1	80,000
				8/5/10	Bank	CB1	60,000
			140,000				140,000
				1/6/10	Balance b/d		140,000

SALES A/C (3)

Date	Details	F	€	Date	Details	F	€
31/5/10	Balance c/d		40,000	31/5/10	Sundry debtors	SB1	20,000
				31/5/10	Bank	CB1	20,000
			40,000				40,000
				1/6/10	Balance b/d		40,000

SALES RETURNS A/C (4)

Date	Details	F	€	Date	Details	F	€
31/5/10	Sundry debtors	SRB1	10,000				

PURCHASES A/C (5)

Date	Details	F	€	Date	Details	F	€
31/5/10	Bank	CB1	20,000				

VAT A/C (6)

Date	Details	F	€	Date	Details	F	€
31/5/10	Sundry debtors	SRB1	1,000	31/5/10	Sundry debtors	SB1	2,000
31/5/10	Cash purchases*	CB1	4,200	31/5/10	Cash sales*	CB1	2,000
			1,200	31/5/10	Balance c/d		1,200
1/6/10	Balance b/d		5,200				5,200

*Instead of *Cash purchases* and *Cash sales* you could insert *as per cash book*.

WAGES A/C (7)							
Date	Details	F	€	Date	Details	F	€
31/5/10	Bank	CB1	5,000				

Debtors ledger

P. POWER A/C (1)							
Date	Details	F	€	Date	Details	F	€
1/5/10	Balance	GJ1	45,000	5/5/10	Returns	SRB1	11,000
2/5/10	Sales	SB1	22,000	9/5/10	Bank	CB1	56,000
			67,000				67,000

Creditors ledger

S. SMITH A/C (1)							
Date	Details	F	€	Date	Details	F	€
12/5/10	Bank	CB	15,000	1/5/10	Balance	GJ1	35,000
31/5/10	Balance b/d		20,000				
			35,000				35,000
				1/6/10	Balance b/d		20,000

Step 3: Extract trial balance

TRIAL BALANCE AT 31/5/10		
	Dr €	Cr €
Bank	123,800	
Machinery A/C	40,000	
Issued share capital A/C		140,000
Sales A/C		40,000
Sales returns A/C	10,000	
Purchases A/C	20,000	
VAT A/C	1,200	
Wages A/C	5,000	
S. Smith A/C		20,000
	200,000	200,000

EXAMPLE 2: NO OPENING GENERAL JOURNAL

Junior Certificate Examination, Paper, 2 Higher Level 2008

Kelly Ltd is a retail store.

(a) Record the following credit transactions in the purchases and purchases returns books of Kelly Ltd for the month of April 2010. Post relevant figures from the books to the ledger accounts.

- 3/4/10 Purchased goods on credit from Nee Ltd, Invoice no. 12 €16,000 + VAT 13.5%
- 9/4/10 Purchased goods on credit from Hay Ltd, Invoice no. 67 €22,600 + VAT 13.5%
- 15/4/10 Returned goods to Nee Ltd, Credit note no. 5 € 7,000 + VAT 13.5%

(b) Record the following bank transactions for the month of April in the analysed cash book of Kelly Ltd. Post relevant figures to the ledger accounts.

Analyse the bank transactions using the following money headings:
Debit (receipts) side: *Bank Sales VAT Share capital*
Credit (payments) side: *Bank Purchases VAT Light and heat Creditors*

- 1/4/10 Shareholder invested €150,000 and this was lodged. Receipt no. 24
- 2/4/10 Purchases for resale (Cheque no. 45) €70,000 + VAT 13.5%
- 13/4/10 Paid electricity bill (Cheque no. 46) €1,700
- 19/4/10 Cash sales lodged €90,800 (€80,000 + VAT €10,800)
- 28/4/10 Paid Hay Ltd (Cheque no. 47) €17,500

(c) Balance the accounts on 30 April 2010 and extract a trial balance as at that date.

Solution

Step 1: Write up the required day books

In this case you are asked to write up the **purchase book**, the **purchases returns book** and the **analysed cash book**.

PURCHASES BOOK

Date	Details	F	Net €	VAT €	Total €
3/4/10	Nee Ltd, Invoice no. 12	CL1	16,000	2,160	18,160
9/4/10	Hay Ltd, Invoice no. 67	CL2	22,600	3,051	25,651
			38,600	5,211	43,811
			GL1	GL4	

PURCHASES RETURNS BOOK

Date	Details	F	Net €	VAT €	Total €
15/4/10	Nee Ltd, Credit note no. 5	CL1	7,000	945	7,945
			7,000	945	7,945
			GL2	GL4	

Dr side (money received) — **ANALYSED CASH BOOK** — **Cr side (money paid out)**

Date	Details	F	Bank	Sales	VAT	Share capital	Date	Details	F	Bank	Purchases	VAT	Light & heat	Creditors
2010		€	€	€	€	€	2010		€	€	€	€	€	€
1/4	Shareholders, Rec. 24		150,000			150,000	2/4	Purchases, Chq. no. 45	GL3	79,450	70,000	9,450		
19/4	Sales		90,800	80,000	10,800		13/4	Electricity, Chq. no. 46		1,700			1,700	
							28/4	Hay Ltd, Chq. no. 47	CL2	17,500				17,500
							30/4	Balance c/d		142,150				
			240,800	80,000	10,800	150,000				240,800	70,000	9,450	1,700	17,500
1/5	Balance b/d		142,150	GL3	GL4	GL5					GL3	GL4	GL6	

Step 2: Write up the ledgers

As there is no general journal in this exercise you skip point (a) for the general ledger given in the guidelines on page 343 and proceed as per the rest of the guidelines.

Debit side — **PURCHASES A/C (1)** — **Credit side**

Date	Details	F	€	Date	Details	F	€
30/4/10	Sundry creditors	PB1	38,600	30/4/10	Balance c/d		108,600
30/4/10	Bank	CB1	70,000				
			108,600				108,600
1/5/10	Balance b/d		108,600				

PURCHASES RETURNS A/C (2)

Date	Details	F	€	Date	Details	F	€
				30/4/10	Sundry creditors	PRB1	7,000

SALES A/C (3)

Date	Details	F	€	Date	Details	F	€
				30/4/10	Bank	CB1	80,000

VAT A/C (4)

Date	Details	F	€	Date	Details	F	€
30/4/10	Sundry creditors	PB1	5,211	30/4/10	Sundry creditors	PRB1	945
30/4/10	As per cash book	CB1	9,450	30/4/10	As per cash book	CB1	10,800
				30/4/10	Balance c/d		2,916
			14,661				14,661
1/5/10	Balance b/d		2,916				

SHARE CAPITAL A/C (5)

Date	Details	F	€	Date	Details	F	€
				30/4/10	Bank	CB1	150,000

LIGHT AND HEAT A/C (6)							
Date	Details	F	€	Date	Details	F	€
30/4/10	Bank	CB1	1,700				

Creditors ledger

NEE LTD A/C (1)							
Date	Details	F	€	Date	Details	F	€
15/4/10	Returns	PRB1	7,945	3/4/10	Purchases	PB1	18,160
30/4/10	Balance c/d		10,215				
			18,160				18,160
				1/5/10	Balance b/d		10,215

HAY LTD A/C (2)							
Date	Details	F	€	Date	Details	F	€
28/4/10	Bank	CB1	17,500	9/4/10	Purchases	PB1	25,651
30/4/10	Balance c/d		8,151				
			25,651				25,651
				1/5/10	Balance b/d		8,151

Step 3: Extract the trial balance

TRIAL BALANCE AT 30/4/10		
	Dr €	Cr €
Bank	142,150	
Purchases A/C	108,600	
Purchases returns A/C		7,000
Sales A/C		80,000
VAT A/C	2,916	
Capital A/C		150,000
Light and heat A/C	1,700	
Nee Ltd A/C		10,215
Hay Ltd A/C		8,151
	255,366	255,366

QUESTIONS

Note: In all of these exercises all credit sales and credit purchases are for goods normally traded by the firms.

In questions 1 to 4:

(a) Write up the appropriate day books for the credit transactions. Post the relevant figures to the ledgers.
(b) From the bank transactions given, write up the analysed cash book using the relevant headings, and post the figures to the ledgers.
(c) Balance the ledgers where required.
(d) Extract a trial balance on the last day of the month.

1. During December 2010 B. Early Ltd had the following transactions:

Credit transactions

1/12 Sold goods on credit, Invoice no. 1, to A. Wake Ltd, €19,000 + 13½% VAT
3/12 Sold goods on credit, Invoice no. 2, B. Allwright Ltd, €23,000 + 13½% VAT
8/12 A. Wake Ltd returned goods, Credit note no. 1, €9,000 + 13½% VAT
12/12 B. Allwright Ltd returned goods, Credit note no. 2, €3,000 + 13½% VAT
15/12 Sold goods on credit, Invoice no. 3 to A. Wake Ltd, €37,000 + 13½% VAT

Bank transactions
Debit (receipts) side: *Bank Sales VAT Debtors*
Credit (payments) side: *Bank Purchases VAT Wages*

2/12 Cash sales lodged, €15,000 + 13½% VAT
4/12 Paid wages, Cheque no. 1, €2,500
9/12 Shareholders invested €60,000 which was lodged
14/12 Cash purchases, €13,620 (Purchases €12,000, VAT €1,620)
15/12 Allwright Ltd paid €1,500 by cheque which was lodged
20/12 A. Wake Ltd cleared its account in full. Cheque lodged

2. During October 2010 K. Knows Ltd had the following transactions:

Credit transactions

2/10 Purchased goods on credit from L. Lyons Ltd, Invoice no. 82, €17, 000 + 21% VAT
4/10 Returned goods to L. Lyons Ltd, Credit note no. 34, €7,000 + 21% VAT
7/10 Purchased goods on credit from Q. Quinn Ltd, Invoice no. 54, €28,000 + 21% VAT
12/10 Returned goods to Q. Quinn Ltd, Credit note no. 39, €14,000 + 21% VAT
13/10 Purchased goods on credit from L. Lyons Ltd, Invoice no. 93, €56,000 + 21% VAT
15/10 Purchased goods on credit from Q. Quinn Ltd, Invoice no. 64, €65,000 + 21% VAT

Bank transactions
Debit (receipts) side: *Bank Sales VAT Capital*
Credit (payments) side: *Bank Purchases VAT Wages Creditors*

1/10 Shareholders invested €78,000 which was lodged
4/10 Cash sales lodged, €15,000 + 21% VAT
8/10 Cash purchases for resale, €13,000 + 21% VAT, Cheque no. 32
10/10 Paid wages, €580, Cheque no. 33
19/10 Paid L. Lyons Ltd, €10,000, Cheque no. 34
22/10 Paid Q. Quinn Ltd, €15,000, Cheque no. 35

3. During January 2009 C. Clear Ltd had the following transactions:

Credit transactions

1/1 Purchased goods for resale on credit from J. James, €12,000 + 21% VAT
4/1 Sold goods on credit to a customer P. Plenty, €15,000 +21% VAT
7/1 Returned goods to J. James, €5,000 + 21% VAT
10/1 P. Plenty returned goods, €6,000 + 21% VAT
12/1 Sold goods on credit to P. Plenty, €18,000 + 21% VAT

Bank transactions

Debit (receipts) side: *Bank Sales VAT Debtors*
Credit (payments) side: *Bank Purchases VAT Rent Creditors*

1/1 Bank balance on hand (Dr), €2,000
3/1 Cash sales lodged, €60,000 + 21% VAT
7/1 Paid rent, €500, Cheque no. 20
15/1 Cash purchases for resale, €19,118 (Purchase €15,800 + VAT €3,318)
19/1 Paid J. James €5,000, Cheque no. 21
22/1 P. Plenty paid his account in full. Lodged cheque

4. During February 2009 B. Bright Ltd had the following transactions:

Credit transactions

1/2 Purchased goods on credit from M. Maher Ltd, Invoice no. 34, €25,000 + 21% VAT
2/2 Purchased goods on credit from V. Vaughan Ltd, Invoice no. 43, €16,000 +21% VAT
5/2 Sold goods on credit to F. Flynn Ltd, Invoice no. 12, €34,000 +21% VAT
8/2 Sold goods on credit to C. Curran Ltd, Invoice no. 13, €24,000 + 21% VAT
13/2 Returned goods to M. Maher Ltd, Credit note no. 56, €12,000 + 21% VAT
15/2 F. Flynn Ltd returned goods, Credit note no. 67, €8,000 + 21% VAT

Bank transactions

Debit (receipts) side: *Bank Sales VAT Debtors Share capital*
Credit (payments) side: *Bank Purchases VAT Telephone Creditors*

1/2 Shareholders invested €50,000 share capital. This was lodged
3/2 Paid telephone bill, Cheque no. 34, €1,200
14/2 Cash purchases for resale, Cheque no. 35, €10,000 + 21% VAT
18/2 Cash sales lodged, €32,670 (Sales €27,000, VAT €5,670)
21/2 Paid M. Maher Ltd €10,000. Cheque no. 36
23/2 Received cheque from F. Flynn Ltd to clear its account in full. Cheque was lodged

In questions 5 to 8:

(a) Enter the opening balances in the general journal, calculate the share capital and post the figures to the relevant accounts.
(b) Using the credit transactions post the relevant figures from the sales, sales returns, purchases and purchases returns books (where applicable) to the ledgers. The general ledger account numbers have been omitted to allow you create your own numbering sequence.
(c) Using the bank transactions, write up the analysed cash book, using the relevant headings, and post the figures to the ledgers.
(d) Balance the ledgers where required.
(e) Extract a trial balance on the last date of the month.

5. Recent Ltd had the following balances on 1/1/10:

Motor vehicles €50,000; Debtor D. Dunne €15,000; Bank overdraft €10,000

Credit transactions

SALES BOOK

Date	Details	F	Net €	VAT €	Total €
2/1/10	D. Dunne, Invoice no. 1	DL1	10,000	2,100	12,100
8/1/10	E. Egan, Invoice no. 2	DL2	20,000	4,200	24,200
			30,000	6,300	36,300
			GL	GL	

SALES RETURNS BOOK

Date	Details	F	Net €	VAT €	Total €
5/1/10	D. Dunne, Credit note no. 2	DL1	5,000	1,050	6,050
			5,000	1,050	6,050
			GL	GL	

Bank transactions
Debit (receipts) side: *Bank Sales VAT Share capital Debtors*
Credit (payments) side: *Bank Purchases VAT Light and heat*

1/1 Shareholder invested €100,000 and this was lodged, Receipt no. 12
2/1 Purchases for resale (Cheque no. 11), €60,000 + VAT 21%
8/1 Paid electricity bill (Cheque no. 12), €800
10/1 Cash sales lodged, €121,000 (€100,000 + VAT €21,000)
20/1 Received a payment of €15,000 from E. Egan which was lodged

6. Long Ago Ltd had the following balances on 1/2/10:

Furniture €30,000; Computers €25,000; Bank (Dr) €60,000; Debtor G. Guthrie €5,000; Creditor B. Warren €18,000

Credit transactions

SALES BOOK

Date	Details	F	Net €	VAT €	Total €
4/2/10	G. Guthrie, Invoice no. 11	DL1	30,000	4,050	34,050
			30,000	4,050	34,050
			GL	GL	

PURCHASES BOOK

Date	Details	F	Net €	VAT €	Total €
9/2/10	B. Warren, Credit note no. 21	CL1	23,000	3,105	26,105
			23,000	3,105	26,105
			GL	GL	

Bank transactions
Debit (receipts) side: *Bank Sales VAT Debtors Share capital*
Credit (payments) side: *Bank Purchases VAT Wages Creditors*

4/2 Paid wages (Cheque no. 4), €500
8/2 Purchases for resale (Cheque no. 11), €30,000 + VAT 13.5%
11/2 Paid B. Warren (Cheque no. 12), €40,000
13/2 Cash sales lodged, €113,500 (€100,000 + VAT €13,500)
22/2 Received a payment of €15,000 from G. Guthrie, €25,000 which was lodged

7. Too Soon Ltd had the following balances at 1/3/10:

Bank (Dr) €67,000; Machinery €65,000; Debtor C. Cullen €20,000; Creditor F. Fagan €12,000

Credit transactions

SALES BOOK

Date	Details	F	Net €	VAT €	Total €
10/3/10	C. Cullen, Invoice no. 28	DL1	21,600	4,536	26,136
			21,600	4,536	26,136
			GL	GL	

PURCHASES BOOK

Date	Details	F	Net €	VAT €	Total €
12/3/10	F. Fagan, Invoice no. 82	CL1	39,500	8,295	47,795
			39,500	8,295	47,795
			GL	GL	

Bank transactions
Debit (receipts) side: *Bank Sales VAT Debtors Share capital*
Credit (payments) side: *Bank Purchases VAT Insurance Creditors*

1/3 Shareholders invested €50,000 which was lodged
4/3 Cash purchases for resale, Cheque no. 44, €55,000 + 21% VAT
8/3 Paid Insurance, Cheque no. 45, €1,500
15/3 Received cheque from C. Cullen, €50,000. This was lodged
18/3 Paid F. Fagan the total amount owed to him, Cheque no. 46

8. Too Late Ltd had the following balances on 1/4/10:

Furniture €35,000; Debtor J. Jones €76,000; Bank (Cr) €25,000

Credit transactions

PURCHASES BOOK

Date	Details	F	Net €	VAT €	Total €
12/4/10	G. Griffen, Invoice no. 63	CL1	34,000	4,590	38,950
			34,000	4,590	38,950
			GL	GL	

PURCHASES RETURNS BOOK					
Date	Details	F	Net €	VAT €	Total €
18/4/10	G. Griffen, Credit note no. 97	CL1	10,000	1,350	11,350
			10,000	1,350	11,350
			GL	GL	

Bank transactions
Debit (receipts) side: *Bank Sales VAT Debtors Share capital*
Credit (payments) side: *Bank Purchases VAT Furniture Creditors*

2/4 Cash sales lodged, €85,000 inclusive of €11,475 VAT
4/4 Purchased furniture, Cheque no. 31, €15,500
8/4 Cash purchases for resale, Cheque no. 32, €45,000 + 13.5% VAT
15/4 Received payment, €67,000, receipt no. 3, from J. Jones. The cheque was lodged
20/4 Paid G. Griffen in full, Cheque no. 33

In questions 9 to 12:

(a) Complete the general journal by calculating the share capital and post the figures to the relevant accounts.
(b) Write up the sales, sales returns, purchases or purchases returns books (where applicable) and post to the ledgers.
(c) Using the bank transactions, write up the analysed cash book, using the relevant headings, and post the figures to the ledgers.
(d) Balance the ledgers where required.
(e) Extract a trial balance on the last date of the month.

9. The following transactions appeared in the books of Malone Ltd in January 2010:

GENERAL JOURNAL AT 1/1/10				
Date	Details	F	Dr €	Cr €
1/1/10	Bank	CB1	40,000	
	Computers	GL1	50,000	
	Debtor, S. Smith Ltd	DL1	5,000	
	Creditor, B. Breen Ltd	CL1		8,000
	Share capital	GL2		
	Being assets, liabilities and share capital		95,000	95,000

Credit transactions

2/1 Sold goods on credit to S. Smith Ltd, Invoice no. 23, €10,000 + 21% VAT
4/1 Purchased goods on credit from B. Breen, Invoice no. 32, €6,000 + 21% VAT
6/1 Returned goods to B. Breen Ltd, Credit note no. 54, €3,000 + 21% VAT
8/1 S. Smith Ltd returned goods, Credit no. 67, €5,000 + 21% VAT

(continued overleaf)

Bank transactions
Debit (receipts) side: *Bank Sales VAT Debtors Share capital*
Credit (payments) side: *Bank Purchases VAT Computers Creditors*

2/1 Cash sales lodged, €45,000 plus 21% VAT
4/1 Purchased a computer, Cheque no. 11, €1,500
8/1 Cash purchases for resale, Cheque no. 12, €19,118 (Purchases €15,800, VAT €3,318)
15/1 Received a cheque from S. Smith Ltd in full settlement of its account. The cheque was lodged
20/1 Paid B. Breen Ltd €2,500 on account, Cheque no. 13

10. The following transactions appeared in the books of P. Whelan in February 2010:

GENERAL JOURNAL AT 1/1/10

Date	Details	F	Dr €	Cr €
1/2/10	Debtor, Fixit Ltd	DL1	35,000	
	Machinery	GL1	95,000	
	Bank	CB1		45,000
	Creditor, Fillit Ltd	CL1		23,500
	Share capital	GL2		
	Being assets, liabilities and share capital at 1/2/10		130,000	130,000

Credit transactions
3/2 Sold goods on credit to Fixit Ltd, Invoice no. 76, €25,000 + 21% VAT
4/2 Purchased goods on credit from Fillit Ltd, Invoice no. 53, €6,000 + 21% VAT
6/2 Returned goods to Fillet Ltd, Credit note no. 98, €33,000 + 21% VAT
8/2 Fixit Ltd returned goods, Credit note no. 78, €15,000 + 21% VAT

Bank transactions
Debit (receipts) side: *Bank Sales VAT Debtors Share capital*
Credit (payments) side: *Bank Purchases VAT Machinery Creditors*

2/2 Shareholders invested €35,000. This was lodged
5/2 Purchased a machine, Cheque no. 42, €20,500
8/1 Cash purchases for resale, Cheque no. 12, €38,236 (Purchases €31,600, VAT €6,636)
15/1 Received a cheque from Fixit Ltd, €4,000. The cheque was lodged
20/1 Cash sales €25,000 + 21% VAT, lodged

11. The following transactions appeared in the books of M. O'Malley Ltd in March 2010:

GENERAL JOURNAL AT 1/3/10

Date	Details	F	Dr €	Cr €
1/3/10	Bank	CB1	30,000	
	Office furniture	GL1	76,000	
	Creditor: H. Holmes Ltd	CL1		12,000
	Share capital	GL2		
	Being assets, liabilities and share capital at 1/3/10		106,000	106,000

Credit transactions

2/3 Purchased goods on credit from H. Holmes Ltd, Invoice no. 43, €13,000 + 13½% VAT
4/3 Purchased goods on credit from G. Dwyer Ltd, Invoice no. 89, €18,500 + 13½% VAT
7/3 Returned goods to H. Holmes Ltd, Credit note no. 67, €11,500 + 13½% VAT
9/3 Returned goods to G. Dwyer Ltd, Credit note no. 56, €5,500 + 13½% VAT

Bank transactions

Debit (receipts) side: *Bank Sales VAT Share capital*
Credit (payments) side: *Bank Purchases VAT Office furniture Creditors*

2/3 Cash sales lodged €12,500 + 13½% VAT
5/3 Purchased office furniture, Cheque no. 15, €34,000
8/3 Cash purchases for resale, Cheque no. 16, €53,345 (Purchases €47,000, VAT €6,345)
12/3 Paid H. Holmes Ltd, Cheque no. 17, €15,000
15/3 Shareholders invested €67,000 which was lodged

12. The following transactions appeared in the books of M. O'Malley Ltd in April 2010:

GENERAL JOURNAL AT 1/4/10

Date	Details	F	Dr €	Cr €
1/4/10	Motor vehicles	GL1	200,000	
	Debtor, G. O'Hara Ltd	DL1	30,000	
	Bank	CB1		56,000
	Creditor, N. Garvey Ltd	CL1		44,000
	Share capital	GL2		
	Being assets, liabilities and share capital at 1/4/10		230,000	230,000

Credit transactions

2/4 Sold goods on credit to G. O'Hara Ltd, Invoice no. 34, €76,000 + 21% VAT
4/4 G. O'Hara Ltd returned goods, credit note no. 29, €16,000 + 21% VAT
5/4 Purchased goods on credit from N. Garvey Ltd, Credit note no. 18, €15,000 + 21% VAT

Bank transactions

Debit (receipts) side: *Bank Sales VAT Debtors Share capital*
Credit (payments) side: *Bank Purchases VAT Motor vehicles Creditors*

3/4 Purchased a new motor vehicle, Cheque no. 16, €45,000
5/4 Cash purchases, Cheque no. 17, €13,500 plus 21% VAT
11/4 Cash sales lodged, €18,150 (Sales €15,000, VAT €3,150)
15/4 Received a cheque from G. O'Hara Ltd in full settlement of its account. This was lodged
17/4 Paid N. Garvey Ltd, Cheque no. 18, €35,000

See workbook for more questions.

39 End of year procedure (HL)

This chapter shows the **accounting procedures** a business follows before preparing **the final accounts**.

Up to this point we have recorded all transactions in the books of first entry, posted these to the ledgers and extracted trial balances to ensure we have complied with the double-entry accounting system. However, we do not know how much **profit** our business has made, nor do we know the **value** of our business!

The profit and the value of the business are shown by doing **the final accounts** at the end of every trading period. A **trading period** can be for any period of time decided by the business, e.g. a month, three months, or, more usually, one year. The final accounts will be dealt with in detail in the next three chapters.

Businesses using computerised accountancy programmes can produce these accounts on an on-going basis because they are updated after every transaction is recorded. Well-known computerised accountancy systems include *TASBooks*, *Sage*, *Big Red Book*, and *IRIS Exchequer*.

PROFIT

Businesses distinguish between **gross profit** and **net profit**.

- **Gross profit** is the business's trading profit, i.e. the difference between the income received from the sale of goods and the direct cost of buying these goods (sales *minus* cost of goods sold)
- **Net profit** is gross profit *less* all overhead costs *plus* any other gains.

Gross and net profit are calculated by transferring the balances in the **nominal accounts** (see Chapter 30) to one of two accounts: the **trading account** or the **profit and loss account** (P&L A/C).

This will return the value of all nominal accounts to zero at the start of the next year. This is demonstrated in the following example using only a limited number of accounts.

Example

Debit side		SALES A/C					Credit side
Date	Details	F	€	Date	Details	F	€
31/12/11	to Trading A/C		500,000	31/12/11	Balance		500,000

		STOCK A/C					
Date	Details	F	€	Date	Details	F	€
1/1/11	Opening balance		10,000	31/12/11	to Trading A/C		10,000
31/12/11	Trading A/C		15,000	31/12/11	Balance c/d		15,000
1/1/12	Balance b/d		15,000				

See *Opening and closing stock* on page 358.

		PURCHASES A/C					
Date	Details	F	€	Date	Details	F	€
31/12/11	Balance		200,000	31/12/11	to Trading A/C		200,000

		CARRIAGE INWARDS A/C					
Date	Details	F	€	Date	Details	F	€
31/12/11	Balance		15,000	31/12/11	to Trading A/C		15,000

		INSURANCE A/C					
Date	Details	F	€	Date	Details	F	€
31/12/11	Balance		5,000	31/12/11	to P&L A/C		5,000

		RATES A/C					
Date	Details	F	€	Date	Details	F	€
31/12/11	Balance		12,000	31/12/11	to P&L A/C		12,000

		SALARIES A/C					
Date	Details	F	€	Date	Details	F	€
31/12/11	Balance		9,000	31/12/11	to P&L A/C		9,000

		ELECTRICITY A/C					
Date	Details	F	€	Date	Details	F	€
31/12/11	Balance		6,000	31/12/11	to P&L A/C		6,000

TRADING A/C AND PROFIT AND LOSS A/C AT 31/12/11			
Details	€	€	€
Sales			500,000
Less Cost of sales			
Opening stock		10,000	
Purchases		200,000	
Carriage inwards		15,000	
Cost of goods available for sale		225,000	
Less Closing stock		15,000	
Cost of goods sold			210,000
Gross profit			290,000
Less Expenses			
Insurance		5,000	
Rates		12,000	
Salaries		9,000	
Electricity		6,000	32,000
Net profit			258,000

Opening and closing stock

Stock, in this context, refers only to traded goods, i.e. the goods purchased for resale. It does not include items such as stationery or heating oil. The business's stock is an asset because it owns these goods.

The **opening stock** refers to the amount of goods purchased in the previous year that remained unsold at the end of that year, i.e. the *closing stock* from the previous year.

The **closing stock** in one period becomes the *opening stock* for the next period in the same way that the *closing cash* for one month became the *opening cash* for the next month in your household accounts.

You will recall from Chapter 36 that the opening stock was recorded as one of the opening entries in the general journal and was posted to the *Stock* A/C in the general ledger. This is the €10,000 shown as *Opening balance* in the *Stock* A/C on page 357 and is then also shown in the *Trading* A/C.

The business obviously buys in more goods during the year. A record of this stock (stock record) is kept so that the business knows the quantity of goods it holds at any given time. A value is then established for all these goods, i.e. the €15,000 shown in the *Stock* A/C on page 357. This is the *Closing stock* for 2011 (Balance c/d) and the *Opening stock* for 2012 (Balance b/d).

THE VALUE OF THE BUSINESS

The value or worth of a business at any given time is shown in a **balance sheet**. This is a statement of the net assets (all assets *minus* all liabilities) of the business at that time. It also shows the source of the money used to finance this value. All of this information is extracted from the balances on the real and personal accounts at the time. This will be dealt with in detail in Chapter 42.

ADJUSTMENTS NEEDED AT THE END OF A TRADING PERIOD

1. EXPENSE ACCOUNTS

Expenses due or accruals

Some expenses that apply to a particular trading period may not have been recorded in the books at the end of the trading period. These are known as **expenses due** or **accruals**.

Example

Assume that the end of the trading period is the year ending 31/12/11.

The ESB (*Electricity charges*) sends out its bills at the end of every two-monthly period for, say €200 (six bills per year).

The first bill is received at the end of February and it covers the cost of electricity for January and February. This bill is not paid until early March.

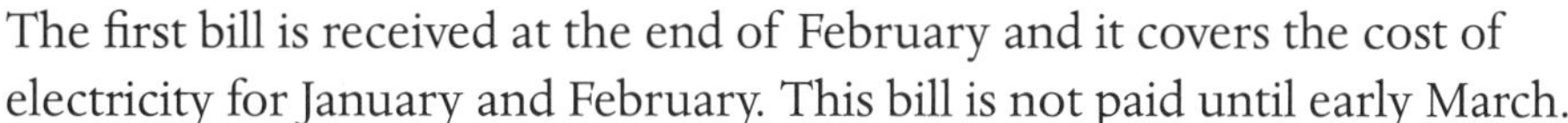

The second bill is received at the end of April and paid in May and so on.

The sixth bill is sent out at the end of December 2011. This covers the charges for electricity used in November and December, but is not paid until January 2012.

Because the bill has not been paid at 31/12/11, there cannot be a record of it in the *Electricity* account. Look at the ledger showing the five accumulated charges.

ELECTRICITY CHARGES A/C

Date	Details	F	€	Date	Details	F	€
1/12/11	Balance b/d		1,000				

However, the true cost for electricity charges for the year is €1,200. This must be shown in the *Profit and loss* account.

Therefore we **debit** the *Profit and loss* account with the true cost of €1,200 and **credit** the *Electricity charges* account with €1,200.

Now look at the *Electricity charges* account at the end of the year.

ELECTRICITY CHARGES A/C

Date	Details	F	€	Date	Details	F	€
1/12/11	Balance b/d		1,000	31/12/11	P&L A/C		1,200
31/12/11	Balance c/d		200				
			1,200				1,200
				31/12/11	Balance b/d		200

This leaves a **credit balance** on the expense account of €200, which indicates that the money is *owed by you* at that time.

This is a **liability** and will appear as such on the balance sheet.

Expenses due summary

1. Calculate the full cost of that expense for the year.
2. Credit the expense account with this amount (write in 'P&L A/C').
3. Balance the account.
4. Bring the balance down on the credit side to indicate the amount owed.
5. The balance appears as a liability in the balance sheet.

Expenses prepaid

Sometimes the very opposite can happen, i.e. you pay an expense in *this* trading period and some of the money paid relates to the expenses of the *next* trading period.

Assume that the end of the trading period is the year ending 31/12/11.

You purchased a new delivery van on 1/11/11 and paid the insurance on it, say €600, for a full year's insurance cover. Only one-sixth (two months) of this amount applies to this trading period, i.e. €100. This is the amount that must be entered in the *Profit and loss* account for the year ending 31/12/11.

Therefore you must **debit** the *Profit and loss* account with €100 and **credit** the *Insurance* account with €100.

INSURANCE A/C

Date	Details	F	€	Date	Details	F	€
1/12/11	Balance b/d		600	**31/12/11**	**P&L A/C**		**100**
				31/12/11	Balance c/d		500
			600				600
31/12/11	Balance b/d		500				

This leaves a **debit balance** on the expense account indicating that this amount of money is *prepaid by you*.

This is an **asset** and will appear as such on the balance sheet.

Expenses prepaid summary

1. Calculate the full cost of that expense for the year.
2. Credit the expense account with this amount (write in 'P&L A/C').
3. Balance the account.
4. Bring the balance down on the debit side to indicate the amount prepaid.
5. The balance appears as an asset in the balance sheet.

2. GAINS ACCOUNTS

Gains prepaid (to you)

Assume, again, that the end of the trading period is the year ending 31/12/11.

Example

On 1/7/11 you sub-let a part of your offices to a tenant who pays you an annual rent (rent receivable), in full, of €3,600. Only half of this is applicable to the trading period end 31/12/11. Therefore only €1,800 can be entered in the *Profit and loss* account for that year.

Therefore you **credit** the *Profit and loss* account with €1,800 and also **debit** the *Rent receivable* account with this amount.

RENT RECEIVABLE A/C

Date	Details	F	€	Date	Details	F	€
31/12/11	P & L A/C		1,800	1/12/11	Balance b/d		3,600
31/12/11	Balance c/d		1,800				
			3,600				3,600
				31/12/11	Balance b/d		1,800

This leaves a **credit balance** on the gain account indicating that this amount of money has been *prepaid to you.*

This is a **liability** and will appear as such on the balance sheet.

Gains (incomes) prepaid summary

1. Calculate the full amount of the gain due for the year.
2. Debit the gain account with this amount (write in 'P&L A/C').
3. Balance the account.
4. Bring the balance down on the credit side to indicate the prepayment.
5. The balance appears as a liability in the balance sheet.

Gains due (to you)

Again our trading period is the year ending 31/12/11.

Assume a tenant pays you €400 a month for the lease of part of your office. However, for some reason, the tenant fails to pay the amount due in December but agrees to pay the outstanding amount in January 2012. The €400 due is part of the income for 2011 and must be included in the amount shown for *rent receivable* in the *Profit and loss* account.

Therefore you must credit the *Profit and loss* account with the total amount due for the year, €4,800, and debit the *Rent receivable* account with this amount. *(See overleaf.)*

RENT RECEIVABLE A/C							
Date	Details	F	€	Date	Details	F	€
31/12/11	P & L A/C		4,800	1/12/11	Balance b/d		4,400
				31/12/11	Balance c/d		400
			4,800				4,800
31/12/11	Balance b/d		400				

This leaves a **debit balance** on the gain account, indicating that this amount of money is *owed to you.*

This is an **asset** and so will appear as such in the balance sheet.

Gains due summary

1. Calculate the full amount of the gain due for the year.
2. Debit the gain account with this amount (write in 'P&L A/C').
3. Balance the account.
4. Bring the balance down on the debit side to indicate money owed to you.
5. The balance appears as an asset in the balance sheet.

3. DEPRECIATION OF FIXED ASSETS

Straight-line method

A **fixed asset** is an asset owned by a business whose value is not directly affected by the normal daily trading transactions of the business, e.g. computers and delivery vans (more about these in Chapter 42).

These assets lose value over time due to wear and tear or obsolescence. Businesses record the **annual loss in value** of these fixed assets as an expense known as **depreciation**.

The **original value** of the fixed asset is shown at its **cost price** each year. Therefore there is never any adjustment to the asset account itself.

However, the yearly loss in value of the asset is recorded in a *Depreciation* account and the accumulated loss, over a number of years, is recorded in a *Provision for depreciation* account.

Example

- A delivery van is purchased on 1/1/11 for €90,000. It is expected to last for five years and to have a scrap value of €10,000 at the end of that period.
- The loss in value, €80,000, is spread evenly over the five-year period.
- Therefore €16,000 deprecation is written off as an expense each year.

Depreciation = Cost price of the asset **minus** its scrap value **divided by** the expected life of the asset.

This is recorded over the first two years as follows:

Step 1
Record the purchase of the delivery van and carry the balance down each succeeding year.

DELIVERY VAN A/C

Date	Details	F	€	Date	Details	F	€
1/11/11	Bank	CB1	90,000	31/12/11	Balance c/d		90,000
			90,000				90,000
1/1/12	Balance b/d		90,000	31/12/12	Balance c/d		90,000
			90,000				90,000
1/1/13	Balance b/d		90,000				

This balance will appear as a **fixed asset** on the balance sheet each year.

Step 2
Record the amount of **depreciation** written off each year by:
- Debiting the *Depreciation* account with the amount written off *and*
- Crediting the *Provision for depreciation* account with the same amount.

Step 3
- Close off the *Depreciation* account to the *Profit and loss* account each year *and*
- Balance the *Provision for depreciation* account and bring the balance down to the next year.

DEPRECIATION A/C

Date	Details	F	€	Date	Details	F	€
31/12/11	Prov. for depreciation		16,000	31/12/11	P&L A/C		16,000
			16,000				16,000
31/12/12	Prov. for depreciation		16,000	31/12/12	P&L A/C		16,000
			16,000				16,000

The €16,000 will appear as **depreciation** in the *Profit and loss* A/C **each year**.

PROVISION FOR DEPRECIATION A/C

Date	Details	F	€	Date	Details	F	€
31/12/11	Balance c/d		16,000	31/12/11	Depreciation A/C		16,000
			16,000				16,000
31/12/12	Balance c/d		32,000	1/12/12	Balance b/d		16,000
				31/12/12	Depreciation A/C		16,000
			32,000				32,000
				1/12/13	Balance b/d		32,000

The **balance** on this account will appear on the **balance sheet** each year.

Depreciation summary

1. **Debit** the asset account with the cost price of the asset when the asset is purchased. Carry this balance on to each year after that.
2. **Calculate** the amount of depreciation to be written each year.
   Debit the *Depreciation* account and **credit** the *Provision for depreciation* account with this amount each year.
3. **Close off** the *Depreciation* account each year, i.e.
   debit the *Profit and loss* account and **credit** the *Depreciation* account with this same amount each year.
4. **Balance** the *Provision for depreciation* account each year and carry this balance forward to the next year.

4. BAD DEBTS

These were dealt with in Chapter 36, *The General Journal*, page 325.

QUESTIONS

1. Quick Transport Ltd purchased a new van on 1/9/11. It also paid the **annual** insurance on it of €2,400 on that date. Show, in your ledger, the *Insurance* A/C at 31/12/11. How will the balance on this account be treated in the balance sheet?
2. Properties Ltd leased a property to a client on 1/6/11 and received the **annual** rent of €24,000 on that date. Show, in your ledger, the *Rent receivable* A/C at 31/12/11. How will the balance on this account be treated in the balance sheet?
3. Having paid €11,000 for stationery during 2011, Marsh Ltd still owed €1,000 for stationery supplied during the year. Show the *Stationery* A/C for the year ending 31/12/11. How will the balance on this account be treated in the balance sheet?
4. Caffery Ltd receives its ESB bill of €400 at the end of every two months (for the previous two months) starting at the end of February. It pays each of these bills on the 5th of the following month. Show Caffery Ltd's *Electricity* A/C for the year ending 31/12/11.
5. Murphy Ltd purchased a new computer on 1/1/11 for €8,000. Depreciation of 20% is to be written off the computer each year. Show, in your ledgers, the *Computer* A/C, the *Depreciation* A/C and the *Provision for depreciation* A/C for the years ending 31/12/11 and 31/12/12.
6. Quick Transport Ltd purchased a new delivery van for €90,000 on 1/9/11. The van is expected to have a useful life of 5 years, at which time it will have a scrap value of €10,000. Show, in your ledgers, the *Delivery van* A/C, the *Depreciation* A/C and the *Provision for depreciation* A/C for the years ending 31/12/11 and 31/12/12.

See workbook for more questions.

Final accounts 1: **The trading account**

Any business that trades in goods, i.e. buys goods for resale, must calculate its **gross profit** or **gross loss**.

Gross profit = Value of sales – Cost of goods sold

SALES

- The value of sales is found by subtracting the balance in the *Sales returns* account from the balance in the *Sales* account. This is often referred to as **net sales**.
- The costs involved in buying the goods that are sold is known as the **cost of sales**, or the **cost of goods sold**.

COST OF GOODS SOLD

Let us assume that a firm calculates its gross profit or loss once a year. The costs to the firm of the goods it sells in a year are made up of:

1. The cost of the **opening stock**, i.e. the goods purchased the previous year that remained unsold that year, but were sold in the current year.
2. The cost of **purchases** in the current year, i.e. the cost of the goods bought for resale in the current year. (Again, *Purchases* minus *Purchases returns* equals *Net purchases.*)
3. Any **carriage inwards** paid by the firm in the current year, i.e. the transport costs paid by the firm on goods purchased by it.
4. Any **import duty** paid by the firm in the current year, i.e. taxes on imported goods that were purchased for resale.

When these four costs are added together the total is known as the **cost of goods available for sale**.

Note: If the seller does not charge the buyer for the cost of delivering goods then there are is no figure for *carriage inwards*. Likewise not all goods purchased are subject to *import duties*. Therefore one or both of these figures may not appear in any given exercise you are asked to do.

Some of the goods purchased for resale during the current year remain unsold at the end of the current year. These are known as the firm's **closing stock**. As these goods were not sold during the current year they are not part of the *cost of goods sold*. Therefore their value must be subtracted from the *cost of goods available for sale*. Thus:

Cost of goods sold = Cost of goods available for sale – Closing stock

Note: *Opening* and *Closing stock* refer only to goods purchased for resale. They do not include such items as stationery, heating oil or office equipment.

GROSS PROFIT OR LOSS

- A **gross profit** occurs when the value of sales is *greater* than the value of the cost of goods sold.
- A **gross loss** occurs when the value of sales is *less* than the value of the cost of goods sold.

THE TRADING ACCOUNT

The trading account is part of a set of inter-related accounts known as the **final accounts**. This set of accounts is made up of the:

1. trading account
2. profit and loss account
3. profit and loss appropriation account
4. balance sheet

The **trading account** is used to calculate the **gross profit** or **loss** for a particular period of time known as the **trading period**.

The trading account can refer to any period of time, e.g. a month, a quarter, a six-month period or a year.

Therefore a trading account must have a title showing the date of the end of the trading period, e.g. *Trading Account at 31/12/11.*

The figure for sales can be either the value of goods sold for cash (cash sales) or the combined figure of cash sales *plus* credit sales (sales). Also, allowance may have to be made for sales returns.

Likewise the figure for purchases can be either the value of goods purchased by cash (cash purchases for resale) or the combined figure of cash purchases *plus* credit purchases (purchases). Again allowance may have to be made for purchases returns.

Record Book No. 2 can be used for the trading account. Your teacher will advise.

Example 1: Ordinary level

From the following figures prepare a **trading account** for O'Gorman Ltd for the year ending 31/12/11.

- Cash sales €300,000
- Opening stock at 1/1/11 €15,000
- Cash purchases for resale €150,000
- Carriage inwards €6,000
- Import duties €11,000
- Closing stock at 31/12/11 €17,000

Layout of the trading account

The trading account is presented in a *statement* format using Record Book No. 2.

TRADING A/C AT 31/12/11			
Details	**€**	**€**	**€**
Cash sales			300,000
Less Cost of sales			
Opening stock		15,000	
+ Cash purchases for resale		150,000	
+ Carriage inwards		6,000	
+ Import duties		11,000	
= Cost of goods available for sale		182,000	
Less Closing stock		17,000	
= Cost of goods sold			165,000
Gross profit (sales *less* cost of goods sold)			135,000

Gross profit percentage or gross profit margin

Sometimes the gross profit is expressed as a percentage of the sales to show the percentage of sales earned as gross profit. This is known as **gross profit percentage** or **gross profit margin**.

$$\textbf{Gross profit percentage/margin} = \frac{\text{Gross profit}}{\text{Sales}} \times 100$$

In the example above this is: $\frac{135,000}{300,000} \times 100 = 45\%$

Example 2: Higher level

From the following figures prepare a trading account for Mi-Class Ltd for the year ending 31/12/11.

- Sales €700,000
- Sales returns €12,000
- Opening stock at 1/1/11 €30,000
- Purchases €300,000
- Purchases returns €11,500
- Carriage inwards €7,500
- Import duties €9,000
- Closing stock at 31/12/11 €19,000

TRADING A/C AT 31/12/11

Details	€	€	€
Sales	700,000		
Less Sales returns	12,000		688,000
Less Cost of sales			
Opening stock		30,000	
Purchases	300,000		
Less Purchases returns	11,500	288,500	
Carriage inwards		7,500	
Import duties		9,000	
Cost of goods available for sale		335,000	
Less Closing stock		19,000	
Cost of goods sold			316,000
Gross profit			372,000

Note: The first of the three money columns is *usually* reserved for any calculations that need to be shown. However, this is not *always* the case. For example, the figures for sales *less* sales returns are sometimes shown in the second column. Your teacher will guide you on this.

Example 3

This example shows a case where a **gross loss** occurs. Note that the value of the cost of goods available for sale is *greater* than the value of the sales. This gives a negative number when the cost of goods available for sale is subtracted from the sales.

TRADING A/C AT 31/12/11			
Details	€	€	€
Sales	500,000		
Less Sales returns	50,000		450,000
Less Cost of sales			
Opening stock		40,000	
Purchases	400,000		
Less Purchases returns	5,000	395,000	
Carriage inwards		10,000	
Import duties		20,000	
Cost of goods available for sale		465,000	
Less Closing stock		9,000	
Cost of goods sold			456,000
Gross loss			(6,000)

Gross profit mark-up

Sometimes the gross profit is expressed as a **percentage of the cost of goods sold** to find the **percentage return** earned on money spent buying the goods. This is known as the **gross profit mark-up**.

$$\textbf{Gross profit mark-up} = \frac{\text{Gross profit}}{\text{Cost of goods sold}} \times 100$$

In Example 2 on page 368 this is: $\frac{372{,}000}{316{,}000} \times 100 = 117.72\%$ (to two decimal places),

i.e. the gross profit represents 117.72% of the **cost of goods sold**. It is *not* a gross profit of 117.72%

Average stock

Average stock is the opening stock *plus* the closing stock *divided by* 2.

In Example 3 above, average stock is calculated as follows:

Opening stock €40,000 + Closing stock €9,000 = €49,000

$$\frac{€49{,}000}{2} = €29{,}500$$

STOCK RECORDS

When a firm takes delivery of goods it is supplied with a **delivery note** that gives details of the goods delivered. These details are entered on **stock sheets** that are used to monitor stock levels in the store room or warehouse. Thus each time a new delivery is made, the increase in stock is recorded on the stock sheets.

As goods are taken from the store room or warehouse the decrease in stock is recorded on the stock sheets.

The use of bar-coded goods helps to keep accurate stock records. As goods are taken into stock, the bar code reading adds them to the stock level. As goods are sold, the bar code reading at the check-out deducts the quantity sold from the stock.

STOCKTAKING

Stocktaking is the counting and valuing of (trading) stock held by a business at a given time.

At the end of the year, or the end of a trading period, a business should do a stocktake.

A typical stocktaking method

1. People are assigned to count all the goods held in given areas of the shop or store rooms.
2. This information is called out to other people who record the counts on a stock sheet.
3. All the individual stock sheets are transferred to a master sheet and the final total of all goods held is calculated.
4. This should tally with the total on the store rooms' stock sheets.

Evaluating stock

Stock can be evaluated (priced) in a number of different ways. The most commonly used methods are:

1. Apply the selling price of the goods to all goods in stock.
2. Apply the cost price of the goods to all goods in stock.
3. Apply the replacement price of the goods for all goods in stock.
4. Best-possible value, i.e. apply any price other than the three named above to **distressed stock** (the modern description for stock that may be difficult to sell). Examples of distressed stock include goods that have reached their 'use-by date', damaged goods, clothes that have gone out of fashion and goods that are no longer being produced by the original manufacturer and don't carry a manufacturer's guarantee.

Firms normally use the method that gives the lowest stock value.

Example

A firm sells overcoats at €200 each. The coats cost €120 each, but would now cost €150 to restock. In most cases all the overcoats would be evaluated at €120 each, i.e. the lowest value.

However, some of the overcoats may soon go out of fashion and be difficult to sell (distressed stock). The firm may decide to sell these at a price below the cost price, e.g. €90, to ensure that it at least gets some money for them.

Importance of stocktaking

1. To calculate closing stock
2. To identify understocking of goods and so avoid the loss of possible future sales
3. To identify overstocking and so not waste money by having it tied up in stock that won't be sold
4. To detect theft of stock
5. To detect distressed stock

LEARN THE KEY TERMS

- A **gross profit** occurs when the income received from the sale of goods is greater than the costs involved in buying those goods.
- A **gross loss** occurs when the costs involved in buying goods is greater than the income received from the sale of them.
- The **cost of sales** or **cost of goods sold** refers to the costs involved in buying the goods that are sold.
- **Gross profit** or **gross loss** = Sales – Cost of goods sold.
- The **trading account** is used to calculate the gross profit or loss for a particular period of time.
- **Gross profit percentage** or **margin** is the gross profit expressed as a percentage of the sales.
- The **gross profit mark-up** is the gross profit expressed as a percentage of the cost of goods available for sale.
- **Average stock** is the opening stock *plus* the closing stock *divided by* 2.
- **Stocktaking** is the counting and valuing of (trading) stock held by a business at a given time.

QUESTIONS

In Questions 1 to 6 calculate the cost of goods available for sale.

1. Opening stock €25,000; Purchases €50,000; Carriage inwards €3,500; Closing stock €14,000
2. Opening stock €20,000; Purchases €45,000; Import duties €2,000; Closing stock €6,000
3. Opening stock €45,000; Purchases €65,500; Carriage inwards €5,500; Import duties €2,500; Closing stock €14,000
4. Opening stock €35,000; Purchases €65,500; Carriage inwards €5,000; Import duties €12,500; Closing stock €11,000
5. Opening stock €45,000; Purchases €85,500; Purchases returns €12,000; Carriage inwards €5,000; Closing stock €18,000
6. Opening stock €29,000; Purchases €55,500; Purchases returns €12,000; Carriage inwards €3,000; Closing stock €27,000

In Questions 7 to 16 prepare a trading account at 31/12/12 and answer the sub-question in questions 13 to 16.

7. Cash sales €500,000; Opening stock €15,000; Cash purchases €425,000; Carriage inwards €5,500; Closing stock €12,000
8. Cash sales €235,000; Opening stock €36,000; Cash purchases €150,000; Import duties €8,000; Closing stock €18,500
9. Cash sales €325,000; Opening stock €12,000; Cash purchases €230,000; Carriage inwards €6,300; Import duties €3,200; Closing stock €9,000
10. Cash sales €200,000; Opening stock €52,000; Cash purchases €190,000; Carriage inwards €7,000; Import duties €6,500; Closing stock €8,000
11. Sales €123,500; Sales returns €25,000; Opening stock €37,000; Purchases €56,000; Purchases returns €7,000; Carriage inwards €6,000; Closing stock €28,000
12. Sales €321,500; Sales returns €52,000; Opening stock €45,000; Purchases €80,000; Purchases returns €7,000; Carriage inwards €3,500; Import duties €1,500; Closing stock €25,000
13. Sales €400,000; Sales returns €40,000; Opening stock €30,000; Purchases €380,000; Purchases returns €12,000; Carriage inwards €5,500; Import duties €2,300; Closing stock €8,000.

    Calculate the average stock held by this firm.
14. Sales €600,000; Sales returns €30,000; Opening stock €20,000; Purchases €290,000; Purchases returns €16,500; Carriage inwards €7,500; Import duties €4,400; Closing stock €68,000

    Calculate the gross profit mark-up.

15. Sales €430,000; Sales returns €23,500; Opening stock €40,000; Purchases €170,550; Purchases returns €10,500; Carriage inwards €3,100; Import duties €2,900; Closing stock €28,600

Calculate the gross profit margin/percentage.

16. Purchases €56,700; Closing stock €22,200; Sale returns €36,500; Purchases returns €15,700; Carriage inwards €1,500; Opening stock €23,300; Sales €125,000; Import duties €2,100

Calculate:
- **(a)** the average stock
- **(b)** the gross profit margin/percentage
- **(c)** the gross profit mark-up

17. What is stocktaking?

18. Outline a suitable method of stocktaking.

19. Outline four different methods of evaluating (pricing) goods held in stock.

20. Give three reasons why it is important to undertake the task of stocktaking.

See workbook for more questions.

41 Final accounts 2: **Profit and loss accounts**

This chapter is divided into two closely related parts. Part A deals with the profit and loss account and Part B deals with the profit and loss appropriation account.

PART A
THE PROFIT AND LOSS ACCOUNT

The second part of the final accounts mentioned in the last chapter is the profit and loss account. This is used to calculate the **net profit**.

Net profit = Gross profit + Gains (other income) – Expenses

From the statement above you can see that the profit and loss account can only be done **after** the trading account is completed because we need to know the gross profit before we can calculate the net profit.

Gains or other income

Gains are any income the business receives other than the income received directly from the sale of goods.

1. An example of a gain is rent the business may receive from leasing part of its premises to another business. This is normally referred to as *rent receivable* to distinguish it from any rent the business itself may have to pay.
2. Likewise any interest received by the business on money lodged to its bank account would be regarded as a gain.
3. Sometimes a firm that buys goods for resale from an agent will receive a commission from the agent when the firm exceeds a certain level of sales. This is additional to the income received directly from the sale of goods and is therefore regarded as a gain.

All **gains** are recorded on the **credit side** of their respective ledger accounts (*remember:* credit gains!) and so will also appear as **credits** in any **trial balance** you may be given as part of an exercise.

Expenses

Expenses are regular, ongoing payments that must be made when running a business. These are the overhead expenses mentioned in Chapter 35 and are sometimes called revenue expenditure. Some of the most common are:

EXAMPLES OF EXPENSES	
Light and heat	Commission paid
Stationery	Wages/Salaries
Rent (paid)	General/Office expenses
Rates	Travel expenses
Taxes (other than import duties)	Insurance
Advertising	Bad debts
Depreciation	Bank interest paid/Interest on overdraft
Carriage outwards	Telephone/email/Internet expenses
Postage	Cleaning
Water charges	Auditor's fees

All **expenses** are recorded on the **debit side** of their respective ledger accounts (*remember:* debit expenses!) and so will also appear as **debits** in any **trial balance** you may be given as part of an exercise.

Revenue expenditure vs. capital expenditure

It is important to understand, clearly, the difference between revenue expenditure and capital expenditure.

Capital expenditure is spending on fixed assets that will benefit the business, hopefully, for a number of years, e.g. the purchase of a delivery van.

This form of expenditure **does not** go into the profit and loss account but will appear in the balance sheet (this will be dealt with in the next chapter).

Revenue expenditure, which is included in the profit and loss account, is day-to-day spending by the business.

The business only benefits from this expenditure in the year the money is spent, e.g. repairs to a delivery van, or stationery.

Layout of the profit and loss account

The profit and loss account is presented in a *statement* format using record book no 2.

Example 1: Ordinary level (no gains)

A firm had the following balances on its accounts on 31/12/12:

- Travelling expenses €2,000
- Advertising €12,000
- Light and heat €4,600
- Rent €4,500
- Interest on overdraft €1,500
- Wages €10,000
- Bad debts €500

- The firm's gross profit for the year was €40,500.

PROFIT AND LOSS A/C AT 31/12/12			
Details	**€**	**€**	**€**
Gross profit			40,500
Less Expenses			
Travelling expenses		2,000	
Advertising		12,000	
Light and heat		4,600	
Rent		4,500	
Interest on overdraft		1,500	
Wages		10,000	
Bad debts		500	35,100
Net profit (gross profit – total expenses)			5,400

Notes

1. The gross profit is entered in the third column.
2. All the expenses are listed in the second column.
3. The total of the expenses is entered in the third column in line with the last expense listed.
4. Subtract the total expenses from the gross profit to calculate the net profit.

Example 2: Higher level (including gains)

A firm had the following balances on its accounts on 31/12/12:

Gains

- Rent receivable €3,500
- Commission receivable €15,000

Expenses

- Stationery €4,000
- Advertising €11,500
- Insurance €8,300
- Rates €2,700
- Interest on overdraft €3,500
- Wages €25,000
- Water charges €1,800

- The firm's gross profit for the year was €70,500.

PROFIT AND LOSS A/C AT 31/12/12			
Details	**€**	**€**	**€**
Gross profit			70,500
Plus Gains			
Rent receivable			3,500
Commission receivable			15,000
			89,000
Less Expenses			
Stationery		4,000	
Advertising		11,500	
Insurance		8,300	
Rates		2,700	
Interest on overdraft		3,500	
Wages		25,000	
Water charges		1,800	56,800
Net profit			32,200

Notice this time that the figure for total expenses (€56,800) is subtracted from the total figure for *Gross profit plus gains* (€89,000) to get the net profit of €32,200.

COMBINED TRADING ACCOUNT AND PROFIT AND LOSS ACCOUNT

At the start of Chapter 40 we saw that the **trading account** and the **profit and loss account** were two elements of the **final accounts** that are inter-related. Shown here is a combined trading account and profit and loss account for a limited company.

TRADING AND PROFIT AND LOSS ACCOUNTS AT 31/12/12			
Details	**€**	**€**	**€**
Sales	700,000		
Less Sales returns	12,000		688,000
Less Cost of sales			
Opening stock		30,000	
Purchases	300,000		
Less Purchases returns	11,500	288,500	
Carriage inwards		7,500	
Import duties		9,000	
Cost of goods available for sale		335,000	
Less Closing stock		19,000	
Cost of goods sold			316,000
Gross profit			372,000
Plus Gains			
Rent receivable			4,500
			376,500
Less Expenses			
Light and heat		3,500	
Carriage outwards		4,600	
Advertising		20,000	
Wages and salaries		25,500	
Postage		1,700	
Bad debts		3,000	58,300
Net profit			318,200

THE NET PROFIT PERCENTAGE/MARGIN

The **net profit percentage** or **net profit margin** is the net profit expressed as a *percentage* of the *net sales* (sales *minus* sales returns).

$$\textbf{Net profit percentage/margin} = \frac{\text{Net profit}}{\text{Net sales}} \times 100$$

In the previous example this is: $\frac{318,200}{688,000} \times 100 = 46.25\%$

The net profit percentage figure in any given year should be compared with the previous years' figures. A decrease in the figure would indicate that overhead costs are increasing or that sales are decreasing.

The figure should also be compared with that of other firms in the same industry to assess the company's efficiency relative to its competitors.

PART B
THE PROFIT AND LOSS APPROPRIATION ACCOUNT

The third element of the final accounts is the **profit and loss appropriation account**. One of the meanings of the verb *to appropriate* is to put something in a suitable or fitting place. In a financial sense it means to allocate money for a particular usage.

The **profit and loss appropriation account** is used to show the distribution of the net profit.

POSSIBLE MEANS OF DISTRIBUTING THE NET PROFIT

1. **The entire profit can be reinvested in the business.**
   This would mean that the business may not have to borrow to finance the expansion of the business; but the owners (shareholders) may not be too pleased with this as they would not get any return on their investment.
2. **The entire profit can be given to the owners (shareholders).**
   This would mean that there would be no money set aside (reserves) for the future needs of the business. This, obviously, would make it difficult to improve and expand the business.
3. **Some of the profit can be reinvested in the business and the remainder given to the owners (shareholders).**
   This would mean that there would be money available to the business for expansion and that the owners (shareholders) would receive some return on their investment.

Dividends

When a limited company allocates part of its profit to its shareholders the business is said to be issuing a dividend. Thus **dividends** are the **share of the profits** paid to the **shareholders**.

Dividends are always expressed as a **percentage of the issued share capital** of the business. If the issued share capital is €100,000 (e.g. 100,000 shares at €1 each) and the dividend is 5%, then the business will pay out a total dividend of €5,000.

In this case, each shareholder would receive 5c for every share he or she holds.

If you had 5,000 shares in this business you would receive (5,000 × 5c) €250.

Reserves or retained earnings

The part of the profit retained by the business (not given to the shareholders) is known by many different names. The two most commonly used terms are:

- profit and loss balance
- profit and loss reserve

Your teacher will guide you. This textbook will use the term **profit and loss reserve**.

HL only

The amount of money reserved in any one year is added to any reserves from previous years and is shown in the balance sheet as money owed to the shareholders (see next chapter). It is also shown as the *opening profit and loss reserve* in the profit and loss appropriation account the following year.

Record Book No. 2, again, is a convenient copy to use for the profit and loss appropriation account.

Example 1: Ordinary level

On the year ending 31/12/12, T. Taylor Ltd had a net profit of €250,000. It paid the shareholders a total dividend of €130,000. Prepare a profit and loss appropriation account for the year ending 31/12/12.

PROFIT AND LOSS APPROPRIATION A/C AT 31/12/12			
Details	€	€	€
Net profit			250,000
Less dividends paid			130,000
Closing profit and loss reserve			120,000

Example 2: Higher level

The issued share capital of P. Power Ltd is 200,000 ordinary shares of €1 each. The company had a profit and loss reserve of €50,000 on 1/1/12. The net profit for the year ending 31/12/12 was €80,000. It declared a dividend of 15% for the year. You are required to prepare a profit and loss appropriation account for the year ending 31/12/12.

PROFIT AND LOSS APPROPRIATION A/C AT 31/12/12			
Details	€	€	€
Net profit			80,000
Plus Opening profit and loss reserve			130,000
			210,000
Less dividend declared*			30,000
Closing profit and loss reserve			180,000

Alternative presentation

PROFIT AND LOSS APPROPRIATION A/C AT 31/12/12			
Details	**€**	**€**	**€**
Net profit			80,000
Less dividend declared*			30,000
			50,000
Plus Opening profit and loss reserve			130,000
Closing profit and loss reserve			180,000

* The issued share capital is 200,000 × €1 = €200,000.
The dividend declared is 15% of the issued share capital. 15% of €200,000 = €30,000.

As we have seen, all sections of the final accounts are inter-related. Below is a full trading, profit and loss and profit and loss appropriation account for a company at 31/12/12.

TRADING, PROFIT & LOSS AND PROFIT & LOSS APPROPRIATION A/C AT 31/12/12			
Details	**€**	**€**	**€**
Sales	700,000		
Less Sales returns	12,000		688,000
Less Cost of sales			
Opening stock		30,000	
Purchases	300,000		
Less Purchases returns	11,500	288,500	
Carriage inwards		7,500	
Import duties		9,000	
Cost of goods available for sale		335,000	
Less Closing stock		19,000	
Cost of goods sold			316,000
Gross profit			372,000
Plus Gains			
Rent receivable			4,500
			376,500
Less Expenses			
Light and heat		3,500	
Carriage outwards		4,600	
Advertising		20,000	
Wages and salaries		25,500	
Postage		1,700	
Bad debts		3,000	58,300
Net profit			318,200
Plus Opening profit and loss reserve			50,000
			368,200
Less Dividends declared			56,000
Closing profit and loss reserve			312,200

LEARN THE KEY TERMS

- The **profit and loss account** is used to calculate the net profit.
- **Net profit** = Gross profit + Gains (other income) – Expenses.
- **Gains** are any income the business receives other than the income received directly from the sale of goods.
- **Capital expenditure** is spending on fixed assets that will benefit the business, hopefully, for a number of years.
- **Revenue expenditure** is day-to-day spending by the business.
- The **net profit percentage** or **net profit margin** is the net profit expressed as a percentage of the net sales (sales *minus* sales returns).
- The **profit and loss appropriation account** is used to show the distribution of the net profit.
- **Dividends** are the share of the profits paid to the shareholders.
- **Reserves/retained earnings/profit and loss reserve** is the part of the profits retained by the business (not given to the shareholders).

QUESTIONS

Questions 1 to 16 refer to Part A.

1. What is the purpose of the profit and loss account?
2. What is net profit?
3. Distinguish between capital expenditure and revenue expenditure.
4. What is the net profit percentage/margin?

In Questions 5 to 12 prepare a profit and loss account for the year given.

5.

Year ending 31/12/10	€
Gross profit	40,000
Light and heat	6,000
Insurance	3,000
Bad debts	1,500
Wages	10,500
Rates	3,200

6.

Year ending 31/12/11	€
Gross profit	36,000
Travelling expenses	5,300
Insurance	2,500
Light and heat	5,600
Telephone	2,800
Rent and rates	8,600

7.

Year ending 31/12/12	€
Gross profit	24,000
Interest on overdraft	7,000
Rates	3,200
Wages	5,000
Telephone	1,600
Insurance	1,600

8.

Year ending 31/12/12	€
Gross profit	20,000
Light and heat	5,300
Interest on overdraft	2,500
Insurance	5,600
Telephone	2,800
Rent and rates	8,600

9.

Year ending 31/12/12	€
Gross profit	87,000
Commission received	4,300
Bad debts	1,500
Office expenses	6,400
Stationery	5,000
Wages	18,500
Cleaning	3,200

10. Year ending 31/12/11

	€
Gross profit	29,000
Commission received	1,300
Rent receivable	8,500
Insurance	6,100
Postage	3,900
Light and heat	7,500
Interest on overdraft	3,200

11. Year ending 31/12/12

	€
Gross profit	28,500
Interest received	4,300
Rent receivable	5,200
Office expenses	2,800
Stationery	6,000
Light and heat	9.100
Travelling expenses	6,100

12. Year ending 31/12/12

	€
Gross profit	45,100
Commission received	2,300
Rent receivable	2,600
Insurance	5,800
Wages	6,000
Interest on overdraft	3,200
Repairs	8,100

In Questions 13 to 16 prepare a trading account and profit and loss account for the year given.

13. Year ending 31/12/10

	€
Cash sales	100,000
Opening stock 1/1/10	20,000
Cash purchases	45,000
Carriage inwards	27,200
Closing stock 31/12/10	18,000
Office expenses	6,000
Interest on overdraft	3,600
Travelling expenses	5,200
Bad debts	1,600

Calculate the gross profit percentage and the net profit percentage.

14. Year ending 31/12/11

	€
Cash sales	250,000
Opening stock 1/1/11	36,300
Cash purchases	112,000
Import duties	11,100
Closing stock 31/12/11	25,000
Light and heat	4,300
Advertising	15,400
Travelling expenses	16,100
Insurance	12,000

Calculate the gross profit percentage and the net profit percentage.

15. Year ending 31/12/12

	€
Sales	400,000
Sales returns	15,000
Opening stock 1/1/12	36,300
Purchases	200,000
Purchases returns	8,000
Carriage inwards	11,100
Closing stock 31/12/12	25,000
Commission received	5,500
Light and heat	7,600
Cleaning	1,200
Travelling expenses	5,400
Bad debts	3,000

Calculate the gross profit percentage, the gross profit mark-up and the net profit percentage.

16. Year ending 31/12/13

	€
Sales	350,000
Sales returns	25,000
Opening stock 1/1/13	25,000
Purchases	150,000
Purchases returns	6,000
Import duties	3,400
Closing stock 31/12/13	12,500
Rent receivable	3,700
Insurance	5,300
Wages	12,200
Repairs	4,700
Office expense	2,300
Bad debts	1,000

Calculate the average stock, the gross profit percentage, the gross profit mark-up and the net profit percentage.

Questions 17 to 27 refer to Part B.

In Questions 17 to 23 prepare a profit and loss appropriation account at the date given.

17. 31/12/10: Net profit €120,000; Dividend paid €12,000

18. 31/12/11: Net profit €35,000; Dividend paid €20,000

19. 31/12/11: Net profit €85,000
Closing profit & loss reserve €65,000
There was no opening profit and loss reserve.

20. 31/12/10
Opening profit and loss reserve €15,000
Net profit €65,000
Dividend paid €12,000

21. 31/12/11
Issued share capital €400,000
Dividend paid 10%
Profit and loss reserve at 1/1/11 €28,000
Net profit €90,000

22. 31/12/12
Issued share capital €350,000
Dividend paid 12%
Profit and loss reserve at 1/1/12 €83,000
Net profit €60,000

23. 31/12/13
Issued share capital €250,000
Dividend paid 15%
Profit and loss reserve at 1/1/13 €65,000
Net profit €95,000.

In Questions 24 to 27 prepare a trading, profit and loss and profit and loss appropriation account at the date given.

24.

Year ending 31/12/10	€
Cash sales	300,000
Opening stock 1/1/10	35,000
Cash purchases	150,000
Carriage inwards	6,000
Closing stock 31/12/10	30,000
Office expenses	5,000
Interest on overdraft	2,000
Travelling expenses	4,500
Bad debts	4,000
Dividend paid	7,000

25.

Year ending 31/12/11	€
Cash sales	480,000
Opening stock 1/1/11	42,000
Cash purchases	200,000
Import duties	5,500
Closing stock 31/12/11	12,000
Advertising	8,700
Wages	10,100
Light and heat	3,000
Insurance	2,500
Dividends paid	10,000

26.

Year ending 31/12/10	€
Issued share capital	200,000
Sales	450,000
Sales returns	45,000
Opening stock 1/1/10	25,000
Purchases	350,000
Purchases returns	70,000
Carriage inwards	5,000
Closing stock 31/12/10	50,000
Commission received	50,000
Interest on overdraft	2,000
Wages	11,000
Office expenses	2,500
Advertising	5,000
Opening P&L reserve 1/1/11	45,000
Dividend declared	2%

27.

Year ending 31/12/11	€
Issued share capital	100,000
Sales	750,000
Sales returns	27,000
Opening stock 1/1/11	20,000
Purchases	400,000
Purchases returns	35,000
Import duties	5,500
Closing stock 31/12/10	40,000
Interest received	15,000
Advertising	11,000
Wages	18,000
Light and heat	3,000
Insurance	2,500
Opening P&L reserve 1/1/11	13,500
Dividends declared	4%

See workbook for more questions.

Final accounts 3: **The balance sheet**

42

The balance sheet is the fourth and last part of the final accounts.

The two functions of a balance sheet

1. It is used to show the **net assets** (**value**) of a business at any given moment in time.
2. It is used to show the **capital employed** in the business, i.e. the sources of the money used to finance the net assets.

The totals at (**1**) and (**2**) should equal each other because all the money received by a business is used to finance its assets.

All the figures required for the balance sheet are taken from the debtors and creditors ledgers as well from the real accounts in the general ledger. These figures are normally presented to you in the form of a trial balance as the other figures in the trial balance can be used for the trading, profit and loss and profit and loss appropriation accounts.

VALUE OR NET ASSETS OF A BUSINESS

Assets

Assets are sub-divided into **fixed assets** and **current assets**.

Fixed assets

A **fixed asset** is any asset whose value **is not** directly affected by the *normal daily transactions* of the business, e.g. land, buildings, machinery, motor vehicles and fixtures and fittings.

Current assets

A **current asset** is an asset whose value **is** directly affected by the *normal daily transactions* of the business, e.g. bank/cash, stock and debtors (money owed by customers).

Liabilities

Liabilities are sub-divided into current (short-term) liabilities and long-term liabilities.

Current liabilities

A **current liability** is any debt owed by the business that is due for repayment within one year. The two most common current liabilities are: creditors (money owed to suppliers) and a bank overdraft.

Note: Long-term liabilities will be explained later in this chapter and other current liabilities will be dealt with in the next chapter.

Working capital

Working capital refers to the amount of money available to a business to pay for its normal daily transactions. It is calculated as follows:

Working capital = Current assets – Current liabilities

Working capital will be dealt with in more detail in Chapter 44.

Calculating the value of the net assets

Net assets = Fixed assets + Working capital

CAPITAL EMPLOYED OR SOURCES OF FINANCE

The main sources of finance are:

1. the **issued share capital**
2. the **closing profit and loss balance/reserves/retained earnings**
3. any **long-term loans** taken out by the business

A **long-term liability** is any debt that is not due for repayment within the coming twelve months.

The three sources of finance are regarded as **long-term liabilities** because:

1. The **issued share capital** is not repaid to the shareholders until the company closes down. Thus, this could be owed for a very long time, hopefully!
2. The **profit and loss balance/reserves** etc are only repaid to the shareholders at the discretion of the directors of the business. This usually remains unpaid for a long time because the money is used to purchase assets.
3. **Long-term loans** may not have to be repaid for a 3–5 or even 20-year period.

Now let us use all this information to see a typical balance sheet. Remember that a balance sheet shows us the net assets and the capital employed **at any given moment in time**. Therefore it is essential to show the date of the balance sheet, e.g. *Balance sheet as at 31/12/12.*

A **balance sheet** has been described as a **snap shot** of a company at a given moment in time.

DRAWING UP A BALANCE SHEET

1. Make a list of the **fixed assets** and show the total of them.
2. List the **current assets** and show a total for them.
3. List the **current liabilities** and show a total for them.
4. Subtract the **current liabilities** from the **current assets** = **working capital**.
5. Add the **working capital** to the **fixed assets** = **net assets**.
6. Show and total the **issued share capital**, **reserves** and **long-term loans** (where applicable) = **capital employed**.

All of these figures are highlighted in the following example by the insertion of the relevant number. The total of the two underlined figures should equal each other, as highlighted in the example.

Example

BALANCE SHEET AS AT 31/12/12			
	Cost €	Depreciation €	Net value €
Fixed assets			
Land			400,000
Buildings			650,000
			(1) 1,050,000
Current assets			
Debtors	50,000		
Closing stock	70,000	(2) 120,000	
Less Current liabilities			
Creditors	30,000		
Bank overdraft	15,000	(3) 45,000	
Working capital			(4) 75,000
Net assets			(5) 1,125,000
Financed by:			
Authorised share capital	2,000,000		
Issued share capital			1,000,000
Closing profit and loss reserve			100,000
Ten-year loan			25,000
Capital employed			(6) 1,125,000

Notes

1. Headings for *Cost* and *Depreciation* have been inserted here. These will be dealt with in the next chapter.
2. Note that the *Current assets* and *Current liabilities* are listed in the first column and their totals are entered in the second column. If there is only one of these, e.g. only one current liability, then it is entered in the second column.
3. There is a legal requirement to enter the value of the authorised share capital.

A full worked example of final accounts (Ordinary level)

Adapted from 1999 Junior Certificate Ordinary Level Paper

This company has an authorised share capital of 200,000 ordinary shares at €1 each.

TRIAL BALANCE AT 31/12/98		
	Dr €	Cr €
Cash sales **(T)**		185,000
Carriage inwards **(T)**	450	
Cash purchases for resale **(T)**	106,000	
Opening stock 1/1/98 **(T)**	28,500	
Dividend paid **(APR)**	8,000	
Rent and rates **(P&L)**	1,250	
Telephone **(P&L)**	850	
Wages **(P&L)**	15,500	
Interest on overdraft **(P&L)**	650	
Heating and lighting **(P&L)**	1,850	
Bank overdraft **(CL)**		7,200
Cash in hand **(CA)**	1,600	
Issued share capital **(F)**		90,000
Machinery **(FA)**	57,200	
Motor vans **(FA)**	60,350	
	282,200	282,200

The closing stock at 31/12/98 was €16,000 (**T** and **CA**).

From the above figures, prepare a trading, profit and loss, and profit and loss appropriation account for the year ended 31/12/98 and a balance sheet as at that date.

Notes

1. The closing stock is always shown **after** the trial balance and is entered twice into the final accounts, i.e. in the trading account and as part of the current assets in the balance sheet.
2. The authorised share capital is always shown in the introduction to the question.
3. When undertaking an exercise like this you should mark each item in the trial balance, indicating where each item is to be entered in the final accounts.

   The following abbreviations have been used here:

   T Trading account
   P&L Profit and loss account
   APR Profit and loss appropriation account
   FA Fixed asset
   CA Current asset
   CL Current liability
   F Finance section.

TRADING, PROFIT & LOSS AND PROFIT & LOSS APPROPRIATION A/CS AT 31/12/98			
	€	€	€
Cash sales			185,000
Cost of sales			
Opening stock 1/1/98		28,500	
Cash purchases for resale		106,000	
Carriage inwards		450	
Cost of goods available for sale		134,950	
Less Closing stock		16,000	
Cost of goods sold			118,950
Gross profit			66,050
Less Expenses			
Rent and rates		1,250	
Telephone		850	
Wages		15,500	
Interest on overdraft		650	
Heating and lighting		1,850	20,100
Net profit			45,950
Less Dividend paid			8,000
Closing profit and loss reserve			37,950

BALANCE SHEET AS AT 31/12/98			
	Cost €	Depreciation €	Net value €
Fixed assets			
Machinery			57,200
Motor vans			60,350
			117,550
Current assets			
Cash in hand	1,600		
Closing stock	16,000	17,600	
Less Current liabilities			
Bank overdraft		7,200	
Working capital			10,400
Net assets			127,950
Financed by:			
Authorised share capital	200,000		
Issued share capital			90,000
Closing profit and loss reserve			37,950
Capital employed			127,950

(see Notes overleaf)

Notes

1. In this case there was only one *Current liability* and so was entered directly into the second column.
2. Always remember to include the *Closing profit and loss reserve* in the *Financed by* section.
3. In this case there were no long-term loans, but if there were they too should be included in the *Financed by* section.

LEARN THE KEY TERMS

- The **balance sheet** is used to show the net assets (value) of a business at any given moment in time and to show the sources of the capital employed in the business.
- An **asset** is anything a business owns *plus* any debts owed to it.
- A **fixed asset** is any asset whose value **is not** directly affected by the normal daily transactions of the business.
- A **current asset** is any asset whose value **is** directly affected by the normal daily transactions of the business.
- A **liability** is any debt owed by the business.
- A **current liability** is any debt owed by the business that is due for repayment within one year.
- A **long-term liability** is any debt that is not due for repayment within the coming twelve months.
- **Working capital** = Current assets – Current liabilities
- **Net assets** = Fixed assets + Working capital

QUESTIONS

Complete the balance sheet for Questions 1 to 4 as at the date stated.

1. Year ending 31/12/10
   Authorised share capital:
   300,000 €1 ordinary shares

	€
Machinery	80,000
Land	120,000
Cash in hand	80,000
Closing stock	40,000
Bank overdraft	15,000
Issued share capital	235,000
Closing profit & loss reserve	70,000

2. Year ending 31/12/11
   Authorised share capital:
   400,000 €1 ordinary shares

	€
Fixtures and fittings	100,000
Motor vehicles	95,000
Cash in hand	30,000
Closing stock	25,000
Bank overdraft	80,000
Issued share capital	125,000
Closing profit & loss reserve	45,000

3. Year ending 31/12/12
Authorised share capital:
500,000 €1 ordinary shares

	€
Premises	200,000
Computers	40,000
Cash in hand	35,000
Closing stock	84,000
Bank overdraft	59,000
Issued share capital	240,000
Closing profit & loss reserve	60,000

4. Year ending 31/12/13
Authorised share capital:
400,000 €1 ordinary shares

	€
Delivery vans	150,000
Buildings	250,000
Cash in hand	50,000
Closing stock	100,000
Bank overdraft	80,000
Issued share capital	300,000
Closing profit & loss reserve	170,000

In Questions 5 to 12 prepare the trading, profit and loss and profit and loss appropriation accounts for the year ending as stated and a balance sheet as at that date.

5. Year ending 31/12/10
Authorised share capital: 20,000 €1 shares

TRIAL BALANCE AT 31/12/10		
	Dr €	Cr €
Cash sales		350,000
Opening stock	25,000	
Cash purchases	150,000	
Carriage inwards	5,000	
Rent	15,000	
Wages	10,000	
Electricity	12,000	
Insurance	7,000	
Dividends paid	5,000	
Cash	15,000	
Bank overdraft		10,000
Issued share capital		4,000
Furniture	80,000	
Machinery	40,000	
	364,000	364,000
Closing stock	15,000	

6. Year ending 31/12/11
Authorised share capital: 40,000 €1 shares

TRIAL BALANCE AT 31/12/11		
	Dr €	Cr €
Cash sales		500,000
Opening stock	3,000	
Cash purchases	300,000	
Carriage inwards	3,000	
Light and heat	10,000	
Wages	15,000	
Advertising	22,000	
Rates	6,000	
Postage	2,000	
Dividends paid	8,000	
Cash	10,000	
Bank overdraft		15,000
Issued share capital		33,000
Land	108,000	
Equipment	61,000	
	548,000	548,000
Closing stock 31/12/11	€35,000	

7. Year ending 31/12/12
Authorised share capital: 200,000 €1 shares

TRIAL BALANCE AT 31/12/12		
	Dr €	Cr €
Cash sales		250,000
Opening stock	1,500	
Cash purchases	120,000	
Carriage inwards	5,000	
Telephone	3,000	
Rent	6,000	
Insurance	6,000	
Stationery	2,500	
Postage	2,000	
Dividends paid	15,000	
Cash	10,000	
Bank overdraft		20,000
Issued share capital		150,000
Premises	200,000	
Fixtures and fittings	49,000	
	420,000	420,000
Closing stock	2,500	

8. Year ending 31/12/10
Authorised share capital: 500,000 €1 shares

TRIAL BALANCE AT 31/12/10		
	Dr €	Cr €
Cash sales		350,000
Opening stock	12,000	
Cash purchases	250,000	
Import duties	8,500	
Bad debts	2,300	
Advertising	12,000	
Office expenses	2,500	
Printing expenses	6,700	
Rent	5,500	
Dividends paid	2,000	
Cash	35,000	
Bank overdraft		45,000
Issued share capital		190,500
Delivery vans	200,000	
Computer equipment	49,000	
	585,500	585,500
Closing stock	16,500	

9. Year ending 31/12/11
Authorised share capital: 600,000 €1 shares

TRIAL BALANCE AT 31/12/11		
	Dr €	Cr €
Cash sales		450,000
Opening stock	15,000	
Cash purchases	194,500	
Carriage inwards	5,200	
Telephone	5,000	
Bad debts	2,400	
Light and heat	3,450	
Wages	10,600	
Rates	1,500	
Dividends paid	3,500	
Cash in hand	45,000	
Bank overdraft		35,000
Issued share capital		200,000
Land	320,000	
Office equipment	80,000	
	686,150	686,150
Closing stock	24,000	

10. Year ending 31/12/13
Authorised share capital: 200,000 €1 shares

TRIAL BALANCE AT 31/12/13		
	Dr €	Cr €
Cash sales		250,000
Opening stock	3,000	
Cash purchases	80,000	
Import duties	1,500	
Wages	6,500	
Electricity	3,000	
Advertising	2,400	
Stationery	5,000	
Rent	4,000	
Dividends paid	4,500	
Cash in hand	21,000	
Bank overdraft		10,900
Issued share capital		200,000
Premises	200,000	
Office equipment	130,000	
	460,900	460,900
Closing stock	18,000	

11. Year ending 31/12/12
Authorised share capital: 400,000 €1 shares

TRIAL BALANCE AT 31/12/12		
	Dr €	Cr €
Cash sales		451,000
Opening stock	5,000	
Cash purchases	220,000	
Carriage inwards	2,000	
Wages	10,500	
Carriage outwards	3,400	
Light and heat	4,300	
Interest on overdraft	2,500	
Water charges	1,800	
Dividends paid	6,000	
Cash in hand	51,000	
Bank overdraft		5,500
Issued share capital		180,000
Land	150,000	
Office equipment	180,000	
	636,500	636,500
Closing stock	21,000	

12. Year ending 31/12/12
Authorised share capital: 400,000 €1 shares

TRIAL BALANCE AT 31/12/12	Dr €	Cr €
Cash sales		600,000
Opening stock	2,500	
Cash purchases for resale	350,000	
Import duty	2,500	
Light and heat	4,200	
Water charges	2,500	
Insurance	3,000	
Wages	40,000	
Postage	2,000	
Dividends paid	15,000	
Cash	5,000	
Bank overdraft		3,000
Issued share capital		150,000
Premises	277,000	
Fixtures and fittings	49,300	
	753,000	753,000
Closing stock	4,500	

13. Year ending 31/12/11
Authorised share capital €300,000

TRIAL BALANCE AT 31/12/11	Dr €	Cr €
Cash sales		400,000
Opening stock	3,500	
Cash purchases for resale	250,000	
Carriage inwards	1,800	
Motor insurance	2,500	
Wages	25,000	
Light and heat	2,600	
Interest on overdraft	2,200	
Stationery	4,300	
Dividends paid	18,000	
Bank overdraft		10,600
Issued share capital		133,300
Cash	4,000	
Delivery vans	150,000	
Fixtures and fittings	80,000	
	543,900	543,900
Closing stock	1,800	

14. Year ending 31/12/10
Authorised share capital €900,000

TRIAL BALANCE AT 31/12/10	Dr €	Cr €
Cash sales		750,000
Cash purchases for resale	450,000	
Opening stock	40,000	
Carriage inwards	3,600	
Import duties	4,200	
Wages	50,000	
Rent	25,000	
Interest on overdraft	3,400	
Telephone charges	2,500	
Dividends paid	71,300	
Cash	5,000	
Issued share capital		160,000
Bank overdraft		35,000
Premises	230,000	
Computers	60,000	
	945,000	945,000
Closing stock	19,000	

15. Year ending 31/12/11
Authorised share capital €700,000

TRIAL BALANCE AT 31/12/11	Dr €	Cr €
Cash sales		345,000
Cash purchases for resale	215,000	
Stock 1/1/11	12,000	
Carriage inwards	1,500	
Wages	24,000	
Insurance	5,000	
Light and heat	16,000	
Interest on overdraft	1,200	
Travelling expenses	1,800	
Dividends paid	22,000	
Bank overdraft		22,000
Issued share capital		333,500
Cash	12,000	
Fixtures and fittings	190,000	
Premises	200,000	
	700,500	700,500
Stock 31/12/11	23,500	

43 Final accounts with adjustments (HL)

In a typical examination question on company final accounts you are given a trial balance and a **list of adjustments** that must be taken into consideration. The adjustments are made by you in the final accounts as you proceed through them. You do not have to do the ledger account adjustments.

In order to comply with the double-entry system, each adjustment appears *twice* in the final accounts: *once* in the balance sheet and *once* in either the **trading**, **profit and loss** or **profit and loss appropriation account**.

GENERAL GUIDELINES

Adjustments for expenses

1. Any expense **due** is **added** to that expense in either the trading account or the profit and loss account, and is also entered as a **current liability** in the balance sheet.
2. Any expense **prepaid** is **subtracted** from that expense in either the trading account or the profit and loss account, and is also entered as a **current asset** in the balance sheet.

Adjustments for gains

1. Any gain **due** is **added** to that gain in the profit and loss account and is also entered as a **current asset** in the balance sheet.
2. Any gain **prepaid** is **subtracted** from that gain in the profit and loss account and is also entered as a **current liability** in the balance sheet.

Closing stock

Closing stock is entered as part of the **cost of sales** in the trading account and as a **current asset** in the balance sheet.

Dividends declared

Dividends are recorded in the **profit and loss appropriation account** and as a **current liability** in the balance sheet.

It is helpful, at least initially, to mark the destiny of each item listed in the trial balance and also to mark each item that requires adjustment. The abbreviations shown below are used in the example that follows.

- T — Trading account
- P&L Ex — Expenses in the profit and loss account
- P&L G — Gains in the profit and loss account
- APR — Appropriation account
- BS, FA — Fixed asset in the balance sheet
- BS, CA — Current asset in the balance sheet
- BS, CL — Current liability in the balance sheet
- BS, F by — Entered in the *Financed by* section of the balance sheet
- Adj — The item needs to be adjusted

Example

From the following information prepare a **trading, profit and loss and profit and loss appropriation account** and a **balance sheet** for Quinn Ltd as at 31/12/12.

- Year ending 31/12/12
- Authorised share capital: 200,000 €1 ordinary shares

TRIAL BALANCE AT 31/12/12			
	Dr €	Cr €	Destination
Purchases and sales	300,000	590,000	T
Sales returns and Purchases returns	10,000	12,000	T
Opening stock 1/12/12	25,000		T
Carriage inwards	30,000		T
Debtors and creditors	50,000	40,000	BS, CA & CL
Import duty	6,000		T
Equipment	180,000		BS, FA
Bad debts	4,200		P&L Ex
Rent receivable		8,000	P&L G (Adj)
Machinery	110,000		BS, FA
Carriage outwards	5,000		P&L Ex (Adj)
Cash in hand	15,000		BS, CA
Bank overdraft		8,000	BS, CL
Wages	38,000		P&L Ex (Adj)
Reserves/profit and loss balance		10,000	APR
Issued share capital		110,000	BS, F by
Carriage outwards	12,000		P&L Ex (Adj)
15-year long-term loan		10,000	BS, F by
Interest on overdraft	2,800		P&L Ex
	788,000	788,000	

You are given the following information as on 31/12/12:

1. Closing stock	€40,000	T and BS, CA
2. Wages prepaid	€4,000	P&L Ex and BS, CA
3. Carriage outwards due	€4,500	P&L Ex and BS, CL
4. Rent receivable due	€2,000	P&L G and BS, CA
5. Dividends declared	10%	APR and BS, CL
6. Depreciation	Equipment 10%; Machinery 5%	P&L Ex and BS, FA

Depreciation

- **Profit and loss account.** Depreciation is the loss in value of a fixed asset due to wear and tear or obsolescence. This is an expense to the business and so will appear as an expense in the profit and loss account. The value shown in the trial balance is the cost of the asset. The value shown in the profit and loss account is the stated percentage of this cost. *(continued overleaf)*

- **Balance sheet.** The balance sheet shows the fixed assets at their cost price (as per trial balance). The value of the depreciation for that year (as per profit and loss account) is also shown. Finally the depreciation is subtracted from the cost price to give the net value (or book value).

Solution

TRADING, PROFIT & LOSS AND PROFIT & LOSS APPROPRIATION A/CS AT 31/12/12

	€	€	€
Sales	590,000		
Sales returns	10,000		580,000
Cost of sales			
Opening stock		25,000	
Purchases	300,000		
Less Purchases returns	12,000	288,000	
Carriage inwards		30,000	
Import duty		6,000	
Cost of goods available for sale		349,000	
Less Closing stock		40,000	
Cost of goods sold			309,000
Gross profit			271,000
Plus Gains			
Rent receivable	8,000		
Plus Rent receivable due	2,000		10,000
			281,000
Less Expenses			
Bad debts		4,200	
Carriage outwards	5,000		
Plus Carriage outwards due	4,500	9,500	
Wages	38,000		
Less Wages prepaid	4,000	34,000	
Light and heat		12,000	
Interest on overdraft		2,800	
Depreciation			
Equipment 10%	18,000		
Machinery 5%	5,500	23,500	86,000
Net profit			195,000
Less dividends declared			11,000
			184,000
Plus Opening profit & loss balance			10,000
Closing profit and loss reserve			194,000

BALANCE SHEET AS AT 31/12/12			
	Cost €	Depreciation €	Net value €
Fixed assets			
Equipment	180,000	18,000	162,000
Machinery	110,000	5,500	104,500
	290,000	23,500	266,500
Current assets			
Debtors	50,000		
Cash in hand	15,000		
Closing stock	40,000		
Wages prepaid	4,000		
Rent receivable due	2,000	111,000	
Less Current liabilities			
Creditors	40,000		
Bank overdraft	8,000		
Carriage outwards due	4,500		
Dividends declared	11,000	63,500	
Working capital			47,500
Net assets			314,000
Financed by			
Authorised share capital	200,000		
Issued share capital			110,000
Plus Closing profit and loss reserve			194,000
Plus 15-year long-term loan			10,000
Capital employed			314,000

QUESTIONS

In each of the following questions you are required to prepare a trading, profit and loss and profit and loss appropriation account and a balance sheet as at the date shown.

1. **(a)** Year ending 31/3/09
Authorised share capital:
500,000 €1 ordinary shares

TRIAL BALANCE AT 31/3/09	Dr €	Cr €
Purchases and sales	120,000	340,000
Sales returns	10,000	
Opening stock 1/4/08	12,000	
Carriage inwards	3,000	
Debtors and creditors	12,000	18,000
Advertising	4,000	
Rent receivable		23,000
Bank overdraft		11,000
Wages	40,000	
Buildings	420,000	
Motor vehicles	180,000	
Bad debts	2,000	
Machinery	135,000	
Reserves/profit and loss balance		55,000
Issued share capital		433,000
10-year loan		58,000
	938,000	938,000

You are given the following information as on 31/3/09.

(i) Closing stock €25,000
(ii) Advertising due €3,000
(iii) Rent receivable due €2,000
(iv) Dividends declared 10%
(v) Depreciation:
Motor vehicles 5%
Machinery 10%

(b) Explain the term **depreciation**.

2. **(a)** Year ending 31/5/09
Authorised share capital:
200,000 €1 ordinary shares

TRIAL BALANCE AT 31/5/09	Dr €	Cr €
Opening stock 1/6/08	30,000	
Purchase returns		12,000
Debtors and creditors	70,000	40,000
Purchases and sales	150,000	420,000
Import duty	11,000	
Land	300,000	
Rates	15,000	
Computer equipment	90,000	
Commission receivable		20,000
15-year loan		68,000
Cash	10,000	
Telephone	3,000	
Bank overdraft		10,000
Wages	30,000	
Reserves/profit and loss balance		30,000
Issued share capital		110,000
Interest on overdraft	1,000	
	710,000	710,000

You are given the following information as on 31/5/09.

(i) Closing stock €20,000
(ii) Import duty due €3,000
(iii) Wages prepaid €4,000
(iv) Dividends declared 5%
(v) Depreciation:
Computer equipment 10%

(b) Identify three long-term sources of finance used by this company.

3. (a) Year ending 31/12/09
Authorised share capital:
400,000 €1 ordinary shares

TRIAL BALANCE AT 31/12/09	Dr €	Cr €
Purchases and sales	130,000	460,000
Sales returns	15,000	
Opening stock 1/1/09	13,000	
Carriage inwards	2,000	
Debtors and creditors	80,000	60,000
Carriage outwards	2,500	
Insurance	12,000	
Light and heat	12,700	
Machinery	185,000	
Buildings	250,000	
Interest receivable		10,000
Bank	180,000	
Reserves/profit and loss balance		30,000
Wages	27,800	
Issued share capital		300,000
20-year loan		50,000
	910,000	910,000

You are given the following information as on 31/12/09.

(i) Closing stock €21,000
(ii) Light and heat prepaid €1,700
(iii) Interest receivable due €600
(iv) Dividends declared 2%
(v) Depreciation:
Machinery 5%

(b) Calculate the average stock held by this company.

4. (a) Year ending 31/1/10
Authorised share capital:
450,000 €1 ordinary shares

TRIAL BALANCE AT 31/1/10	Dr €	Cr €
Purchases returns		15,000
Opening stock 1/2/09	30,000	
Purchases and sales	120,000	350,000
Import duty	1,500	
Insurance	5,000	
Debtors and creditors	35,000	67,000
Wages	25,000	
Bad debts	2,500	
Delivery vans	350,000	
Buildings	250,000	
Commission receivable		24,000
Bank overdraft		40,000
Reserves/profit and loss balance		20,000
Interest on overdraft	3,000	
Issued share capital		400,000
20-year loan		56,000
Land	150,000	
	972,000	972,000

You are given the following information as on 31/1/10.

(i) Closing stock €38,000
(ii) Commission receivable due €2,000
(iii) Wages due €800
(iv) Dividends declared 12½%
(v) Depreciation:
Delivery vans 10%

(b) Why is it important for a business to have reserves?

5. **(a)** Year ending 31/3/10
Authorised share capital:
350,000 €1 ordinary shares

TRIAL BALANCE AT 31/3/10	Dr €	Cr €
Purchases and sales	96,000	310,000
Purchases returns		8,000
Import duty	2,400	
Wages	28,000	
Insurance	7,000	
Repairs	16,500	
Commission receivable		5,000
Rent receivable		18,000
Office equipment	450,000	
Machinery	140,000	
Debtors and creditors	25,000	18,000
Light and heat	20,000	
Opening stock 1/4/09	20,000	
Bank	9,100	
Issued share capital		300,000
20-year loan		80,000
Reserves/profit and loss balance		75,000
	814,000	814,000

You are given the following information as on 31/3/10.

(i) Closing stock €25,000
(ii) Commission receivable prepaid €2,000
(iii) Repairs due €800
(iv) Dividends declared 6%
(v) Depreciation:
Office equipment 5%
Machinery 10%

(b) Calculate the gross profit mark-up (to two decimal places).

6. **(a)** Year ending 31/12/10
Authorised share capital:
350,000 €1 ordinary shares

TRIAL BALANCE AT 31/12/10	Dr €	Cr €
Purchases and sales	250,000	500,000
Sales returns	7,000	
Opening stock 1/1/10	5,000	
Bad debts	6,000	
Rent receivable		10,000
Stationery	8,000	
Carriage inwards	2,000	
Carriage outwards	4,000	
Premises	400,000	
Computer equipment	150,000	
Debtors and creditors	30,000	20,000
Repairs	15,000	
Delivery vans	80,000	
Bank	28,000	
Issued share capital		300,000
15-year loan		60,000
Reserves/profit and loss balance		95,000
	985,000	985,000

You are given the following information as on 31/12/10.

(i) Closing stock €15,000
(ii) Rent receivable due €4,000
(iii) Repairs due €900
(iv) Dividends declared 8%
(v) Depreciation:
Computer equipment 5%
Delivery vans 15%

(b) List three means by which this company could minimise its bad debts.

7. (a) Year ending 31/12/11
Authorised share capital:
200,000 €1 ordinary shares

TRIAL BALANCE AT 31/12/11	Dr €	Cr €
Purchases and sales	350,000	700,000
Sales returns	10,000	
Insurance	9,000	
Advertising	9,000	
Commission receivable		5,000
Wages	18,000	
Motor vehicles	60,000	
Import duty	6,000	
Machinery	250,000	
Debtors and creditors	60,000	90,000
Cash in hand	5,000	
Bank overdraft		15,000
Premises	120,000	
Reserves/profit and loss balance		10,000
Issued share capital		120,000
Opening stock 1/1/11	25,000	
Rent	18,000	
	940,000	940,000

You are given the following information as on 31/12/11.

(i) Closing stock €30,000
(ii) Commission receivable prepaid €1,500
(iii) Import duty due €700
(iv) Dividends declared 10%
(v) Depreciation:
Motor vehicles 10%
Machinery 2%

(b) Calculate the net profit percentage.

8. (a) Year ending 31/12/12
Authorised share capital:
300,000 €1 ordinary shares

TRIAL BALANCE AT 31/12/12	Dr €	Cr €
Opening stock 1/1/12	18,000	
Sales returns and purchases returns	15,000	24,000
Printing	7,000	
Purchases and sales	250,000	755,000
Rent receivable		8,000
Carriage inwards	9,000	
Office furniture	195,000	
Insurance	7,000	
Delivery vans	300,000	
Debtors and creditors	90,000	50,000
Cash in hand	8,000	
Bank	25,000	
Wages	35,000	
Reserves/profit and loss balance		13,000
Issued share capital		150,000
Carriage outwards	25,000	
Advertising	16,000	
	1,000,000	1,000,000

You are given the following information as on 31/12/12.

(i) Closing stock €35,000
(ii) Rent receivable due €1,500
(iii) Insurance prepaid €1,000
(iv) Dividends declared 10%
(v) Depreciation:
Office furniture 10%
Delivery vans 15%

(b) Identify two long-term sources of finance in the above trial balance.

9. **(a)** Year ending 31/12/10
Authorised share capital:
300,000 €1 ordinary shares

TRIAL BALANCE AT 31/12/10		
	Dr €	Cr €
Opening stock 1/1/10	35,000	
Sales returns and purchases returns	12,000	18,000
Advertising	11,000	
Purchases and sales	300,000	700,000
Commission receivable		11,000
Import duty	3,000	
Premises	250,000	
Rent	10,000	
Machinery	250,000	
Debtors and creditors	40,000	50,000
Cash in hand	7,000	
Bank overdraft		15,000
Interest on overdraft	1,000	
Reserves/profit and loss balance		6,000
Issued share capital		150,000
Carriage outwards	10,000	
Stationery	21,000	
	950,000	950,000

You are given the following information as on 31/12/10.

(i) Closing stock €42,000
(ii) Advertising due €1,200
(iii) Rent prepaid €1,000
(iv) Commission receivable due €2,100
(v) Dividends declared 5%
(vi) Depreciation:
Machinery 10%

(b) Explain the term **import duty**.

10. **(a)** Year ending 30/11/11
Authorised share capital:
500,000 €1 ordinary shares

TRIAL BALANCE AT 30/11/11		
	Dr €	Cr €
Issued share capital		400,000
Purchases returns		13,000
Opening stock 1/12/10	12,000	
Import duty	6,000	
Debtors and creditors	25,000	45,000
Purchases and sales	80,000	320,000
Commission receivable		5,000
Bank overdraft		30,000
Interest on overdraft	3,000	
Wages	25,000	
Buildings	500,000	
Motor vehicles	210,000	
Bad debts	5,000	
Machinery	80,000	
Printing	22,000	
Reserves/ profit and loss balance		65,000
10-year loan		90,000
	968,000	968,000

You are given the following information as on 30/11/11.

(i) Closing stock €10,000
(ii) Wages due €3,000
(iii) Interest on overdraft due €1,000
(iv) Commission receivable due €2,500
(v) Dividends declared 10%
(vi) Depreciation:
Machinery 10%
Motor vehicles 5%

(b) Distinguish between *authorised* and *issued* share capital.

11. (a) Year ending 31/12/12
Authorised share capital:
200,000 €1 ordinary shares

TRIAL BALANCE AT 31/12/12	Dr €	Cr €
Opening stock 1/1/12	30,000	
Purchase returns		18,000
Debtors and creditors	80,000	35,000
Purchases and sales	250,000	600,000
Import duty	13,000	
Land	350,000	
Rates	12,000	
Computer equipment	94,000	
Commission receivable		35,000
15-year loan		50,000
Cash	5,000	
Telephone	8,000	
Bank overdraft		17,000
Wages	45,000	
Reserves/profit and loss balance		25,000
Issued share capital		110,000
Interest on overdraft	3,000	
	890,000	890,000

You are given the following information as on 31/12/12.

(i)	Closing stock	€25,000
(ii)	Import duty due	€5,000
(iii)	Wages prepaid	€5,000
(iv)	Dividends declared	5%
(v)	Depreciation: Computer equipment	15%

(b) Identify three long-term sources of finance used by this company.

12. (a) Year ending 31/12/10
Authorised share capital:
400,000 €1 ordinary shares

TRIAL BALANCE AT 31/12/10	Dr €	Cr €
Purchases and sales	120,000	460,000
Sales returns	13,000	
Opening stock 1/1/10	15,000	
Carriage inwards	3,000	
Debtors and creditors	90,000	45,000
Carriage outwards	5,500	
Insurance	8,500	
Office expenses	11,000	
Machinery	90,000	
Buildings	300,000	
Interest receivable		10,000
Bank	180,000	
Reserves/profit and loss balance		25,000
Wages	54,000	
Issued share capital		
20-year loan		300,000
		50,000
	890,000	890,000

You are given the following information as on 31/12/10.

(i)	Closing stock	€21,000
(ii)	Carriage outwards due	€7,000
(iii)	Wages due	€8,000
(iv)	Dividends declared	5%
(v)	Interest receivable due	€1,500
(vi)	Depreciation: Machinery	15%

(b) Calculate the net profit percentage.

13. **(a)** Year ending 31/12/11
Authorised share capital:
450,000 €1 ordinary shares

TRIAL BALANCE AT 31/12/11		
	Dr €	Cr €
Purchases returns		7,000
Opening stock 1/1/11	14,000	
Purchases and sales	200,000	540,000
Import duty	2,000	
Advertising	9,000	
Debtors and creditors	45,000	60,000
Wages	18,000	
Bad debts	1,000	
Delivery vans	210,000	
Buildings	320,000	
Commission receivable		12,000
Bank overdraft		10,000
Reserves/profit and loss balance		15,000
Interest on overdraft	5,000	
Issued share capital		300,000
20-year loan		30,000
Land	150,000	
	974,000	974,000

You are given the following information as on 31/12/11.

(i) Closing stock €15,000
(ii) Advertising prepaid €2,000
(iii) Wages due €4,000
(iv) Dividends declared 10%
(v) Commission receivable prepaid €1,000
(vi) Depreciation:
Delivery vans 8%

(b) Calculate the gross profit margin.

14. **(a)** Year ending 31/12/12
Authorised share capital:
300,000 €1 ordinary shares

TRIAL BALANCE AT 31/12/12		
	Dr €	Cr €
Opening stock 1/1/12	7,000	
Sales returns and purchases returns	14,000	11,000
Advertising	5,000	
Purchases and sales	260,000	480,000
Rent receivable		10,000
Carriage inwards	4,000	
Fixtures and fittings	120,000	
Rent	6,000	
Machinery	140,000	
Debtors and creditors	56,000	43,000
Cash in hand	6,000	
Bank overdraft		10,000
Interest on overdraft	1,000	
Reserves/profit and loss balance		6,000
Issued share capital		100,000
Office equipment	23,000	
Stationery	18,000	
	660,000	660,000

You are given the following information as on 31/12/12.

(i) Closing stock €9,000
(ii) Stock of stationery on hand €3,000
(iii) Dividends declared 10%
(iv) Rent receivable prepaid €1,000
(v) Depreciation:
Fixtures and fittings 10%
Machinery 5%

(b) Calculate the average stock of this company.

15. (a) Year ending 31/12/12
Authorised share capital:
200,000 €1 ordinary shares

TRIAL BALANCE AT 31/12/12	Dr €	Cr €
Stationery	18,000	
Sales returns and purchases returns	12,000	19,000
Printing	6,000	
Purchases and sales	300,000	550,000
Rent receivable		10,000
Import duty	8,000	
Office furniture	100,000	
Office expenses	5,000	
Delivery vans	150,000	
Debtors and creditors	45,000	25,000
Cash in hand	10,000	
Bank	40,000	
Wages	27,000	
Reserves/profit and loss balance		10,000
Issued share capital		160,000
Opening stock 1/1/12	30,000	
Advertising	23,000	
	774,000	774,000

You are given the following information as on 31/12/12.

(i) Closing stock €20,000
(ii) Stock of stationery on hand €5,000
(iii) Wages prepaid €2,500
(iv) Dividends declared 10%
(v) Rent receivable due €2,000
(vi) Depreciation:
Delivery vans 10%
Office furniture 2%

(b) Why are retained earnings/reserves important to a company?

16. (a) Year ending 31/12/12
Authorised share capital:
200,000 €1 ordinary shares

TRIAL BALANCE AT 31/12/12	Dr €	Cr €
Purchases and sales	250,000	570,000
Sales returns and purchases returns	12,000	16,000
Opening stock 1/1/12	30,000	
Carriage inwards	2,000	
Debtors and creditors	40,000	25,000
Import duty	6,000	
Equipment	250,000	
Bad debts	1,500	
Commission receivable		10,000
Machinery	100,000	
Carriage outwards	3,000	
Cash in hand	19,000	
Bank overdraft		6,000
Wages	40,000	
Reserves/profit and loss balance		10,000
Issued share capital		110,000
Light and heat	12,000	
Long-term loan		20,000
Interest on overdraft	1,500	
	767,000	767,000

You are given the following information as on 31/12/12.

(i) Closing stock €40,000
(ii) Wages prepaid €4,000
(iii) Carriage outwards due €4,500
(iv) Dividends declared 10%
(v) Commission receivable due €5,000
(vi) Depreciation:
Equipment 5%

(b) Explain the difference between carriage inwards and carriage outwards.

17. Year ending 30/11/13
Authorised share capital:
200,000 €1 ordinary shares

TRIAL BALANCE AT 30/11/13		
	Dr €	Cr €
Issued share capital		150,000
Sales returns	15,000	
Opening stock 1/12/12	18,000	
Import duty	3,000	
Debtors and creditors	15,000	50,000
Purchases and sales	70,000	220,000
Commission receivable		20,000
Bank overdraft		30,000
Interest on overdraft	2,500	
Wages	22,000	
Buildings	250,000	
Motor vehicles	22,000	
Bad debts	2,500	
Machinery	150,000	
Advertising	10,000	
Reserves/profit and loss balance		60,000
10-year loan		50,000
	580,000	580,000

You are given the following information as on 30/11/13.

(i)	Closing stock	€25,000
(ii)	Wages due	€3,000
(iii)	Import duty due	€4,500
(iv)	Dividends declared	10%
(v)	Commission receivable due	€2,000
(vi)	Depreciation:	
	Motor vehicles	10%
	Machinery	5%

18. Year ending 31/12/12
Authorised share capital:
200,000 €1 ordinary shares

TRIAL BALANCE AT 31/12/12		
	Dr €	Cr €
Purchases and sales	250,000	550,000
Sales returns and purchases returns	12,000	15,000
Stock 1/1/12	16,000	
Carriage inwards	6,000	
Debtors and creditors	56,000	26,000
Insurance	5,500	
Rent receivable		15,000
Bank	25,500	
Issued share capital		105,000
Rates	12,000	
Wages and salaries	45,000	
Buildings	250,000	
Motor vehicles	60,000	
Advertising	11,000	
Machinery	100,000	
Advertising	22,000	
Reserves/profit and loss balance 1/1/12		60,000
20-year loan		100,000
	871,000	871,000

You are given the following information as on 31/12/12.

(i)	Closing stock	€20,000
(ii)	Wage and salaries due	€12,000
(iii)	Rates prepaid	€2,500
(iv)	Rent receivable prepaid	€5,000
(v)	Dividends declared	5%
(vi)	Advertising due	€3,500
(vii)	Depreciation:	
	Motor vehicles	10%
	Machinery	5%

See workbook for more questions.

Assessment and interpretation of accounts

WHO IS INTERESTED IN A COMPANY'S FINAL ACCOUNTS?

The final accounts of a company are of interest to many people and organisations other than just the company managers.

FINAL ACCOUNTS	
Shareholders (or potential shareholders) will want to know:	(a) How profitable is the business? (b) Are profits increasing or decreasing? (c) Is it making a good return on the amount of money already invested in it? (d) How much of the authorised share capital is already issued?
Banks and financial institutions (before giving a loan or overdraft to the company) will want to know:	(a) The company's credit rating (b) The company's existing level of debt (c) The company's liquidity (its ability to pay debts when due) (d) The true value of the company's fixed assets
The Revenue Commissioners (the taxman!) will want to know:	(a) Is the company paying the correct level of corporation tax? (b) Is the company paying the correct level of VAT? (c) Is the company liable to pay any capital gains taxes? (d) Is the company complying with all tax laws?
Creditors will want to know:	(a) The company's credit rating (b) How quickly does the company pay its creditors?
Employees and trade unions will want to know:	(a) The ability or otherwise of the company to continue to pay the existing wages of employees (b) The management of pension funds used by the company (c) The security of employment for the employees

However, the final accounts do not give all the information that these people and organisations need.

Limitations of final accounts

1. The trading and profit and loss accounts give financial information related to one trading period only, usually one year.
2. The balance sheet gives information related to only one moment in time.
3. The final accounts do not give any information about the changing nature of the market in which the company is operating. For example, are new firms entering the market? Is the firm's product going out of fashion?
4. The final accounts do not give any information about the state of industrial relations within the business.
5. The final accounts do not show how profitable the company is relative to similar companies in that market.

To gain a better insight into a company we need to analyse its accounts under a number of different headings:

- Liquidity and solvency
- Profitability
- Dividend policy
- Efficiency

LIQUIDITY AND SOLVENCY

Liquidity refers to the company's ability to pay its debts when they become due for payment. (The information for this is found in the balance sheet.)

To assess the liquidity and solvency of a company we look at:

1. **Current ratio** or **working capital ratio**
2. **Acid test ratio** or **quick ratio**
3. **Total value of the company's assets in relation to its external liabilities**

1. Current ratio or working capital ratio

Current ratio is the ratio of **current assets** to **current liabilities**.
Ideally this should be 2:1, but its minimum should be 1.5:1.

This is used to see whether or not the business can pay its day-to-day debts from its own current assets. A company is said to be **liquid** when the ratio of current assets to current liabilities is at least 1.5 to 1.

If this ratio reflects a negative working capital (e.g. 0.5:1) it shows that the company is **overtrading**. This means that the money available to the company on a daily basis is not sufficient to finance the quantity of goods the firm is buying and selling.

Current ratio example

A company has the following current assets and current liabilities:
- *Current assets:* Debtors €20,000; Bank €30,000; Closing stock €30,000
- *Current liabilities:* Creditors €40,000

This gives a ratio of **80,000** : **40,000** = **2:1**

Total current assets : Total current liabilities

2:1 is the ideal ratio.

2. Acid test ratio/quick ratio

The **acid test ratio** is the ratio of **total current assets, less closing stock,** to **current liabilities**. This should be a minimum of 1:1.

This ratio is particularly important for firms selling perishable goods or goods whose demand is subject to changes in fashion, e.g. designer clothes. It is unrealistic for these firms to rely on money from the sale of this stock to meet its debts.

Acid test ratio example

- *Current assets:* Debtors €20,000; Bank €40,000; Closing stock €40,000
- *Current liabilities:* Creditors €120,000

This gives a ratio of **60,000** : **120,000** = **1:2**

Total current assets *less* Closing stock : Total current liabilities

1:2 is below the minimum requirement.

3. Solvency

A company is said to be **solvent** when the value of its **total assets** is *greater* than the value of its **outside (external) liabilities**.

Outside or external liabilities are current liabilities plus long-term liabilities, excluding money owed to the shareholders. The money owed to the shareholders is the issued share capital and the closing profit and loss reserve / retained earnings.

A company is said to be **insolvent** when the value of its total assets is less than the value of its outside (external) liabilities. In such a situation the company is said to be **bankrupt** and would go out of business.

Insolvency example

INSOLVENCY		
Total assets		
Fixed assets	€100,000	
Current assets	€40,000	€140,000
Less Total liabilities		
Current liabilities	€80,000	
Long-term liabilities (e.g. 20-year loan)	€100,000	€180,000
= Insolvency		(€40,000)

PROFITABILITY

Profitability examines the **return** (percentage profit) to the business on the money available to it and the return on its sales. (The information for this is found in the balance sheet and in the trading and profit and loss account.)

To assess the profitability of a company we look at:

1. Gross profit percentage or gross profit margin
2. The net profit percentage or net profit margin
3. The return on capital employed
4. Return on shareholders' funds

1. Gross profit percentage or gross profit margin

This is the gross profit expressed as a percentage of the net sales.

Gross profit percentage/margin $= \dfrac{\text{Gross profit}}{\text{Net sales}} \times 100$

Example

Gross profit €135,000; Net sales €300,000

$$\frac{135{,}000}{300{,}000} \times 100 = 45\%$$

This figure should be compared with previous years' figures and the figures of similar firms in the same industry.

Fall in gross profit percentage

The gross profit percentage could decrease if:

1. the price received per unit of the good sold decreased
2. the cost of goods sold increased.

2. Net profit percentage or net profit margin

The net profit percentage is the net profit expressed as a percentage of the net sales.

Net profit percentage/margin $= \dfrac{\text{Net profit}}{\text{Net sales}} \times 100$

Example

Net profit €60,000; Net sales €300,000

$$\frac{60{,}000}{300{,}000} \times 100 = 20\%$$

This figure should also be compared with previous years' figures and the figures of similar firms in the same industry.

Fall in net profit percentage

The net profit percentage could decrease if:

1. the gross profit percentage decreased while there was no change in overhead costs
2. the gross profit percentage remained unchanged while the overhead costs increased and/or the gains decreased.

3. Return on capital employed

The return on capital employed is the net profit expressed as a percentage of the capital employed. Remember that the capital employed is the issued share capital + retained earnings (closing profit and loss reserve) + long-term loans.

$$\textbf{Return on capital employed} = \frac{\text{Net profit}}{\text{Capital employed}} \times 100$$

Example

Net profit €60,000; Capital employed €1,200,000

$$\frac{60,000}{1,200,000} \times 100 = 5\%$$

This figure should be compared with the rate of interest that could be received from a financial institution for a deposit of €1,200,000. It should also be compared to the return earned by other firms investing a similar amount of money.

4. Return on shareholders' funds

This is the net profit expressed as a percentage of the shareholders' funds.

Shareholders' fund = *issued share capital + closing profit and loss reserve (retained earnings).*

$$\textbf{Return on shareholders' funds} = \frac{\text{Net profit}}{\text{Shareholders' funds}} \times 100$$

Example

Net profit €100,000; Shareholders' funds €1,000,000

$$\frac{100,000}{1,000,000} \times 100 = 10\%$$

This is of interest to existing and potential shareholders. They should compare this with interest rates available to them from financial institutions and to returns earned by other similar businesses. All shareholders should be aware of the opportunity cost of their investment.

DIVIDEND POLICY

The dividend is the payment made by the company to the shareholders in a given year. It is normally expressed as a **percentage of the issued share capital**. We examined this in Chapter 41 when we looking at the appropriation account.

Investors buy shares for one or both of the following reasons:

- **To receive an annual income from the dividend**. People who buy shares for this purpose are interested in the **dividend percentage** (the dividend paid expressed as a percentage of the issued share capital).
- **To make a capital gain**, i.e. to make a profit on the sale of their shares.

$$\textbf{Dividend percentage} = \frac{\text{Dividend paid}}{\text{Issued share capital}} \times 100$$

Example

Dividend paid €20,000; Issued share capital €800,000

$$\frac{20{,}000}{800{,}000} \times 100 = 2.5\%$$

Again this is of interest to existing and potential shareholders. They should compare this with interest rates available to them from financial institutions and to returns earned by other similar businesses.

However, some investors may accept a very low, or even a zero dividend percentage if the company is earning a substantial net profit and reinvesting it in the business to make it more efficient and profitable in the future. This will drive up the value of the shares, which the investors can then sell at a profit.

EFFICIENCY

The efficiency of a business is assessed by using the following:

1. Rate of stock turnover
2. The gross profit mark-up or the mark-up on cost
3. The net profit percentage

1. The rate of stock turnover

The **rate of stock turnover** is the number of times in a year the firm sells its average stock.

- The **annual turnover** of a business is it annual sales.
- **Average stock** is opening stock *plus* closing stock *divided by* 2.

Rate of stock turnover $= \dfrac{\text{Cost of goods sold}}{\text{Average stock}} =$ times per year

Example

Opening stock €20,000; Closing stock €30,000; Cost of sales €250,000

(**a**) Average stock $= \dfrac{€20{,}000 + €30{,}000}{2} = \dfrac{€50{,}000}{2} = €25{,}000$

(**b**) Rate of stock turnover $= \dfrac{\text{Cost of goods sold}}{\text{Average stock}} = \dfrac{250{,}000}{25{,}000} = 10$ times per year

A business will improve the return on the money tied up in its average stock if it can increase the number of times it sells this average stock per year.

It is more important for firms that sell *perishable goods*, e.g. grocers, to have a **high rate of stock turnover** than for firms that sell non-perishable goods, e.g. furniture shops.

Likewise it is more important for firms that have *small gross profit mark-up*, e.g. supermarkets, than for firms that have a big gross profit mark-up, e.g. jewellers.

2. Gross profit mark-up

The gross profit mark-up is the gross profit expressed as a **percentage of the cost of goods sold**.

$$\textbf{Gross profit mark-up} = \frac{\text{Gross profit}}{\text{Cost of goods sold}} \times 100$$

Example

Gross profit €100,000; Cost of goods sold €500,000

$$\frac{100{,}000}{500{,}000} \times 100 = 20\%$$

This can be used to show the efficiency of the managers in controlling the cost of sales.

3. The net profit percentage

Net profit percentage was explained on page 410. In the context of efficiency it can be used to assess how efficiently the overhead costs of running the business are being controlled.

ASSESSING AND REPORTING ON A BUSINESS

Exam question

Sarah Hurley, a Business Consultant of 20 High Street, Newbridge, Co. Kildare, received the following figures from a client, Goode Ltd, Main Street, Naas, Co. Kildare.

GOODE LTD		
	2009 **€**	**2010** **€**
Sales	700,000	770,000
Net profit	175,000	231,000
Current assets	50,000	96,000
Current liabilities	25,000	80,000
Capital employed	437,500	924,000

The directors of Goode Ltd wish to receive a report from Sarah Hurley commenting on its performance, with particular attention being paid to its **net profit percentage**, **return on capital employed** and **current ratio**.

Write the report Liam Hurley sends the directors on 1/1/11.

Note: It may be advisable, at this point, to revise *Report writing* on page 242.

Solution

Guidelines

1. Calculate the required information.
2. Refer to these calculations as an attachment to the report.
3. Draw up the report.

Net profit percentage	Formula	Calculations	Answer	Change
2009	$\frac{\text{Net profit} \times 100}{\text{Sales}}$	$\frac{175{,}000 \times 100}{700{,}000}$	25%	
2010	$\frac{\text{Net profit} \times 100}{\text{Sales}}$	$\frac{231{,}000 \times 100}{770{,}000}$	30%	+5%

Return on capital employed	Formula	Calculations	Answer	Change
2009	$\frac{\text{Net profit} \times 100}{\text{Capital employed}}$	$\frac{175{,}000 \times 100}{437{,}500}$	40%	
2010	$\frac{\text{Net profit} \times 100}{\text{Capital employed}}$	$\frac{231{,}000 \times 100}{924{,}000}$	25%	–15%

Current ratio	Formula	Calculations	Answer	Change
2009	Current assets : Current liabilities	50,000 : 25,000	2:1	
2010	Current assets : Current liabilities	96,000 : 80,000	1.2 :1	–40%

SARAH HURLEY
Business Consultant
20 High Street, Newbridge, Co. Kildare

Report re: Goode Ltd for the Years 2009 and 2010

1/1/11

To: The Directors
Goode Ltd
Main Street, Naas, Co. Kildare

Based on your instructions and the figures supplied by you I have examined the performance of your company for the years ending 2009 and 2010. I have enclosed a detailed copy of my calculations for your attention.

My findings are:

Net profit percentages
Year 2009 25% Year 2010 30%

This is an increase of 5%, which is a good improvement.

Return on capital employed
Year 2009 40% Year 2010 25%

Although the 25% return in 2010 is a good return, it is 15% lower than the return in 2009.

Current ratio
This fell from the ideal ratio of 2:1 in 2009 to an unsatisfactory ratio of 1.2:1 in 2010.

Overall comment
Your business is making good progress. However, there are now signs that you may be overtrading. This indicated by the poor current ratio in 2010. This should be rectified as soon as possible.

I can be contacted at the above address if you have any queries on this report.

Yours faithfully,

Sarah Hurley

Business Consultant

LEARN THE KEY TERMS

- **Current ratio** or **working capital ratio** is the ratio of current assets to current liabilities.
- **Acid test ratio** or **quick ratio** is the ratio of total current assets, less closing stock, to current liabilities.
- **Solvency** means that the value of total assets is greater than the value of outside (external) liabilities.
- **Number of days credit given to debtors** $= \frac{\text{Debtors}}{\text{Credit sales}} \times 365$ (days)
- **Number of days credit received from creditors** $= \frac{\text{Creditors}}{\text{Credit purchases}} \times 365$ (days)
- The **gross profit percentage** or **gross profit margin** is the gross profit expressed as a percentage of the net sales.
- The **net profit percentage** or **net profit margin** is the net profit expressed as a percentage of the net sales.
- The **return on capital employed** is the net profit expressed as a percentage of the capital employed.
- **Shareholders funds'** = issued share capital + closing profit and loss reserve (retained earnings).
- **Return on shareholders funds'** is the net profit expressed as a percentage of the shareholders' funds.
- **Dividend percentage** $= \frac{\text{Dividend paid}}{\text{Issued share capital}} \times 100$
- **Average stock** is opening stock plus closing stock divided by 2.
- The **rate of stock turnover** is the number of times the firm sells its average stock in a year.
- The **gross profit mark-up** is the gross profit expressed as a percentage of the cost of goods sold.

QUESTIONS

1. Other than the managers of a business, name five other groups of people or organisations that may take an interest in the final accounts of a business and state why they would take this interest in the accounts.
2. Explain five limitations on the use of final accounts as a means of assessing a business.

Calculations in all of the following questions should, where necessary, be to two decimal places.

3. In each of the following cases calculate the rate of stock turnover.

Business A		Business B		Business C	
Cost of goods sold	€240,000	Opening stock	€50,000	Closing stock	€15,000
Average stock	€80,000	Cost of goods sold	€160,000	Opening stock	€30,000
		Closing stock	€30,000	Cost of goods sold	€78,750

4. In each of the following cases calculate the current ratio (working capital ratio). Make an appropriate comment on each case.

Business A		Business B		Business C	
Current assets	€80,000	Current liabilities	€30,000	Current assets	€60,000
Current liabilities	€40,000	Current assets	€45,000	Current liabilities	€72,000

5. In each of the following cases calculate the acid test ratio/quick ratio. Make an appropriate comment on each case.

Business A		Business B		Business C	
Current assets	€40,000	Closing stock	€20,000	Current liabilities	€50,000
Closing stock	€10,000	Current liabilities	€60,000	Current assets	€70,000
Current liabilities	€20,000	Current assets	€80,000	Closing stock	€30,000

6. In each of the following cases calculate the gross profit percentage or gross profit margin.

Business A		Business B		Business C	
Sales	€500,000	Gross profit	€75,000	Sales	€240,000
Gross profit	€50,000	Sales	€1,500,000	Gross profit	€60,000

7. In each of the following cases calculate the net profit percentage or the net profit margin.

Business A		Business B		Business C	
Sales	€500,000	Net profit	€50,000	Sales	€240,000
Net profit	€25,000	Sales	€1,500,000	Net profit	€30,000

8. In each of the following cases calculate the return on capital employed.

Business A		Business B		Business C	
Capital employed	€100,000	Net profit	€25,000	Capital employed	€330,000
Net profit	€25,000	Capital employed	€1,500,000	Net profit	€30,000

9. In each of the following calculate the gross profit mark-up.

Business A		Business B		Business C	
Cost of goods sold	€95,000	Gross profit	€22,000	Cost of goods sold	€110,000
Gross profit	€32,000	Cost of goods sold	€110,000	Gross profit	€60,000

10. In the two cases below fill in the missing figures and state, giving a reason in each case, whether the business is solvent or insolvent.

(a)

Assets		Totals
Fixed assets	€180,000	
Current assets	€60,000	?
Total liabilities		
Current liabilities	40,000	
Long-term liabilities (20-year loan)	?	210,000
= **Solvent or insolvent?**		?

(b)

Assets		Totals
Fixed assets	€310,000	
Current assets	?	420,000
Total liabilities		
Current liabilities	40,000	
Long-term liabilities (e.g. 20-year loan)	350,000	?
= Solvent or insolvent?		?

11. Fill in the missing figures in each of the following:

Business A		Business B		Business C	
Issued share capital	€100,000	Dividend paid	€80,000	Dividend percentage	15%
Dividend paid	€25,000	Dividend percentage	12.5%	Issued share capital	€90,000
Dividend percentage?		Issued share capital?		Dividend paid?	

12. Joseph O'Bloggs, of 284 Navan Rd, Dublin 7, an investor, wishes to invest in one of three companies. He supplies you, Michelle Hobbs, a business consultant of 34 Nephin Rd, Dublin 7, with the data below concerning the three companies. He is particularly concerned about the liquidity of each of the companies as well as the return on issued share capital of each.

Business A		Business B		Business C	
Issued share capital	€100,000	Issued share capital	€100,000	Issued share capital	€100,000
Dividend paid	€25,000	Dividend paid	€5,000	Dividend paid	€10,000
Net profit	€75,000	Net profit	€75,000	Net profit	€10,000
Current assets	€30,000	Current assets	€30,000	Current assets	€20,000
Current liabilities	€20,000	Current liabilities	€25,000	Current liabilities	€30,000

Using today's date, write up the report you would send to Joseph O'Bloggs, commenting on **(i)** the working capital ratio, **(ii)** the net return on capital employed, and **(iii)** the dividend percentage of each firm. Conclude your report by recommending him to invest in the company you think is the best of the three.

13. Imelda Sharp, a business consultant of 20 Low Street, Newtown, Co. Donegal, received the following figures from a client, Blunt Ltd, High Street, Lifford, Co. Donegal.

	2010 €	2011 €
Sales	140,000	213,000
Net profit	35,000	71,000
Current assets	100,000	70,000
Current liabilities	50,000	80,000
Capital employed	500,000	900,000

The directors of Blunt Ltd wish to receive a report from Imelda Sharp commenting on its performance, with particular attention being paid to its net profit percentage, its return on capital employed and its current ratio.

Write the report Imelda Sharp sends the directors on 1/1/12.

See workbook for more questions.

45 Club accounts

Club accounts are used by **not-for-profit** organisations, i.e. voluntary organisations whose primary purpose is not profit making, but providing a service to groups or individuals.

Typical examples are:

1. Sporting organisations (non-professional)
2. Social organisations
3. Charitable organisations
4. Representative organisations (e.g. residents associations)

These clubs are usually run by voluntary committees who hold regular ordinary meetings as well as annual general meetings.

An **annual general meeting (AGM)** is a meeting of **all** members of the organisation that must be held once a year. Notice of the time and date of an AGM must be sent to all members in advance. The officers (see below) of the organisation are elected at this meeting.

An **extraordinary general meeting (EGM)** is a meeting of all members, in addition to the AGM, that is held to allow members to vote on an important issue. For example, the club may wish to amalgamate with another one during the year, or it may want to change the rules on who may become a member of the club.

Agendas

An agenda is drawn up for every meeting to allow it to function efficiently.

An **agenda** is a list of the topics to be discussed at a meeting, in the order in which they will be discussed.

Example agenda for an AGM

Agenda for AGM 31/12/2010

1. Minutes of the last AGM
2. Matters arising from the minutes
3. Secretary's report
4. Treasurer's report
5. Chairperson's address
6. Election of officers
7. AOB

OFFICERS OF THE CLUB

The three main officers of a club are the chairperson, secretary and treasurer.

Role of the chairperson

- Responsible for leading the club
- Ensures that club policy is carried out
- Draws up the agenda for meetings in conjunction with the secretary
- He/she keeps order at meetings
- He/she ensures that the agenda for a meeting is followed

Role of the secretary

- Is in charge of all correspondence
- Is in charge of making and filing all club records
- Draws up, in conjunction with the chairperson, the agenda for meetings
- Notifies relevant people of meetings
- Keeps the minutes of meetings, i.e. records the topics discussed and decisions taken

Role of the treasurer

- Operates a deposit and a current account for the club
- Ensures all members pay their subscriptions
- Lodges all receipts in the bank
- Pays all expenses for the club
- Records all financial transactions
- Draws up the final accounts for the club
- Prepares an end-of-year financial report for the annual general meeting

FINANCIAL RECORDS

These are very similar to company accounts but the language used is slightly different because the clubs are not commercial concerns.

The following are the main records kept by most small- to medium-sized clubs:

1. Statement of accumulated fund
2. Analysed cash book
3. Receipts and payments account
4. Shop/bar/restaurant trading account (if the club operates any of these)
5. Income and expenditure account
6. Balance sheet

Firstly we will incorporate all of these into one full set of club accounts.

1. Statement of accumulated fund

You will recall that we calculated a company's capital in the general journal at the start of a trading period by subtracting the firm's *opening liabilities* from its *opening assets*. We do the same thing in club accounts but use the term **accumulated fund** rather than *capital* to describe the difference in value of the opening assets and opening liabilities.

Example

STATEMENT OF ACCUMULATED FUND AT 1/12/2010		
	Dr €	Cr €
Clubhouse (1)	180,000	
Bar opening stock (2)	5,600	
Cash (3)	1,700	
5-year loan (1)		14,000
Accumulated fund (1)		173,300

Notes

1. All of these figures will appear in the club's balance sheet at the end of the month because there is no change in their values during the month.
2. This figure will be used later on as the *Opening stock* in the bar trading A/C.
3. This figure will be used as the *Opening cash* in the analysed cash book.

2. Analysed cash book

The analysed cash book shows:

(a) **Opening cash**
(b) **All money received** and **all money paid out** (recorded under analysed headings), regardless of whether it is current or capital in nature
(c) **Closing cash**

Example

The club had the following incomes and payments for December 2010. These are to be recorded in the club's analysed cash book.

- 1/12/10 Opening balance, €1,700
- 1/12/10 Paid telephone bill, €300, Cheque no. 1
- 3/12/10 Paid rent, €500, Cheque no. 2
- 8/12/10 Received membership fees, €800
- 8/12/10 Purchased equipment, €1,000, Cheque no. 3
- 11/12/10 Purchased raffle prizes, €200, Cheque no. 4
- 12/12/10 Match receipts, €400
- 13/12/10 Paid rent, €500, Cheque no. 5
- 18/12/10 Purchased raffle prizes, €200, Cheque no. 6
- 21/12/10 Received membership fees, €600
- 21/12/10 Paid insurance premium, €800, Cheque no. 7
- 24/12/10 Paid telephone bill, €300, Cheque no. 8
- 25/12/10 Match receipts, €300
- 28/12/10 Receipts from sale of raffle tickets, €700
- 31/12/10 Bar purchases, €28,000, Cheque no. 9
- 31/12/10 Bar receipts for the month of December, €45,000

The following analysed columns are to be used:

- **Dr side:** *Total Membership fees Raffle receipts Match receipts Bar receipts*
- **Cr side:** *Total Telephone Rent Equipment Raffle prizes Insurance Bar purchases*

Dr side (money received)							ANALYSED CASH BOOK AT 31/12/2010							Cr side (money paid out)		
Date	Details	Total	Membership fees	Raffle receipts	Match receipts	Bar receipts	Date	Details	Chq	Total	Telephone	Rent	Equipment	Raffle prizes	Insurance	Bar purchases
2010		€	€	€	€	€	2010			€	€	€	€	€	€	€
1/12	Balance	1,700					1/12	Telephone	1	300	300					
8/12	Membership fees	800	800				3/12	Rent	2	500		500				
12/12	Match receipts	400			400		8/12	Purchase of equipment	3	1,000			1,000			
21/12	Membership fees	600	600				11/12	Purchase of raffle prizes	4	200				200		
24/12	Raffle receipts	900		900			13/12	Rent	5	500		500				
25/12	Match receipts	300			300		18/12	Purchase of raffle prizes	6	300				300		
28/12	Raffle receipts	700		700			21/12	Insurance	7	800					800	
31/12	Bar receipts	45,000				45,000	24/12	Telephone	8	300	300					
							31/12	Bar purchases	9	28,000						28,000
							31/12	Balance c/d		18,500						
		50,400	1,400	1,600	700	45,000				50,400	600	1,000	1,000	500	800	28,000
1/1/11	Balance b/d	18,500														

The totals of the individual analysed columns are now used to draw up the receipts and payments account.

3. Receipts and payments account

The *Receipts and payments* account is a summary of the analysed cash book. It shows:

(a) **Opening cash**
(b) A summary of the **total of money received** under various headings
(c) A summary of the **total of money paid out** under various headings
(d) **Closing cash**

Example

The *Receipts and payments* account associated with the above analysed cash book is shown below.

RECEIPTS AND PAYMENTS A/C AT 31/12/10							
Date	Details	F	€	Date	Details	F	€
1/12/10	Balance		1,700	31/12/10	Telephone		600
31/12/10	Membership fees		1,400	31/12/10	Rent		1,000
31/12/10	Raffle receipts		1,600	31/12/10	Equipment		1,000
31/12/10	Match receipts		700	31/12/10	Raffle prizes		500
31/12/10	Bar receipts		45,000	31/12/10	Insurance		800
				31/12/10	Bar purchases		28,000
				31/12/10	Balance c/d		18,500
			50,400				50,400
31/12/10	Balance b/d*		18,500				

Note: *The *Closing cash* will appear as a *Current asset* in the balance sheet.

4. Shop/bar/restaurant trading account

Many clubs run a shop, bar, canteen or restaurant and use the profit earned as income for the club.

The club (shop/bar/canteen/restaurant) trading account is used to calculate the gross profit (surplus) earned from the club's trading activity.

In this example the *Closing bar stock* was €13,000.

Example club trading account

BAR TRADING ACCOUNT AT 31/12/10		
Details	€	€
Bar receipts		45,000
Less Cost of sales		
Opening stock	5,600	
Bar purchases	28,000	
	33,600	
Less Closing stock*	13,000	
Cost of goods sold		20,600
Bar surplus**		24,400

Note: * The *Closing stock* will appear as a current asset in the balance sheet.
**The *Bar surplus* will appear as an *Income* in the *Income and expenditure* account.

5. Income and expenditure account

Instead of preparing a *Profit and loss* account (remember that these are 'not-for-profit' organisations), clubs prepare an *Income and expenditure* account.

An **income and expenditure account** is used to show all **current income** and **current expenditure,** allowing for depreciation, items of income and expenditure due, and items of income and expenditure prepaid. It calculates the club's surplus or deficit for the year/month.

The terms *net profit* and *net loss*, as used in the profit and loss account, are replaced with **surplus of income over expenditure** and **surplus of expenditure over income** in the *Income and expenditure* account.

Example

The following example takes into account:

- Membership fees due €800
- Rent due €200
- Insurance prepaid €100
- Depreciation: 20% of the equipment purchased

INCOME AND EXPENDITURE ACCOUNT AT 31/12/2010

Details	€	€	€
Income			
Bar surplus		24,400	
Membership fees	1,400		
Plus membership fees due	800	2,200	
Raffle receipts*	1,600		
Less Raffle prizes*	500	1,100	
Match receipts		700	**28,400**
Less Expenses			
Telephone		600	
Rent	1,000		
Plus rent due	200	1,200	
Insurance	800		
Less Insurance prepaid	100	700	
Depreciation			
Equipment 20%		200	**2,700**
Surplus income over expenditure			25,700

Notes

1. The purchase of equipment does not go in the income and expenditure account. This account is only for current income and current expenditure. Therefore transactions for the purchase or sale of assets are not entered here. They feature in the balance sheet.
2. The *Bar sales* and the *Bar purchases* are not entered as they have already been used to calculate the *Bar surplus.*
3. The *Surplus of income over expenditure* is carried forward to the financing section of the balance sheet.

*When there is income from and expenditure on a given activity the difference between them should be shown as either a net income or a net expenditure. See the case of the raffle in the income and expenditure account.

6. Balance sheet

Many clubs do not have enough assets and liabilities to justify preparing a balance sheet.

Example

The local bridge club may rent a room each week. It may take in membership fees and charge for entry to competitions. Finally it may pay for prizes for each competition. There is no need for this club to prepare a balance sheet because its only asset is its cash balance.

When a club balance sheet is required, it is almost identical to a balance sheet for a limited company, i.e.

- **Part 1:** Fixed assets + Working capital = Net assets
- **Part 2:** *Financed by* section:
  Instead of *Issued share capital* we use *Accumulated fund.*
  Instead of adding the *Closing profit and loss reserve* we add the *Surplus of income over expenditure* to the *Accumulated fund.*

Example club balance sheet

BALANCE SHEET AS AT 31/12/10			
	€	€	€
Fixed assets	Cost	Depreciation	Net value
Clubhouse	180,000		180,000
Equipment	1,000	200	800
	181,000	200	180,800
Current assets			
Cash at bank	18,500		
Membership fees due	800		
Insurance prepaid	100		
Bar closing stock	13,000	32,400	
Less Current liabilities			
Rent due	200	200	
Working capital			32,200
Net assets			213,000
Financed by:			
Accumulated fund			173,300
Surplus of income over expenditure			25,700
5-year loan			14,000
Capital employed			213,800

TREASURER'S REPORT

One of the responsibilities or functions of the treasurer is to present a financial report to the AGM. This report should contain:

- a brief summary of the club's financial performance for the past year
- future financial requirements, if any, of the club
- recommendations to the members concerning these requirements.

This report should be laid out like any other official report as shown on page 242.

Example treasurer's report

THE COMMUNITY SPORTS CLUB

Treasurer's Report for Year Ending 31/1/2010

31/12/2010

To all members:

It is my pleasure to present the treasurer's report for the year ending 31/12/2010. Enclosed are copies of the Receipts and Payments Account, the Income and Expenditure Account and the Balance Sheet.

The accounts show that the club had an operating surplus of €25,700 for the year and the bank balance increased to €18,500. The club also purchased new equipment.

I would like to draw your attention to a number of important points:

1. The bulk of the year's surplus was generated from the bar surplus, i.e. €24,400. Due to the opening of the new local hotel we can no longer rely on this income as many local organisations are likely to use this hotel for their annual functions.
2. The club intends to purchase an adjoining field at a cost of €25,000. This is to be used to provide more playing pitches. The development work on this project is estimated to be a further €35,000.
3. There is therefore an obvious need for the club to undertake a new fund-raising project. I recommend that a sub-committee be set up as soon as possible to organise this.

I will be available at the AGM to answer any questions concerning the details of the accounts.

Joseph Murray

Treasurer

ABBREVIATED ACCOUNTS

Many examination questions skip much of the process of drawing up all of the club's accounts and present you with summarised figures showing the **payments made** and the **income received** by the club. Additional adjustment figures are also supplied.

From these figures you are required to do the **trading account** and the **income and expenditure account** of the club at a given date (Type 1), ***or*** an **income and expenditure account** and a **balance sheet** (Type 2).

Examination question type 1

From Junior Certificate Higher Paper 2, Question 5, 2001

The Knockbrack Mountaineering Club was formed on 1 May 2000. Officers were elected at its first meeting. The club had the following financial transactions for its first year to 30 April 2001:

Payments	€
Insurance	2,714
Rent	1,275
Purchase of equipment	3,400
Canteen purchases	2,647
Travel expenses	1,688
Telephone	493
Receipts	
Subscriptions	2,418
Raffle income	3,786
Canteen sales	8,193
Flag day collection	1,959

The following additional information is also available at the end of the year:

- Telephone bill due, €84
- Rent prepaid, €350
- Subscriptions prepaid, €180
- Equipment to be depreciated by 15%
- Canteen stock, €575

From this information prepare:

(a) a **canteen trading account** and

(b) an **income and expenditure account** for the year ending 30/4/2001.

Solution

(a)

CANTEEN TRADING ACCOUNT AT 30/04/2001		
Details	€	€
Canteen sales		8,193
Cost of sales		
Canteen purchases	1,688	
Less Canteen closing stock	575	
Cost of goods sold		1,113
Canteen surplus		7,080

Note: There is no *Opening canteen stock* in this question because it is the first year of the club's existence.

(b)

INCOME AND EXPENDITURE ACCOUNT AT 30/04/2001			
Details	**€**	**€**	**€**
Income			
Canteen surplus		7,080	
Subscriptions	2,418		
Less Subscriptions prepaid	180	2,238	
Raffle income		3,786	
Flag day collection		1,958	15,062
Less Expenditure			
Insurance		2,714	
Rent	1,275		
Less rent prepaid	350	925	
Travel expenses		1,688	
Telephone	493		
Plus telephone bill due	84	587	
Depreciation of equipment 15%		510	6,424
Surplus income over expenditure			8,638

Examination question type 2

From Junior Certificate Higher Level Paper 1, Question 2, 2007

On 1 June 2006, Greenfield Golf Club had an accumulated fund of €305,770. The following is a summary of the club's financial transactions for the year ended 31 May 2007:

Receipts	**€**
Competition fees	34,400
Subscriptions	89,550
Annual sponsorship	17,650
Payments	
Repairs	1,850
Stationery	2,460
Wages	27,800
Competition expenses	6,200
Insurance	1,440
General expenses	25,000

Additional information at 31 May 2007:

- Subscriptions prepaid, €1,450
- Stationery on hand, €240
- Wages due, €2,400
- Cash at bank, €15,620
- Depreciation: Clubhouse, 2% of €252,000; Equipment, 15% of €115,000

Prepare:
(a) an **income and expenditure account** for the year ended 31 May 2007
(b) a **balance sheet** as at 31 May 2007.

Note: Some very big clubs may post the analysed cash book to ledger accounts (see Chapter 34, *The analysed cash book*). In particular this will happen where the club is using a computerised accounting package. In these situations you will be presented with a trial balance and from that you extract the information required to do the bar account, the income and expenditure account and the balance sheet.

Solution

(a)

INCOME AND EXPENDITURE ACCOUNT AT 31/05/2007			
Details	€	€	€
Income			
Competition fees	34,400		
Less Competition expenses	6,200	28,200	
Subscriptions	89,550		
Less Subscriptions prepaid	1,450	88,100	
Annual sponsorship		17,650	133,950
Less Expenditure			
Repairs		1,850	
Stationery	2,460		
Less Stationery on hand	240	2,220	
Wages	27,800		
Plus Wages due	2,400	30,200	
Insurance		1,440	
General expenses		25,000	
Depreciation			
Clubhouse 2%	5,040		
Equipment 15%	17,250	22,290	83,000
Surplus income over expenditure			50,950

(b)

Preparatory work

Identify each of the adjustments as an element of the balance sheet.

1. *Clubhouse* and *Equipment* are **fixed assets** and they have also been depreciated.
2. *Stationery on hand* and *Cash at bank* are **current assets**.
3. *Subscriptions prepaid* and *Wages due* are **current liabilities**.
4. Remember, the accumulated fund was given in the introduction to the question.

BALANCE SHEET AS AT 31/05/2007			
	€	€	€
Fixed assets	Cost	Depreciation	Net value
Clubhouse	252,000	5,040	246,960
Equipment	115,000	17,250	97,750
	367,000	22,290	344,710
Current assets			
Stationery on hand	240		
Cash at bank	15,620	15,860	
Less Current liabilities			
Subscriptions prepaid	1,450		
Wages due	2,400	3,850	
Working capital			12,010
Net assets			356,720
Financed by:			
Accumulated fund			305,770
Surplus of income over expenditure			50,950
Funds/capital employed			356,720

LEARN THE KEY TERMS

- An **annual general meeting (AGM)** is a meeting of all members of the organisation that must be held once a year.
- An **extraordinary general meeting (EGM)** is a meeting of all members, in addition to the AGM, that is held to allow members to vote on an important issue.
- An **agenda** is a list of the topics that are to be discussed at a meeting, in the order in which they will be discussed.
- The **minutes** of a meeting is a record of the topics discussed and decisions taken.
- The **officers** of a club are the chairperson, secretary and treasurer.
- The **accumulated fund** of a club is its opening assets *less* its opening liabilities.
- The **analysed cash book** is used to record **all** money received and **all** money paid out under various headings.
- The **receipts and payments account** is a summary of the analysed cash book.
- The **club trading account** is used to calculate the gross profit (**surplus**) earned from the club's trading activity.
- The **income and expenditure account** is used to show all current income and expenditure and to calculate the club's surplus or deficit for the period.

QUESTIONS

1. Distinguish between an AGM and an EGM.
2. Name three functions of the chairperson of a club.
3. Name three functions of the secretary of a club.
4. What are the functions of the treasurer?
5. What is an agenda for a meeting?
6. What are the minutes of a meeting?
7. What is a receipts and payments account?
8. What is an income and expenditure account?
9. What is the accumulated fund of a club?

In Questions 10 and 11 you are required to write up the club's *analysed cash book* for the period shown.

10. All money received is lodged in a current account and all bills are paid by cheque. The annual membership fee is €80 per member.

    Use the following analysed columns:
    Debit (receipts) side: *Bank, Competitions, Lotto, Membership fees*
    Credit (payments) side: *Bank, Competitions, Lotto, Wages, Other*

    Total **each** analysis column and balance the *Bank* columns at the end of July.

    On 1 July 2010, the club had a balance of €500 in the bank. The club had the following transactions during July 2010:

    July 2010
    2 Paid for competition prizes, €120, Chq. no. 1
    3 Received annual membership fee from 40 members
    4 Received competition entry fees, €100
    6 Received annual membership fee from 10 members
    8 Paid lotto advertising costs, €190, Chq. no. 2
    10 Received money from sale of club lotto tickets, €1,200
    11 Paid ESB bill, €120, Chq. no. 3
    12 Paid cleaners' wages, €220, Chq. no. 4
    13 Received annual membership fee from 15 members
    14 Received competition entry fees, €200
    15 Received money from sale of club lotto tickets, €2,550
    16 Paid for competition prizes, €150, Chq. no. 5
    17 Received competition entry fees, €450
    22 Paid lotto winner, €2,000, Chq. no. 6
    26 Paid lotto advertising costs, €190, Chq. no. 7

11. All money received is lodged in a current account and all bills are paid by cheque.

    Use the following analysed columns:
    Debit (receipts) side: *Bank, Subscriptions, Competitions, Disco*
    Credit (payments) side: *Bank, Disco, Prizes, Rent, Others*

    Total **each** analysis column and balance the *Bank* columns at the end of November.

    The following transactions took place in the month of November 2010:

    November 2010
    1 Opening balance, €3,500
    3 Received annual subscriptions, €1,500
    4 Received competition entry fees, €240
    6 Income from disco, €560
    8 Paid for competition prizes, €120, Chq. no. 1
    9 Received annual subscriptions, €1,800
    10 Paid disco expenses €250, Chq. no. 2
    11 Paid rent of hall, €210, Chq. no. 3
    13 Paid ESB bill, €140, Chq. no. 4
    14 Received competition entry fees, €150
    15 Income from disco, €550
    16 Paid for competition prizes, €130, Chq. no. 5
    18 Paid rent of hall, €210, Chq. no. 5
    19 Received competition entry fees, €450
    22 Paid disco expenses, €250, Chq. no. 6
    26 Received annual subscriptions, €900

In Questions 12 and 13 you are required to prepare *Receipts and payments* account and an *Income and expenditure* account on the last day of the stated month for the local football club.

12.

May 2010		€
1/5	Opening cash balance	600
	Incomes	
31/5	Membership fees	1,500
	Dinner dance receipts	5,600
	Raffle income	8,700
	Match day receipts	2,500
	Sale of old club bus	3,100
	Payments	
	Caretaker's wages	2,300
	Light and heat	1,600
	Maintenance of pitches	1,000
	Stationery	500
	Dinner dance expenses	2,300

13.

July 2010		€
1/7	Opening bank balance (Cr)	4,500
	Incomes	
31/7	Subscriptions	3,200
	Annual fundraiser	8,950
	Income from disco	2,700
	Bar receipts	8,100
	Donations	670
	Payments	
	Yearly lease on premises	4,500
	Printing expenses	1,200
	Travelling expenses	830
	Referees' expenses	840
	Purchase of equipment	3,200

All the figures are bank transactions.

In Questions 14 and 15 you are required to calculate the *Accumulated fund* of the club on the first day of the month.

14. On 1/1/11, St Mary's Club had the following assets and liabilities:

Bank overdraft	€3,000
Clubhouse	€150,000
Bar stock on hand	€3,500
Furniture and equipment	€23,000

15. On 1/10/11, The Putters Golf Club had the following assets and liabilities:

Cash at bank	€15,000
Land	€450,000
15-year loan	€500,000
Machinery	€45,000
VAT due (to be paid by club)	€5,000

In Questions 16 and 17 you are require to prepare a *Trading account* and an *Income and expenditure account* for the club on the stated date.

16. The Hurlers Club, whose bar stock was valued at €600 on 1/1/09, had the following financial transactions for the year ending 31/12/09:

Payments	€
Light and heat	2,100
Administration expenses	4,200
Purchase of equipment	7,000
Bar purchases	8,500
Stationery	3,200
Telephone	500
Receipts	**€**
Membership fees	5,500
Club lotto income	8,300
Bar sales	13,500
Annual sponsorship	4,000

The following additional information is also available at the end of the year:

(i) Telephone bill due, €75
(ii) Stock of stationery on hand, €2000
(iii) Membership fees prepaid, €180
(iv) Equipment to be depreciated by, 15%
(v) Bar stock, €575

17. The Highlanders Club, whose shop stock was valued at €300 on 1/1/10, had the following financial transactions for the year ending 31/12/10:

Payments	€
Repairs	4,200
Printing	3,600
Purchase of equipment	10,000
Shop purchases	11,200
Light and heat	2,300
Annual website expenses	300
Receipts	**€**
Subscriptions	6,000
Profit from annual raffle	8,300
Shop sales	15,000
Annual sponsorship	7,000

The following additional information is also available at the end of the year:

(i) Printing due, €155
(ii) Light and heat due, €150
(iii) Subscriptions prepaid, €200
(iv) Equipment to be depreciated by, 10%
(v) Shop closing stock, €950

In Questions 18 and 19 you are required to prepare an *Income and expenditure account* and a *Balance sheet* for the club as at the date stated.

18. On 1/1/09 The Hockey Club had an accumulated fund of €216,260. The following is a summary of the club's financial transactions for the year ended 31/12/09:

Receipts	€
Annual fundraiser	94,400
Membership fees	12,500
Raffle income	7,700
Payments	**€**
Maintenance of grounds	4,500
Stationery	2,460
Light and heat	15,200
Travelling expenses	8,200
Insurance	2,500
General expenses	35,000

Additional information at 31/12/09:

(i) Membership fees prepaid, €1,500
(ii) Insurance prepaid, €500
(iii) Light and heat due, €4,500
(iv) Cash at bank, €18,000
(v) Depreciation:
Clubhouse 2% of €150,000
Equipment 15% of €95,000

19. On 1/1/10 The Golf Club had an accumulated fund of €104,100. The following is a summary of the club's financial transactions for the year ended 3112/10:

Receipts	€
Green fees	110,000
Annual subscriptions	95,000
Bar profit	105,000
Payments	**€**
Maintenance	7,500
Greenkeeper's wages	15,500
Telephone	6,500
Administration expenses	12,500
Insurance	4,500
Printing	5,600

Additional information at 31/12/10:

(i) Annual subscriptions prepaid, €1,500
(ii) Printing due, €400
(iii) Insurance prepaid, €1,500
(iv) Cash at bank, €12,000
(v) Depreciation:
Clubhouse 2% of €300,000
Motor mowers 12% of €50,000

See workbook for more questions.

Accounts for service firms

46

SERVICE FIRMS

Service firms don't buy goods for resale; instead they provide services for people: e.g. hairdressers, accountants, doctors, entertainers, solicitors, dentists, travel agents, insurance brokers, painters, etc.

Most service firms charge a fee for the services they provide. Many service firms operate on a cash basis, i.e. they do not provide services on credit.

RECORDS OF SERVICE FIRMS

1. Analysed cash book
2. Operating statement
3. Balance sheet

Service firms need to keep records to:

(a) keep track of all income and expenditure (**analysed cash book**)

(b) calculate profit or loss (**operating statement**)

(c) establish the value (i.e. net assets) of the business (**balance sheet**)

(d) use as support for loan applications

(e) provide the Revenue Commissioners with the information or data necessary to calculate the amount of tax due by the business

Analysed cash book

You should recall that the analysed cash book is used to record, under appropriate headings, all income received and all payments made by a business.

Service firms use the **debit side** analysed columns to distinguish between the various sources of their **incomes**, e.g. a doctor may receive income from private patients, public patients and insurance companies.

The **credit side** is used to record the normal overhead **expenses** of running the business.

Operating statement

The details from the analysed columns of the analysed cash book are used to draw up an operating statement.

An **operating statement** is part of the final accounts of a service firm that is used to calculate the firm's **operating profit** or **net profit**.

The operating statement of a service firm is the equivalent to a *profit and loss account* of a trading company. Service firms **do not** draw up a *trading account* for the obvious reason that they are not traders, i.e. they do not buy goods for resale.

Note: Many large service firms post the analysed cash book to the ledgers to complete the double-entry system. These firms then extract a trial balance and use this to draw up the operating statement and balance sheet.

Balance sheet

The balance sheet drawn up by a service company is the same as the balance sheet drawn up by a trading company.

SAMPLE QUESTION TYPE 1

Analysed cash book and income and expenditure account

The Regional Healthcare Clinic, a medical practice, cares for private patients and public patients, and undertakes work for insurance/assurance companies. It had the following transactions during the month of April 2010.

You are required to record these in its **analysed cash book** and prepare an **operating statement** at the end of the month. Use the following analysed columns:

Dr side (receipts): *Bank Private Public Insurance*
Cr side (payments): *Bank Wages Electricity Travel Telephone*

- 1/4/10 Opening balance €1,500
- 2/4/10 Income from private patients €1,200
- 4/4/10 Travelling expenses, Cheque no. 1 €120
- 8/4/10 Secretary's wages, Cheque no. 2 €340
- 12/4/10 Income from public patients €900
- 15/4/10 Secretary's wages, Cheque no. 3 €340
- 16/4/10 Paid telephone bill, Cheque no. 4 €220
- 19/4/10 Income from private patients €1,400
- 21/4/10 Paid electricity bill, Cheque no. 5 €250
- 22/4/10 Secretary's wages, Cheque no. 6 €340
- 23/4/10 Travelling expenses, Cheque no. 7 €180
- 25/4/10 Income from insurance company €750
- 27/4/10 Income from public patients €660
- 28/4/10 Travelling expenses, Cheque no. 8 €250
- 29/4/10 Secretary's wages, Cheque no. 9 €340
- 30/4/10 Income from private patients €900

Solution

Dr side (money received)							ANALYSED CASH BOOK AT 30/04/10							Cr side (money paid out)
Date	Details	F	Bank	Private	Public	Insurance	Date	Details	Chq	Bank	Wages	Electricity	Travel	Telephone
2010		€	€	€	€	€	2010		€	€	€	€	€	€
1/4	Balance		1,500				4/4	Travel expenses	1	120			120	
2/4	Private patients		1,200	1,200			8/4	Wages	2	340	340			
12/4	Public patients		900		900		15/4	Wages	3	340	340			
19/4	Private patients		1,400	1,400			16/4	Telephone	4	220				220
25/4	Insurance		750			750	21/4	Electricity	5	250		250		
27/4	Public patients		660		660		22/4	Wages	6	340	340			
30/4	Private patients		900	900			23/4	Travel expenses	7	180			180	
							28/4	Travel expenses	8	250			250	
							29/4	Wages	9	340	340			
							30/4	Balance c/d		4,930				
			7,310	3,500	1,560	750				7,310	1,360	250	550	220
1/5	Balance b/d		4,930											

Note: Remember that two separate books – an **analysed cash receipts and lodgement book** and an **analysed cheque payments book** – can also be used instead of this format. See Chapter 34.

OPERATING STATEMENT AT 30/4/10			
Details	€	€	€
Income			
Private patients		3,500	
Public patients		1,560	
Insurance		750	5,810
Expenditure			
Wages		1,360	
Electricity		250	
Travel		550	
Telephone		220	2,380
Operating profit* or Net profit			3,430

Notes

1. Neither the *opening cash* nor the *closing cash* is entered.
2. *Purchases* or *sale of fixed assets* are not entered.
3. If there are any adjustments (Higher Level only) remember '**Add** anything due; **Subtract** anything prepaid.'

***Operating profit** is often used to describe the difference between a service firm's *current income* and *current expenditure*. It is the equivalent to the **net profit** of a trading company.

SAMPLE QUESTION TYPE 2

Preparing an operating statement and balance sheet from a trial balance

From Junior Certificate Ordinary Level Paper, 2004, Question 2 (altered to include adjustments)

Blue Cabs Ltd is a firm that provides a taxi service in three different towns. The firm prepares an operating statement (profit and loss account) and a balance sheet at the end of each year. The following trial balance was taken from the books on 31 December 2010, the end of its financial year:

TRIAL BALANCE AT 31/12/10		
	Dr €	Cr €
Income from Naas		130,000
Income from Navan		125,700
Income from Mullingar		103,500
Insurance	35,920	
Light and heat	3,900	
Telephone	14,750	
Drivers' wages	47,300	
Petrol and car service	28,180	
Road tax	6,450	
Advertising	5,300	
Bank overdraft		4,950
Cash on hand	6,350	
Ordinary share capital (80,000 €1 shares)		80,000
Premises and equipment	70,000	
Motor vehicles	226,000	
	444,150	444,150

You are also provided with the following information on 31/12/10:

- Light and heat due, €1,100
- Insurance prepaid, €1,920
- Depreciation of motor vehicles 20%

(a) Prepare an **operating statement** for Blue Cabs Ltd for the year ended 31 December 2010 and a **balance sheet** as at that date.

(b) What percentage of the total income is insurance? Show your workings.

Solution

(a)

OPERATING STATEMENT AT 31/12/10			
Details	€	€	€
Income			
Income from Naas		130,000	
Income from Navan		125,700	
Income from Mullingar		103,500	359,200
Expenditure			
Insurance	35,920		
Less insurance prepaid	1,920	34,000	
Light and heat	3,900		
Plus Light and heat due	1,100	5,000	
Telephone		14,750	
Drivers' wages		47,300	
Petrol and car service		28,180	
Road tax		6,450	
Advertising		5,300	
Depreciation: motor vehicles 20%		45,200	186,180
Operating profit/Net profit			173,020

BALANCE SHEET AS AT 31/12/10			
	€	€	€
Fixed assets	Cost	Depreciation	Net value
Premises and equipment	70,000		70,000
Motor vehicles	226,000	45,200	180,800
	296,000	45,200	250,800
Current assets			
Cash on hand	6,350		
Insurance prepaid	1,920	8,270	
Less Current liabilities			
Bank overdraft	4,950		
Light and heat due	1,100	6,050	
Working capital			2,220
Net assets			253,020
Financed by:			
Issued share capital			80,000
Operating/Net profit			173,020
Capital employed			253,020

Note: As there is no appropriation account the entire **operating profit** (net profit) is added to the *Issued share capital* in the balance sheet.

(b)

Insurance for the year ending 31/12/10 was €34,000 (*Insurance* €35,920 less *Insurance prepaid* €1,920).

Total income for the year was €359,200.

Therefore, **insurance** as a **percentage of total income** equals:

$\frac{34{,}000}{359{,}200} \times 100 = 9.47\%$ (to 2 decimal places)

LEARN THE KEY TERMS

- An **operating statement** is part of the final accounts of a service firm that is used to calculate the firm's **operating profit** or **net profit**.
- **Operating profit** is the difference between a service firm's current income and its current expenditure.

QUESTIONS

1. Write up the **analysed cash book** (analysed receipts and payments book) of Smith, Will and Fight, solicitors, for the month of July from the information supplied. They receive fees for private conveyance work, commercial conveyance and insurance claims. All money received is lodged that day. Use the following analysed columns:

   Dr (receipts) side: *Bank, Private conveyance, Commercial conveyance, Insurance*
   Cr (payments) side: *Bank, Wages, Stationery, Light and heat, Travel expenses*

July 2010		€
1	Opening bank balance	€5,000
3	Fees for private conveyance work	€2,500
4	Paid wages, Chq. no. 1	€450
6	Purchased stationery, Chq. no. 2	€150
9	Fees for commercial conveyance work	€6,500
10	Paid for heating oil for office, Chq. no. 3	€580
11	Paid wages, Chq. no. 4	€450
12	Paid annual car road tax, Chq. no. 5	€330
13	Fees for insurance claims	€1,000
15	Fees for private conveyance work	€1,400
16	Purchased stationery, Chq. no. 6	€200
18	Paid wages, Chq. no. 7	€450
20	Paid ESB bill for light, Chq. no. 8	€280
22	Fees for insurance claims	€800
24	Fees for commercial conveyance work	€1,600
25	Paid wages, Chq. no. 9	€450

2. Write up the **analysed cash book** (analysed receipts and payments book) for the month of May of Joe White and Co., painters and decorators, who undertake work in Bandon, Kinsale and Youghal. All money received is lodged that day. Use the following analysed columns:

Dr (receipts) side: *Bank, Bandon, Kinsale, Youghal*
Cr (payments) side: *Bank, Wages, Office expenses, Paint, Travel expenses*

May 2011		€
1	Balance at bank	€1,300
2	Paid travelling expenses, Chq. no. 20	€100
4	Purchased paint, Chq. no. 21	€850
5	Paid wages, Chq. no. 22	€520
9	Income from Youghal	€1,600
10	Income from Bandon	€2,400
11	Paid office expenses, Chq. no. 23	€780
12	Paid wages, Chq. no. 24	€520
15	Income from Kinsale	€2,300
16	Purchased paint, Chq. no. 25	€850
17	Paid travelling expenses, Chq. no. 26	€120
19	Paid wages, Chq. no. 27	€520
20	Income from Kinsale	€1,300
21	Income from Bandon	€870
22	Income from Youghal	€1,700
25	Paid office expenses, Chq. no. 28	€450

3. Shift It Ltd, a common carrier, provides a waste disposal service in three towns, Tuam, Ballinasloe and Athenry. The firm prepares an operating statement (profit & loss account) and a balance sheet at the end of each year. The following trial balance was taken from the books on 31 December 2010, the end of its financial year.

TRIAL BALANCE AT 31/12/10

	Dr €	Cr €
Income from Tuam		160,000
Income from Ballinasloe		114,600
Income from Athenry		125,500
Annual vehicle insurance	40,000	
Office expenses	7,800	
Annual servicing of trucks	18,000	
Drivers' wages	56,000	
Diesel for trucks	45,000	
Annual road tax	6,450	
Advertising	7,500	
Bank overdraft		7,000
Cash on hand	6,350	
Ordinary share capital (300,000 €1 shares)		300,000
Premises	120,000	
Motor vehicles	400,000	
	707,100	707,100

Prepare the firm's **operating statement** and its **balance sheet** as at 31/12/10.

Higher Level students should also take the following factors into account:

At 31/12/10 wages due amounted to €4,000 and advertising prepaid totalled €1,500. Depreciation of 10% is to be written off the motor vehicles.

4. Comfort Holidays Ltd, a travel agent, sells holidays to three destinations, Monaco, Morocco and Miami. The firm prepares an operating statement (profit and loss account) and a balance sheet at the end of each year. The following trial balance was taken from the books on 31 December 2011, the end of its financial year.

TRIAL BALANCE AT 31/12/11		
	Dr €	Cr €
Income sale of holidays to Monaco		150,000
Income sale of holidays to Morocco		180,000
Income sale of holidays to Miami		109,000
Insurance	17,000	
Administration expenses	23,400	
Annual bonding fee	30,000	
Light and heat	20,000	
Printing	23,000	
Telephone	5,200	
Advertising	43,000	
Bank overdraft		14,700
Cash on hand	2,100	
Ordinary share capital (100,000 €1 shares)		100,000
Premises	300,000	
Office equipment	90,000	
	553,700	553,700

Prepare the firm's **operating statement** and its **balance sheet** as at 31/12/2011.

Higher Level students should also take the following factors into account:

At 31/12/11, *Insurance prepaid* amounted to €4,000 and there was an overpayment of €800 on the telephone account. Depreciation of 5% is to be written off the office equipment.

5. T. Fawcet Ltd operates a central heating systems maintenance service in Dublin, Meath and Kildare. The firm prepares an operating statement (profit & loss account) and a balance sheet at the end of each year. The following trial balance was taken from the books on 31 December 2012, the end of its financial year.

TRIAL BALANCE AT 31/12/12		
	Dr €	Cr €
Income from Dublin		80,000
Income from Meath		70,000
Income from Kildare		60,000
Advertising	5,600	
Travelling expenses	6,100	
Parts used in services	21,500	
Stationery	3,400	
Printing	5,100	
Administration costs	4,200	
Maintenance of vehicles	2,200	
Bank overdraft		10,600
Cash on hand	2,500	
Ordinary share capital (70,000 €1 shares)		70,000
Premises	150,000	
Motor vehicles	90,000	
	290,600	290,600

Prepare the firm's **operating statement** and its **balance sheet** as at 31/12/12.

Higher Level students should also take the following factors into account:

At 31/12/12, *Advertising prepaid* amounted to €1,600 and there was a stock of stationery on hand of €500. Depreciation of 15% is to be written off the motor vehicles.

6. Murphy, Kelly and Co. operates an accountancy practice. The firm prepares an operating statement (profit & loss account) and a balance sheet at the end of each year. The following trial balance was taken from the books on 31 December 2010, the end of its financial year.

TRIAL BALANCE AT 31/12/10		
	Dr €	Cr €
Income from auditing		100,000
Income from tax consultancy		70,000
Income from investment consultancy		90,000
Wages	54,000	
Travelling expenses	11,100	
Stationery	2,300	
Administration expenses	5,400	
Light and heat	7,900	
Insurance	5,200	
Software licence fees	1,100	
Bank overdraft		2,100
Cash on hand	5,100	
Ordinary share capital (70,000 €1 shares)		70,000
Premises	200,000	
Computers	40,000	
	332,100	332,100

Prepare the firm's **operating statement** and its **balance sheet** as at 31/12/10.

Higher Level students should also take the following factors into account:

At 31/12/12, *Wages prepaid* €4,000; Interest on overdraft due €100; Depreciation of 25% is to be written off the computers.

7. Callaghan, Cunningham and Co. operate a veterinary practice. The firm prepares an operating statement (profit & loss account) and a balance sheet at the end of each year. The following trial balance was taken from the books on 31 December 2010, the end of its financial year.

TRIAL BALANCE AT 31/12/10		
	Dr €	Cr €
Income from Bandon		100,000
Income from Cobh		90,000
Income from Cork city		150,000
Insurance	45,000	
Telephone	5,000	
Light and heat	35,000	
Travel expenses	12,000	
Medications	11,000	
Premises	220,000	
Equipment	95,000	
Motor vehicles	60,000	
Bank overdraft		15,000
Cash on hand	6,500	
Ordinary share capital		134,500
	489,500	489,500

Prepare the firm's Operating Statement and its Balance Sheet as at 31/12/10.

Higher Level students should also take the following factors into account:

At 31/12/10, Insurance prepaid €5,000; Light and heat due €600; Depreciation of 25% is to be written off motor vehicles.

See workbook for more questions.

47 Farm accounts

Agriculture is still a very important industry in Ireland. In 2009 it accounted for 8.4% of our GDP, 9.5% of total employment and 7.12% of total exports. Therefore it is very important to our economy to have financial information on industry.

Farmers need to keep accounts to:

1. keep a record of all money received and all money paid out by them
2. calculate their net profit or loss
3. calculate the net value of the farm / business
4. use as a basis for cash flow forecasts
5. act as evidence of ability to repay any loans they may seek
6. use as evidence of qualification for grants and subsidies.

ACCOUNTS KEPT BY FARMERS

Many large-scale farmers keep a full set of day books and ledgers just like the trading companies we dealt with in previous chapters. Most medium- and small-sized farms confine their record keeping to:

(a) an **analysed cash book** for day-to-day transactions
(b) an **income and expenditure account** to calculate their net profit
(c) a **balance sheet**

SAMPLE QUESTION

An analysed cash book and related income & expenditure account

Based on Junior Certificate Ordinary Level Paper, Question 6, 2004

Kate Sullivan is a farmer who keeps an **analysed receipts and payments book**. All money received is lodged in her bank current account on the same day and all payments are made by cheque. She had the following transactions during May 2010:

- 1/5/10 Balance in bank €3,500
- 4/5/10 Sold cattle at the mart for €8,500 (Receipt no. 401)
- 5/5/10 Purchased cattle feed for €925 (Cheque no. 811)
- 6/5/10 Received an EU grant of €1,750 (Receipt no. 402)
- 11/5/10 Purchased cattle (calves) for €3,000 (Cheque no. 812)
- 12/5/10 Paid for repairs to tractor €850 (Cheque no. 813)
- 14/5/10 Purchased diesel oil for machinery €550 (Cheque no. 814)
- 17/5/10 Paid fees to vet €475 (Cheque no. 815)
- 18/5/10 Sold cattle at the mart for €7,500 (Receipt no. 403)
- 19/5/10 Purchased cattle feed for €2,400 (Cheque no. 816)

- 20/5/10 Received a state grant of €1,000 (Receipt no. 404)
- 25/5/10 Purchased cattle (calves) for €4,800 (Cheque no. 817)
- 28/5/10 Purchased diesel oil for machinery €700 (Cheque no. 818)

(a) Write up the **analysed receipts and payments book** (analysed cash book) of Kate Sullivan for the month of May 2010, using the following money column headings:

Dr (receipts) side: *Total Cattle Grants*
Cr (payments) side: *Total Cattle Feed Diesel Other*

Total each analysis column and balance the total columns at the end of May.

(b) Write up the **income and expenditure account** for the month of May.

Solution

(a)

Dr side		ANALYSED RECEIPTS AND PAYMENTS BOOK (ANALYSED CASH BOOK)												Cr side
Date	Details	Rcpt	Total	Cattle	Grants	Date	Details	Chq	Total	Cattle	Feed	Diesel	Other
2010		€	€	€	€	2010		€	€	€	€	€	€
1/5	Balance		3,500			5/5	Cattle feed	811	925		925		
4/5	Sale of cattle	401	8,500	8,500		11/5	Purchase of calves	812	3,000	3,000			
6/5	EU grant	402	1,750		1,750	12/5	Repairs to tractor	813	850				850
18/5	Sale of cattle	403	7,500	7,500		14/5	Purchase of diesel oil	814	550			550	
20/5	State grant	404	1,000		1,000	17/5	Vet fees	815	475				475
						19/5	Cattle feed	816	2,400		2,400		
						25/5	Purchase of calves	817	4,800	4,800			
						28/5	Purchase of diesel oil	818	700			700	
						31/5	Balance c/d		8,550				
			22,250	16,000	2,750				22,250	7,800	3,325	1,250	1,325
1/6	Balance b/d		8,550										

(b)

INCOME AND EXPENDITURE ACCOUNT AT 31/5/10			
Details	**€**	**€**	**€**
Income			
Sale of cattle	16,000		
Less purchase of cattle (calves)	7,800	8,200	
Grants		2,750	10,950
Expenditure			
Feed		3,225	
Diesel		1,250	
Other		1,325	5,800
Surplus of income over expenditure (net profit)			5,150

GRANTS

Grants or payments received from the government or the EU can be classified as sources of **current finance** or as sources of **long-term finance** (see Chapter 18).

Annual payments received such as those from the REPS (Rural Environment Protection Scheme) are treated as **current income** and would be included in the *Income and expenditure* account.

Once-off payments received to aid on-farm investment such as the IAFWM (Investment Aid For Farm Waste Management) scheme are treated as **long-term sources of finance** and would not be included in the *Income and expenditure* account. These should be shown as sources of finance in the balance sheet.

Example of a balance sheet for a large-scale farm

BALANCE SHEET AS AT 31/12/11			
	€	€	€
Fixed assets	Cost	Depreciation	Net value
Land	500,000		500,000
Buildings	800,000		800,000
Machinery	100,000	40,000	60,000
Motor vehicles	50,000	35,000	15,000
	1,450,000	75,000	1,375,000
Current assets			
Livestock	150,000		
Stocks of materials	3,000		
Crops	15,000		
REPS income due	1,000		
Cash	1,500	170,500	
Less Current liabilities			
Bank overdraft	20,000		
Electricity due	450	20,450	
Working capital			150,050
Net assets			1,525,000
Financed by:			
Capital			1,300,000
Surplus of income over expenditure			75,000
10-year loan (e.g. mortgage)			100,000
Government and EU grants			50,000
Capital employed			1,525,000

QUESTIONS

1. State five reasons farmers should keep accounts.
2. List three types of accounts farmers might keep.

In Questions 3 and 4 prepare the *analysed cash book* for the month concerned. All income received is lodged that day.

3. Dr side: *Bank, Cattle, Milk, Grants*
   Cr side: *Bank, Feed, Tractor, Electricity*

May 2010		€
1	Bank balance (Dr)	5,000
3	Sold cattle	12,000
5	Purchased diesel for tractor, Cheque no. 1	120
8	Received creamery cheque (milk)	3,500
11	Purchased feed for cattle, Cheque no. 2	900
15	Paid for electricity, Cheque no. 3	320
19	Sold cattle	3,000
21	Received EU grant (REPS)	700
23	Received creamery cheque (milk)	1,500
24	Paid insurance for tractor, Cheque no. 4	400
25	Purchased feed for cattle, Cheque no. 5	400
27	Paid for electricity, Cheque no. 6	230

4. Dr side: *Bank, Cattle, Crops, Grants*
   Cr side: *Bank, Diesel, Vet fees, Cattle, Seed*

July 2010		€
1	Bank balance, overdraft (Cr)	3,500
3	Purchased seed, Cheque no. 20	1,200
5	Sold cattle	10,500
8	Sale of crops	4,500
12	Paid vet's fees, Cheque no. 21	250
16	Purchased diesel, Cheque no. 22	540
18	Sold cattle	4,500
20	Purchased seeds, Cheque no. 23	500
21	Purchased calves (cattle), Cheque no. 24	2,500
25	Sale of crops	2,700
28	Purchased diesel, Cheque no. 25	440
29	Received grant, Single Farm Payment Scheme	3,700

In Questions 5 to 10 you are required to make out an *income and expenditure account* at the end of the month stated.

5. Farmer A, May 2010

Income	€
Sale of potatoes	3,000
Sale of cabbage	2,500
Sale of turnips	2,700
Expenditure	**€**
Purchase of seeds	2,100
Light and heat	450
Diesel	670
Repairs	260
Fertilisers	1,500
Insurance	760

6. Farmer B, July 2010

Income	€
Sale of milk	6,400
Sale of cattle	7,800
Farmers' Market	1,100
Expenditure	**€**
Vet's fees	400
Repairs	890
Feed	1,200
Rent of stall	200
Insurance	650
Transport	720

7. Farmer C, August 2010

Income	€
Sale of cattle	9,500
Sale of eggs	1,500
Sale of turkeys	4,200
Expenditure	**€**
Light and heat	600
Feed	820
Diesel	320
Maintenance	950
Vet's fees	420
Purchase of calves	820

8. Farmer D, October 2010

Income	€
Sale of sheep	3,500
Sale of fleece	1,200
Sale of crops	3,400
Expenditure	**€**
Fertilisers	1,100
Insurance	600
Maintenance	450
Transport	280
Pesticides	500
Waste charges	240

9. Farmer E, November 2010

Income	€
Cattle	40,000
Pigs	35,000
Mushrooms	85,000
Expenditure	**€**
Heating	12,000
Water charges	3,000
Wages	35,000
Transport	13,000
Repairs	3,000
Depreciation of equipment	8,000

10. Farmer F, December 2010

Income	€
Milk	60,000
Crops	22,000
Poultry	44,000
Expenditure	**€**
Heating	27,000
Electricity	9,000
Delivery costs	8,000
Rates	4,500
Telephone and Internet	2,200
Wages	40,000

See workbook for more questions.

Information technology

48

The word *technology* refers to devices developed by the applied sciences that have a practical or industrial use. Machines that accept data (information), process it and display the end result have become our **computers** or **information technology** (**IT**).

A **computer** is an electronic device that accepts **input**, **processes** it as per a set of instructions and displays the end result as **output**.

Because computers also allow people to communicate with each other, we now use the term **information communication technology** (**ICT**).

Firstly let us distinguish between the terms *hardware* and *software*.

- **Hardware** refers to the physical components of the computer – either the computer itself or **peripherals** connected to it such as keyboards and printers.
- **Software** is a set of instructions, usually in the form of a programme, given to the computer to perform some task. These instructions are stored electronically on the computer (see page 450).

THE COMPOSITION OF A COMPUTER

The central processing unit (CPU)

The CPU is often called the 'brain' of the computer. It accepts information or data (from an input device), processes it and displays the result through an output device. See also page 448.

Input devices

An input device is used to give information and signals to the computer. The most commonly used input devices are:

- **Keyboards**: used to input letters, numbers, symbols and computer commands.
- **Pointing devices** (mice, joysticks, trackballs): used to input spatial data, i.e. to indicate the point in a document, worksheet etc., where data is to be placed.

- **Video input devices** (webcams, barcode readers): used to change an image, graph or video into a form that can be processed by the computer.
- **Audio input devices** (microphones, CDs and MIDI (musical instrument digital interface) keyboards): used to either input or create sounds.
- **Touch screens**: (visual display units) show pre-programmed information or choices for the user. When the user touches a particular part of the screen the computer stores this information or reacts to the touch to carry out a given function. Many vending machines (e.g. train ticket selling machines) use touch screens.
- **Scanners**: devices that read text, images or barcodes and store the information on the computer.
- **CDs/DVDs**: information can be copied from these onto a computer's hard drive (the main storage area of the computer). A **hard drive** is a circular disk in the hardware that stores changing digital information in a permanent form. It enables the computer to retain information after it has been shut down.
- **Memory sticks/USB flash drives**: external storage devices that are connected to the computer via a USB (universal serial bus) port. USB has become a standard system for connecting devices to computers, e.g. cameras, printers, MP3 players, scanners.

Output devices

An output device is used to display information from the computer to the user or to an audience. The most commonly used output devices are:

- **Monitors** (screens) or visual display units (VDUs)
- **Printers**: the printed information from a computer is called 'hard copy'
- **Projectors**
- **Synthesizers**: these create sounds from digital instructions
- **Speakers**

A computer's output can be stored externally on items such as CDs, DVDs and memory sticks (described earlier).

Modems

Computer information is stored digitally, whereas information transmitted over telephone lines is transmitted in the form of analogue waves. A modem is used to convert digital information to analogue and vice versa.

THE CPU REVISITED

The central processing unit is divided into three units:

1. **Control unit:** controls the rest of the computer so that it will produce the desired results from information inputted and from programmed information.
2. **Arithmetic unit:** processes information and does calculations to arrive at the desired end result.
3. **Memory unit:** stores data and programmes. Memory capacity is measured in **bytes**. A byte is a unit of storage capable of holding a single character.
   1024 bytes = 1 kilobyte (Kb) 10242 = 1 megabyte (MB) 10243 = 1 gigabyte (GB)

Computers use two forms of memory:

1. **Read only memory** (ROM) stores essential programmes for loading the operating system and other basic software packages. It is normally preloaded by the computer manufacturer and cannot be altered or removed. It can only be 'read'. This memory is permanent and remains on the computer, even after shutdown.
2. **Random access memory** (RAM) is used by programmes. If you are using memory-intensive software you may require a lot of RAM. RAM is not permanent memory, and information stored there is lost when the computer is shut down unless you save it to the hard drive or a storage device.

Processor speed

CPU speed is measured in megahertz (MHz). A 1 MHz CPU can perform one million operations in one second. In general, the greater the MHz rating, the faster the processor will work.

KEYBOARDING SKILLS

This textbook does not set out to teach keyboard skills, nor could it do so in one chapter. However, it is essential to acquire these if you intend to use computers on a regular basis. As well as acquiring typing skills you should also learn about the function keys (F1, F3 etc.), the shortcut keys and basic skills such as how to *cut* and *paste* (Ctrl-X for cut and Ctrl-V for paste).

COMMONLY USED SOFTWARE

Word processing programmes

A word processor enables you to create a text document, e.g. a letter or a report, edit it, correct mistakes without rewriting it, check grammar and spelling, print it and save it. The saved document can be used as a template (model) for further documents that would then only need slight alterations, e.g. replace the name of the addressee and the date.

Spreadsheets

Spreadsheets are used to perform mathematical exercises with data and formulae. The results can then be displayed in many different forms, e.g. as line graphs, pie charts or bar charts. Spreadsheets are regularly used for calculating the full cost of money borrowed or the monthly repayments on a loan. Many small businesses prepare their own spreadsheets for their final accounts and wage calculations rather than purchasing full accounting programmes.

$0.00	$0.90	8.97	5720.79	6.47	16.52	14.21	30.73	33.69	$1,010.
$1.40	$0.00	15.17	5735.96	11.2	17.00	14.02	31.02	32.55	$976.43
$0.70	$0.30	33.07	5768.73	15.1	17.65	14.09	31.74	33.15	$994.37
$1.40	$0.00	46.87	5815.60	22.9	18.14	14.38	32.52	34.08	$1,022.43
$3.15	$0.00	33.84	5849.44	13.6	17.49	14.39	31.88	33.58	$1,007.52
$4.20	$0.90	44.57	5893.11	26.3	17.76	14.34	32.10	33.45	$1,003.55
$1.05	$0.00	37.27	5930.38	10.3	16.40	15.13	31.52	33.09	$992.62
$0.35	$0.60	10.51	5940.29	4.51	16.16	15.23	31.39	31.51	$945.38
$1.05	$0.00	14.05	5954.34	7.05	16.08	15.27	31.35	29.91	$897.27
$0.70	$0.30	48.07	6002.11	25.9	16.85	15.71	32.56	31.06	$931.67
$1.05	$0.00	42.68	6044.79	23.8	17.44	15.65	33.09	32.04	$961.09
$4.20	$0.30	43.95	6088.44	19.7	17.12	16.17	33.28	32.28	$968.37
$1.05	$0.00	44.63	6133.07	15.8	16.78	16.94	33.72	32.34	$970.29
$0.70	$0.00	36.50	6169.57	11.9	15.31	17.55	32.87	31.79	$953.70
$0.35	$0.00	10.96	6180.53	2.86	15.06	17.95	33.01	30.95	$928.44
$1.40	$0.90	18.63	6198.26	9.63	14.95	18.31	33.26	30.91	$927.25
$1.40	$0.00	42.44	6240.70	22.6	15.49	18.44	33.93	31.78	$953.46
$1.40	$1.20	41.87	6281.37	18.8	15.19	18.38	33.57	32.81	$984.22
$5.25	$0.00	49.78	6331.15	24	15.94	18.77	34.71	33.70	$1,011.02
$21.00	$0.00	72.20	6403.35	41	16.99	19.70	36.68	34.91	$1,047.20
$3.50	$0.00	40.52	6443.87	14.1	17.26	19.65	36.91	34.83	$1,044.93

Databases

A database is an organised filing system that allows information to be retrieved in many different ways. A firm may keep information concerning their customers on a database in such a manner that it can instantly identify all its customers in a given region and so send information to them that is relevant only to those customers. The database can also be used in conjunction with a word processor to send multiple copies of the same document to many different people. This is known as mail merge.

Desktop publishing

Desktop publishing software is software for producing programmes, leaflets, greetings cards, brochures, books, magazines, manuals, etc. This entails combining computer skills in one package. Traditionally desktop publishing uses six skills, i.e. design, set-up, text, images, file preparation (pre-press stage) and printing. There are many packages available on the market, some free and some that must be purchased.

Computer aided design (CAD)

CAD is a computerised method of creating plans and drawings for design purposes, e.g. house plans, factory layouts, clothes patterns and engineering concepts.

Computer aided manufacture (CAM)

CAM uses a computer programme to operate a machine to perform specific tasks.

Accounting packages

These are linked series of databases and spreadsheets used to keep a full set of accounts and produce business documents such as invoices, credit notes and statements.

Presentation packages

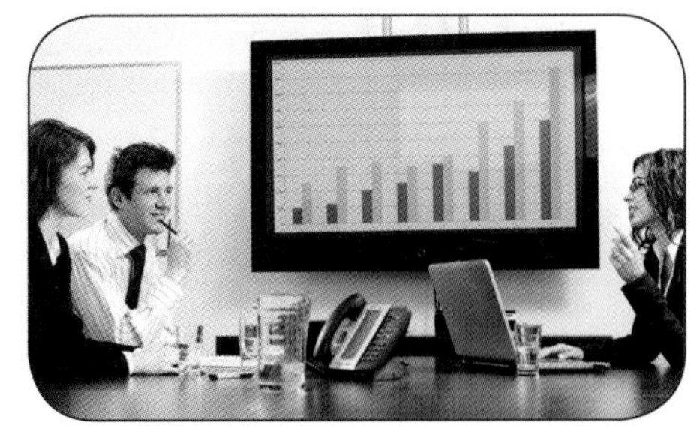

These are multi-media (can include text, images, sound, movement etc,) packages that create 'slide shows' which can be used for meetings and presentations, e.g. sales presentations, lectures, information meetings etc.

THE INTERNET

A computer **network** allows many computers to be connected to each other. This enables them to share common programmes and material provided by a **server**. The server manages the network and provides information and software to the other computers on the network.

A **local area network** (**LAN**) is a computer network covering a small geographical area, e.g. the connection of all the computers in a school. A number of different LANs may be connected to form a **wide area network** (**WAN**).

The Internet is a worldwide interconnection between a very large number of network connections. This is normally known as the **worldwide web** (**WWW**).

All computers using the Internet must have their own **IP address** (internet protocol address). This is a unique identifying numeric address for a computer. All computers are assigned this address at time of manufacture.

To access the worldwide web your computer must be connected to an Internet service provider (ISP) such as Eircom. By using a search engine or browser (such as Google, Yahoo! or Mozilla Firefox) you can access information from other computer networks through the worldwide web.

The Internet service provider usually offers its customers an e-mail account that allows them to send electronic mail (e-mail) to each other via the Internet.

Broadband Internet normally refers to high-speed, large-capacity internet connections (i.e. as well as a high-speed modem a high-speed line feeding the modem is also needed). 'Dial-up' connections can only transfer 56 kilobits per second, whereas broadband can transfer a minimum of 256 kilobits per second.

Wireless Internet (wi-fi)

A wireless Internet connection allows a computer to receive signals from a modem without directly connecting it to the computer. The computer receives the signal via the airwaves. This gives the computer user the freedom to move the computer anywhere (within a certain range) without having to move the modem at the same time. All modern computers have the facility to do this. Wireless connections are available for many other devices, e.g. printers, keyboards, mice, cameras.

Webcams

Webcams are video cameras that can be connected to or built into a computer to allow you to send and receive video images over the Internet. These are used for video conferencing and VOIP (voice over Internet protocol) networks such as Skype.

COMPUTER APPLICATIONS		
Homes	Banks	Businesses
Personal e-mails	On-line banking	Databases
Family budgets	Prepare statements	Process statements, credit notes etc.
Internet shopping	Process loan applications	Accounting packages for all day books, ledgers and final accounts
Databases for addresses, telephone numbers etc.	Check customer/potential customer credit ratings	E-mail for contacting customers and suppliers
Operation of home alarm/ security systems	ATM services	Video conferencing
Filing of medical records and school reports	Electronically transfer money between banks	On-line banking
Payment of bills on-line	Mail merges to customers	Internet advertising and websites* for publicity and on-line trading
Internet banking	EFTPOS facilities for customers, both hardware and software facilities	EFTPOS terminals

*A **website** is, literally, a site on the worldwide web. A person, company or organisation can have its own website with its own web address. These sites are usually used to create publicity, to provide information or to sell products.

BUYING A COMPUTER

1. If and when you decide to purchase a computer you should, firstly, follow the *Guidelines for the wise consumer* on page 58. (It might be a good idea to revise these now!)
2. Know exactly what specifications you require, in particular re processor, amount of RAM and hard drive capacity, because these are essential guides to the overall capability of the computer.
3. Know what programmes it can support.
4. Because technology changes so rapidly you should buy the latest technology that your budget permits.
5. Ensure you obtain a good anti-virus software package that can identify and remove a known or potential computer virus and also a firewall system designed to prevent unauthorised access to or from your network.

RECORDING A COMPUTER PURCHASE

1. The credit purchase of a computer

Remember that a computer is an asset in a business. You will recall from Chapter 36 that the credit purchase of an asset must first be recorded in the general journal before being posted to the ledgers.

Rule: **Debit** the item received. **Credit** the giver.

Example: Purchased a computer on credit for €1,000 from Computer Suppliers Ltd on 1/1/10.

General journal

GENERAL JOURNAL (page 1)				
Date	Details	F	Dr €	Cr €
1/1/10	Computer A/C	GL1	1,000	
	Computer Suppliers Ltd	CL1		1,000
Narration	**Being the credit purchase of a computer**			

General ledger

COMPUTER A/C (1)							
Date	Details	F	€	Date	Details	F	€
1/1/10	Computer Supplies Ltd	GJ1	1,000				

Creditors ledger

COMPUTER SUPPLIERS A/C (1)							
Date	Details	F	€	Date	Details	F	€
				1/1/10	Computer Supplies Ltd	GJ1	1,000

2. Purchase of a computer by cheque

As this is a cheque transaction it must be entered in the *Bank* account as well as the *Computer* account.

Rule: **Debit** the item received. **Credit** the bank account for money paid out.

Example: Purchased a computer on 1/1/10 by cheque no. 2.

COMPUTER A/C (1)							
Date	Details	F	€	Date	Details	F	€
1/1/10	Bank A/C	CB1	1,000				

ANALYSED CASH BOOK (1) (Bank column only)							
Date	Details	F	€	Date	Details	F	€
				1/1/10	Computer A/C	GL1	1,000

LEARN THE KEY TERMS

- **Arithmetic unit**: Part of the CPU that processes information and does calculations to arrive at the desired end result
- **Broadband**: High-speed, large capacity Internet connections
- **Byte**: Unit of storage capable of holding a single character
- **Central processing unit (CPU)**: Part of the computer that accepts information or data, processes it and gives the result by means of an output device
- **Computer**: Electronic device that accepts input, processes it as per a set of instructions and displays the end result as output
- **Computer aided design (CAD)**: Computerised method of creating plans and drawings for design purposes
- **Computer aided manufacture (CAM)**: Using a computer programme to operate a machine to perform specific tasks
- **Control unit**: Part of the CPU that controls the rest of the computer
- **Database**: Organised filing system that allows information to be retrieved in different ways
- **Desktop publishing**: Software designed to produce leaflets, books, posters, etc.
- **Hardware**: Physical components of a computer
- **Input device**: Device used to give information and signals to the computer
- **Internet**: Worldwide interconnection between a very large number of network connections
- **Keyboard**: Device used to input letters, numbers, commands and signs
- **Local area network (LAN)**: Computer network covering a small geographical area
- **Memory unit**: Part of the CPU that stores data and programmes
- **Modem**: Device that converts digital signals to analogue signals and vice versa.
- **Network**: Many computers connected to each other, enabling them to share common programmes and material provided by a server
- **Random access memory (RAM)**: Temporary memory used by programmes
- **Read only memory (ROM)**: Permanent memory that stores essential programmes for loading the operating system and other basic software packages
- **Server**: Computer that manages a network and provides information and software to the other computers on the network
- **Software**: Set of instructions, usually in the form of a programme, given to the computer to perform a task
- **Spreadsheet**: Programme that can perform mathematical exercises with data and formulae
- **Webcam**: Video cameras that can be connected to, or built into, a computer to allow you to send and receive video images over the Internet
- **Wide area network (WAN)**: Different LANs connected to each other to form a wider area network

- **Wireless Internet (wi-fi)**: Allows a computer to receive signals from a modem without directly connecting the modem to the computer
- **Word processor**: Programme that can create, edit and proof text documents

QUESTIONS

1. What is technology?
2. What is a computer?
3. Distinguish between an input device and an output device. Give two examples of each.
4. What is a hard drive?
5. In relation to computers, what are **peripherals**?
6. What is the central processing unit (CPU) of a computer?
7. Name and describe the three units or components in a CPU.
8. Identify the parts of a computer marked A, B, C and D in the picture.

9. You are the chairperson of your local club. An EGM is to be held shortly. You want the secretary to write a well-presented report, the treasurer to provide a well-presented set of financial details and the PRO to produce a brochure (containing photographs, tables and diagrams) outlining the history of the club. What software would you make available to each to accomplish the tasks you set them? Give a brief explanation of each.
10. What is the difference between CAD and CAM?
11. Explain the difference between RAM and ROM.
12. What is a modem? When are you most likely to use one?
13. What is a network?
14. What is a server (computer)?
15. What is an IP address?
16. Distinguish between LAN and WAN networks.
17. What is the Internet?
18. What is a website? What advantages may there be to your school to have its own website?
19. Outline any three uses of a computer in **(a)** the home, **(b)** a bank and **(c)** business.
20. What advice would you give to a person who is thinking about buying a computer?

See workbook for more questions.

A
accounting 31
double-entry 164
software 450
accounts
abbreviated 425
audited 179
balancing 263
nominal 259
personal 259
real 259
accruals/expenses due 166, 359
accumulated fund 419
acid test ratio 409
actuaries 75
adjustments 359
to final accounts 394
advertising 209
media 210
misleading 62
recording in accounts 212
AER 117
after-sales service 212
agenda 418
AGM 163, 418
analysed cash book 31, 33, 246, 302
bank account 31
bank statements and 105
bank transactions 38
basic entries 33
cash account 31
closing balance 36
club accounts and 420
contra entries 36
double-page layout 303
farm accounts and 442
ledger accounts and 306
opening cash 34
service firms and 433
source documents for 302
two separate books 303
analysed cash receipts and lodgement book 303
analysed cheque payments book 303
annual general meeting (AGM) 163, 418
An Post 114
communications services 244
savings schemes 116
APR 118
arbitration 233
articles of association 160
assessors 77
assets 34
current 385
fixed 165, 324, 385
assurance 71, 116
applying for 75
contracts 73
life assurance 80, 116
ATMs 89, 100
average clause 77
average stock 369, 412

B
bad debts 325
balanced current budget 138
balance of payments 145
balance of trade 146
balance sheet 359, 385
club accounts and 424
depreciation and 396
drawing up 387
farm accounts and 442
service firms and 434
banking, business 178
account application 178
loan applications 179
overdrafts 166
banking, personal 93
24-hour banking 101
account application 94
banker's card 94
cheques 96
current accounts 93
deposit accounts 115
drafts 88
overdrafts 100, 119
overdrawn accounts 110
reconciliation statements 109
saving 113
statements 105
bankruptcy 325, 409
bar charts 240
bar codes 60
barter 85
benefit-in-kind 3
bookkeeping 31
rules 260
books of original (first) entry 246
borrowing 118
branding 211
brand names 59
broadband 451
budgets
analysing 28
budgeting 1, 15, 23
comparison statements 45, 318
estimating figures 23
household 1
national budget 136
preparing 15
revised budgets 26
building societies 113
business
definition 1
documents 247, 255
efficiency 412
finance 165
net assets (value) 385
ownership 155
plans 170
profitability 410
value of 359
byte 448

C
capital 128, 156
calculating 308
employed 385, 411
expenditure 375
gains 116
working capital 386
capitalism 129
CAR 117
carriage 197
paid 248
carriers 197
cash 87
closing 16, 36, 47
correction accounts 108
discounts 248
flow forecasts 174
net 16, 47
opening 16, 34
purchases for resale 276
transactions 246
cash and carry wholesalers 190
certificate of incorporation 162
chain of production 187
chairperson 419
channels of distribution 188
charge cards 89
cheques 87, 96
ante-dated 97
counterfoil 97
crossing 98
dishonouring 99
drawee 96
drawer 96
guarantee card 94
payee 96
post-dated 97
stale 97
traveller's 88
wages payment by 227
Child Benefit 2
chip and PIN 89
Cirrus cards 89, 100
closing
cash 16, 36, 47
stock 358, 394
club
accounts 418
officers 419
trading accounts 422
COD 248
collateral 119, 179
commission 2, 223
communication 236
external 239
internal 239

oral 236
visual aids 240
written 237
communism 129
companies
limited 156, 160
organisational chart 216
promoters of 160
state-owned 158
complaints 64, 66
compound interest 117
computers 447
buying advice 452
CAD/CAM 450
CPU 447, 448
input devices 447
memory 448
networks 451
output devices 448
peripherals 447
recording purchase in accounts 452
servers 451
conciliation 233
consumer durable goods 13
consumer price index (CPI) 130
Consumer Protection Act 61
consumers 58, 188
complaints 64, 66
EU Directives 63
guidelines 58
law and 60
organisations 68
rights 61, 64
Consumers' Association of Ireland 68
containers 196
continuous balance accounts 253, 294
general ledger and 298
from T-ledger 294
to T-ledger 297
contracts 60
consideration 60
implied conditions 61
contra entries 36
control accounts
creditors 335
debtors 330
co-operatives 157
cost of goods sold 365, 366
cost of sales 365
couriers 197
CPU 447, 448
credit 246
cards 89, 122
notes 65, 252
purchases returns book and 271
sales returns book and 284
purchasing 118
side of accounts 31, 259
transfers 90
unions 113
deposit accounts 115
loans 119
worthiness 249
creditors 90, 166
control accounts 335
ledger 263
credits 31, 34
currency exchange 101, 151
current
accounts 93
national 146, 147
assets 385
liabilities 385
ratio 408
curriculum vitae (CV) 221
customs duty 137
CWO 248

D
databases 450
day books 246
combined with ledgers & trial balances 341
folio column 268
days of grace 83
debentures 168
debit
cards 88
notes 253
side of accounts 31, 259
debits 31, 34
debtors 90
control accounts 330
factoring 166
ledger 263
debt servicing 139
deductions
statutory 4, 224
voluntary 5, 224
deficit
current national budget 138
household budget 16
national current account 147
deflation 131
delivery notes 250
delivery systems 194
calculating cost 200
calculating time 198
van purchase 203
deposit accounts 115
depreciation 362, 395
desktop publishing 450
direct debits 90
direct foreign investment 147
DIRT 115
distribution channels 188
dividends 3, 117, 156, 379
percentage 411
recording 394
double-entry accounting 164, 260
double-time 3

E
EAR 117
economics 125
economic growth 131
economic systems 129
government and 135
efficiency 412
EFTPOS 88
EGM 418
electricity bills 10
e-mail 237
employees 215
records 221
recruiting 221
rights and responsibilities 216
employers 215, 220
equal opportunity 220
rights and responsibilities 220
employment 215
self employment 217
Employment Appeals Tribunal 234
end of year procedure 356
endowment policies 116
enquiry 247
enterprise 128
entrepreneurs 128
E&OE 248
equality officers 233
EU, Ireland and 148
excess clauses 80
exchange rates 101
exchequer balance 138
excise duties 137
exclusion clauses 80
expenditure 8
capital 13, 136, 165, 375
current 13, 136, 165
discretionary 11
fixed 11
government 136
irregular 11
long-term 165
medium-term 165
recording 11
revenue 375
short-term 166
unplanned 9
expense accounts 359
expenses due 359
expenses prepaid 360
expenses
adjustments for 394
recording 375
exports 144, 147
invisible 145
visible 144
extractive industries 187

extraordinary general meeting (EGM) 418
ex works 248

F
facsimiles (fax) 237
factoring, of debtors 166
factors of production 126
false economies 8
farm accounts 442
ferries 196
filing 6
final accounts
  adjustments 394
  assessment and interpretation 407
  balance sheet 385
  limitations of 408
  profit and loss account 374
  trading account 365
finance
  business 165
  internal/external 166
  long-term 167
  medium-term 167
  short-term 166
  sources of 386
financial institutions 113
fixed assets 165, 324, 385
  depreciation 362
fixed costs 173
flexitime 228
folio columns 268
foreign currency exchange 101, 151
forklifts 197
franchising 178
freehold properties 180
freight 197

G
gains 374
gains accounts 361
  gains due 361, 394
  gains prepaid 361, 394
GDP 131
general government debt 139
general journal 246, 321
  bad debts 325
  fixed assets 324
  narration 322
  opening entries 322
general ledger 263
  continuous balance accounts and 298
GNP 131
government
  capital expenditure 136
  current expenditure 136
  economy and 135
  national budget 136
grants 168, 444
gross domestic product 131
gross loss 366
gross national product 131
gross pay 4
gross profit 356, 365, 366
  mark-up 369, 413
  percentage/margin 367, 410
guarantees 65
guarantor 179

H
hard drive 448
hardware 447
hire purchase 121, 167
household
  budgets 1, 23
  expenditure 1, 8
  insurance 78

I
import agents 189
imports 144, 147
  import substitution 147
  invisible 145
  visible 145
imprest system 314
impulse buying 9
income 2
  benefit-in-kind 3
  irregular 3
  recording 6
  regular 2
income and expenditure account
  in club accounts 422
  in farm accounts 442
indemnity 74
industrial relations 230
  disputes 232
  strikes 233
inflation 130
  imported 130
information communication technology (ICT) 447
infrastructure 136
insolvency 409
insurance 71
  agents 78
  applying for 75, 78
  average clause 77
  brokers 78
  for businesses 182
  claims 76
  compulsory policies 183
  contracts 73
  cover note 75
  excess clauses 80
  exclusion causes 80
  loading 72
  motor 80
  non-insurable risks 81, 182
  personal 78
  premium 71, 72
  premium calculations 81, 184
  principles 73
  property 79
  proposal form 75
interest 2, 117
  flat rate 118
Internet 451
investment 114
  schemes 116
invoices 251
  purchases book and 267
  sales book and 280
IP addresses 451
Ireland
  economy 129, 135
  EU and 148
  imports and exports 148, 151
  trading partners 148, 150
Irish Business and Employers Confederation (IBEC) 232
Irish Congress of Trade Unions (ICTU) 231
issued share capital 163

J
Jobseeker's Benefit 2

K
keyboard skills 449

L
labour 127
  force 215
Labour Court 233
Labour Relations Commission (LRC) 233
land 127
Laser cards 88
leasing 122, 167
  sale and leaseback 168
ledgers 259
  folio column 268
legal tender 91
letters
  formal 238
  of complaint 67
  of enquiry 247
liabilities 34
  current 385
  long-term 386
life assurance 80, 116
limited companies 156, 160
limited liability 156
line graphs 240
liquidity 408
Live Register 218
loading 72
loans 119, 179
  applications 120, 180
  receipts in accounts 180

local area network (LAN) 451
loss adjusters 77
loss leaders 60

M
MABS 29
manufacturers 188, 190
marketing 206
  advertising 209
  after-sales service 212
  distribution 212
  market research 208
  mix 206
  sales promotion 211
markets 206
  segmentation 207
  target 207
media 210
memorandum of association 160, 161
memos 237
merchandising 211
merit goods 135
minutes 419
mixed economies 129, 135
modems 448
money 85
  cash 87
  cheques 87
  laundering 94
  legal tender 91
  lenders 122
mortgages 113, 121

N
national budget 136
  capital budget 138
  current account deficit 147
  current budget 137
  exam question 139
National Consumer Agency (NCA) 64
national debt 139
National Employment Rights Authority (NERA) 221
nationalisation 158
needs 125
net assets 385
  calculating 386
net cash 16, 47
net direct foreign investment 147
net pay 5
net profit 356, 374
  distributing 379
  percentage/margin 378, 410, 413
net sales 365
night safes 100
no-claims bonus 73
not-for-profit organisations 418

O
Ombudsmen 68
opening cash 16, 34
operating profit 433
operating statement 433, 436
opportunity cost 8, 129
orders 249
overdrafts 100, 119, 166
overdrawn accounts 110
overheads 317
overtime 3
overtrading 408

P
pallets 197
pay
  gross 4
  net 5
  slips 5
PAYE 4
  calculating 223
PayPal 91
Paypath 91, 178, 227
personal loans 119
petty cash
  book 246, 314
  vouchers 314
pictograms 241
piece rates 222
pie charts 241
PIN numbers 88
pipelines 196
plastic money 88
PowerPoint® presentations 241
PPS number 222
premium 71
prices 62
price tags 61
primary industry 187
private limited companies 156, 160
privatisation 158
production chain 187
product labelling 60
profitability 410
profit and loss account 356, 358, 374
  depreciation and 395
  trading account and 378
profit and loss appropriation account 379
profit and loss reserve 380
PRSI 4
public private partnerships 158
public relations 212
public services/utilities 136
purchases book 246, 266, 267
purchases returns book 246, 271
purveyors 191
pyramid schemes 63

Q
Quarterly National Household Survey 218
quick ratio 409
quotations 248

R
RAM 449, 454
rate of stock turnover 412
receipts 59, 254
receipts and payments account 421
recessions 133
recruitment 221
remittance advice slips 254
report writing 242
  on business performance 413
REPS 444
resources 126
retailers 190, 191
  in Ireland 192
retained earnings 380
retained profits 167
return on capital employed 411
return on shareholders' funds 411
revenue expenditure 375
Rights Commissioners 233
ROM 449, 454
RTÉ 244

S
salaries 2, 222
sale and leaseback 168
Sale of Goods and Supply of Services Act 61
sales book 246, 280
sales promotion 211
sales returns book 246, 284
savings 113, 114
  schemes 115
secondary industry 188
secretary 419
self employment 217
service firms' accounts 433
service industry 188
shareholders 156
  funds 411
shares 116, 156
  issue of 167
  share capital 163
shop stewards 231
simple interest 117
Small Claims Court 68
smart cards 89
sociably desirable goods 135
software 447
  common programmes 450
sole traders 155
solvency 408, 409
spending. *See* expenditure
spreadsheets 450
stamp duty 137
standing orders 90
statements 253
  of accumulated fund 419
  operating 433, 436
state-owned companies 158

stock
  average 369, 412
  closing 358
  distressed 370
  opening 358
  records 370
  turnover rate 412
stocktaking 370
store cards 122
strikes 233
subrogation 74
surplus
  current national budget 138
  household budget 16
  of expenditure over income 422
  of income over expenditure 422

T

tachographs 195
tax
  capital acquisition 137
  capital gains 137
  corporation 137
  levies 224
  PAYE calculation 223
  VAT 248, 266
technology 447
term loans 119, 167
tertiary industry 188
time-and-a-half 3
time rates 222
T-ledger
  from continuous balance ledger 297
  to continuous balance ledger 294
trade
  associations 66
  discounts 248
  free 150
  international 144, 147
  invisible 145
  unions 230
  visible 144
aders 58
trading account 356, 358, 366
  profit & loss account and 378
trading period 356
transport 194
  air 196
  calculating costs 200
  calculating delivery times 198
  Irish developments 202
  pipelines 196
  rail 195
  road 195
  sea 196
  timetables 201
traveller's cheques 88
treasurer 419
  treasurer's report 425
trial balance 264
  ledgers, day books and 341
  purchases book and 269, 274
  purchases returns book and 272, 274
  sales book and 282, 287
  sales returns book and 285, 287
turnover 412

U

underwriters 71
unemployment 217
uninsurable risks 81
unions 230
USC 4

V

variable costs 173
VAT 248, 266

W

wages 2, 222
  book 225
  calculating 222
  cash analysis statement 226
  payment 226
  recording payment 225
  slips 5
wants 125, 126
warranties 65
webcams 451
websites 452
wholesalers 189, 190
  cash and carry 190
wide area network (WAN) 451
wi-fi 451
word processors 450
work 215
working capital 386
  ratio 408
workplace
  industrial relations 230
  organisation structure 216
work to rule 233
worldwide web 451